THE SCOTS GUARDS IN THE GREAT WAR
1914–1918

THE SCOTS GUARDS
IN THE GREAT WAR 1914-1918

BY F. LORAINE PETRE : WILFRID EWART

AND

MAJOR-GENERAL SIR CECIL LOWTHER

K.C.M.G., C.B., C.V.O., D.S.O.

LONDON

JOHN MURRAY, ALBEMARLE STREET, W.

1925

FOREWORD

By FIELD-MARSHAL LORD METHUEN,
G.C.B., G.C.M.G., G.C.V.O.

THE history of the part that the Scots Guards took in the Great War is one that will at all times remain as a record of works performed worthy of the great traditions of the Regiment.

Though this long, wearisome war was full of suffering and discomfort in front of an enemy known for its perfect organization, discipline, and courage, the Regiment never lost heart, and felt that in the good cause for which they were fighting the end would never be in doubt.

The high opinion of the Guards in the Peninsular War, expressed by the Duke of Wellington, was held by those officers under whom we served in the late war, and by the country.

May our high sense of duty, our fine state of discipline, our happy relations between all ranks, for ever remain as they are now, and were during the late war, is the earnest hope of their Colonel.

12th October, 1925.

PREFACE

THE history of the Scots Guards has been most unfortunate in only reaching completion so long after the conclusion of the war.

The Regimental Committee for the history consisted of experienced officers: Colonel F. W. Romilly, C.V.O., C.B., D.S.O., Colonel G. C. Paynter, C.M.G., D.S.O., Colonel S. H. Godman, D.S.O., Lieut.-Colonel J. A. Stirling, D.S.O., M.C., Lieut.-Colonel Sir Victor Mackenzie, Bart., D.S.O., M.V.O., and Lieut.-Colonel G. Loder, M.C.

Providence combated the efforts of this committee. Their first selection was Captain Wilfrid Ewart, who had been in the Scots during part of the war, and who, in his early twenties, wrote the great war book, *The Way of Revelation.* He made a start by getting through about the first two months of the war. Then he was killed by an accidental bullet in Mexico City on New Year's Eve, 1922-3.

Men able to do the sort of work required are not to be found at every corner. Mr. F. Loraine Petre, O.B.E., who consented to carry on the book, got most of the war diaries put together extremely well. But there was still much left to do, when he died after an operation in May 1925.

The Committee in July 1925 kindly accepted the services of the writer of this preface, who offered himself to do the work when he heard of its suspension. The Committee here desire to express their thanks to the Lady Grizel Hamilton for the use of several maps from the *War Diary of the Master of Belhaven,* and also to Major-General the Lord Ruthven, C.B., C.M.G., D.S.O., for the use of maps from the *Guards Divisional History.*

vii

This is the proper place to say how the Regiment, like the whole army of the Empire, kept up its courage and cheerfulness in face of the awful dangers and discomforts they suffered.

All honour to the dead of the several ranks of the Scots Guards, who, like other gallant soldiers of the British Army, had the conviction in their minds that in the end victory would crown their sacrifice, and so gave their lives for their country.

H. CECIL LOWTHER,
Major-General.

CONTENTS

CHAPTER I

THE 1ST BATTALION SCOTS GUARDS TO THE END OF THE BATTLE OF THE AISNE

CHAPTER II

THE 2ND BATTALION SCOTS GUARDS

CHAPTER III

THE FIRST BATTLE OF YPRES

CHAPTER IV

TRENCH WARFARE, 1914–1915

CHAPTER V

NEUVE CHAPELLE AND FESTUBERT, AND DOWN TO THE FORMATION OF THE GUARDS DIVISION

ix

CHAPTER XII

THE THIRD BATTLE OF YPRES (*continued*)

CHAPTER XIII

THE BATTLE OF CAMBRAI

CHAPTER XIV

THE EARLY MONTHS OF 1918 AND THE GERMAN OFFENSIVE IN THE SPRING

CHAPTER XV

FROM THE END OF THE GERMAN SPRING OFFENSIVE TO THE COMMENCEMENT OF THE FINAL BRITISH ADVANCE

CHAPTER XVI

THE COMMENCEMENT OF THE FINAL ADVANCE

CHAPTER XVII

THE PASSAGE OF THE CANAL DU NORD AND OF THE SELLE

CHAPTER XVIII

FROM THE PASSAGE OF THE SELLE TO COLOGNE AND HOME

CHAPTER XIX

THE RESERVE BATTALION

CHAPTER XX

LIST OF MAPS

ERRATA

Page 50, line 37. Delete footnote 3 after "Lieutenant B. G. Jolliffe."
(To stand after Lieutenant C. F. F. Campbell.)
For "Lieutenants B. G. Jolliffe and C. F. F. Campbell, and R. H.
FitzRoy" substitute "Captains B. G. Jolliffe and C. F. F. Campbell,
and Lieutenant R. H. FitzRoy."
Page 53, line 27. For "Lieutenant B. Winthrop Smith" substitute
"Captain B. Winthrop Smith."
Page 55, line 4. For "Major A. V. Poynter, D.S.O." substitute "Captain
A. V. Poynter, D.S.O."
Page 57, line 6. Delete hyphen between "Captain" and "Bagot"
and insert it between "Bagot" and "Chester."
Page 90, line 6. For "2nd-Lieutenants Hon. A. P. Methuen" substitute
"2nd-Lieutenant Hon. A. P. Methuen."
Page 95, line 34. For "W. G. A. Garforth" substitute "W. G. W.
Garforth."
For "W. C. Hope" substitute "A. C. Hope."
Page 95, line 35. For "A. N. Hepbrune-Scott" substitute "A. N. Hep-
burne-Scott."
Page 106, line 14, and Page 120, line 12. For "Ferguson" substitute
"Fergusson."
Page 117, line 23. For "Lieutenant MacDonald" substitute "Lieutenant
Macdonald."
Page 174, line 14. For "Captain M. Barne" substitute "Major M.
Barne."
Page 183, line 32. For "Private Creig" substitute "Private Greig."
Page 218, line 39. Insert "H" before "L. N. Dundas."
Page 334. After "Balfour, Captain C. J." delete "96."
After "Balfour, 2nd-Lieutenant E. M. M. and detail" insert
"Balfour, Lieutenant J., 96."
Page 336. Delete "138" from detail after "Clarke, Lieutenant E."
Page 337. "Coke, Captain Hon. R. and detail." Pages 55, 170 and 325
refer to the Hon. Reginald Coke. Pages 57, 60, 160 and 161 refer
to the Hon. Richard Coke.
After "Dawkins, Lieutenant G. S., wounded" for "121" substitute
"120."
Page 343. After "Mackenzie, Lieutenant-Colonel Sir Victor A. F., vii"
insert "3" and substitute "120" for "126," and after "231"
insert "325."
After "Monckton, Lieutenant F. A." insert "11."
Page 344. Delete "Monckton, Lieutenant F. A., and detail."
For "Moncur, Sergeant-Majo" substitute "Moncur, Sergeant-
Major."

THE SCOTS GUARDS

CHAPTER I

THE 1ST BATTALION SCOTS GUARDS TO THE END OF THE BATTLE OF THE AISNE

Mobilization—Billets in France—Advance just into Belgium—Retreat to Rozoy, 40 miles east by south of Paris—Advance over Aisne—First Battle of Aisne—To Hazebrouck.

THE history of a regiment during a great war begins only with its declaration, and the story that is to be told here is that of the sword after it has been drawn, not of the quarrel which led to its drawing.

The days preceding the declaration of war by the British Government will be looked back upon by most of those who remember them as amongst the most anxious of the whole period. There were few probably who did not suffer from the terrible fear lest the way of peace with dishonour should be chosen, or who did not heave a sigh of relief when the only honourable course was pursued and war was declared against Germany. An officer of the Regiment, who soon afterwards made the sacrifice of his life in battle, expresses in a private letter of the 2nd August, 1914, what was probably the general feeling, not only of himself and his brother officers, but of the great majority of Englishmen. He writes:

" It is hardly possible to speak calmly of what appears to be our policy in this terrible crisis. It really looks, during the last twenty-four hours, as if Great Britain was going to stand aside and not go to the help of France ; it seems to all of us the most insane action, whether we have or have not given a promise. While I write, a telephone message has come through to send fifty men and three officers at once to the London Docks; but even that excitement does not lift the gloom off one's mind."

His mind was relieved, on this score at any rate, when he again writes on the 5th August, after the declaration of war :

" London is agog with excitement. I really think and hope that the vast majority of the nation will enthusiastically support the war. Hundreds are coming to join the Colours ; but alas ! it is almost too late for them to be of any use, however good a spirit it shows."

Another officer writes, also in a private letter :

" Overwhelming opinion amongst the ' men in the street ' that we must help France. It is not a question of national honour any longer, but of national welfare and actual life in the future. If we climb down (which is thought almost impossible, as it is completely unthinkable), then we must be done. Canada might join U.S.A., Australia set up on its own, anything, in short, might be the outcome of such a degrading performance. As you will see, abroad all socialists and syndicalists have regretted mobilization, but state that, as it is an accomplished fact, it is the duty of every man, etc.—in fact, patriotism. If we can't do the same, we had better go to bed ! "

These quotations are given as showing the spirit which pervaded the officers of the Regiment, and indeed of the army generally. Here is none of the bloodthirsty idea, so often and so wrongly attributed to the professional soldier, of war for the sake of fighting. It is recognized by both writers that war is necessary, not only for the maintenance of British honour, but for the very existence of the nation and the Empire.

When the die was cast and mobilization commenced, the two then existing battalions of the Scots Guards were quartered, the 1st at Aldershot, the 2nd at the Tower of London. There was no 8rd Battalion then. The 1st Battalion, being a unit of the 1st (Guards) Brigade of the 1st Division of the British Expeditionary Force, was bound to be sent abroad at once ; the 2nd Battalion was not destined to leave England till two months after the declaration of war, and it is, therefore, necessary to treat

Zeebrugge
Ostend
Bruges
Nieuport
Ghen
Dunkirk
Dixmude
Calais
Houthulst Forest
Langemarck
Roulers
E
L
YPRES
Menin
F
A
N
D
R
St Omer
Cassel
Bailleul
Armentières
Boulogne
Hazebrouck
Fleurg
Lille
Tournai
M
Merville
Bois Grenier
A
St Venant
Neuve Chapelle
Étaples
Robecq
Julg
La Bassée
R
Bethune
Brocourt
Condé
Valencie
Montreuil
Agincourt
Loos
Douai
T
Festu
Lens
G
Crécy
Vimy
ARRAS
Le Quesnoy
Doullens
Quéant
Cambrai
Mort
Bapaume
Moeuvres
Fore
Abbeville
Thiepval
Gouzeaucourt
Le Cateau
P
Albert
Marfeta
Etreu
Dieppe
Corbier
SOMME
Péronne
AMIENS
C
St Quentin
Villers-Bretonneux
A
Ham
R
D
Nesle
Guise
Royc
Tergnier
le Havre
Montdidier
Noyon
La Fère
St Gobain
Lassigny
Forest
Laon
Rouen
OISE
Chemin Troyo
des Dames
Compiègne
Forest
Soissons
Villers
Néry
Cotterets
La Fère
Forest
OURCQ
en Tardenois
Château Thierry
Dormans
PARIS
Claye
MARNE
Épern
Versailles
La Ferté
Montmi
Lagny
PETIT MORIN
GRAND MORIN

Roulers
Langemarck
Passchendaele
Miles
5 4 3 2 1 0   5
Broodseinde
Zonnebeke
YPRES
Hooge
Veldhoek
Beaumont Hamel
Dickebusch
Gheluvelt
Klein Zillebeke
Thiepval
Cassel
Zandvoorde
Poziéres
Mont
Hollebeke
Rouge
Kemmel
Kruiseik
Menin
Albert
Baa
Mont-des-Cats
Wytschaete
Fricourt
Locre
Messines
Comines
to Amiens
Meteren
Neuve
Église
R. Ancre
Bailleul
Ploegsteert
Hazebrouck
R.
S o m L
R. Lys
Armentières

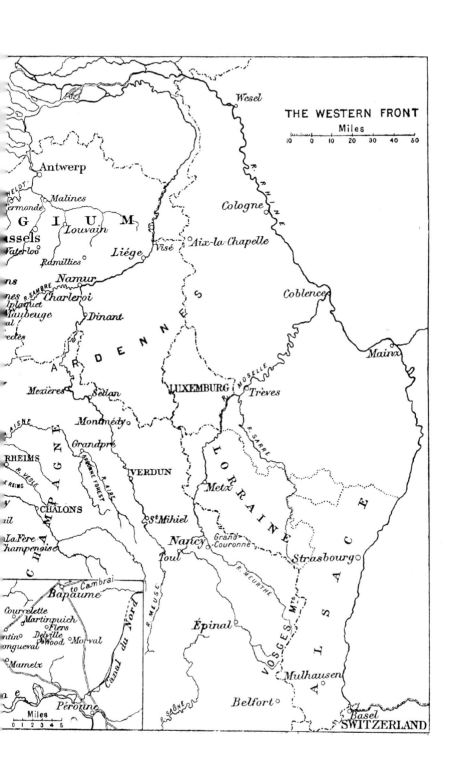

THE WESTERN FRONT

Miles
10 0 10 20 30 40 50

Wesel

Antwerp

Malines

Cologne

ermonde
HELDT

G I U M

ssels
Louvain

Vaterloo

Ramillies

Liége   Visé   Aix-la-Chapelle

ns
R.SAMBRE   Namur   Coblence

nes   Charleroi
Iplaquet
Maubeuge
al
ectes   Dinant

A R D E N N E S

Mainx

Meziéres   Sedan   LUXEMBURG   Tréves

MOSELLE

AISNE   Montmédy

RHEIMS   Grandpré

EING   R.VESLE   ARGONNE FOREST   R.AIRE   VERDUN

R. SARRE

L O R R A I N E

Metz

CHÂLONS

y

uil

LaFere   St Mihiel

hampenoise

Nancy   Grand-
Couronne   Strasbourg

Toul

R. MEURTHE

A L S A C E

to Cambrai

Bapaume

Courcelette
Martinpuich   Flers   Épinal
ntin   Delville
ongueval   Wood   Morval

VOSGES Mts

R. MEUSE

Canal du Nord

Mametz

Mulhausen

n   e

Péronne

Belfort   Basel

Miles
0 1 2 3 4 5   SWITZERLAND

SAÔNE

the two separately until at least the time of the first Battle of Ypres, when both were in the same neighbourhood, though in different divisions and brigades. Mobilization was hurried up with the greatest enthusiasm. War Diaries are generally rather prosaic documents, often speaking of the most heroic deeds in the most matter-of-fact terms. That of the First Battalion Scots Guards waxes enthusiastic on the 5th August when it says: "Three parties of reservists arrived. Magnificent, clean, steady men." The mobilization order had reached the battalion at 4 p.m. on the previous day. (The mobilization of this battalion was so far advanced that every officer, including the Adjutant, had a few days' leave to say *au revoir* to his relations and friends.) By the 6th the battalion had been completed to war strength, and by the 7th the last details had been worked out, and it could be recorded that it was ready to move by midnight. On the 13th the battalion left Farnborough by two trains, of which the second started at 6.25 a.m. and reached Southampton at 8 a.m. Four hours later the battalion sailed on the s.s. *Dunvegan Castle*,[1] and reached Havre at 1 a.m. on the 14th, the horses following in another steamer. From Havre it marched six miles to camp near Harfleur. The officers who sailed for France were:

Lieut.-Colonel H. C. Lowther, C.B., C.V.O., C.M.G., D.S.O.
Major J. T. Carpenter-Garnier, second-in-command.
Major B. G. Van De Weyer.
Captain and Adjutant A. A. L. Stephen, D.S.O.
Captain R. G. Stracey.
Captain W. J. Wickham.
Captain C. E. de la Pasture.
Captain C. F. P. Hamilton.
Captain Sir V. A. F. Mackenzie, Bart., M.V.O.
Captain R. F. Balfour.
Captain J. D. P. Astley-Corbett.
Lieutenant B. G. Jolliffe.
Lieutenant C. F. F. Campbell.
Lieutenant H. C. E. Ross.

---

[1] This vessel had hardly any ballast, and the troops had to be distributed equally, so as to balance the ship.

Lieutenant G. F. de Teissier.
Lieutenant C. J. Balfour.
Lieutenant Sir I. Colquhoun, Bart.
Lieutenant R. N. Gipps.
Lieutenant H. R. Inigo-Jones.
2nd-Lieutenant R. A. Compton-Thornhill.
2nd-Lieutenant W. B. W. Lawson.
2nd-Lieutenant Sir G. N. Ogilvy, Bart.
2nd-Lieutenant G. V. F. Monckton.
2nd-Lieutenant A. G. Menzies.
2nd-Lieutenant E. D. Mackenzie.
2nd-Lieutenant J. Stirling-Stuart.
2nd-Lieutenant W. G. Houldsworth.
Lieutenant and Quartermaster D. Kinlay.

Marching from Harfleur at 9 p.m. on the 15th, the 1st Battalion entrained at Havre and, passing by Rouen, Amiens, Arras, and Cambrai, reached Nouvion, where it was billeted for the night of the 16th, and marched to Boué four miles to the west on the morning of the 17th. At Boué the battalion was received with enthusiasm, and made as comfortable as was possible under the circumstances. Indeed, so friendly were the people that an officer's private diary records that the motherly old lady who had looked after him insisted on being kissed before he left. Here it remained in billets till the 21st, when it marched ten miles to Cartignies. On the 22nd it had reached Grand Reng, at about 4 a.m., just over the Belgian frontier, after passing the French fortress of Maubeuge during the night. The 1st (Guards) Brigade was at this time commanded by Brigadier-General F. I. Maxse. The battalions that constituted it were :

1st Coldstream Guards.
1st Scots Guards.
1st Black Watch (Royal Highlanders).
2nd The Royal Munster Fusiliers.[1]

The brigade, with the 2nd and 3rd, formed the infantry of the 1st Division commanded by Major-General S. H.

[1] Replaced in September by the 1st Queen's Own Cameron Highlanders.

Lomax, which, with the 2nd, made up the I Corps under Lieut.-General Sir D. Haig.

The I Corps was the right of the British force in France, the 1st Division was on the extreme right rear of the corps, with the French 5th Army on its right. It was posted about Grand Reng and Vieux Reng, and the 1st (Guards) Brigade was on its right at the former place. The I Corps faced generally to the north-east, whilst the II looked due north, thus forming an obtuse angle about Mons.

On the 22nd guns were heard for the first time in the direction of Charleroi, from the battle in which the 5th French Army had been defeated and forced back to its present position on the right rear of the British. The sound had had the effect of bringing home to all the reality of the war, and that it was not the sort of picnic that it had hitherto seemed.

The history of an individual regiment in a campaign has little or no connexion with its strategy, a matter which concerns the history of the campaign generally, and is almost irrelevant to that of regiments, brigades, and even larger units. Strategy only concerns them when acting as an independent force detached from the main army. The story of a regiment deals chiefly with its technical employment in furtherance of strategical operations directed by the Higher Command. Still less do comments or criticisms on strategical decisions find a suitable place in dealing with the operations of a minor unit.

All that can appropriately be said on general situations affecting the whole army is to give a brief outline, sufficient to enable the reader to understand the main situation and to see how the particular unit in which he is interested fits into it.

Speaking quite generally in this sense, the German design at the outset of the war in Belgium was the turning of the left flank of the Anglo-French armies, their separation from the English overseas base in northern France, and the rolling up of the left on the centre. A new Sedan on a gigantic scale was the hope of the German leaders, a hope which, fortunately, was not destined to be realized. As with Napoleon in Russia in 1812, the means were inadequate to the end; von Kluck found himself without sufficient troops to encircle Paris from the west, and was compelled to change the direction of his march to the left, with the result that, when the end of the retreat from Mons was reached, the German Army found itself in a position analogous to that which it had intended for the allies. Its right, instead of turning the allied left, had itself been turned, with the result that it was forced, by the battle of the Marne, to retrace its steps till it could again halt on the strong position of the Aisne. In pursuance of the original design, von Kluck's attention was directed to the II Corps of the British Army, standing as it did on the left of that small but highly efficient force. The British II Corps west of Mons on the 22nd August, 1914, faced north, whilst the I Corps faced generally north-east. When, therefore, the German advance against the British Army first came into contact with it on the 23rd, the onslaught fell mainly on the II Corps. On the first day of the battle of Mons the Scots Guards, in reserve on the right of the I Corps, knew practically nothing about the battle going on far away on their left. The battalion diary passes it unnoticed, and an officer's private diary describes it as " a day of rest " after the last two days of heavy and trying marching in very hot weather. The next day (24th), whilst the German attack on the British left was raging, was almost equally quiet. The battalion was ordered to hold the line of the main Rouveroi–Erquelines road four miles north of Grand Reng, but on reaching that point was ordered back to dig deep trenches west of Villers Sire Nicole.[1] The digging was done by the flank companies, and " B " with " C " in reserve. At 5 p.m. it marched again to La Longueville, three miles west of Maubeuge, round the north side of which it had passed. A fight had been expected, and there was much disappointment when nothing happened. The retreat from Mons had begun on the 24th, and was continued on the 25th, when the 1st Scots Guards had a march of fifteen miles to Taisnières, where they were separated from the rest of

[1] A terribly hot day, and men digging without their shirts could not carry their packs the next day.

the brigade, which had reached Dompierre. The heat and the dust were terrible. In the afternoon the battalion stood to arms on account of rifle fire heard in the neighbourhood ; but again it had no fighting.

The start on the 26th was delayed by having to wait whilst two French regiments passed. This was the day of the battle of Le Câteau on the British left, but of that the Scots Guards saw nothing, as they had seen nothing, but heard the noise, of the fight at Landrecies in the previous night. They had now rejoined the brigade, and were ordered to hold a line covering the retirement of the 3rd Brigade. Right Flank and " B " Companies dug trenches, with the other two in reserve.

At 3.30 p.m. they marched to Rejet de Beaulieu, acting as rearguard, with " C " Company acting as right-flank guard of the division. It was an exhausting day, and many men fell out on the march, but rejoined later. It was not till 10 p.m. that billets were reached.

At 8 a.m. on the 27th the men were hard at work digging trenches till noon, when a very heavy shower soaked them to the skin. At 2 p.m. the retreat continued, and the trenches which had been dug with so much labour were abandoned. The battalion, assembled in Etreux, was about to rejoin the rest of the brigade, when enemy patrols were seen to the east, and " B " Company had to be detached to block the roads in that direction till the rearguard had got clear on its way to Guise.

For a mile and a half after passing Etreux the battalion had to move in artillery formation on both sides of the road, to leave it clear for the British batteries, which had taken up a position and were engaged for a quarter of an hour in a brisk duel with German guns.

Just before the third company crossed the Iron stream, the Germans began firing with howitzers and long-range rifle fire. Little harm was done by this fire, which lasted till dusk, but failed to impede the retreat. The only casualties, the first sustained by the battalion, were two men slightly wounded. The Black Watch had suffered more severely, with two killed and ten wounded.

On arrival at the bivouac at Jonqueuse on the Guise–St.

Quentin road at 11 p.m., the men were thoroughly exhausted; for the shower had failed to lower the temperature, and marching in soaked clothes added to the trials of the day.

The Munsters had met with disaster, being surrounded and overwhelmed in a desperate struggle with six German battalions at Etreux.

On the 28th a forced march of thirty-one miles carried the Scots Guards as far as St. Gobain, south of La Fère and west of Laon. The enemy was not seen, and the 29th was one of rest after the great march. The march of the 28th, in the great heat which still continued, had been a specially long and fatiguing one. The men were almost worn out by it.

The 30th was another day of hard marching, unmolested by the enemy.[1] Starting at 12.30 a.m. Terny was reached after a march of eighteen miles at 8 a.m. Here the battalion bivouacked till 5 p.m. to guard headquarters of the I Corps.

In the evening another stage was covered before billets at Allemant were reached.

On the 31st Soissons was passed, after a halt in a rearguard position to the north of it, where two platoons covered the preparations for blowing up the bridges over the Aisne. Vauxbuin, a couple of miles on the road to Paris from Soissons, was reached. On the 1st September the retreat was through the Forest of Villers Cotterets to that town, whence, after a halt for food, it continued to La Ferté Milon on the river Ourcq. The men were relieved during this march by their packs being carried on wagons.

This relief was very acceptable at the time, but later on, when the weather changed from intense heat and drought to cold and wet, it was found that the men's great-coats were missing, and their sufferings under the changed circumstances were considerable, till the great-coats lost, or others, came up.

---

[1] On the march down the steadily sloping road at night, the French guide showed the C.O. the entrance to caves he said were a kilometre in length inside the limestone line. These the Germans lighted up and used as entire protection from any known shell. On their retirement these vandals did all they could to destroy the fine old Château of Coucy.

The 4th (Guards) Brigade, on this day, was heavily engaged in the forest, and about 1 p.m. the 1st Scots Guards were ordered up to cover its retirement. But the Germans had had enough of it, and did not attempt to follow up the brigade. The 2nd Brigade, acting as rearguard, was still engaged to the north-west at 7 p.m. The battalion was ordered to dig in at Marolles in anticipation of an attack at dawn.[1] At 11.30 the battalion was told that it would have to march again at 1.30 a.m. There was no time for repose, and the over-wrought men almost walked in their sleep. When they reached Chambry, a little north of Meaux, at 4 p.m. on the 2nd September, nothing on earth could have set them marching again. Nevertheless, after a few hours' rest, they took up a rearguard position at 3 a.m. to cover the passage of the Marne by the 1st Division and at 7 a.m. set out south-eastwards for Jouarre, which was reached at 7 p.m. after many delays, and it was hoped there might at last be a good night's rest. The whole battalion was billeted in a Benedictine Monastery, which had recently been dismantled when threatened with seizure by the State. It was so large that it could have accommodated 2,500 men. The hope of rest proved vain, for a fresh start was made at 3 a.m., and Coulommiers was reached by 8 a.m. on the 4th. Here at last there was some rest, though the machine-guns under Lieutenant Balfour, sent in support of a company of the Black Watch at a stream on the Coulommiers–Boissy road on the right, had a rather disturbed night and he was much disappointed when thirty Uhlans arrived on the farther side of a stream in his front, but got away unscathed, because some of our own men were on the road along which his guns were trained, and masked their fire till too late and the Germans had disappeared. " B " Company also was approached by some German cavalry, who, again, owing to a misapprehension, were not fired on till too late. In another case an opportunity was lost of shooting a German cyclist and six others with him, who escaped in the woods without being fired on.

[1] Fortunately the C.O. anticipated events, and only let the men dig a line a few inches deep to mark the line of the battalion at night.

An early morning march of twelve miles on the 5th September took the battalion to Nesles, east of Rozoy, where R.F. "B" and "C" Companies were on outposts with L.F. Company in reserve. Here at last, to the universal joy of the British Army, ended the great retreat from Mons.

Though the Scots Guards had seen no serious fighting, they had experienced a very rough and trying time in the many long, wearing marches in great heat, and the inevitable discouragement of the knowledge that they were retiring nearer to Paris every day. Yet they, like the rest of the army, had never for a moment lost heart or shown any symptom of indiscipline or disorder. In a private letter, their Colonel wrote that the men had been throughout cheerful, though dog-tired. What kept them cheery was that they had always had full rations and plenty of extras, such as bacon and cheese. One of the most trying things had been the impossibility of getting a good wash. The officers had been told to shave, and the men followed their example without orders. Now all was changed, the joy of advance succeeded the depressing conditions of retreat. At Nesles, too, the first reinforcement was received on the arrival of Lieutenant Gordon Ives with ninety-one rank and file.

Next day the outposts were relieved by the 3rd Coldstream Guards of the 4th Brigade north-east of Rozoy. Presently the advanced guard of the Coldstream Guards encountered the enemy, and Lieutenant Balfour, with his machine-guns, was ordered to their support, and was soon under a hail of bullets and then of shells from a German battery. Though the machine-gun section was fortunate enough to have no casualties, it was compelled to retire when the Coldstream Guards did so under the shell fire, having suffered a loss of four officers wounded and forty-two other ranks killed or wounded. German infantry in motor lorries were seen and shelled, as was a farm from which about fifty German cyclists issued and made off along the road as fast as they could pedal.

After an artillery duel at 2 p.m., in which the German guns were silenced, the general advance commenced at

4 p.m., and the Scots Guards that night slept at Le Plessis, nine miles northwards. German limbers, rifles, and other material found in the night showed that the enemy had suffered heavily and were retreating in some haste and disorder.

The advance continued, without opposition so far as the Scots Guards were concerned, on the 7th September to Le Frenois. On the 8th the Grand Morin was crossed at Jouy, and the march proceeded to Sablonnières on the Petit Morin. The Scots Guards, on reaching Bellot a short way south of Sablonnières, came under shell fire from the right. There was also rifle fire from a thick clump nearer in the same direction. Lieutenant Balfour with his machine guns was at first with the Black Watch south of Sablonnières. He then went to assist the Camerons on his right, who had now replaced the Munster Fusiliers in the 1st Brigade. The thick clump was beaten out by the machine-guns of the Black Watch and Lieutenant Balfour, and a good bag of Germans was secured from it—15 killed, 12 wounded, and 14 prisoners. A wounded German offered Balfour his watch to spare his life, saying he " had heard that the British killed all the wounded and prisoners." He was relieved to find that neither the watch nor his life was to be forfeited. The rest of the battalion then passed on to Sablonnières without further adventure.

Only one man was wounded. Colonel Lowther had a narrow escape when a German shell, bursting near him, killed five men and wounded three Coldstream stretcher-bearers.[1] On this day, too, the first dead and wounded Germans left behind in the precipitation of the retreat were found. The brigade bivouacked astride of the road to Nogent l'Artaud on the Marne. The battalion was on outpost, with cavalry in front and the 4th Brigade on the left. Here the second reinforcement, of Lieutenant F. A. Monckton and ninety-eight men, arrived.

On the 9th September the Scots Guards crossed the Marne at Nogent l'Artaud unopposed, passed through Charly-sur-Marne and up the steep hill on the right bank,

[1] Fortunately the Scots Guards companies had been moved away, two each side of the road.

and eventually, at the end of a fourteen-mile march, bivouacked at La Marette. Heavy firing had been heard on the right towards Château Thierry, but, beyond an overhead visit from a Taube, nothing had been seen of the enemy. At midnight it began to rain, and was still raining when the battalion resumed its advance at 7 a.m. on the 10th. Marching by Le Thiolet, Torcy, and Courchamps, the 3rd Brigade on the left was seen to be heavily engaged, and on reaching Sommelans a halt was made to await developments. About 9 p.m. billets were reached at Latilly, a little farther on. The place had only been evacuated six hours earlier. Here the inhabitants gave a better account than usual of their uninvited German guests, saying that they had behaved well and paid for everything.

The battalion had not been engaged, though the machine-guns were brigaded near Latilly to support the fight on the left. Some German infantry on the left retreated northwards.

The advanced guard had been heavily attacked at Licy, and among other losses had suffered that of Brigadier-General N. D. Findlay, C.B., the C.R.A. 1st Division.[1]

Next day (11th) the direction of march was turned from north to north-east, and by 9 a.m. Bruyères on the Meaux to Fismes railway was reached. Here the battalion halted, and it rained heavily in the afternoon. Bazoches was reached on the 12th, and the ensuing night was very wet. There were no billets, and the battalion was conducted to a muddy orchard and the ditch of the château. Shelter was at last found for half a company, and a room for the officers, but all others passed a miserable night. The Germans in front were crossing the Aisne, which flows generally from east to west at the foot of the high ridge on the plateau at the top of which is the Chemin des Dames, a road famous since the days when Napoleon won his victory of Craonne in 1814, fighting with his line astride it. It was now to be the objective of a great attack from the south.

In the early morning of September 13th the 1st Scots

---

[1] This was the first time the battalion saw the heavy German field howitzers used.

Guards marched due north from Bazoches-en-Bourg, a village just beyond the Aisne and at the foot of the heights forming the northern side of the valley. The southern side here also is formed of heights, with an elevation the same as that of the Chemin des Dames, seven miles to the north beyond the river. The northern heights run down to the river in numerous spurs separated from one another by small lateral valleys running generally from north to south. The first obstacle to be passed after crossing the valley from south to north was the Aisne canal, running parallel to the river and south of it. The canal bridges had not all been destroyed, those over the Aisne itself had everywhere been more or less blown up. On the 13th September the 2nd was the leading brigade of the 1st Division, and when the 1st Brigade reached the crossing, the 2nd was already beyond it, covering the passage for the 1st, followed by the 3rd. Where the Scots Guards crossed there were three waterways to be passed, first the Aisne canal, secondly the Aisne itself, and thirdly the Aisne et Oise canal, which passes by a tunnel under the Chemin des Dames heights, and crosses the Aisne on an aqueduct to join the Aisne canal. This aqueduct had two shell holes in it, but was utilised for the passage of the battalion.

Having passed the Aisne et Oise canal, the Scots Guards moved eastwards to Oeuilly, under German shell fire. The battalion reached Pargnan, at the toe of the spur leading down by Paissy from the Chemin des Dames, and took shelter on the road under the hill, ready to assist the British artillery close by. At 5 p.m. orders were received to move up to Paissy. This was done in artillery formation. French Turcos and Spahis were close on the right, and partially mixed up with the battalion during this advance, which at one time got half a mile beyond Paissy. At Paissy the battalion bivouacked for the night. It had not been under rifle fire, but the shelling had been heavy at long range, and caused the following casualties:

Killed : 2nd-Lieutenant W. G. Houldsworth (died five days later) and three men.

Wounded : Lieutenant C. J. Balfour, 2nd-Lieutenant G. V. F. Monckton, and eleven men.

Lieutenant Balfour was wounded by shrapnel, which killed his pony under him and wounded five of his men. The pony had got some thirty shrapnel bullets in him, whilst his master fortunately was only wounded and still able to give instructions. He was first taken to a French dressing-station near by, and later to the English one near Vendresse. There he had a terrible time during the shelling of the next day (14th), till he was moved from under fire. As the British artillery was firing within 40 yards of the dressing-station, the feelings of the wounded in it may be imagined.

That night (13th) the French XVIIIth Corps was on the right of the 1st Brigade, the rest of the 1st Division on the left on a line passing through Moulins and Oeuilly to Bourg.

The battle of the 14th September began at 3 a.m., in rain and mist, when the 2nd Infantry Brigade advanced to seize the Chemin des Dames, with its right directed on the village of Cerny beyond it on the farther side of the ridge, looking down on the valley of the Ailette. Its left was directed on a point a mile west of Cerny. Covered by this attack, the 1st (Guards) Brigade was to move leftwards through Moulins, which was to be passed about 7.30 a.m., and then turn northwards over the ridge through Cerny-en-Laonnais, down to Chamouille on the farther side of the Ailette valley on the direct road to Laon.

The leading troops of the 1st Brigade reached Vendresse about 7 a.m. The day had broken in thick mist and rain, which, once troops were in action, rendered almost inevitable the mixing of companies and battalions through losing direction.

Meanwhile the 2nd Brigade had been fighting strenuously on the plateau of the Chemin des Dames, but had not made progress beyond the crest. Brigadier-General Bulfin commanding it had now received orders not to attempt a further advance when he had secured his hold on the ridge.

The 1st Brigade was coming into action on the left of the 2nd, with the 1st Coldstream Guards on the right. The 3rd Brigade was in reserve at Moulins. The Coldstream Guards on the right of the 1st Brigade, as they mounted towards the plateau from Vendresse, had found themselves in a terribly steep and thick wood, and by the time they reached the top found that the battalions on their left, the Black Watch and the Camerons beyond them, had found a clearer way and were already in position. Between the right of the Black Watch and the left of the 2nd Brigade, the Coldstream Guards found room. Everywhere on the ridge there was the confusion of companies and battalions, which could not be avoided in the mist in an unknown country. The mist only lifted about 10.30 a.m.

The 1st Scots Guards sent two companies ("B" and "C") as escort to the guns at the Tour de Paissy, the other two (R.F. and L.F.) acting as Brigade Reserve.

Soon after 1 p.m. a great German counter-attack on the 1st and 2nd Brigades drove back the troops to the right of the Camerons, exposing the right flank of that battalion, which suffered heavy losses. A gap had developed between them and the Black Watch, and into this were sent the two reserve companies of the Scots Guards. The Scots Guards companies deployed, under cover of the Troyon ridge, about half a mile west of Vendresse. Each had two platoons in front and two in support. They were heavily shelled, but had few casualties before the crest was reached. They then extended and pushed forward by rushes. One shell burst in the midst of a R.F. platoon, wounding 2nd-Lieutenant E. D. Mackenzie and killing or wounding several N.C.O.s and men. Another killed Sergeant Royall and seven men. The leading platoons went on, under heavy rifle and machine-gun fire, but without many casualties, until they came in touch with the Camerons on the right and the Black Watch on the left, both of whom had already suffered severely and could get no farther forward. Captain Sir V. Mackenzie (R.F. Company) then sent back a message explaining the situation ; but two minutes later received an order which had crossed his messenger, that no advance was to be made beyond a hedge about 200 yards behind the village of Chivy, where his company already was. Some 200 yards in front of him was thick wood.

In this position R.F. remained, helping to repel the

counter-attacks which were made up till about 3 p.m. At dusk the fighting was over for the day, and the company was ordered to withdraw and rejoin the rest of the battalion on the Troyon Ridge. It was at that time mixed up with battalions of the 3rd Brigade. L.F. Company was on the right of R.F., out of touch, and about 200 yards farther forward.

The following account probably refers, in so far as the Scots Guards are mentioned, to men of L.F. It was given by Lieut.-Colonel J. Ponsonby of the 1st Coldstream Guards to Lieutenant C. J. Balfour, when they were both in hospital in Paris a few days after the battle. Here is the story practically as told by Lieutenant Balfour in his diary :

" Ponsonby had two Coldstream companies in the firing line. He went along from the left company, with which he was, to the right. There he found it lining a wall near a factory chimney, evidently the Troyon sugar factory near the southern edge of the plateau. The chimney was brought down by the German artillery, and as the position was too hot, Ponsonby determined to go forward, and took with him his right company and an odd lot of men, numbering about fifty, whom he found at hand. The fifty comprised an officer and ten men of the Camerons, nine of the Black Watch, a few Coldstreamers, and the remainder men of the 1st Scots Guards, who, presumably, had got separated from L.F. Company. With this odd lot Colonel Ponsonby went across the plateau to the point where a side road leaves the main road to Laon to go to the right through the village of Cerny-en-Laonnais. He sent his company along the main road, and himself went with the fifty men to Cerny. Two men were sent ahead as an advanced guard, and as the fifty approached Cerny, these two signalled to them to come forward. On reaching the village they found about two battalions of Germans having dinner in the middle of the street. These of course were helpless against even fifty men armed and ready. They were promptly fired on and dispersed, with the loss of five machine-guns, besides casualties.

" Then a German officer, with the Red Cross on his arm and his breast covered with medals and decorations, came out of a house. With him were about forty others, apparently medical officers. The officer, whom we cannot help suspecting to have been General von Zwehl commanding the 27th Reserve Infantry Brigade about here, begged Colonel Ponsonby to spare the house, as they had over 1,000 wounded there. He was assured that it would not be molested. Ponsonby then discovered that Cerny was surrounded, so he and his men made for a wood, where he found a ditch with a hedge in front of it. In this they established themselves, surrounded on three sides by Germans. They gave all their ammunition, except ten rounds per man, to one of their number, who was a marksman. For seven hours they lay here under fire, but whenever a German showed himself he was picked off by the marksman, and the enemy never dared to close. Colonel Ponsonby had the small bone of his leg broken by a bullet as he got to the ditch. At dark the Germans ceased firing. Then Ponsonby and his men saw German carts with dead and wounded, and presently a large body of the enemy bivouacked on the farther side of the hedge and posted sentries. The British scarcely dared to breathe till, fortunately, about midnight a gale sprang up and they were able to take advantage of the noise and crawl up the ditch, dodging the sentries. Colonel Ponsonby was the only one of the party who had been hit, and he had to be carried by four men, which added to the difficulty of moving undiscovered. Nevertheless, the whole party got safely away and back to their own lines."

The rest of L.F. had been withdrawn at dusk to the general line. This had been the heaviest fighting the 1st Scots Guards had yet had, and their losses for the first time were really serious. They were :

Killed : Major J. T. Carpenter-Garnier, 2nd-Lieutenant Compton-Thornhill, 2nd-Lieutenant Inigo-Jones, and 16 other ranks.

Wounded : 2nd-Lieutenants E. D. Mackenzie, J. Stirling-Stuart, and 86 other ranks.

Missing : 12 other ranks.[1]

[1] These are the casualties according to the Adjutant's diary. Sir V. Mackenzie estimated them at about 120 for L.F. and 70 for R.F., besides the officers. This appears to justify the statement in the text that the heaviest losses were in L.F. When it is remembered that the losses were practically confined to these two companies, it will be seen how heavy, proportionately, they were.

Major Carpenter-Garnier was mortally wounded, and died about eight hours later. He was hit just behind the Troyon Ridge, when temporarily commanding the battalion, Colonel Lowther having been summoned to Brigade Headquarters. Early on the 15th " B " and " C " Companies rejoined, having a few casualties on the way up.

The night of the 14th–15th was spent under cover of the Troyon Ridge.

The position of the British at 8 p.m. on the 14th ran S.W. to N.E. along the heights above Vendresse, from Beaulne through Chivy and Troyon. The 5th French Army was on the right. The right of the British 1st Division was on the Chemin des Dames, 1,000 yards east of the sugar factory of Troyon. Thence the line extended leftwards along the ridge into the valley south of Chivy. At the head of that valley were two advanced detachments. The 2nd Brigade was on the right, with the 1st on its left.

Both on the 13th and the 14th the points to be reached had been indicated as far beyond the Chemin des Dames, on the way to Laon. Those points were not reached till the final advance of the French army in the late summer and autumn of 1918. It had been at first supposed that the Germans meant to continue their retreat beyond the ridge of the Chemin des Dames, but it was now found that they were determined to defend that strong position. The French on the right were at Craonnelle on the southern slope of the ridge near its eastern extremity. From that point they extended almost straight in a south-easterly direction to Rheims, which had been recaptured from the enemy. The line held by the 1st British Division was the extreme limit reached at this period of the war, and on it the situation began to pass from one of open war to trench warfare, which for so long afterwards was the outstanding feature of the struggle on the Western Front. The German orders for the 15th were for the 7th Army on the ridge opposite to the British 1st Division to drive the British over the Aisne and to support the 1st German Army on its right. All attempts to carry out this order failed, but, on the other hand, the British were unable to make any further advance. The great deadlock had begun. The battle that began this day continued night and day till the termination of the war.

The weather on the 15th was still atrocious. Rain had begun on the 10th September, and went on almost continuously for the next ten days, with the result that every road and trench was inches deep in mud. From the great heat of the end of August, the weather had now changed to cold as well as wet. The unpleasant conditions were aggravated by the fact that at first the men had no greatcoats. These had probably, as was the case with at least one other regiment, been turned off vehicles on which they were being carried during the retreat, in order to make room for the wounded of Mons, Le Câteau, and other actions.

On the 14th September the trenches on the Scots Guards' front were in a rudimentary state, and gave little protection from the enemy's artillery. They had been improved by the 15th, and where they were dug into the steep slope below the plateau gave excellent shelter against anything but a direct hit on the trench itself. Whilst the battalion remained in this position, the order was two companies holding trenches, which had been dug at night, just over the ridge ; below the ridge one company in close support, and the fourth in reserve. Brigade Headquarters were in the cave of a quarry, which was perfectly safe. The trenches on the edge of the plateau were, of course, more exposed.

On the 15th most of the infantry fighting was to the left of the I Corps, where little or no progress had been made in the ascent of the heights above the Aisne. On the front of the Scots Guards there appear to have been no infantry attacks by day, though there were constant outbursts of shell fire of all calibres, including the heavy artillery intended for the siege of Paris, which the Germans had looked on as a certainty. Infantry attacks were attempted at night, but invariably beaten off. Of these, no details are on record. The only record in the battalion diary is—" in trenches near Vendresse " ; and there are no further details in officers' diaries.

On the 15th Colonel Lowther was wounded in the hand, chest, and foot by a 5·9-inch explosive shell, but none of

3

the wounds were serious, and he resumed command after the First Battle of Ypres.

The conditions above described, constant shelling by day and occasional infantry attacks at night, continued from the 15th to the 19th September, without any material change of position on the part of either British or Germans, who were separated by a No Man's Land of about 1,000 yards breadth on the front of the Scots Guards. On the 20th the 1st Scots Guards were relieved near Vendresse, and went back to billets at Oeuilly, near Bourg, where they had crossed the Aisne a week before.

The 6th Division, who relieved them, were fresh out from home, and inclined to be jocose over the appearance of men who for a week past had had no chance of a wash or a shave, but that frame of mind did not last long after some experience of the front on the Troyon ridge.

Even Oeuilly was not altogether pleasant or exempt from German shelling.

It was while they were at Oeuilly that Lieutenant Sir E. Hulse wrote the following account of some German atrocities which came within his knowledge :

" This is a true story of ——'s death. He was wounded, and together with some of our men and the Black Watch, and, I believe, a few Coldstream, had crawled into a pit to avoid further fire. The Germans came up and fired on this party of our men (30–40 in all), and all wounded—and a Black Watch officer put up a handkerchief as a signal to them, upon which the Germans walked in and shot the lot point-blank. Two men escaped—and one of them was ours—by feigning to be dead and crawling back by night to the lines ; they had two wounds each. The rest, as I say, were butchered, although already incapacitated completely. Again, a Medical Officer, wounded, lay on the ground, and when the Germans came up, he handed them his revolver, upon which they took it and shot him through both hands, and left him. He is now in England."

The " —— " of this letter was, as appears from a letter of Sir V. Mackenzie, 2nd-Lieutenant Compton-Thornhill.

The battalion was supposed to be going to have three

days' rest at Oeuilly, but only thirty hours hadelapsed when it was sent forward again, this time to trenches at Moussy, a mile and a half south-west of Vendresse, where it relieved the 6th Brigade of the 2nd Division. The position, which was not completely occupied till midnight of the 21st–22nd September, is described as a difficult one, with woods all round. One man was killed by the trench falling in on him. The place is spoken of as Canal Post, which locates it as being on the Aisne et Oise canal about two miles south of Braye-en-Laonnais, where it issues from the tunnel under the ridge. There was a good deal of shelling during the 22nd, but no infantry attack. The next day was fairly quiet, and that night the battalion, on relief by the Coldstream Guards, moved into billets at Verneuil just behind Moussy. It bivouacked on the 24th on the side of the road to Vendresse, a position which is described by an officer as " very smelly but fairly safe." There was the usual shelling all day, and also on the 25th, when three men were killed and an alarm of an attack came to nothing. The three men were absolutely blown to bits by a direct hit. They were in R.F. Sir V. Mackenzie and Captain de la Pasture were at the same time knocked over by a shell burst, but not wounded.

That night the Scots Guards returned to Oeuilly, where General Maxse, on appointment to a Division forming in England, made over the command of the 1st (Guards) Brigade to Brigadier-General Charles Fitz-Clarence.

Next evening (27th) the 1st Scots Guards returned to the Troyon ridge, " C " Company going to the Chivy valley, to a position which was occupied only at night. The next few days were spent north of Vendresse, in trenches under shell fire, and at last, on the 16th October, the battalion left the trenches on the Aisne for good, and marched to billets at Blanzy on the southern slope of the hills dividing the valley of the Aisne from that of the Vesle.

On the 9th October the battalion had received a rein-forcement, consisting of Lieutenants Sir J. S. Dyer, Douglas Dick, J. L. Wickham, and 50 rank and file. Its losses during its service on the Aisne had been 4 officers killed (Major Carpenter-Garnier, 2nd-Lieutenants W. G. Houldsworth, Compton-Thornhill, and Inigo-Jones), and 5 wounded (Lieut.-Colonel Lowther, Lieutenants C. J. Balfour, and 2nd-Lieutenants G. V. F. Monckton, E. D. Mackenzie, and J. Stirling-Stuart). Of other ranks 37 killed, 137 wounded, and 12 missing. Of the 186 other ranks' casualties, 116 are accounted for on the 14th September alone.[1] In addition to the losses, the time on the Aisne had been very arduous. No one had a chance of taking off his boots, and in those days there were few parcels from home to supply consolation in the shape of small comforts. Amongst other things badly missed were matches and tobacco, of which there was a great scarcity.

On the 17th October the battalion marched to Fismes, the railway junction in the Vesle valley, and entrained at 3.30 p.m. for a very different country in Belgium in the Ypres area. The race for the sea had now commenced, and the Allied Armies were striving their utmost to outflank the German right and reach the North Sea coast before it, or at least, if it could not be cut from that coast entirely, to keep it as far east as possible from Calais and Boulogne. With the details of the replacement of British by French troops on the Aisne front we are not concerned. The I Corps was the last of the three British Corps which had existed since the end of August to leave the trenches on the Aisne to their French allies. On the 18th October the 1st Scots Guards detrained at Hazebrouck, and here we will leave them for the moment whilst we bring up to date the history of the 2nd Battalion.

---

[1] It may be noted here that the 1st Guards Brigade—1st Coldstream, 1st Scots Guards, 1st Black Watch, 1st Cameron Highlanders, and 1st London Scottish—had 300 per cent. killed and wounded by March 1st, 1915.

For the information of those who do not know, it should here be stated that "A" and "D" of the 1st Battalion are known as Right- and Left-flank Companies, and in the 2nd Battalion "E" and "H" Companies are similarly known.

CHAPTER II

THE 2ND BATTALION SCOTS GUARDS

Mobilization—To Ostend—In 20th Brigade of 7th Division—Via Ghent to Roulers.

AT the end of July 1914 the 2nd Battalion was quartered at the Tower of London, under the command of Lieut.-Colonel R. G. I. Bolton, doing the ordinary duties of that post in peace time. By the morning of the 4th August it had been called on to send 50 men with 3 officers to the London Docks. War was imminent, and was declared the same night. Everybody belonging to the battalion was busy with mobilization. There were detachments out at such places as the London and Victoria and Albert Docks, the Post Office, the Bank, Woolwich, Abbey Wood Ammunition Factory, and Deptford Storage Wharf.

Mobilization was quickly completed, but the 2nd Battalion still remained at the Tower, eating their hearts out with envy at the better fortune of the 1st in going off with the first four divisions of the B.E.F. The time was enlivened by frequent scares of German invasions on the East Coast, which entailed the recall to barracks of every officer and man not employed elsewhere, but of course all turned out to be unfounded.

Thus passed the whole of August and the first two-thirds of September. By the 20th of that month the 2nd Battalion was in camp at Lyndhurst in the New Forest, where the 7th Division was forming. But, though the 2nd Scots Guards was ready for immediate service, there were other battalions still arriving from Egypt, Malta, and Gibraltar, which had to be awaited before a start could be made. The stoppage of all leave on the 1st October was a sure sign of very early departure, and on the 4th the battalion marched for Southampton at 9 p.m., and began to arrive there half an hour after midnight. The right half battalion, with Colonel Bolton, embarked on the s.s. *Lake Michigan*, the left on the s.s. *Cestrian*. Battalions were embarked in separate halves, because the fleet of transports had to pass through a German mine-field, and if one transport was blown up, it might be hoped that the other would escape, and so one half battalion would be left intact as a nucleus. Leaving Southampton at 7 a.m. on the 5th and passing down Southampton Water, the convoy steamed south past the western end of the Isle of Wight, and then made for the Straits of Dover. It had passed Dover that night, when it was recalled to that port owing to an alarm of submarines. At Dover the whole day of the 6th was passed.

At 7.30 p.m. on the 6th the transports sailed for the Belgian coast, which was sighted before dawn, and an hour later the ships lay alongside the long curved mole of Zeebrugge, which was to acquire such undying fame on the 23rd April 1918. The passage was stated to have been threatened by German submarines, one of which was claimed by the escorting destroyers to have been sunk.

At 7 a.m. disembarkation of the 7th Division began. It could not be commenced earlier, as the supply ships with the disembarking equipment had to be awaited for before the transports would come alongside the mole. Whilst lying outside, the sound of the guns at Antwerp had already been heard.

The 2nd Scots Guards had a strength of 31 officers, 1 warrant officer, 43 sergeants, 30 corporals, 20 drummers, and 879 privates; total, 1,004 all ranks.

The officers were :

Lieut.-Colonel R. G. I. Bolton.
Major Viscount Dalrymple.
Major Hon. H. J. Fraser, M.V.O.
Major Lord E. C. Gordon-Lennox, M.V.O.
Captain T. H. Rivers-Bulkeley, C.M.G., M.V.O.
Captain Hon. J. S. Coke.
Captain C. V. Fox.
Captain Hon. D. A. Kinnaird.
Captain H. L. Kemble, M.V.O.

Captain G. C. B. Paynter.
Lieutenant Sir F. L. F. FitzWygram, Bart.
Lieutenant H. K. Hamilton-Wedderburn.
Lieutenant G. H. Loder.
Lieutenant E. C. T. Warner.
Lieutenant Lord Cochrane.
Lieutenant Lord G. R. Grosvenor.
Lieutenant E. B. Trafford.
Lieutenant H. Taylor.
Lieutenant The Earl of Dalhousie.
Lieutenant D. R. Drummond.
Lieutenant W. H. Holbech
Lieutenant A. R. Orr.
Lieutenant R. Steuart-Menzies.
Lieutenant Hon. J. St. V. B. Saumarez.
Lieutenant R. H. F. Gladwin.
2nd-Lieutenant W. H. Wynne-Finch.
2nd-Lieutenant Lord Garlies.
2nd-Lieutenant C. Cottrell-Dormer.
2nd-Lieutenant Viscount Clive.
2nd-Lieutenant R. C. M. Gibbs.
Lieutenant and Quartermaster T. Ross.

The 2nd Scots Guards were a unit of the 20th Infantry Brigade, the other battalions in it being the :

> 1st Grenadier Guards.
> 2nd Border Regiment.
> 2nd Gordon Highlanders.

The 20th Brigade, with the 21st and 22nd Infantry Brigades, made up the infantry of the 7th Division.

The 20th Brigade was commanded by Brigadier-General Ruggles-Brise, the Division by Major-General T. Capper, and the IV Corps by Lieut.-General Sir H. Rawlinson,Bart.

A short description of the general situation in Belgium is necessary to enable the reader to understand the otherwise somewhat puzzling movements of the British IV Corps commanded by Sir H. Rawlinson, of which the 7th Division was the principal constituent. Any expression of opinion on the controversial question of the authority to which this corps was and should be subordinate is a matter to be avoided in a regimental history; but there appears to be no doubt that, at first, it was intended that Sir H. Rawlinson should be directly under the orders, not of Sir John French, the Commander-in-Chief of the British Expeditionary Force, but of Lord Kitchener, the Secretary of State for War. Lord Kitchener's telegram to Sir John French, quoted on page 177 of " 1914," seems to show that clearly. It says, " Have already given Rawlinson temporary rank. I am sending him instructions regarding his action Antwerp. The troops employed there will not for the present be considered part of your force."

It was not till the 9th October that Rawlinson was definitely placed under the orders of French. Meanwhile, when the 7th Division landed at Zeebrugge on the 7th October, it was to the accompaniment of the thunder of heavy artillery at Antwerp, the fall of which within the next few days was certain. In it were the Belgian field army and the British Naval Division, of which latter a great part was either captured or driven to seek safety in internment in Holland.

Being unable to relieve the fortress, it was the function of the IV Corps and the French Territorials acting with it to cover the retirement of the garrison. It was with this object that Ghent was occupied, as will be narrated presently, and a front was formed facing eastwards beyond it.

Sir John French's first instructions to Sir H. Rawlinson, when the latter was placed under him, were to hold the line of the Lys, if he could do so without risking a big battle. In that event the III Corps, the first to leave the Aisne, would join up with him on the 13th or 14th. If he should find himself forced to leave the line of the Lys, Rawlinson was to fall back in the direction of St. Omer, where the III Corps was detraining after its journey from the Aisne. That was the course which had to be followed, and the line of retreat to St. Omer passed through Ypres. What has been said above accounts sufficiently for the general movements of the 7th Division and the French Territorials, who were in Ghent on the 9th October. On that day Rawlinson had telegraphed to French that he was sending two brigades of the 7th Division to Ghent to cover the retreat of the Belgians to Bruges, and a brigade of the 3rd Cavalry Division to the Lys, towards Courtrai, for the same purpose. The Belgians, having passed through the covering force, fell back to the west bank of the Yser, where they remained till the end of the war.

With this general explanation we may proceed to follow the actual movements of the 2nd Scots Guards and the 20th Brigade, which was one of the two sent, under General Capper, to Ghent on the 9th October.

By 11 a.m. on the 7th October the battalion had arrived at Bruges by rail from Zeebrugge. It appears to have been among the earliest, if not the first, to arrive. The whole 20th Brigade was not assembled at Bruges till 3 p.m.

At Bruges, as on the journey, the British were received with great enthusiasm by the inhabitants, who had never before seen British troops.

Arrangements were made to billet the battalion at Varssenaere, about four miles south-west of Bruges, and towards 6 p.m. news came in that a German force was within about sixteen miles. R.F. and " F " Companies went on outpost duty, " F " guarding the roads towards Ostend and Thourout, whilst R.F. was on its left. Billets were bad and scattered, but the officers had comfortable quarters in a Belgian château.

About 10 a.m. on the 8th the battalion was ordered to join the division on the Bruges–Thourout road. It was necessary to cover the landing of the 3rd Cavalry Division at Ostend, and the battalion arrived there at 4.30 p.m. It was billeted at Steene, a village two miles south of Ostend.

Here it was with Brigade Headquarters in reserve, with the other three battalions farther out to the south and east. Many miserable and frightened Belgian refugees, intermingled with disorganized Belgian troops, had been seen during the march.

Here the battalion had its first sight of a German, in the shape of a " Taube," which flew over, and was pursued by a British aeroplane and a seaplane. In the morning of the 9th the battalion entrained at Ostend at 7.30 for Ghent, which was reached at 11 a.m. There had been much confusion at the start, owing to the disorganization in Ostend and the unsuitability of the station for entraining troops.

At Ghent the battalion was received by the population with great enthusiasm, which took a welcome material shape in gifts of food and tobacco for the men.

It bivouacked in the town, till joined later by the rest of the brigade.

The town was crowded with wounded Belgians and refugees from Antwerp, which was reported to have fallen. In the afternoon the battalion moved out to a position on the Ghent–Antwerp road, with the object of assisting the retirement of the Belgians from Antwerp. A number of Belgian artillery, cavalry, and cyclists passed through, saying they were pursued by large German forces, but not showing many signs of rough usage. The Belgian infantry were just evacuating Loochristy, five miles east of Ghent. The Scots Guards' outposts that night were entrenched astride the road, and extended to the railway on the right.

The Border Regiment was on the right, the Grenadiers on the left of the Scots Guards, the Gordon Highlanders in reserve on the railway embankment. There was no artillery support.

The Belgians had all passed through on their way to the Yser, and there was nothing now between the battalion and the Germans. Next morning they moved forward to a better position. Here entrenchments were made, strengthened by wire attached to trees felled across the road, and empty meat tins were scattered in front, as a means of giving an alarm of an approaching enemy.

That afternoon heavy artillery fire was heard from the direction of Antwerp, which had been evacuated on the 9th October. There was an alarm after midnight, in consequence of which the battalion stood to arms till daybreak, and then proceeded to strengthen its defensive works. A forward post had narrowly missed capturing a German officer seeking food and information as to the British position and strength. The same post also saw half a dozen Uhlans passing along the road on the right. The Scots Guards claimed first blood on this day, when Private Rae stated that he had emptied one saddle of a German patrol towards Loochristy. Practically nothing was known in the battalion as to the enemy's positions and movements. At 9 p.m. it was ordered back to Ghent. The immediate mission of the British force had been fulfilled, by drawing the Germans away and facilitating the retreat of the Belgian army from Antwerp. Artillery fire had been heard on the right, where the transport of the 21st Brigade had been shelled without serious damage. The cold was trying, as was the unaccustomed marching on cobbled roads, which, however excellent for artillery and heavy transport, are a terrible affliction to the feet of the infantry.

The march lasted all night, till Sommergem was reached at 6 a.m. with very sore feet. About fifteen miles of cobbled roads had been traversed in the night, with many delays due to the roads being blocked by artillery and transport. Here it was reported that Sergeant J. G. Burke was missing, and it will be as well here to give briefly the story of what had happened to him.

He, with Privates H. B. Wood [1] and J. O'Halloran, all of them battalion scouts, were in an advanced post one and a half miles in front of the R.F. Company. On the morning of the 11th October, when Burke came in to the company's trenches, he found them empty. He returned to his two men on the advanced post, being fired on by Uhlans just before he reached it. The two men had been hiding in a ditch, watching the passage of German troops on the road, and had had a narrow escape of capture when a dog with the Germans came and sniffed at them, but fortunately made no sign of its discovery. The men were crawling back towards where they supposed R.F. Company to be, when they met the sergeant.

The three then met a Belgian railway man, who beckoned them into his hut and provided them with civilian clothes.

[1] Private Wood afterwards gained the V.C. in September 1918.

They were then taken to a farm, where they buried their uniforms and equipments, and remained in hiding till the 12th, when a Belgian nurseryman of the name of Cannil told them the place was surrounded by Germans. This man and a friend then arranged to get passports for the soldiers in fictitious names. The three, with Cannil, then started across country, pioneered by another Belgian on a bicycle, who kept a look-out ahead. Their further adventures are too long to recount in full. After passing undetected a party of Uhlans, and avoiding a bridge guarded by Germans on the Ghent–Scheldt canal by crossing in a small boat, they had their narrowest escape when a half drunken German cyclist said they were all English. He was just drunk enough to be satisfied with their passports, and to ask them to have a drink with him. The invitation was declined on the ground of teetotalism, and the Dutch frontier was reached. The Dutch and Germans there were so busy looking after other travellers that the three Englishmen and their Belgian friend succeeded in slipping by unnoticed. Taking the train from Sas van Ghent to Terneuzen, they applied to the British Consul there, who saw to their papers and shipped them off in a small British steamer to England.

After this digression we return to the battalion, which we left at Sommergem at 6 a.m. on the 12th October. That afternoon the march was continued to Thielt. It was delayed by the roads being blocked by transport and ammunition columns. Thielt was not reached till 6 p.m., though the march had started at 2 p.m. Altogether, since the start in front of Ghent, thirty-two miles of cobbled roads had been covered. R.F. Company, owing to insufficient information about this flat and featureless country, had another four or five miles before finding its position on outpost.

Before the outposts were called in next morning, a German aeroplane, flying very low, was fired at and winged, and was eventually found, by the cavalry east of Thielt, smashed up and with its aviator and observer dead. That day (13th) the battalion marched from Thielt to Roulers. During the march there had been an alarm of German troops in the north, north-east, and south-east. This was at Pilkem. The baggage was sent on, and the 20th and 22nd Brigades were ordered to cover it in reconnoitred position. The Germans, however, failed to put in an appearance. The whole 20th Brigade only reached Roulers at 10 p.m., where it found comfortable billets.

CHAPTER III

Ypres : description of area—7th Division joins main army just south of Ypres—Battalions meet at Gheluvelt—Account of first battle.

BATTLES in ancient warfare, and even down to the Napoleonic era, had rarely extended over more than a single day ; many had been decided in an hour or two. With the advent of Napoleon they had occasionally extended to two or even three days. There were two days at Wagram and again at Bautzen, and Leipzig, the greatest battle so far between the armies of civilized powers, was spread over three. The Russo-Japanese war gave us the first instance of battles extending over many days and weeks. It was not till the greatest of all wars yet known that what was called a battle came to mean a series of struggles, each of them often greater than what used to be called a battle, spread over many weeks, and even months.

The first battle of Ypres lasted from the 19th October till the 22nd November 1914.

It is difficult for a traveller visiting Ypres for the first time in 1924 to imagine the abomination of desolation which represented the ancient town and the country surrounding it only five years before. Hardly a house was then anything but ruins for miles around. Forests and woods were wiped out, save for some blasted trunks of the gas-poisoned trees. The famous Cloth Hall was a hideous ruin, as indeed it still is.

Now all is changed again, and it is not difficult to conjure up a picture of what the neighbourhood must have been like in 1914. There are only two things which recall the desolation of 1918—the ruined Cloth Hall and Cathedral of Ypres, and the woods. In the latter the undergrowth flourishes, but the white, leafless and torn trunks and stumps of the larger trees recall the days of war. Elsewhere the fields are cultivated, the farms, the villages,

the churches rebuilt by the energy of an industrious population, who turned to, man, woman, and child, to repair the
damage. The one jarring note is the present brilliancy of
the new tiles and bricks. In places one has the impression
of being in a newly built garden settlement. Details of
trenches and dug-outs can only be seen in some places
where ground is useless or covered with undergrowth, but
the general lie of the country is of course unchanged.

Perhaps the first thing that strikes one from the military
point of view is that Ypres itself is the bottom of all things.
It is commanded from everywhere. Leaving out of consideration the Paschendaele ridge, overlooking the plain
at a considerable distance and nowhere by more than 150
feet, the command is generally small, often but a few feet
or metres ; but in modern war even that command is important, not as in the old days, because it is more difficult
to attack up a hill than down, but because the slight
command makes all the difference in the world to the
possibility of supporting infantry or cavalry by artillery
in their rear, and to the power of observation.

Again, a few feet of elevation will make all the difference,
in this low-lying country, between comparatively dry
trenches and places where trenches are impossible and a
line has to be held by detached posts sited where it is a
little drier, or the remains of an old building give something
of a firm foundation. Poelcappelle village, for instance,
stands only 20 to 30 feet above the marshy country of the
outskirts of the Forest of Houthulst. Yet the former is
comparatively dry, the latter, in wet weather or winter,
a mere marsh. In the majority of cases, for a great part
of the war, it was the Germans who held the dry places,
the British the wet ones. The edge of the Houthulst
Forest was an exception ; for there the conditions for
both sides were almost equally intolerable.

The heaviest fighting in the early days of the First Battle
of Ypres was in the southern portion of the forty miles
of front, towards Armentières. In it neither battalion of the
Scots Guards was engaged. The 2nd Battalion was the
first to come into action, on the 15th October, in the
Ypres neighbourhood. The first on that day was, as we

know, still on the Aisne, and it was only on the 21st October that it came on to the Ypres front with the I Corps, on the left of the IV, on the right of which was the Cavalry Corps. From Roulers, where it was on the 13th October, the march of the 2nd Battalion continued at 9.30 a.m. on the 14th via Moorslede to near Ypres, a distance of about twelve miles. Half a dozen Uhlans were seen north-east of Ypres. The Scots Guards themselves could not capture these mounted men, but they shepherded them into the arms of the Grenadiers, who duly took them. The Scots Guards now entrenched themselves hastily, as there was a good deal of movement of troops on their left, the nature of which was doubtful. Presently some cavalry appeared in that direction. The battalion knew nothing of the movements of the 3rd British Cavalry Division, but luckily it was perceived in time that this cavalry belonged to it. Entrenching continued till dark, but it was not till 1 a.m. on the 15th that the Scots Guards were relieved by French troops, who had been expected much earlier.

The 7th Division was now in touch with the advanced posts of the British army moved up from the Aisne and detrained in the Hazebrouck area.

The battalion got some rest in a neighbouring farmyard before marching again, at 7 a.m., to rejoin the brigade. When relieved by the French, they had been on outposts near Zillebeke. A move was then made to Verbranden Molen, a mile and a half south of Ypres, where the battalion entrenched itself in brigade reserve, the front line being held by the Border Regiment. This day was one of comparative rest after recent heavy marching with very little sleep. A badly wounded Uhlan was brought in, and the battalion was visited by Prince Arthur of Connaught. By 4 a.m. on the 16th October the 2nd Scots Guards were again on the move. There was a thick fog in the early morning when they passed through the Border Regiment to take up an outpost position about Gheluvelt, with R.F., "F," and "G" Companies in front and L.F. in reserve. The 1st Grenadier Guards were on the right about Zandvoorde, the Border Regiment in brigade reserve, and the Gordon

THE YPRES SALIENT, OCT. 1914.

Highlanders in divisional reserve. The 20th Brigade was now facing east, with the 21st on its left north of the Ypres–Menin road. On its right British cavalry continued the line, with outposts pushed out to Tenbrielen towards Vervicq. Soon after midnight of the 16th–17th the sounds were heard of a German attack on the 21st Brigade. The battalion stood to in trenches till 3 a.m., when the flank companies, under Major the Hon. H. Fraser, were sent forward to the village of Kruisecke, two miles in front of the centre, which was not occupied by the enemy. The two companies entrenched east of the village, R.F. on the right, L.F. on the left.

L.F. Company's trenches in front of Kruisecke extended from the entrance of the Klein Zillebeke road for about 700 yards south; R.F. was entrenched on the right of L.F. in a semicircle just short of the village of America on the Vervicq-Becelaere road.

It was learnt from refugees that the enemy was entrenching the line Menin–Vervicq–Comines. The entrenchments had been commenced by R.F., and it was not till about 9 a.m. that L.F. came into position and completed the line up to the Ypres–Menin road. In this position the two companies stood all day, suffering annoyance from snipers and enemy patrols. On two occasions enemy cavalry patrols were seen, one about 1,000 yards off in the direction of Vervicq and Comines, and the second almost in rear of the position. The latter were driven off by fire, but apparently without loss. By 4 p.m. the Germans were seen to be burning everything they could lay hands on towards Comines. The remaining two companies joined the flank companies soon after midnight of the 17th–18th. At this time the enemy were reported to be occupying the village of America, and a windmill about half a mile in front. An advance had been made earlier on the 17th by Captain Rivers-Bulkeley, with the object of clearing a wood which was unpleasantly near the front, but he had to withdraw, without loss, under the fire of a horse artillery gun. This wood was cleared about 9 a.m. on the 18th by the Bedfords (21st Brigade) sent up for the purpose. They came under very heavy shell fire as they attempted to

4

advance towards Gheluvelt and were forced to retire with some loss.[1]

To help this retirement, a party of R.F. Company of the Scots Guards went out under 2nd-Lieutenant Wynne-Finch. It covered the Bedfords right in the retirement and brought in a number of their wounded. There had been very little rifle fire from the enemy; the fire being almost entirely shrapnel. The Scots Guards party had no casualties.

The Gordon Highlanders now came up on the right of the Scots Guards, and entrenched facing south-east, with their left near the Kruisecke–Vervicq road. Beyond them the Border Regiment extended back to Zandvoorde.

The Scots Guards, after the clearing of the wood by the Bedfords, moved to a position farther forward, with their left touching the right of the 21st Brigade at the tenth kilometre stone from Ypres. Here they dug trenches, covered by R.F. Company, and, when this was completed, were sent to reserve at Kruisecke. The night of the 18th–19th was quiet. On the latter day a projected attack towards Menin was abandoned, and, owing to German threats towards the left, the Scots Guards and Gordons were sent to Reutl, a mile north of Gheluvelt as divisional reserve. They went to Zandvoorde during the following night. C.S.M. Wilson appears to have lost his way going round his company, and to have got in front of the trenches, where he was shot by a sentry who took him for an enemy. His dead body was found next morning. On that morning (20th) a reconnaissance in force was ordered towards Gheluvelt, with the object of making the enemy disclose his dispositions. The Scots Guards were to lead, with the Gordon Highlanders supporting. Assembly positions being reached about 9 a.m., the men took off their packs to facilitate their movements. The advance began, under very heavy shell fire, over a rise of the ground in a series of lines of platoons extended from 6 to 10 paces. The companies were disposed from right to left in the order G, F, L.F., R.F. When the second line of R.F. was crossing a ploughed field half a mile on the near side of

---

[1] Major Warner's diary attributes the loss to a spy dressed as a Belgian officer, but does not explain further.

America, it ran into a storm of shell fire concentrated on a small area from a range of 6,000 or 7,000 yards towards Vervicq. Thanks to the smallness of the area, and the fact that percussion and not shrapnel shells were used, there was only one casualty—Drummer Steer, who received a direct hit from a shell. The advance proceeded for about one and a half miles without any enemy infantry being seen and then was withdrawn after reaching America.

One section with Captain Kemble got into a farm, where it was cut off from direct retreat on " G " Company by heavy shelling. They managed to get out in another direction, but Warner says he and Captain Paynter had a nervous time waiting for them, and only got back behind the trenches just before a German attack, which was driven off by the Grenadiers and Gordon Highlanders. The battalion was fortunate in suffering only the one casualty just mentioned. The night was spent at Zandvoorde with L.F. Company on outposts.

The positions held by the 20th Brigade at this time were these : The 2nd Scots Guards at Zandvoorde had the Gordon Highlanders in front of them ; the Border Regiment was at Kruisecke, with its left on the Kruisecke–Menin road ; the Grenadier Guards were in front of them, east of Kruisecke. The line was continued to the left by the 21st Brigade. The trenches on the right of the 20th Brigade were in short lengths, not continuous, on the forward slope facing Vervicq and Comines. They were deep and narrow, with but little head cover.

At 8 a.m. on the 21st October R.F. Company was ordered to move up to support the Gordons. The Germans, however, were on the alert, and no sooner did the movement commence than they began to shell heavily the road of approach. Fortunately the shells were high, and passed over the Guards' heads to wreck a farm fifty yards west of the road. They were evidently percussion again. It was necessary to make a circuit to reach the Gordons. That battalion had suffered some casualties from Germans crawling close up to their trenches and had to clear their front by a bayonet charge.

The adventures of R.F. Company on this day were not

ended, for it was presently sent to fill a gap on the right of the brigade towards Hollebeke, where it found itself holding about a mile of front, with the Divisional Cyclists Company on its right and L.F. and " F " Companies of its own battalion on its left. Here it had to dig trenches under shell fire. About 3.30 p.m. Lieutenant Warner, in command of the company, learnt that the cavalry of the 3rd Cavalry Division at Hollebeke Château were hard pressed. To their aid he sent two of his platoons under Captain Fox and Lieutenant Holbech, and with this help the Germans were driven from the château, but any further advance was stopped by the British artillery fire still falling on the château. In the heavy shelling during the afternoon Major Lord Esmé Gordon-Lennox and eight men were wounded.

That night the battalion was relieved in its trenches by the Royals and 10th Hussars of the 3rd Cavalry Division. Orders now came sending the brigade forward again towards Gheluvelt. The 2nd Battalion was marching most of the night, reaching Veldhoek, just north of the Menin road, at 5 a.m., and being there in Divisional Reserve in a field close to the Ypres–Menin road.

Shelling began at 6 a.m. on the 22nd, and a German attack was launched against the 21st and 22nd Brigades.

The battle on the front of the 22nd Brigade, which was on the left of the division, was in Polygon Wood, a mile north of Veldhoek, and about 8 a.m. the battalion was ordered to move northwards to support the 22nd Brigade. In doing so they had to pass over a mile of shell-swept country, which they were fortunate to accomplish without casualties, except seven men in " F " Company. The new position, in thick wood, was entrenched in support of the Warwickshire and Wiltshire Regiments. Here the Scots Guards remained all day till 3 p.m., when R.F. and " G " Companies were ordered back to Kruisecke to support the Grenadiers and Gordons of the 20th Brigade, who were being hard pressed.

The shell-swept area passed over from south to north in the morning had again to be traversed in the reverse direction in order to reach Brigade Headquarters between

Zandvoorde and Kruisecke. Only three men were wounded in passing the main road. Whilst these two companies were returning southwards under Major Fraser, Colonel Bolton went with " F " and L.F. to support the 21st Brigade. " F," under Captain the Master of Kinnaird, was sent to support the Wiltshires, by whose Colonel he was required, despite his protest, to entrench his company in a position which he considered unsuitable. Beyond occupying this position of support, " F " Co. seems not to have been actively engaged during the rest of the day. L.F., in Polygon Wood, suffered the loss of its commander, Captain T. Rivers-Bulkeley,[1] who was killed by shell in the afternoon whilst making a reconnaissance. The company was taken over by Captain Fox on Captain Rivers-Bulkeley's death. The battalion was now divided into two halves, R.F. and " G " Companies being between Zandvoorde and Kruisecke, south of the Menin road, whilst " F " and L.F. were north of it, in support of the 21st Brigade, " F " being in trenches in close support of the Wiltshires.

R.F. and " G " had a very disturbed night, with Zandvoorde in flames behind them and frequent alarms in front.

As soon as it was light on the 23rd October, this half battalion in reserve was ordered to dig itself into shallow trenches to form a second line position in rear of Kruisecke, and by noon had made itself quite comfortable, and the trenches more or less shell-proof. Out of these they were brought about 1.30 p.m. to support the Gordons, who, however, were able to hold their own against the German attack, and the reserve returned to their new trenches.

Lieutenant Warnerof R.F., on going up to his outpost

[1] Of Captain Rivers-Bulkeley's death a brother officer wrote at the time : " The battalion has lost its very best officer—the best I ever served with. The Germans had got a brigade of maxims and some guns right up to our position, when we were hanging on for dear life till reinforcements arrived, under a withering gun and maxim fire. Our line was broken and Tommy with his own company was sent in to fill the gap—I after him, supporting him with " F " Company. He never looked behind, with six men he went forward, followed by the company. He walked right on and was shot at not more than 100 or 200 yards' range. His advance was magnificent, it stopped a gap being forced in our line, regiments behind took heart and poured into the breach."

trenches, found them occupied by Scots Guards and Gordons, rather mixed up, but behaving well. When ordered to stop the retirement, he found himself with a mixed section of Gordons and his own men.

At 7 p.m. this half battalion was sent into front line to relieve some of the Grenadiers who had had a heavy day and unavoidable losses. The night was disturbed, and the men had to turn out twice on heavy fire being heard at the outposts.

We must now return to the other half battalion north of the main road, where disaster overtook " F " Company. It will be remembered that that company was holding trenches of which its commander, the Master of Kinnaird, considered the position very dangerous. The Wiltshires were heavily attacked on the 24th and badly cut up, whilst the trenches held by " F " Company were blown in, with the result that nearly the whole of the company was either buried alive or taken prisoners. Amongst the dead was Captain the Master of Kinnaird. Lieutenant Orr was wounded, and 2nd-Lieutenant Lord Garlies taken prisoner, "F" Co. being reduced to a strength of twenty-six men. The other company, L.F., seems not to have been so seriously engaged this day, and returned next morning to Brigade Headquarters with Colonel Bolton.

The 25th October was again a day of tremendous fighting. The front of the 20th Brigade was held by the Grenadier Guards on the left, with the 21st Brigade on their left beyond the main road. The Border Battalion was on their right. The German attack on the point of junction with the 21st Brigade was most violent, and about 3 p.m. the Grenadiers reported that they and the Yorkshires (Green Howards) were heavily attacked by infantry and machine-guns. A splendid counter-attack retrieved the situation and broke the German effort in this direction. This had scarcely been done when Brigade Headquarters received a report from the Border Regiment on the right of the Grenadiers that they were seriously engaged. Two companies of the Scots Guards had already been sent up to the support of the Grenadiers and Yorkshires. Now, when a report, happily untrue, came in that the enemy was pushing through a breach in the Border Regiment, the other two companies (R.F. and " G ") and one of the Gordons, all under Major Fraser of the Scots Guards, were sent up to drive out the intruding Germans. In this operation they suffered some fifty casualties, which was specially to be regretted, seeing that the report of the break-through was false. At 6 p.m. the Grenadiers were again hard pressed, but fortunately it was now reported that the 1st Division had come up and was attacking towards Zonnebeke on the left, which would naturally tend to relieve the pressure on the 7th Division.

At the close of this desperate attack the line of the 20th Brigade was intact, though many of its trenches had been damaged. Of the shelling of this day an officer of Scots Guards writes :

" Never have I been through such a day as it was. It was a veritable hell on earth. There was an incessant shower of shells from 7.30 a.m. till 6 p.m. Luckily, the majority of the shells fell well in rear of the trenches, and, therefore, did little or no damage. However, two shells struck the edge of my trench, knocked over the four of us who were sitting there, and broke down all the loopholes of that section. No one was hurt beyond bruises."

Captain Paynter, with " G " Company,[1] relieved R.F. in the trenches, which ran north and south about 300 yards east of Kruisecke village ; the left trench was still held by Lieutenant Holbech of No. 4 platoon, R.F. Company. On his left were the Grenadiers. Captain Paynter's right was bent back to face south-east and the line was con-tinued, facing in that direction, by the Border Regiment. Of what happened to " G " Company during the day and up to 11.30 p.m., the following account was given by Captain Paynter :

" Our trenches were tremendously shelled all day, some of the trenches being blown in ; Drummond and Kemble, being buried in their trench, had to be dug out. A lot

---

[1] The other officers with " G " Co. were Lieutenants Kemble, Warner, Drummond, and Lord Clive;

of cheering was heard in the distance when it became dark, and it was passed down the trenches that the French were attacking on our right. Then we noticed masses of troops advancing on our trenches. It was extremely dark and raining in torrents. Some got as far as our trenches and were shot down, others lay down in front calling out ' We surrender,' and ' Don't shoot ; we are Allies,' ' Where is Captain Paynter " G " Company ? ' Parties got through the line on my right and left and commenced firing at us from behind, others got into houses. We shot at and silenced all these. Fresh lots kept coming on; but, as our fire was pretty heavy, they seemed to make for the places where others had got through. After about a couple of hours all was quiet. I was very relieved to hear Major Fraser's voice, about 11.30 p.m., calling to me we would be relieved by R.F. and L.F. Companies at dawn on October 26th."

How Major Fraser arrived on the scene, as described by Captain Paynter, must now be explained.

The German break through on the left of " G " Company had been effected by overwhelming Lieutenant Holbech's platoon of R.F. in the darkness. The men were driven out, but Holbech led them back in an attempt to retake it with the bayonet. In this attempt they were practically wiped out, and only Holbech and a few men survived.

News of the break-through had already been brought in to Headquarters by a man, and, though its truth was doubted at first, measures were taken for restoring the line.

The reserves of the Scots Guards available were R.F., less Lieutenant Holbech's platoon, L.F., and the small remains of " F " Company, about 300 strong in all. The two latter companies had just come back from north of the Menin road.

Major Viscount Dalrymple [1] was sent out with his own (R.F.) and L.F. Companies, but gave over command to his senior, Major Fraser, who joined him. As the flank companies approached Kruisecke, they met Lieutenant Holbech with three of his men, who reported the disaster of his platoon and said the Germans were in the north-east

[1] Now Earl of Stair.

part of the village. Major Fraser therefore wheeled to his right and arrived at the south-east end on the Vervicq road. There he heard troops marching along the road northwards. Going forward himself, he found that about 1,000 Germans were marching northwards towards Gheluvelt. Fraser then took forty men and got into communication with Captain Paynter, who was not aware of Lieutenant Holbech's trench having been taken. The trenches here were in small detached portions, and the Germans appear to have penetrated by the space between them. Fraser returned to his companies, which were waiting on the outskirts of Kruisecke. They then advanced to the north-east corner of the village, which the Germans had marched out of. Here they found two houses full of wounded British, mostly of the South Staffords,[1] who informed them that the Germans had gone, leaving them under guard of a sentry, who had also left later. Major Fraser then went off with Lieutenant Holbech and forty men to recapture the lost trench, to which Holbech guided him. Arrived close to it, he gave the order to charge, and at the same moment the Germans in the trench fired, killing Fraser himself, severely wounding Holbech, and killing or wounding most of the party. Presently Sergeant Mitchell and four men, the only survivors, got back and told what had happened. Lord Dalrymple then again took command, in consequence of Major Fraser's death.

Word now came in, from a platoon which had been extended to cover the road by which Major Fraser had gone, saying that a house on their left was occupied by Germans. Lord Dalrymple, wheeling R.F. to the left, sent Captain Fox with L.F. to attack the house from the west whilst he did so from the south. As Lord Dalrymple was going to the extended platoon, he was fired on by Germans issuing from the house. He at once charged with the platoon, killed the Germans outside, and called on the occupants to surrender. Whilst they were coming out and being passed down to Captain Fox, more Germans

---

[1] One company of the South Staffords had been with the 1st Grenadier Guards south of the main road.

fired from outside, east of the house, killing Sergeant Mitchell, who was standing beside his commander, and several others. Lord Dalrymple took prisoner the two nearest Germans, and pushing them before him, made them shout to the others not to shoot, and that they had surrendered.

The firing ceased, and a large number of Germans came out of the bushes and surrendered. Altogether 5 officers and 187 men were taken. Captain Fox and his weak company were sent to take them to Brigade Headquarters and return at once. Lieutenant Hope, Grenadier Guards, then came up, but he also was unaware of the capture of Holbech's trench. He knew its whereabouts, and offered to point out to a platoon a position from which it could be enfiladed at dawn. Lieutenant Wynne-Finch was sent in charge of this platoon. He was severely wounded by a shot from a house ; whereupon Lord Dalrymple, leaving the rest of his force to picket the eastern exits from Kruisecke, followed Lieutenant Hope to where he had posted Lieutenant-Wynne Finch's platoon. Going forward alone towards the trench, he found it empty, save for dead and wounded, both British and Germans, mostly killed or wounded by the bayonet.

Captain Paynter had held his trenches all night, as he had promised Major Fraser he would. He was now relieved by Captain Fox and Lord Dalrymple, the latter taking post in Lieutenant Holbech's trench.

By this time it was too light for it to be feasible to search Kruisecke, but that difficulty was solved by the German artillery, which destroyed every house in it, and must have buried any Germans left behind there. Colonel Bolton was now, with Lieutenant Menzies, the adjutant, in the forward trenches, where he had said he would remain. The German bombardment was terrific, Lord Dalrymple and his C.S.M. counted over 120 shell bursts within 100 yards round them in two minutes. About noon there were reports of giving way on the left, and about 1.30 p.m. some men of the company next to the Border Regiment on the right were seen to be retiring slowly across the rear. Here there was heavy firing along

Kruisecke village, and at the north end Lord Gerald Grosvenor, an officer of the battalion, was taken prisoner in a house to which he had gone to have his wounds dressed.

About 2.30 p.m. the front trenches were heavily fired on from the village in their rear, into which Germans had penetrated through the south face of the salient. The defenders might even then have got away to their left; but their orders were definite—to hold on to the last—and they held. At last the Germans were on them on all sides in overwhelming numbers, and surrender could not be avoided. Bushes and houses in the rear screened the assailants until they were actually on the trenches. Lord Dalrymple never saw them till he saw them mixed up with the British in the next trench. He had only five men at hand, whom he ordered to smash their rifles before he surrendered.

The officers of the battalion taken were Colonel Bolton, Major Viscount Dalrymple, Captain Fox (wounded), Captain Hon. J. S. Coke, Lieutenant Lord Gerald Grosvenor (wounded), and Lieutenant E. Trafford. Lieutenant Cottrell-Dormer and Lieutenant Gladwin (Machine-gun Officer) were killed.

Meanwhile a second line had been established on an arc of a circle, convex towards the enemy, from the left of the Gordons (who had not suffered severely) to Gheluvelt. It was held by the remains of the Scots Guards and the Border and South Staffordshire Regiments. Behind this line were the Grenadier Guards and the guns, as reserve in case of fresh attacks on the weakly held line. Fortunately, the Germans were, for the moment, at the end of their tether, and made no serious attempt on the new line. Nevertheless, at 8 p.m. it was considered to be so hazardously isolated that the brigade was withdrawn without molestation, to the Basseville stream in rear. It had lost one-third of its strength in the last twenty-four hours. The men were utterly exhausted, many of them having been for five days and nights continuously in trenches without relief, constantly shelled, and ending up with a night and a day of strenuous fighting.

Of the 2nd Scots Guards, when mustered next day, there

remained but 12 officers and 460 men, whilst the Border Regiment, whose losses were the next heaviest, had the same number of officers and 583 men.

The officers now left in the battalion were Captain Paynter,[1] commanding since the death or capture of his seniors ; Captain Kemble ; Lieutenants or 2nd-Lieutenants Lord Dalhousie, Warner, Sir F. Fitzwygram, Lord Cochrane, Saumarez, Taylor, Gibbs, and Lord Clive ; Captain Davis (Medical Officer) and Lieutenant and Quartermaster T. Ross.

On the 27th October the brigade was withdrawn to reorganize and report casualties and deficiencies. The 2nd Battalion Scots Guards was at Hooge, on the Menin road, when orders were received in the evening to move forward again and support the Grenadiers, who were at Gheluvelt. About 11 p.m. the Scots Guards were marching in column of route on the main road, when two shells were fired at them at short range. The first burst between the rear of R.F. and the head of " F " Company killing 2nd-Lieutenant Gibbs, six men, and two pack animals, and wounding Captain Kemble, Lieutenant Lord Dalhousie, and eight men. The second burst harmlessly. The battalion picketed the exits of Gheluvelt during the rest of the night, with orders to withdraw at dawn.

The 1st Battalion Scots Guards was now next on the left to the 2nd, holding trenches north of the road. On the 27th the IV Corps had been temporarily broken up, Sir H. Rawlinson and his staff being sent home to organise and bring out the 8th Division, which would form part of the IV Corps when reconstituted. The 7th Division, meanwhile, was put under the orders of Sir Douglas Haig, Commanding the I Corps.

The strength of the 2nd Battalion was 11 officers and 500 men on the 27th.[2]

Of this period of the battle Major-General Capper, commanding 7th Division, afterwards reported :

---

[1] Captain Paynter was awarded the D.S.O. for his conduct in front of Kruisecke.

[2] On the 26th Captain Paynter says he was in command with only 6 officers and 233 men. By November 14th he had 21 officers and about 1,000 men, " practically a new battalion."

" 2nd Battalion Scots Guards—as part of the 20th Infantry Brigade, this battalion assisted to hold the exposed position of Kruisecke in front of Ypres during the week. On the night of the 25th–26th October they were almost completely surrounded by the enemy, and were attacked in front and rear ; nevertheless, their reserve company counter-attacked the enemy and drove them from some houses, capturing 8 officers and 200 other prisoners. During the fighting this battalion lost very heavily.

" On subsequent occasions this battalion showed the greatest tenacity, and, as the fighting went on, this battalion seemed to me actually to gain in cohesion and firmness, in spite of weakened members and severe losses in officers. This testifies more than anything else I can say to the true soldiering spirit with which it is possessed."

Both battalions of the Scots Guards being now on the front about Ypres, it is necessary to recount what had happened to the 1st since we left them just detrained at Hazebrouck on the 18th October. After spending the 19th in billets at Hazebrouck, the battalion marched, on the 20th, to billets at Poperinghe, seven miles west of Ypres.

On the 21st the battalion started at 4.35 a.m. in the direction of Langemarck, a little east of north from Ypres, passing through Elverdinghe and Boesinghe. The Gloucesters of the 3rd Brigade were already fighting beyond Langemarck, in which village several shells burst as the battalion passed through, without doing any damage to it. To support the Gloucesters, " B " and L.F. Companies were sent forward from Pilckem, two platoons being sent to fill a gap between the Gloucesters and the 1st Queens. Two sections of them got into the village of Koekuit, about a mile north of Langemarck, held there as the Gloucesters retired, and fired vigorously on a German trench in front. In this affair L.F., to which the two sections belonged, lost four other ranks killed and five wounded. They took heavy toll of some Germans who got close up to them. They were drawn in at nightfall and rejoined Battalion Headquarters at Steenstverden.

Meanwhile, " C " and R.F. Companies had occupied trenches facing Bixschoote, a village on the left held by the enemy. On the 22nd October French Territorials attacked Bixschoote from the west, across the Scots Guards' front, but failed to drive out the Germans and retired to the west bank of the Yser canal. Whilst trying to explain to them how to change the direction of their attack, Lieutenant W. B. Lawson was killed by a sniper. Some of the retiring French had come right up to the battalion's trenches. Lieutenant G. F. de Teissier was wounded. During this day the enemy heavily attacked the Camerons, Black Watch, and Coldstream Guards and succeeded in taking the Camerons' trenches next on the right of the Scots Guards. In this Captain Stracey's company seems to have been involved, and at one time, when two platoons were sent to help him, the Camerons reported that he was the sole survivor. Fortunately this turned out not to be the case. The battalion spent a miserable, sleepless night, haunted by false accounts saying the rest of the brigade had been separated from them, and that at any moment they might expect to be surrounded by the enemy. On the 23rd October at 6 a.m. a counter-attack was made by the 2nd Brigade, supported by " C " Company Scots Guards, and the Camerons' trenches lost the day before were recovered. A German attack on the left of the Scots Guards at about 1 p.m. was repulsed with heavy loss. Otherwise there was nothing very remarkable on this day, or the 24th, except the usual heavy shelling and a great deal of sniping. At midnight of the 24th–25th the 1st Scots Guards left their trenches, on being relieved by a French Territorial Regiment.

A German attack was in progress during the relief, but was repulsed.

The total losses of the 1st Battalion in the Bixschoote neighbourhood had been 1 officer killed and 1 wounded ; of other ranks 5 killed, 25 wounded, and 5 missing. Help, as we know from what has been said about the 2nd Battalion, was now urgently required by the hard-pressed 7th Division towards Gheluvelt, and the 1st Division was to supply it. On the 25th the 1st Battalion reached Zillebeke, south-east of Ypres, and, marching at 5.30 a.m. next day via Hooge, reinforced the firing-line on the left of the 7th

Division near Gheluvelt. On the way it passed the transport of the 2nd Battalion and heard of its losses.

At Gheluvelt R.F. and L.F. were in front line on the right and left respectively, with "B" and "C" Companies in support. They at once came under heavy shell fire and received orders to attack the village of Poezelhoek, in conjunction with the 2nd Brigade, over open ground, which was already held by the Bedfords. The enemy fire of all sorts was very destructive, and when the battalion had at last got within 200 yards of his trenches and the loopholed buildings of Poezelhoek, it was ordered to hold on, which it did for the rest of the day, though with heavy losses. Captain C. F. P. Hamilton was killed, Lieutenants M. O. Roberts and J. L. Wickham were wounded, and the total casualties were about 130.

That night the battalion took over the trenches of the Bedfords, where they spent the night of the 27th, unable to move during daylight in face of the fierce shelling and sniping. That night Captain R. F. Balfour was killed. The trenches were about half a mile north-east of Gheluvelt. The same situation continued throughout the 28th, when warning was received that the German 27th Reserve Division had been brought up and was expected to attack at 5.30 a.m. on the 29th. The attack began, punctually at the hour predicted, on the north front.

The 1st Battalion Scots Guards was in position with L.F. Company on the left, facing north, and touching the right of the Camerons. On the right of L.F. was " C " Co. beyond it R.F., having on its right the Black Watch and Coldstream Guards. Of " B " Company half was in support, the other half with R.F. on the right. The front of the 1st Scots Guards faced north on its left, north-east on its right.

The German attack came on in overwhelming force till it was within 200 yards of L.F., when it could no longer face the accurate fire, and came to a standstill. The same thing occurred on the front of the other companies.

It was about 1 p.m. when a company of the Gloucesters, who had come up to reinforce the Coldstream, was driven in disorder on L.F. A few of them were collected by Sir V. Mackenzie, together with a few Coldstream. News had come in to him that the Germans had broken through on the right of the battalion, and he was expecting to receive their enfilade fire. The Black Watch and the Coldstream Guards were both reported to have been cut up, thus exposing the right of the 1st Scots Guards. The report proved to be only too near the truth. As a result, R.F. was surrounded and practically destroyed, as well as the half of " B " Company with it, and two sections of " C."

The Gloucesters, on the Menin road, had been broken through, and with their right flank exposed, the two battalions on their left had to fall back.

To meet this position " C " Co. retired about 100 yards, and took up a new position facing right. L.F. held on where it was, with its right flank protected by " C " in its new position. The latter was reinforced on its right by a platoon of L.F. and some of the stragglers picked up by Sir V. Mackenzie and Captain Stephen. The Germans were then within 100 yards of " C " Co., and, says Sir V. Mackenzie, " God knows how many we killed." Here that officer himself was wounded and had to be helped back to the dressing-station at Gheluvelt Château. Before he left, the attack had begun to collapse under the devastating fire of " C " Co., and the Germans were beginning to fall back. Still the situation was desperate, and the news that the 3rd Brigade was at hand to help was received with a sigh of relief. When that brigade came up, the almost desperate situation had been saved by the magnificent constancy of the 1st Scots Guards. But the great deed had cost the battalion very dear. R.F., as has been stated, to all intents and purposes no longer existed, and the half of " B " Co. with it had, of course, suffered almost equally. Of officers Lieutenant Sir G. N. Ogilvy, Bart., had been killed, whilst the wounded were Captain and Adjutant A. A. L. Stephen,[1] Captain Sir V. A. F. Mackenzie, Bart., Lieutenant Hon. G. E. H. Macdonald[2] (missing). The missing were Captain C. de la Pasture, and Lieutenants B. G. Jolliffe,[3] C. F. F. Campbell,[3] and R. H. FitzRoy. Captain

[1] Died of his wounds on the 31st October.
[2] Died 2nd November.
[3] Afterwards found to be dead.

R. G. Stracey took over as second-in-command and adjutant of the 1st Battalion. The casualties of the day were about 240 in all.

The enemy had had enough of it on this day, and next day his infantry were not seen, though the woods to the east were known to be full of them. That did not diminish the artillery fire, which continued all day with unmitigated violence. The 1st Scots Guards now had the South Wales Borderers on their right, with the Welsh Regiment and the Queen's extending to the Menin road.

The 31st October was one of the most critical days of the First Battle of Ypres, days of which Sir John French wrote :

" All said and done, however, the main element of success was to be found in the devoted bravery and the stern unyielding determination to ' do or die ' displayed by the rank and file of the ' contemptible little army ' and its reinforcements."

The battle of the 31st began early, with a more terrible storm of shells than ever, and this was followed up by overwhelming infantry attacks. It was about 11 a.m. when, in consequence of the left of the 7th Division being forced back, and so exposing their right flank, the Welsh Regiment and the Queen's were also driven back, followed shortly by a half battalion of the South Wales Borderers. Half of L.F. Company of the 1st Scots Guards was sent up to reinforce the line, but it still could not stand against the fury of the German infantry attack advancing along the Menin road. Gheluvelt was still in British hands at 11.30, when the 1st (Guards) Brigade, including the remainder of the 1st Scots Guards, less half L.F. Company, stood ready to enfilade the enemy from his right as he advanced. The British artillery also contributed largely to temporarily holding up the German attack at Gheluvelt.

The relief in the situation was only temporary, and soon after noon the enemy was reported to be massing east of Gheluvelt. The attack was met with the greatest obstinacy, but the German superiority of numbers was too great to be resisted, and by 2 p.m. Gheluvelt was in the enemy's

5

possession. It was then that Brigadier-General Fitz-Clarence brought up the last available reserve in this part, in the shape of three companies of the 2nd Worcesters [1] (2nd Division) from behind Polygon Wood. West of Polderhoek Château they deployed to cross another 1,000 yards of open country under a devastating fire. The remainder of the 1st Scots Guards and the South Wales Borderers were still holding back the enemy, who had almost surrounded them near Gheluvelt Château, and the arrival of the three Worcester companies on their right was just in time to save them from complete destruction. The Germans in Gheluvelt were busy looting, and the unexpected arrival of the Worcesters on their right flank took them by surprise, and enabled the British troops west of the village to rally and help in driving the enemy from it. The 1st Scots Guards were able to play their part in completing the discomfiture of the Germans in and about Gheluvelt. The lost positions were recovered, and the British front was advanced beyond its morning position.

It was, however, decided to withdraw from this position to one on the next ridge in rear of Gheluvelt, and there during the night the small remains of the 1st Scots Guards (little over 100 men) dug in north of the Menin road.

On this day of desperate fighting the 1st Battalion lost Captain W. J. Wickham, killed, and Major B. G. Van De Weyer, wounded and captured.

During the ensuing night the battalion dug itself in in new trenches between Gheluvelt and Veldhoek. The 1st November was a fairly quiet day. The Gloucesters were on the right of the battalion. In the evening 200 men of the Coldstream Guards relieved the Gloucesters and occupied a barricade across the Menin road, with the 2nd King's Royal Rifle Corps on their right. In the morning of the 2nd the barricade was destroyed by German artillery, and the Coldstream and K.R.R.s were forced to fall back. The Scots Guards also were badly shelled, their trenches being broken in. Captain Stracey was buried for an hour and a half, hardly able to breathe till he was dug out. The enemy, pushing along the road towards Ypres, opened

---

[1] Only 7 officers and 350 other ranks.

fire on the rear of the Scots Guards with machine-guns and enfiladed them with artillery. To meet this danger " C " Company was thrown back on the right to face the road towards the south. In the evening the line was consolidated 300 yards in rear of its morning position. On this day Lieutenant Sir I. Colquhoun was wounded.

On the 3rd November the 1st Scots Guards, with the Loyal North Lancashires, the Camerons, Black Watch, and a battalion of French Zouaves held the Menin road south of Veldhoek and dug new trenches. The bombardment cost the battalion thirteen men.

The 4th was a comparatively quiet day, on which a *point d'appui* was made at a burnt farm-house near Gheluvelt Wood. In this position the line remained till the 7th, suffering from German artillery fire on each day. On the 4th and 5th reinforcements of 110 men arrived, and Lieutenants R. N. Gipps and F. A. Monckton were killed on the 7th.

On the 8th November the German infantry attacks were renewed. They got into communication trenches of the Loyal North Lancashires and Zouaves on the right, and thence were able to enfilade the trenches of the 1st Scots Guards. A counter-attack by the supports of the Loyal North Lancashires and Scots Guards drove them out, but they still held some trenches on the right, and attempts to drive them out by machine-guns failed. On this day Lieutenant B. Winthrop Smith, who had only just arrived with the last reinforcements, Lieutenant J. Stirling-Stuart, and Lieutenant Sir J. S. Dyer were wounded, the two former mortally. Lieutenant A. W. Douglas Dick was missing and afterwards found to have been killed. Twenty more men were killed and thirty wounded.

The next two days were fairly quiet, but for the usual shelling, causing six casualties, which broke out with redoubled fury at 6.30 a.m. on the 11th and lasted for three hours, ruining the trenches and burying many men. Then the Prussian Guard attacked in great strength through Veldhoek and captured the front trenches on the whole line of the 1st Brigade.

The Scots Guards were at this time holding the burnt

farm near Gheluvelt Wood.[1] This place had been shelled to pieces in the morning bombardment, but the men of the Scots Guards in the orchard held on under Captain Stracey when the trenches to right and left had fallen. They did great execution on the enemy till, attacked by infantry from the wood, they were at last overwhelmed. All that escaped were Battalion Headquarters, 5 men from the fire trench, 30 from the orchard, and 4 from the *point d'appui*. These managed to rejoin the rest of the brigade by evening. The enemy had at one time got to within 200 yards of the British guns, but there they were repulsed with enormous losses. The 1st (Guards) Brigade mustered that night altogether 4 officers and 300 men. It had lost its gallant commander, Brigadier-General Charles FitzClarence, V.C., killed.[2] The 1st Scots Guards had been practically destroyed. Its total casualties from its first entry into the Battle of Ypres up to the 15th November were 9 officers killed, 7 wounded, 5 missing; of other ranks 105 had been killed, 151 wounded, and 430 were missing. On the 12th November the 1st Brigade went into reserve at Hooge, when Captain Stracey and the remaining 69 men of the 1st Battalion, with the rather stronger remains of the Black Watch and Cameron Highlanders, dug themselves in in the wood in front of the château.[3]

The weather had now broken, and storms of snow and rain turned the whole neighbourhood into a sea of mud.

The Battle of Ypres lasted till the 22nd November, but for the shattered remnants of the 1st Scots Guards it ended on the 16th, when they marched via Vlammertinghe to billets at Westoutre, where Lieut.-Colonel H. C. Lowther, on recovery from the wound he had received on the Aisne six weeks before, resumed command. It consisted of one combatant officer, Captain Stracey, the Quartermaster,

---

[1] The whole of the 1st (Guards) Brigade at this time counted only about 800 of all ranks, made up of the 1st Scots Guards, 1st Cameron Highlanders, and 1st Black Watch.

[2] At a point between Polygon Wood and Nonne Boschen, three-quarters of a mile north of the main road at Veldhoek.

[3] In a lecture delivered by Colonel Fortescue, he described the Menin road fight 31st October–11th November of the 1st Bn. Scots Guards as the incident he would choose as most typical of individual performances.

and 73 rank and file. On the 17th the battalion marched to Borre, where it was joined by the 6th and 7th reinforcements of 189 rank and file with the following officers : Major A. V. Poynter, D.S.O., Lieutenants or 2nd-Lieutenants Hon. R. Coke, H. G. E. Hill-Trevor, Hon. R. Norton, Hon. R. Bethell, and R. Dormer.

At Borre the battalion remained, resting and refitting, till the 20th December.

Before quitting the First Battle of Ypres it remains to give the story of the 2nd Battalion Scots Guards since we left it at Gheluvelt on the evening of the 28th October. At dawn on the 29th October the battalion returned to its dug-outs at Veldhoek, and remained there till, at 10 a.m., it received orders to counter-attack.

The German artillery was at this time concentrating its fire on the Menin road. This was the day on which R.F. Company and others of the 1st Battalion were cut off.

Matters were in a bad position between 10 and 11 a.m., when the 1st Grenadiers and 1st Gordon Highlanders of the 20th Brigade had suffered badly and were being driven back. The 2nd Scots Guards (reserve of 20th Brigade) and the 2nd Queens (22nd Brigade) were sent up to counter-attack north-eastwards. The attack of these and other battalions sent up to reinforce the front line was successful, and ended in the evening with the recapture of all the positions lost earlier beyond Gheluvelt. At the end of this advance the 2nd Scots Guards found themselves well in front of the general line regained by other troops and selected for the outpost line during the night. Their withdrawal to that line was disastrous, for in the darkness and rain troops in the line mistook them for the enemy and fired into them, causing considerable casualties. Their losses on this day amounted to 31 killed and 104 wounded. The battalion went into billets for the night at a farm 300 yards in rear of the outpost line. Only 150 men could be mustered that night, though apparently others dribbled in later. It was very dark, and the men were wet through by the pouring rain.

When, about noon on the 30th, the battalion was sent back from the Gheluvelt–Zandvoorde road to the woods in rear to cover the guns, it met the Gordon Highlanders, who had suffered very heavy losses. A battery in a field had been knocked to pieces by the German guns, one gun was upside down and surrounded by dead gunners. A reserve was constituted of the 1st Grenadier Guards with 180, the 2nd Scots Guards with 200, and the Border Regiment with 250 men, whilst the 4th (Guards) Brigade, which had now come up, took post on the right of the Gordons (21st Brigade). The left of the Border Regiment was on the main road, with the 2nd Scots Guards and Grenadiers on the right. In this position, 100 yards in rear of the forward slope to Gheluvelt, the reserve dug itself in in the night. The enemy was in possession of Zandvoorde.

The bombardment, with a reckless expenditure of ammunition, which fell upon this little reserve on the 31st would have broken any but the very best of troops.

On this critical day the 2nd Scots Guards remained in the trenches whilst the Germans made head on the main road till beaten and driven back by the famous charge of the Worcesters falling on their right. At night the 2nd Battalion was relieved in the trenches by the Rifle Brigade, and moved, with the 20th Brigade, more to the right. The casualties were small on this day. The whole brigade was now so weak that it could only hold from 300 to 400 yards of trench.

The next day passed with nothing noticeable for the 2nd Scots Guards, beyond the continued bombardment, by which Lieutenant D. R. Drummond was killed on the 3rd November. On the 5th the battalion was relieved by the 1st Gordon Highlanders (3rd Brigade), and received a reinforcement of Lieutenant C. A. M. Cator and 100 Base details. Since the 27th October it had lost 4 officers and 136 men.

After marching till 6 a.m. on the 6th November, the battalion found itself at Locre. It marched again at noon, and by 5 p.m. was in Army Reserve at Meteren, west of Bailleul, resting and refitting. The march over cobbled roads for about fifteen miles had been very trying. On the 9th General Capper addressed the brigade on parade, and made special remarks to each battalion. We know his opinion of the 2nd Scots Guards from the quotation already made on p. 47.

On the 11th the battalion was joined by a draft of 250 other ranks, with the following officers :

Captain-Bagot Chester, Captain Viscount Coke, Lieutenant Hon. F. Hanbury-Tracy, 2nd-Lieutenants Earl of Lisburne, H. H. Liddell-Grainger, G. C. L. Ottley, and A. H. C. Swinton.

Next day a further draft of 285 arrived, with Captains M. Romer, Hon. R. Coke, Lieutenants Sir E. Hulse, Bart., and Hon. E. Massey, 2nd-Lieutenant R. T. Barry. The battalion was now fairly strong. It was visited on the 13th by Field-Marshal Sir John French, who complimented it on its fine performance at Ypres. Alas ! the numbers who had been present there also were sadly thinned by death and wounds. On the 14th the 2nd Scots Guards marched to a different part of the front. Passing through Bailleul, they reached and took over from the 19th Brigade its trenches at Sailly, on the right bank of the Lys, two miles north-east of Estaires.

CHAPTER IV

TRENCH WARFARE, 1914–1915

Monotony of trench warfare—2nd Battalion at Sailly: raids—1st Battalion at Givenchy December 21st, the "Triangle" January 1st, Brickstacks January 26th.

WE have now arrived at the commencement of the first of the long periods of trench warfare which characterized the greater part of the war on the Western front. There were times when the monotony of life in various degrees of discomfort and misery in the trenches, or in reserve, was only relieved at intervals by the excitements of raids carried out against the enemy's trenches, or of defence against raids in the reverse direction. Raids, too, varied in degree from a mere exploring expedition by a patrol into the enemy's trenches to operations of much larger scope and more elaborate design, aiming at the rectification of the line or the obliteration of an inconvenient or dangerous salient.

Trenches were another variable in the equation of life during the Great War. In the last years, and in the drier parts of the front, they became more tolerable than in the early days, when they were almost unbearably wretched, especially in low-lying tracts, like many of those about Ypres or La Bassée. The following short extracts from the diary of an officer, in June, 1916, may serve to give some idea of these miseries in the Ypres salient, even at that comparatively late date.

" June 15th.—My two platoons, 1 and 2, were supposed to take over a trench behind Maple Copse, but the guide told us it had been blown flat, so we took over from a party of 35 Canadians who were in a shallow communication trench in front of Maple Lodge. My two platoons were about 60 strong. The trench we took over was about 3 feet deep and 7 feet broad, with about a foot of mud at the bottom and a few shelters hollowed out of the sides and in full view of the enemy from both flanks. We spent

58

the night in deepening the trench and making more dug-outs. The other platoons were in holes in the ground about 200 yards in front. R.F. and L.F. Headquarters were in the only dug-out in Maple Copse which had not been blown up. . . . In the dug-out were 7 officers, 2 C.S.M.s and servants, orderlies, and signallers, and about two feet of water, rotten meat, equipment, coats, etc., German and Canadian. . . .

" June 16th.—No. 2 platoon officer and I had a dug-out which we had room to lie in side by side with our feet sticking out into the trench. . . .

" June 19th.—Zillebeke is absolutely flat ; we lived in a dug-out in a ruined house. There were a lot of dead men lying all round and the smell was awful ; also the dug-out would not have kept out a shell of any kind."

Men must have sighed for the good old days of the early nineteenth century, when a truce after a battle so often provided an opportunity for the burial of the dead and the collection of the wounded.

The trenches above described were certainly below the average, especially after the first year of war ; but in these and similar neighbourhoods, where the high level of the water forbade digging to any depth, it was never possible for them to attain the comparative comfort and security of others in such country as the rolling downs above the valleys of the Somme and Ancre. There matters were much better, and, as the war went on, dug-outs, especially those taken from the enemy, were often wonderful excavations, deep enough to be safe against the heaviest shell, and fitted up with electric lighting and furniture.

Bombardment of trenches was a daily characteristic of trench life, with its accompaniment of casualties varying from day to day with the severity of the fire, and with accidental circumstances, such as the explosion of a heavy shell when the trenches were particularly crowded during a relief.

We should soon find ourselves at the limit of our available space were we to attempt to give precise details from day to day of the trenches held by a battalion, of the reliefs between front trenches, support, and reserve, or of the daily casualties. All we can do in these periods is to state generally the position of the battalions and to give some account of the more important raids and incidents.

Most of the available space is generally required for more detailed accounts of the great battles and attacks in which the Scots Guards took part, and the names of which are inscribed on their colours, or added to the list of their battle honours.

The 2nd Battalion was the first to begin its experience of winter trench warfare when it went into trenches at Sailly on the 14th November, 1914, on the left of an Indian Division, who seem to have disturbed what little slumber might be hoped for by firing heavily all night. It was very cold, hailing and snowing, snipers fairly active, trenches muddy, and much work to be done on them in the way of making covered shelters, and generally doing what could be done to improve them. Altogether an unpleasant beginning of the winter. When the rain and snow changed to frost, it was dry, but then digging became difficult. At this time, seven days of trenches were succeeded by three out of them.

On the 24th November Captain Paynter went down with fever, and Captain Hon. R. Coke took over command of the battalion.

The first raid was carried out in the night of the 27th-28th November, by Lieutenant Sir E. Hulse with eight men, on the right of the battalion line. Passing, unobserved by the enemy, over some 200 yards of No Man's Land, the raiders fired several rounds down the enemy's trench. This drew a heavy fire on the returning party, who lost two men missing, besides one killed and four wounded. In broad daylight next day Privates Rae, Robertson, and Ferguson crawled to the German trench to explore. Rae was not noticed till he was practically in the trench. He was killed by a bullet as he attempted to return. On the 30th there was another change in the command, as Captain Coke was wounded, and Captain G. H. Loder took over.

The 1st December was signalized by a visit from H.M. the King, with the Prince of Wales, Sir J. French, and General Joffre. Medals were presented, but the battalion was in trenches and His Majesty expressed his disappointment at not being able to see it or the Grenadier Guards.

After this nothing unusual occurred till the 17th December, except the return of Captain Paynter to command on the 5th. The weather was generally bad. On the 17th Lieutenant Cator was wounded, and 2nd-Lieutenant Barry and the machine-gun section had a narrow escape from a " Jack Johnson " which burst close to them.

On the 18th the first serious attack on the German trenches was led by Captain Loder with two companies (" F " and L.F.). The instructions received by him from Captain Paynter were to keep his right on the Sailly–Fromelles road, his left extending about 400 yards eastwards to the point of junction with the Border Regiment, which was to carry on from this point.

Captain Loder was ordered on the afternoon of the 18th to meet Captain Askew of the Border Regiment and arrange details between the two regiments with him. It was decided that at 6 p.m., or just before, the men were to be hoisted over the parapet, to crawl through the British wire, and lie down outside it. On this being done Captain Loder would sound his whistle and the line would move forward together, walking until the Germans opened fire, and then rushing the front-line trenches. When the German trench was reached, if it was found occupied, Captain Loder would hold it if possible ; if it were not occupied, he would pass on to the second line. The men were to carry spades and sandbags. " F " Company (Lieutenant Sir F. FitzWygram) was on the right, " L.F." (Captain H. Taylor) on the left. The men were hoisted over the parapet about three minutes to 6 a.m. and crawled through the wire.

Unfortunately, owing to the noise of the gunfire, the whistle signal was not heard throughout the line, and by the time it had moved forward about 60 yards it was apparent to Captain Loder, in the centre, that the line was irregular. Collecting the men nearest him, he found himself on the German parapet almost before the enemy had opened fire. There was no wire to be passed. Loder and his men jumped into the trench, bayoneting or shooting all the Germans they could see. There was some shouting and confusion, and Captain Loder could not see far to right or left. Where he was the trench had no traverse for a length of at least 25 yards. He ordered the men, who were carrying spades and sandbags, to make firing positions in the rear face of the trench ; others were posted to watch the flanks, and to make traverses if the enemy appeared on them. After he had been about an hour in the trench, he went to see what was happening elsewhere. He could get no information, but saw many dead bodies of his men lying in front of the German trench.

If the trench was to be held, reinforcements were clearly needed, and Captain Loder returned to get Captain Paynter's orders on this subject. The Brigadier was consulted, and, as it was now clear that the Border Regiment had failed in its attack, and that the right of " F " Co. was only in the German trench in places, it was decided not to send in the other two companies of the battalion from reserve. An attempt was made to sap up to the trench ; but, with 180 yards to cover under a heavy fire, this soon appeared to be out of the question. A supporting attack by a party of " G " Co. had failed to maintain itself in the trench, and had retired, except eleven men who remained with Lieutenant Hon. J. Saumarez, who was wounded. Lieutenant G. Ottley,[1] commanding a reserve, was mortally wounded before reaching the trench, and was brought in with great courage by Corporal Mitchell. Eleven dead Germans on either side, piled up. Lieutenant Saumarez captured one German and kept him all night.

These eleven men with Saumarez were still in the trench when, at 3 a.m., Lieutenant Warner, with Corporal Jones as guide, and ten men went up there. Only six of the men arrived with Warner, who found Saumarez's position untenable and practically surrounded. Just before dawn, Warner's party returned, bringing in one prisoner, the wounded Lieutenant Saumarez, and two wounded men.

It was in the course of this affair that the Victoria Cross was gained by Private James Mackenzie under

[1] Lieutenant Ottley was awarded the D.S.O. for this action.

circumstances which are recorded in the following extract from the *London Gazette* of the 18th February, 1915 :

" No. 8185 Private James Mackenzie, late 2nd Battalion Scots Guards. For conspicuous bravery at Rouges Bancs on the 19th December, 1914, in rescuing a severely wounded man from in front of the German trenches under a very heavy fire, and after a stretcher-bearer party had been compelled to abandon the attempt. Private Mackenzie was subsequently killed on that day whilst in the performance of a similar act of gallant conduct."

The casualties in this attack were about 180 other ranks, nearly 50 per cent. of the number engaged.

The officer casualties were :

L.F. :
  Killed : Captain H. Taylor.
  Missing, killed : 2nd-Lieutenant R. F. R. Nugent.
  Wounded : Lieutenant Hon. J. St. V. B. Saumarez.
" F " Company :
  Killed : Lieutenant Hon. F. Hanbury-Tracy.
  Wounded : Lieutenant Sir F. FitzWygram.
" G " Company :
  Died of Wounds : Lieutenant G. C. L. Ottley.

The failure of the attack appears to have been due to the signal not being heard everywhere, and the men consequently being split up into small groups, of which those farther back were exposed to the full blast of the German fire which had not developed when the leading party with Captain Loder had reached the trench. The heavy losses were mainly due to a cross-fire of machine-guns. The Germans were not using bombs or hand-grenades.

Next day the battalion was withdrawn to Divisional Reserve at Sailly, when an order by General Capper was received saying :

" The IV Corps Commander desires me to say that he has received the report of the gallant conduct of the two companies of the 2nd Battalion Scots Guards under Captain Loder, in the attack last night on the enemy's trenches.

" The Corps Commander is sorry that the trenches could

not be held, and he much regrets the loss of so many gallant officers and men. The attempt, though not completely successful in itself, has been of great use and service in the general plan of the Allied Armies."

The battalion returned to trenches in fine frosty weather on the 23rd December, and were there on the first Christmas Day of the War.

On that day, for the first and almost the last time in this war, an attempt was made to return to the old temporary and informal truces which, as at Talavera, occasionally occurred even in the middle of the fiercest battles. The advances came first from the German side, but were freely reciprocated. What happened on that Christmas Day was learnt with anything but approval at British G.H.Q., and probably did not meet with any better reception by the German authorities, at any rate when they found that they had gained little or nothing from the fraternization. There is a long account of the day in the 2nd Battalion diary, but we prefer to it the following graphic quotations from a printed private letter of Lieutenant Sir E. Hulse :

" We stood to arms as usual at 6.30 a.m. on the 25th, and I noticed that there was not much shooting ; this gradually died down, and by 8 a.m. there was no shooting at all, except for a few shots on our left (Border Regiment). At 8.30 a.m. I was looking out, and saw four Germans leave their trenches and come towards us ; I told two of my men to go and meet them, unarmed (as the Germans were unarmed), and to see that they did not pass the half-way line. We were 350–400 yards apart at this point. My fellows were not very keen, not knowing what was up, so I went out alone, and met Barry, one of our ensigns, also coming out from another part of the line. By the time we got to them they were three-quarters of the way over, and much too near our barbed wire, so I moved them back. They were three private soldiers and a stretcher-bearer, and their spokesman started off by saying that he thought it only right to come over and wish us a happy Christmas, and trusted us implicitly to keep the truce. He came from Suffolk, where he had left his best girl and a 3¼-h.p. motor-bike ! He told me that he could not get a letter to the girl, and wanted to send one through me. I made him write out a postcard in front of me in English and I sent it off that night. I told him that she probably would not be a bit keen to see him again. We then entered on a long discussion on every sort of thing. I was dressed in an old stocking-cap and a man's overcoat, and they took me for a corporal, a thing which I did not discourage, as I had an eye to going as near their lines as possible ! They praised our aeroplanes up to the skies, and said that they hated them and could not get away from them. They would not say much about our artillery, but I gathered that it does good damage, and they don't care for it. The little fellow I was talking to was an undersized, pasty-faced student type, talked four languages well, and had a business in England, so I mistrusted him at once. I asked them what orders they had from their officers as to coming over to us, and they said none ; that they had just come over out of good-will.

" They protested that they had no feeling of enmity at all towards us, but that everything lay with their authorities, and that being soldiers they had to obey. I believe that they were speaking the truth when they said this, and that they never wished to fire a shot again. They said that unless directly ordered, they were not going to shoot again until we did. They were mostly 158th Regiment and Jaegers, and were the ones we attacked on the night of the 18th. Hence the feeling of temporary friendship, I suppose. We talked about the ghastly wounds made by rifle bullets, and we both agreed that neither of us used dum-dum bullets, and that the wounds are solely inflicted by the high-velocity bullet with the sharp nose at short range. We both agreed that it would be far better if we used the old South African round-nosed bullet, which makes a clean hole.

" They howled with laughter at a D.T. of the 10th which they had seen the day before, and told me that we are being absolutely misguided by our papers, that France is done, Russia has received a series of very big blows, and will climb down shortly, and that the only thing which is keeping the war going at all is England ! They firmly believe all this, I am sure. They think that our press is to blame in working up feeling against them by publishing false ' atrocity reports.' I told them of various sweet little cases which I have seen for myself, and they told me of English prisoners whom they have seen with soft-nosed bullets, and lead bullets with notches cut in the nose ; we had a heated, and at the same time, a good-natured argument, and ended by hinting to each other that the other was lying !

" I kept it up for half an hour, and then escorted them back as far as their barbed wire, having a jolly good look round all the time, and picking up various little bits of information, which I had not had an opportunity of doing under fire ! I left instructions with them that, if any of them came out later, they must not come over the half-way line, and appointed a ditch as the meeting place. We parted, after an exchange of Albany cigarettes and German cigars, and I went straight to Headquarters to report.

" On my return at 10 a.m. I was surprised to hear a hell of a din going on, and not a single man left in my trenches ; they were completely denuded (against my orders), and nothing lived ! I heard strains of ' Tipperary ' floating down the breeze, swiftly followed by a tremendous burst of ' Deutschland über Alles,' and as I got to my own Company Headquarters' dug-out, I saw, to my amazement, not only a crowd of about 150 British and Germans at the half-way house which I had appointed opposite my lines, but six or seven such crowds, all the way down our lines, extending towards the 8th Division on our right. I bustled out and asked if there were any German officers in my crowd, and the noise died down (as this time I was myself in my cap and badges of rank).

" I found two, but had to talk to them through an interpreter, as they could talk neither English nor French. They were podgy, fat bourgeois, looking very red and full of sausage and beer and wine, and were not over friendly. I explained to them that strict orders must be maintained as to meeting half-way, and everyone unarmed ; and we both agreed not to fire until the other did, thereby creating a complete deadlock and armistice (if strictly observed).

" Meanwhile, Scots and Huns were fraternizing in the most genuine possible manner. Every sort of souvenir was exchanged, addresses given and received, photos of families shown, etc. One of our fellows offered a German a cigarette : the German said, ' Virginian ? ' Our fellow

said, ' Aye, straight-cut ' : the German said, ' No thanks,
I only smoke Turkish ! ' (Sort of 10s. a 100 !) It gave
us all a good laugh.

" A German N.C.O. with the Iron Cross, gained, he told
me, for conspicuous skill in sniping—started his fellows
off on some marching tune. When they had done I set
the note for ' The Boys of Bonnie Scotland, where the
heather and the bluebells grow,' and so we went on,
singing everything from ' Good King Wenceslaus ' down to
the ordinary Tommies' song, and ended up with ' Auld Lang
Syne,' which we all, English, Scots, Irish, Prussian, Wür-
tembergers, etc., joined in. It was absolutely astounding,
and if I had seen it on a cinematograph film I should have
sworn that it was faked !

" I talked to a lot more Huns and found many very young
fellows, but a good, strong, and pretty healthy lot. Probably only the best of them had been allowed to leave their
trenches ; they included the Jaegers, 158th, 37th, and
15th Regiments.

" Just after we had finished ' Auld Lang Syne ' an old
hare started up, and seeing so many of us about in an
unwonted spot, did not know which way to go. I gave
one loud ' view-hallo,' and one and all, British and
Germans, rushed about giving chase, slipping up on the
frozen plough, falling about, and after a hot two minutes
we killed in the open, a German and one of our fellows
falling together heavily upon the completely baffled hare.
Shortly afterwards we saw four more hares, and killed one
again ; both were good heavy weight, and had evidently
been out between the two rows of trenches for the last
two months, well-fed on the cabbage patches, etc., many
of which are untouched on the ' No Man's Land.' The
enemy kept one and we kept the other."

During one of these Christmas Day interviews the fate
of two of the officers in Captain Loder's attack on the 18th
December was ascertained. A German officer stated
that Lieutenant the Hon. F. Hanbury-Tracy had been
brought into the German trenches very badly wounded,
and had died two days later in hospital. He was buried
in the German cemetery at Fromelles. The German also
described another young officer who had been buried as

6

" fair," and it was believed this was 2nd-Lieutenant R. Nugent, who had been reported missing.

In these trenches the 2nd Battalion passed the last days of 1914, and it only remains to recount the last doings of the 1st Battalion since we left them refitting and recruiting their numbers up till the 20th December.

On that day the battalion, of which command had been assumed on the 6th by Major Hon. W. P. Hore Ruthven, was marched off at short notice to Béthune.[1] It arrived there very tired, after a trying march of twenty-two miles with many checks, at 2 a.m. on the 21st. At noon it set out by the La Bassée road and at Cuinchy crossed to the north bank of the La Bassée canal. Casualties began on the canal bridge, which was under artillery fire. The objective of the 1st Brigade in the attack on this day was the recapture of the trenches about Rue d'Ouvert, which had been lost the day before. The Scots Guards were on the right of the brigade just north of the canal as far as Givenchy ; on their left were the Cameron Highlanders, and beyond them the Coldstream Guards. The Black Watch were in reserve with the London Scottish, who had recently joined the brigade. It was nearly dark at 4.15 p.m., when the battalion was ready for the attack in position west of Givenchy. No opposition was met with till Givenchy was reached. Here there was an unfortunate accident, due to the darkness and the fact that the ground was quite strange to the troops engaged. The right of the Cameron Highlanders lost direction, and they and the Scots Guards narrowly escaped attacking one another, and are believed to have actually exhanged shots before the mistake was discovered.

The losses on this day were not serious—Lieutenant H. G. E. Hill-Trevor, who had only joined the battalion on the 18th November at Borre, and of course was in his first and last action, was killed, with two men. Twenty-three men were wounded or missing.

Givenchy being clear of Germans, the battalion took position in what had formerly been the British support

[1] Colonel Lowther had taken over command of the 1st Brigade on the 24th November.

trenches, with R.F., " B " and " C " Companies 100 yards south of Givenchy, and L.F. 200 yards in rear in dug-outs.

At 5 p.m. on the 22nd, on relief by the Royal Berkshires of the 6th Brigade, the Scots Guards recrossed to the south side of the canal at the Cuinchy bridge. At 10 p.m. two companies relieved French troops, and later another company was sent to fill a gap between the Black Watch and the 3rd Brigade, but was brought back, as the gap was found to be non-existent. The days preceding Christmas Day were uneventful, except for the machine-gun section, which joined the London Scottish for a few hours during which they did some execution on two parties of Germans. On Christmas Day there appears to have been no fraternization such as has been described in the case of the 2nd Battalion.

The 1st Battalion went back, on the 28th, to Béthune for a rest, which was broken, on the afternoon of New Year's Eve, by an order to march off at once to Annequin, half-way to La Bassée. The adjutant's diary remarks significantly that " the battalion had been celebrating the near approach of New Year's Day, and several men had to be left behind."

On the 1st January, 1915, the 1st Battalion was assembled at Cuinchy Church, south of the canal, at 11.30 p.m., for an attack, the details of which were arranged in conference with the K.R.R. Corps. For this the battalion had been lent to the 2nd Brigade. The objective of the attack was a position into which the enemy had pushed forward on the embankment of the railway immediately south of the canal, driving out an observation post and machine gun of the K.R.R., who had failed to retake them.

The battalion was ordered to deploy into four lines facing north, just north of some brickstacks, and to attack at 3 a.m. over a distance of about 400 yards.

The order of the companies in the four lines was " C " (Captain Stracey), " B " (Captain Orr-Ewing), R.F. (2nd-Lieutenant Dormer), with L.F. (2nd-Lieutenant Hon. R. Coke), carrying entrenching tools, in reserve. The K.R.R. Corps was on the right.

The British artillery opened at 2.45, and on the stroke

of 8 a.m. Captain Stracey led the advance against the observation post, whilst " B " Co. was directed on the machine-gun emplacement. No trouble was experienced till a point was reached within 100 yards of the railway. Here the advance was met by heavy fire from in front and enfilading fire on the right, where the embankment runs east, then curves south-east. The attackers, nevertheless, got right forward over the embankment, beyond which both Captain R. Stracey and Lieutenant A. G. Menzies were killed. The position had been taken, but was found to be quite untenable, owing to the enfilade fire of machine-guns on the right and right rear. It had, therefore, to be abandoned, and the troops withdrawn to the starting-point. They had held it for an hour. Owing to the position where they fell being north of the embankment, it was not possible to bring back the bodies of the two dead officers. Captain N. A. Orr-Ewing and 2nd-Lieutenant R. S. Dormer were wounded. The numbers of other ranks are not stated.

During the day a party was left at the starting-point, collecting wounded, etc., whilst the rest of the battalion went back to Cuinchy. The communication trench between these points, about 1,000 yards, had from one to three feet of mud, and a great deal of labour was required to make it passable. There was a good deal of shooting on the 2nd January at Germans on the embankment trying to avoid British lyddite shells. A welcome reinforcement of 200 men with Captain J. S. Thorpe and Lieutenant G. V. F. Monckton (just recovered from his wound) was received.

The weather at this time was very wet, and the trenches were in a terrible state. One officer remarks that two days in trenches and one out " might be worse, although forty-eight hours of standing up to one's knees in cold liquid mud is not very pleasant."

There were frequent artillery duels, and the time was generally a very unpleasant one.

The battalion was now returned to the 1st Brigade, and trenches north of the canal, stretching 800 yards towards Givenchy. These were held by 200 men, with the rest

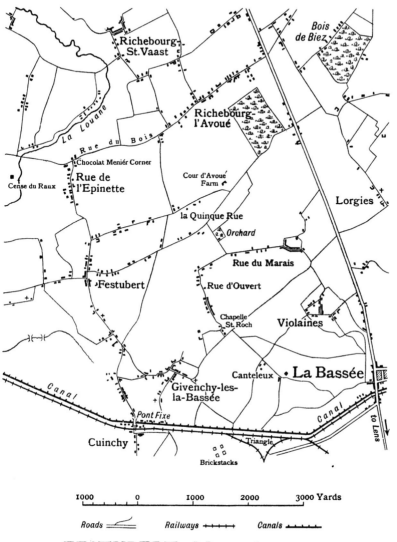

FESTUBERT, May 10th. 1915.

of the battalion in reserve—only 167 men. On the 4th January more officers arrived, and another 100 men as reinforcement with 2nd-Lieutenant G. E. V. Crutchley. The new fire trenches were no better than those of the south bank, and in one place 30 yards had to be left unoccupied, as the water was 4½ feet deep in the trench.

There was constant fighting for the embankment on the south of the canal, in which the troops on the north took a hand with rifles when opportunity offered.

At last, on the night of the 13th-14th, the battalion was relieved and sent back to Béthune. It took two hours to rescue two men who had got up to their armpits in mud. But the prospect of Béthune was welcome. As one officer writes : " What joy ! Bath ! Sleep ! And change of clothes ! I have not had my shirt or trousers off since New Year's Eve." Of the spirit of the men the same officer writes : " The new men, although they have not quite got the discipline of the old lot, are at least wonderful, and have still the spirit of the Brigade of Guards, and their cheerfulness in all the mud and slime is marvellous."

After a week of clearing up, refitting, and being inspected at Béthune, the battalion returned, on the 23rd January, to Cuinchy trenches. It had been reinforced on the 11th by Major A. C. Morrison-Bell and Lieutenant H. Hammersley with 160 men. The position now held by the battalion began on the right at the La Bassée road, where it touched the left of the French, extended northwards about 500 yards, and then bent back westwards. The Coldstream Guards held the left of the line. Behind the Scots Guards' trenches, at a distance of about 500 yards, was the " Keep," formed by linking up four brickstacks with walls of loose bricks, so as to form a square fort with the brickstacks as the corners. The sides faced the points of the compass.

The 1st Scots Guards were thus disposed on the night of the 24th-25th January. In the fire-trenches the two flank companies—of " B " two platoons were in the Keep with Major B. H. Romilly, the other two in dug-outs in support at the brickstacks immediately north of the Keep ; " C " in reserve. At 6.30 a.m. on the 25th a German deserter stated to the officer commanding L.F. Company that in an hour [1] the enemy would begin bombardment, and then fire mines blowing up the British trenches, after which there would be an assault. Sure enough, heavy fire broke out at 7.30 along the front. The supporting platoons of " B " Co. had been warned to be ready. At 7.30, too, a big explosion of a mine occurred at the angle in the British front trenches, followed by about twenty more at different points of the line. The infantry attack followed at once, and very soon it was reported to Major Romilly that the men were retiring from the trenches east of the Keep. Almost simultaneously news came from the north front of the Keep that the enemy were approaching it on that side, and a similar report came from the south front. There was some confusion in the Keep, the garrison of which found it difficult to fire. Major Romilly at once turned the mountain gun which was with him on the northern gate. It blew two breaches in the wall, which gave a good field of fire to north and north-east. It also alarmed the Germans and gave Major Romilly time to organize his defence by rifle fire, and to get together a concealed reserve for use in the event of the enemy reaching the Keep. He also had at his disposal some of the supports who had come in from the north with 2nd-Lieutenants Bury and Denny, as well as some of the Coldstream Guards from the left trenches. Meanwhile Sergeant McPherson of " B " Company had organized the second platoon of his company and some Coldstream in a line facing north and north-east across the tramway running north from the Keep. This line he had handed over to Lieutenant Viscount Acheson of the Coldstream Guards. The firm resistance of this line was of the greatest value in preventing the Germans from surrounding the Keep from the north or pressing on to Cuinchy village from that side. The line formed a semicircle running north from the west gate

---

[1] What occurred in this case was that the Brigadier, knowing that the German time was an hour in front of ours, ordered his artillery to open at 7.30 a.m. punctually on the railway bridge under which a road passed from inside the " triangle " towards the brickstacks, and also at the southern corner of the triangle, where the road from La Bassée passes. This was done, but the terrible shortage of field-gun ammunition at that time made the effect of the artillery very poor.

and then bending round in front of the north face of the Keep. Major Romilly felt safe on this side. There was now, however, a great gap between the south of the Keep and the French beyond the La Bassée road. The Germans were massing opposite this gap ; but reinforcements arrived in the nick of time. The gap was partly filled by two (later three) platoons of " C " Company, and the French were asked to fill the rest of it. Brigadier-General Lowther, now commanding the 1st Brigade, also ordered up two companies of London Scottish.

By 10.50 Major Romilly was able to report the situation satisfactory, and that the time was propitious for a counter-attack. At this time the enemy north and east of the Keep appeared to be somewhat disorganized and to have given up attempting to attack the Keep.

Presently, however, they were reinforced with men and machine-guns, and at 1 p.m. the situation again seemed critical.

The left of the line, north-west of the Keep, was under heavy rifle fire, but Major Romilly wisely refused to draw on his small reserve of one company London Scottish to comply with the demands for reinforcements which came in. He judged rightly that the line could hold on till the counter-attack was made at 1 p.m.

Before that the rifle fire had eased and the enemy were seen running from west of the tramway eastwards, across the British line on the south. The counter-attack, in which the 2nd Brigade came up to the support of the 1st with the K.R.R. Corps and the Royal Sussex, was made by the Cameron Highlanders and the Black Watch, with the two battalions just named. It was not altogether successful, and could not regain the trenches lost in the morning. But the Keep was safe after it began, and its retention by Major Romilly had saved the situation.

There were alarms during the ensuing night, but Major Romilly thinks that no serious attempt to take the Keep was made. A party of bombers on one of the brickstacks north of it prevented the Germans from entering the communication trench (" High Street ") running round its north-east corner. During the night a small enemy party attempted an entrance by the north gate, but fled when their leader was shot by the sentry there. Major Romilly gives great praise to the detachment with the mountain gun, to which he attributes much of his successful defence. Sergeant McPherson also did splendid service in organizing the defensive line north-west of the Keep.

So far we have dealt mainly with the defence of the Keep, in which " B " Company at first was alone concerned. We must now state, as far as possible, what happened to the two flank companies which were practically knocked out at the beginning of the action, and to " C," which was in reserve at Cuinchy.

For the flank companies holding the front trenches we are mainly dependent on letters written from Germany by Major Morrison Bell, who was taken prisoner. No officer got back from the front trenches, and very few men. The officers with the two companies were :

R.F. : Major A. C. Morrison-Bell, 2nd-Lieutenant A. H. Lang (Grenadier Guards), 2nd-Lieutenant G. Hamilton-Fletcher (Grenadier Guards), and 2nd-Lieutenant J. C. Thompson (Artists' Rifles).

L.F. : Lieutenant G. V. F. Monckton, 2nd Lieutenant G. E. V. Crutchley, and 2nd-Lieutenant H. E. Wild (Artists' Rifles).

When Major Morrison-Bell went into trenches on the left of the Scots Guards' line, he found his company had to work hard all night at improving trenches and loopholes.

One third of the company spent the night sniping in outposts. The story of the deserter who came in to L.F. Company in the night, and the news he brought of the impending attack, has already been told. When Major Morrison-Bell got the news, he made all preparations for meeting the attack. All was quiet till suddenly a mine blew up just round a bend in the trench near where he was standing. The debris knocked him down, but did not bury him. Simultaneously with this, and other mines exploding about the same time, the German shelling began, falling chiefly on the left of R.F. and the Coldstream Guards beyond it.

The Germans were not 100 yards off, and the explosion

of the mines was the signal for them to rush the trenches. They came across in hundreds, and stopped on the edge of the trench to shoot down into it. There were but 130 men of R.F. left, and the odds were terrible, but they fought splendidly. Major Morrison-Bell describes specially one young fellow next to him, who was so worn out that he stopped shooting for a moment, but went on again when Major Morrison-Bell offered to take his rifle. The other three officers were all killed, and probably about 100 of the men. 2nd-Lieutenant Hamilton-Fletcher was said, like the others, to have fought like a hero, and Major Morrison-Bell heard of his being twice wounded before the end. The Germans, as the British fire died down, broke into the trench on the left, and Major Morrison-Bell found himself at last with only three men left, and they were picked off one by one. He was now quite alone, covered by the revolvers of two Germans who had jumped into the trench, and there was nothing for it but to declare his rank and surrender. After that he spent a very unpleasant hour in the trench, which was now under fire from the British artillery. When he arrived at Friedberg, in Hesse, he found thirty-two of his men with Sergeant Young were his fellow prisoners. Only about forty men of L.F. got back alive from the trenches.

To supplement this we may quote the account gathered by Captain Kingsmill (Grenadier Guards, attached Scots Guards, temporarily commanding " C " Co.) from some of the men who managed to escape from the disaster, the men of the flank companies. They said the Germans first threw in some "minen-werfer" bombs, and then crawled up to the trenches and threw in bombs and hand-grenades. Then they blew up the trench with mines, and at once issued in swarms from their own trenches, moving slightly across the British front towards the left and the junction with the right of the Coldstream Guards. Then they swept behind the Coldstream trenches, and down the British trenches from left to right. What happened afterwards is uncertain, but many men were killed by the mines and bombs, and when the Germans came up they shot or bayoneted many more.

Captain Kingsmill himself commanded " C " Company, from which R.F. took over the trenches on the 24th. He then went back in reserve to Cuinchy, which was in ruins, and at last found some shelter for his company, in case of bombardment, in three dry cellars and one wet one. The chief objection to the cellars was the presence in Captain Kingsmill's of over 100 big bombs and hand-grenades, which, if hit, would have brought the career of all in the cellar to a sudden close. Fortunately, though the house was hit three times, the cellar escaped.

About 10 a.m. two platoons of " C " were ordered up by the Commanding Officer to trenches south of the Keep, and a third followed them later. The part they played there has already been described. Captain Kingsmill was apparently left behind in reserve with the fourth platoon. 2nd-Lieutenant Thompson went up with the first two platoons apparently, and 2nd-Lieutenant Hammersley with the third.

The casualties of the battalion on this day were naturally heavy.

Of officers, Lieutenant H. S. Bury[1] was killed ; 2nd-Lieutenant J. A. Denny[1] was wounded, and the following were missing :

Major A. C. Morrison-Bell, Lieutenant G. V. F. Monckton,[2] 2nd-Lieutenant G. E. V. Crutchley, 2nd-Lieutenant A. H. Lang,[1] 2nd-Lieutenant J. C. Thompson,[3] and 2nd-Lieutenant H. E. Wild.[1]

The total casualties in this tour of service near Cuinchy had been 4 officers killed, 3 wounded, and 7 missing. Other ranks, 27 killed, 120 wounded, 235 missing.

This account of the fighting on the 25th January may be suitably closed by the following extract from a letter of a German engineer, a former resident in Bâle, who joined up at the beginning of the war and was through the fighting of this day. He writes :

" We got orders to lay mines, and the day before the attack I myself, with my section, under the command of

[1] Grenadier Guards, attached 1st Scots Guards.
[2] Afterwards recorded as killed.
[3] Artists' Rifles, attached 1st Scots Guards.

a first lieutenant, was entrusted with the work of laying the charges in the mine which was to blow them up. On the morning of January 25th we were all at our posts waiting for the command. At 8.30 the order came, and we set fire to the fuse. At the same moment our mine-throwers were busy. Suddenly there was an explosion, which shook the earth for miles around. Our attacking columns instantly rushed forward to take the Scots by surprise, whilst they were still under the effect of the explosion and stunned. I could not take part in the attack myself, as I had to see to removing our instruments to a place of safety.

" Immediately after, there was a pandemonium of rifle fire and of machine-gun discharges that bordered on the incredible. The hand-to-hand combat had begun almost instantly. The Scots fought like demons. Many of their comrades had been blown into the air with the earth of their trenches. The British artillery joined in, and fired with remarkable precision and a rapidity that gave us the shivers. Whilst I was busy withdrawing our mine installation, a British shell burst inside the trench in which our reserves were waiting. It killed every man within a radius of twenty feet, and I escaped as by a miracle. I immediately helped to attend the wounded.

" Our troops continued the attack for two hours, and succeeded in pushing on to the second line of the British entrenchments. Our operations were considerably hampered by a number of brickstacks and sheds which the British had turned into fortifications. At three o'clock in the afternoon we were still fighting, and I had to make an inspection of one of the trenches. I had to do so crawling, as the enemy sniped us mercilessly. I have already seen many horrors of the war, but I never saw any horror like this. The dead lay sometimes in twos and threes on each other, and I had to crawl over them. At 1.30 the British brought up reserves. They rushed to the attack in columns along a road where they were exposed to a murderous fire from our machine-guns.

" As soon as we opened fire on them they dropped down and took to shelter, so that in an instant the whole column seemed to have disappeared. The troops that faced were entirely fresh, and had never before been in action, and they behaved wonderfully well."

In the evening of the 25th the battalion was relieved and marched back to Béthune in billets in the Montmorency Barracks. Here and at Burbure, near Lillers, and at Oblinghem, the 1st Battalion remained refitting and resting till it again went into reserve trenches on the 28th February, at the Rue de l'Epinette, north of Festubert. Here, taking their turn with other battalions of the brigade in front line, the 1st Scots Guards were reinforced by 241 other ranks, with Lieutenant E. P. Orr-Ewing and 2nd-Lieutenant E. D. Mackenzie, who had recovered from his wound received on the 14th September, in the Battle of the Aisne.

Beyond the ordinary incidents of trench life, there is little to record up to the 10th March, and we will take the opportunity to bring the doings of the 2nd Battalion up to date.

We last saw it in the trenches near Sailly, at the end of 1914. In this neighbourhood it remained, with intervals of brigade or divisional reserve, till the 15th January, when we come across the first mention of anything in the way of sports, in the shape of a boxing tournament. Hitherto there had been little time for anything of the sort, but with the settling down to trench warfare it became necessary, when troops were not actually in trenches, to keep up their spirits in their monotonous life, and to divert their minds from brooding over the past and future miseries and sufferings inseparable from these novel conditions of warfare.

Sports during periods of comparative inaction in long wars are an old institution in the British Army. There were many such periods in the Peninsular War, and the officers at any rate had some amusements during them. Sir Rowland Hill's pack of hounds brought out to Portugal afforded amusement and healthy diversion for every officer in its neighbourhood who could rake up a mount of any sort. Even the Commander-in-Chief found time for fox hunting. As for the men, it is to be feared they had not so much care taken for them as is the case in modern times. Still, when Sir William Gomm writes that the officers " played cricket till our legs were tired and chess till our heads were aching," we may feel sure that the men also shared to some extent in the former game.

Football was apparently not so popular then as it was in the Great War, when it was a godsend to all ranks, and from 1915 onwards was constantly played between different companies of the same regiment, between regiments of the same or other brigades, or between brigades of the same division. Even for the many variety entertainments which were so popular at the front in the Great War there were precedents in the Peninsula, though there, of course, reliance had to be placed on local talent, and it was out of the question to have anything like the visits of the many professional or amateur companies who so generously helped to dissipate the tedium on the Western front in the last war.

Of a different class of diversion were lectures delivered by all sorts of people, from Army Chaplains to General Officers, sometimes on topics of the day, sometimes on professional subjects.

The whole of January and February 1915 was passed by the battalion in and out of these trenches near Sailly, which were particularly bad and waterlogged, so much so that, instead of going underground as was done on higher ground, much reliance had to be placed on breastworks raised above the level.

The trenches in wet weather were often knee-deep in water, and as the men laboured at draining and baling them, their only consolation was in hearing the Germans on the other side hard at the same work. Gum-boots were a welcome article of wear, and " trench feet " was the fashionable complaint. Days when there were baths are always noted in diaries as a luxury.

On the 1st March orders were received to march to Vieux Berquin, which was reached on the 3rd, via Estaires and Neuf Berquin. The Scottish heart was cheered on this march by the music of two sets of pipes, which had just arrived.

Rumours of a coming attack were rife next day, and after the battalion moved to Estaires on the 7th, in very cold weather, practice for the attack, which was now said to be fixed for the 10th, was carried out daily.

CHAPTER V

2nd Battalion at Neuve Chapelle and Festubert—1st Battalion in and
out of trenches between Rue du Bois and Loos till August 1915.

THE first great offensive operation by the British Army
in 1915 was the attack, by the 8th Division on the left
and the Indian Division on the right, directed on Neuve
Chapelle and the German lines north and south of it.
There had been much fighting here in October 1914, of
which we have had nothing to say, since both battalions
of the Scots Guards were then engaged in the desperate
struggle farther north about Ypres. In the end, Neuve
Chapelle remained in the hands of the enemy, and was so
still in the beginning of March 1915, when Sir John French
planned his attack on it, to be followed by an advance as
far as possible beyond it, across the Aubers Ridge in rear
of it, and into the plain of Lille beyond that. Arrangements, with which we need not concern ourselves, were
made for compelling the Germans to maintain themselves in
strength to the north and south of the front of attack and
to prevent them sending reinforcements to it. The
enemy's front was very strongly defended by every device
in the way of trenches, machine-gun posts, and artillery.
Against it, on the other hand, was concentrated the most
powerful artillery force the British had yet brought to
bear in any attack, though but a small one when compared with what came later, when guns and ammunition
had been increased to an almost unlimited extent.

Neuve Chapelle itself formed a salient in the German
line. North and south of the village the main points of
resistance were respectively about the hamlet of Piétre
and the Bois du Biez.

The attack of the 8th Division was to be directed by
two brigades (24th and 25th) on the head of the salient

and the village, whilst the third brigade (23rd) operated against the northern face of the salient towards Piétre. The Indian Division was to storm the southern face of the salient and the Bois du Biez.

The function of the 7th Division was to support the 8th, and the 20th Infantry Brigade was destined to deal with the left towards Piétre.

The battle, which extended over three days, commenced on the 10th March. On that day the 2nd Scots Guards and the 20th Brigade were in Corps Reserve and were not engaged at all.

Leaving Estaires at 6 a.m. on the 10th and halting for two hours in a field outside, the 2nd Battalion marched to dug-outs in Cameron Lane, near Pont du Hem, on the east side of the Estaires–La Bassée road. Whilst they were halted they had been listening to the heaviest bombardment yet carried out by British artillery, with every weapon from 18-pdr. field-gun to the gigantic 15-inch howitzer " Granny."

Here they remained all day, listening to the sounds of the battle in front, and seeing signs of it in the British wounded and German prisoners who passed to the rear along the road. Another sight was that of a British aeroplane which crashed close by, both its pilot and its observer being killed. The night after was spent on the La Bassée road, where it was difficult to find shelter, owing to the cavalry occupying the billets. Many of the officers and men slept in the open. During the day Neuve Chapelle and many trenches had been taken by the 8th Division, large numbers of prisoners had been captured, and tremendous losses inflicted on the enemy.

On the 11th it was the turn of the 20th Brigade to go into the fight. At 4 a.m. the battalion was moved up to breastworks on the road running from Bont Lody (on the La Bassée road) north-east towards Fauquissart. Their orders were to attack at 7 a.m. in support of the 1st Grenadier Guards, in the direction of Piétre on the right and Aubers on the left, both villages lying north-east of Neuve Chapelle. A few men were lost by shells bursting in the breastworks. The advance, in line of half companies, was led by R.F. at 7.10 a.m. When 1,000 yards had been covered, the attack of the Grenadiers was held up. The 2nd Scots Guards halted in and were mixed up with the rearmost line of the Grenadiers, which was in the German front line taken the day before. Here they remained all day under a fairly heavy shell fire, digging themselves in as best they could, and completing the operation after dark. In addition to shells, they received rifle bullets fired at the Grenadiers in front, and enfilade fire at times from the right. During the day Lieutenant C. H. Seymour and Lieutenant W. H. Ewart were wounded, and there were about fifty casualties in other ranks.

At 10.30 p.m. orders were received to attack next morning, the objectives being a fort and a house held by the enemy at Moulin du Piétre, north of the village of the same name. These had defied the attacks during the previous day by troops on the right. The day had been so misty that full support by artillery was not possible, and this no doubt contributed to the holding up of the Grenadiers' attack. Lieutenant H. Bullock was wounded during the night.

Before dawn on the 12th, when it was still foggy, the battalion moved out under shell fire to a point where the Neuve Chapelle–Fauquissart road was met by a communication trench taken from the enemy. There the battalion halted in shallow trenches on either side of the road. On their left was the Border battalion, with the Grenadiers in support, the Gordons on the right. Here Captain G. H. Loder was injured by tearing his hand with barbed wire.

The enemy's shell fire was heavy from 5 to 8 a.m. About 8.30 the battalion moved forward along the communication trench, which in places was waist deep in water, till it reached some shallow trenches which had been made the night before, at right angles to the communication trench. The Borderers on the left were in similar trenches farther forward. The formation was lines of half-companies, L.F. being the leading line.

Brigade orders required the Border Regiment to storm the fort, whilst the defended house was assigned to the Scots Guards, who were to push up as the attack com-

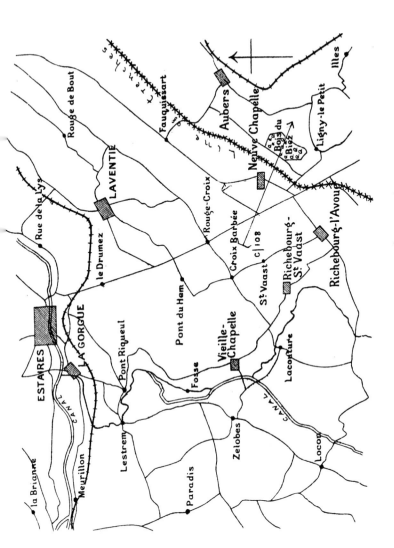

NEUVE CHAPELLE, SEPT. 1915.

menced and pass on to the house, which was 300 yards beyond the fort. The attack, which had been ordered for 10.30, was now postponed for two hours by brigade orders ; but unfortunately the orderlies carrying the orders were killed, and the message never reached the attacking troops. As a consequence, when the latter went forward in accordance with the original orders, at 10.30, they did so entirely without preparation by the artillery, who had duly received the orders of postponement. Soon after the advance began, the battalion was delayed by the difficulty of crossing a deep ditch. By the time 150 yards had been covered in the advance, it was brought to a standstill by very heavy machine-gun and rifle fire. It had already lost three officers and about 100 men. The Border Regiment, on the left, had suffered much more heavily in their advance on the fort.

The 2nd Scots Guards were represented by little more than two companies in this attack ; for in the early morning darkness and mist most of R.F. and the whole of " F " got separated from L.F. and "G," lost their way, and could not be found. Eventually they got back to their starting point, where they remained all day under shell fire, which cost them some losses. At 11.30 the artillery had been turned on to the enemy's first line and the fort. The miscarriage of the postponement orders had been discovered meanwhile, and fresh instructions issued to the artillery. When it did open fire it was so accurate and heavy for two hours that the enemy began to show white flags, and some came out of the trenches and the fort with their hands up. The capture of the fort was a necessary preliminary to an attack on the house, and the Scots Guards united with the Borderers in the assault of the former. The two battalions arrived in it intermingled with one another. L.F. Company had been led with great gallantry and success by Lieutenant A. Swinton, and the attack had resulted in the capture of about 300 Germans and a machine-gun.

The defended house, which had been assigned as the objective of the 2nd Scots Guards, was not reached.

From the fort some of the battalion, with the Borderers,

7

continued for a short distance along a German communication trench leading southwards, but soon found it impossible to advance across the open in the face of machine-guns in the houses in front and enfilade fire from the right. Progress was arrested at the fort, where, and in the trenches in rear of it, the two companies remained consolidating the position gained, till they were withdrawn to Cameron Lane before daybreak on the 13th.

The attack of the 12th had caused the battalion heavy losses, especially in the advance without artillery support. In that Captain Sir E. Hulse was killed and Major Paynter (commanding the battalion) and 2nd-Lieutenant Barry were wounded. Of other ranks, during the day, there were 22 killed, 35 missing, and 132 wounded. The loss is said to have been caused largely by two machine-guns on the left during the first advance. Sir E. Hulse met his death in an endeavour to help Major Paynter, who was lying with a bullet through his lungs. The latter had been hit at the beginning of the 10.30 attack, soon after he left the trench. Sir E. Hulse crawled out to help him, and was killed whilst talking to him.

Of him Paynter wrote to Lady Hulse :

" He was a grand fellow, that son of yours . . . He was with me, trying to help me, when he was hit. There was no finer soldier in the battalion, and his men would do anything for him."

We will conclude this account of the battle by quoting the following graphic extract from a private letter written by Lieutenant Swinton on the 18th March, giving an account of his doings :

" We fell in at 4.30 a.m., and started marching round to a point given to me the night before. We had to go along a typical French road, straight with trees on each side—you know them. Several trees had fallen across the road, shrapnel was bursting over it, it ran parallel to our lines, so there was a cross fire over it, also the Huns were using trench mortars, and chucking bombs by them on and over the road ; how we got along I don't know, but no one was hit. Anyway, I got down to our meeting

point and found George (Major Paynter) ; we lay down,
but had not been there more than five minutes, when they
began to shell like the devil.   The only thing we could do
was to try to get the battalion into the trenches from which
we were to make our attack, so George and I led on,
hoping that the men would follow, as the distance was some
500 yards.   The company got terribly strung out ; several
were hit, and the shells were bursting like the devil.   You
cannot imagine anything worse than being shelled in the
dark, it is much worse than in daylight.   Eventually
George, Barry, and I got to the place with about six men,
the remainder being strung out behind.   Anyway, we
got under cover and sat there till daylight.

" We were to have attacked at 8, but an order came along
to say that, owing to the fog, it was put off till 10.30, so
at 9 we managed to collect L.F. and ' G.'   ' F ' Company
was lost, and R.F. had scattered when the shelling first
began, and was lost except for Pip (Warner) and 12 men.
We scrambled out into the open alongside the trench,
ready to start off ; Barry in front with 15 and 16 Platoons,
then I with 13 and 14, and ' G ' behind me.   At 10.30
we got up and advanced ; we were greeted at once by
rapid rifle and machine-gun fire.   I honestly wouldn't
have believed it possible that anything could have lived
in that fire ; lots were hit, amongst them George, Teddy
(Sir E. Hulse), and Barry, but I ran on until I found a
trench, or rather ditch, 2 feet deep and 2 feet wide ; into
this I dropped and started to dig myself in with my bayonet ;
here I stayed until 1.30.   In the meantime we learnt that
we had attacked too early ; that orderlies had been sent
to George and the Colonel of the Borderers postponing the
attack till 12.30, because the artillery could not see to
bombard ; both these orderlies had been killed, so we had
never got the message, and we had attacked too early ;
hence the fire against us.   Anyway, at noon the bombardment began, we of course were all lying flat in our
scrapes, as the Huns were shooting all the time.   I never
heard such a noise as this bombardment in my life, one
continuous roar the whole time.   Soon it was passed along
that the Huns were putting up white flags.   I looked up
and saw that they were coming out of their trenches on
the left ; at that moment Pip Warner got up and shouted
to me to come on, so I followed him with about 4 men,

and we assisted taking in the prisoners—some 500–600. We then went on, and formed a firing line in the old German trench, firing at the retreating Huns. I was then sent back for reinforcements, and, having seen those all off, found I could not get back, as the fire was too heavy from the right, so I had to sit in the trench till dark. Later on in the night we were withdrawn, cold and weary, and this ends my experience in the Battle of Neuve Chapelle."

Owing to Major Paynter's disablement, Captain Warner found himself in command of the battalion, which was ordered, on the 15th, to man breastworks near Brigade Headquarters in support of the firing line. It was found that there was only room for R.F. Company, which remained there till dark, when it rejoined the rest, now moving from Cameron Lane to billets at Laventie. The rest of March was spent in this area, in the usual routine of trench warfare. A reinforcement of 100 men under 2nd-Lieutenant Hope came in on the 27th, and several other officers joined. On the 19th the battalion had the remarkable luck to be able to describe the trenches taken over from the 21st Brigade as " very comfortable," which was certainly exceptional near Neuve Chapelle. On the 27th a letter from General Capper commanding the division said :

" The conduct of the 2nd Battalion Scots Guards on the 12th March in an attack was very gallant and devoted. Owing to messengers being killed, the postponement of the attack was not notified to this battalion, which consequently attempted most gallantly to advance without artillery support. In spite of losses caused by this, the battalion gallantly and successfully attacked later on in the same day and captured several hundred prisoners."

The weather was still very cold and frosty at the end of the month.

On April 1st Major A. B. Cator, D.S.O., took over command of the battalion, which at this time was in bad trenches in a salient, with a parapet which was not bullet-proof and had to be strengthened during the night. Another good reinforcement of 165 men, under 2nd-Lieutenant Clarke, joined on the 4th.

There was a great deal of route marching at this time when out of trenches, and training of all sorts. Fatigue parties for digging with the R.E. Mining Company were constantly employed, and if there was no fighting, there was plenty of hard work when in reserve areas. On the 17th April the two battalions of the Scots Guards arranged a route march by Vieux Chapelle enabling them to meet.

Next day, to the great regret of the battalion, Major-General Sir T. Capper, commanding the 7th Division, was invalided in consequence of his wounds. He had led the division since October 1914 with conspicuous gallantry and ability, and was as much appreciated by the battalion as it was by him. He was succeeded by Major-General H. Gough.

On April 19th the 20th Brigade was inspected by Field-Marshal Sir John French, who afterwards addressed each battalion. The Scots Guards he congratulated on their smart appearance and the fine work they had done in the field, especially at Neuve Chapelle.

The route march meeting arranged on the 17th took place on the 20th. The occasion was believed to be the first on which the two battalions had ever met on active service. Of the officers who had originally gone abroad, only two in the 2nd Battalion (Captain Warner and Lieutenant and Quartermaster Ross) and one in the 1st (Lieutenant and Quartermaster Kinlay) had been continuously with their unit, and were present on that day.

Trenches were returned to on April 20th, after which nothing worth notice happened till the end of the month, except the arrival of a reinforcement of 125 men under Captain C. Rivers-Bulkeley, and the first days of May were equally uneventful. From the 5th May onwards there were various conferences on the method of a projected attack on the enemy trenches. The 2nd Battalion was then in billets at Laventie.

On the 9th there was an attack by the 8th Division, which was in most places a failure. During this day the battalion remained in dug-outs near the Rue du Bois, to which they had moved in the small hours.

The battle of this day is officially known as the Battle

of Aubers Ridge, and was one of terrible losses for the 8th
Division ; but, looking to the fact that the 2nd Scots
Guards were, as shown by their small loss (only one man
wounded), not actively engaged, it is beyond our province
to describe it.

That night the battalion was ordered to relieve part of
the 8th Division and attack at dawn. But, when Lieutenant Swinton went out to reconnoitre the way to these
trenches, it was found impossible to reach them through
the heavy shelling. The orders were cancelled, and the
battalion went back to Laventie. On the 12th it marched
four miles to Hinges, and went into billets a mile beyond
the village. The 15th was to be the first day of the ten
days' Battle of Festubert,[1] and before describing this great
struggle, in so far as it concerns the Scots Guards, the
movements of the 1st Battalion had better be accounted
for in the period from the 10th March to the middle of
May. March 10th had opened with the very heavy
bombardment of the enemy's trenches by the whole of the
artillery of the 1st Army preceding the Battle of Neuve
Chapelle. The 1st Scots Guards were held in readiness
all day to move at very short notice. At 5 p.m. orders
called them forward towards Richebourg l'Avoué in support
of an Indian Brigade. They halted by the roadside about
a kilometre short of Richebourg l'Avoué, till 11 p.m.,
when they were ordered back to Rue de l'Epinette.
Though they were under artillery fire only, one unlucky
shell wounded Major Romilly and Captain A. Kingsmill
(Grenadier Guards attached), these being the only casualties
noted in the diary. Two days later another shell hit
headquarters and wounded four signallers. The shelling
was very heavy on this day, many shells, as an officer
records, " missing our house by inches every time." On
the 13th, orders being received from brigade to see if
the German trenches were still occupied, Corporals Spence
and Collins volunteered for the service. They crawled to
within twenty yards of the trench, when they were heavily
fired on and had to return. There was no doubt about the
presence of the enemy. On the 13th, headquarters again

[1] See map facing p. 70.

had a fortunate escape. Twelve officers were having lunch when a 6-inch shell came through the room. Everyone was knocked about, but the only casualty was the colonel's servant, Locke, an old soldier of thirty years' service, who was killed when standing by Captain Balfour, who was carving a turkey.

We must refrain from recounting more incidents of this sort which occurred whilst the battalion continued in this neighbourhood south of Neuve Chapelle. Shelling was always heavy, and the ground being very wet in most parts, breastworks insufficiently shell-proof had to supply the cover which could not be got by digging down.

In this turn of service about the Rue de l'Epinette, the total casualties up to the 22nd March were two officers wounded, and of other ranks 12 killed and 40 wounded. Reinforcements of about 170 men came in.

About this time, too, platoons of Territorials or the New Army began to be attached to the older regiments for training. After a rest in the back areas, the battalion returned to trenches in the Richebourg St. Vaast area on the 30th March till the 11th April, during which period they lost 2 men killed and 25 wounded. Reinforcements continued to come in, and by the 1st May the battalion mustered 19 officers and 934 other ranks.

There is nothing special to be noted in April or the first days of May. On the 8th of that month arrangements were being completed for the attack from Richebourg at the same time as that of the 8th Division farther north, which has been mentioned in connexion with the 2nd Battalion.

At 5.40 a.m. on the 9th the battalion moved in artillery formation to trenches behind some houses on the Rue du Bois. The attack by the 2nd and 5th Brigades failed, and the Camerons and Black Watch were sent into front line, whilst the Coldstream and Scots Guards supplied two companies each to the second line. A second attack in the afternoon having again failed, the brigade was withdrawn to Hinges. The Germans had evidently had a good shock, as the battalion moved along the Rue du Bois in platoons by fours and not a shot was fired at them.

Though the battalion only came under shell fire on this day the casualties were :

Captains C. J. Balfour and Egerton-Warburton; 2nd-Lieutenants Hon. A. P. Methuen wounded.

Other ranks : Sergeant Garroway and 5 men killed, and 45 men wounded.

On the 12th May the battalion took over trenches from the Irish Guards in front of Givenchy, and returned on the 14th to Béthune, where it was on the 15th.

As at Neuve Chapelle, the brunt of the fighting at Festubert [1] fell upon the 2nd Battalion Scots Guards.

In the early evening of the 15th May the battalion marched from Hinges. By 8.40 p.m. it had reached, after a march of six miles, the junction of the Rue du Bois with the Rue de l'Epinette. There the German fire was heavy enough to forbid further progress above ground, and the battalion now moved by the communication trench leading to Indian Village, which was just to the right of the trenches it was to occupy, stretching west from Prince's Road, which runs nearly due south from the Rue du Bois to the Rue des Cailloux. These trenches, from which the attack was to proceed, at first parallel to Prince's Road, were occupied by 11 p.m. The general plan of operations in this part was for the 20th Brigade to attack on a front of two battalions, the Scots Guards on the right (west), and the Border Regiment on the left, Prince's Road being the dividing line at first between the two battalions. The Scots Guards to be supported by the 2nd Gordon Highlanders, the Border Regiment by the Grenadier Guards, with the 6th Gordon Highlanders in reserve. There was at starting a gap of about a quarter of a mile between the right of the Scots Guards and the left of the Royal Fusiliers (22nd Division), which would be closed as the advance proceeded.

When the first line of German trenches should be taken, the Borderers would swing to their left, leaving the Scots

---

[1] The village through which d'Artagnan rode in pursuit of " Milady " from Béthune towards Armentières.

Guards to cross the road and also swing to their left, having as their next objective the orchard on the east of Prince's Road close to its junction with the Rue des Cailloux. This would eventually bring the 20th Brigade into a line facing east, with the right of the Scots Guards about La Quinque Rue, and the 22nd Brigade prolonging the line to the right.

Half an hour's bombardment, commencing at 2.45 a.m., would prepare the way for the infantry attack at 3.15. In the assembly trenches the companies were lined up in two ranks along the parapet, in the order from right to left L.F., "G," "F," R.F., and the platoons were posted with that of the lowest number in each company on the right. Thus the right platoon of L.F. was No. 13, the left No. 16, the right of R.F. was No. 1, the left of No. 4, and so on.

The German wire was cut only for about 100 yards opposite the left of the Scots Guards, and it was therefore necessary to make the attack in depth on this space. It was arranged to be in eight waves. The first would consist of No. 4 platoon on the left of R.F. and No. 8 on the left of "F." This would be followed, as second wave, by Nos. 2 and 6. As each pair of platoons left the trench, the rest of the battalion would close to its left, so that when the last pair (Nos. 9 and 13) started they would do so from the left of the line.

During the night the British wire was cleared in front of the position, and ladders were placed to facilitate getting over the breastwork.

The first two platoons started over the parapet three minutes before the bombardment ended, so as to be as close as possible to the German trench when it did cease. This first line was too rapid in its movements, and R.F. was held up momentarily by British shells bursting on the German parapet. Captain Bagot-Chester rushing forward then, led the first line into the trench, where the few Germans still left were bayoneted or captured. The other lines followed at intervals of about 50 yards, all of them passing forward from the German first line, except the last, which was ordered to consolidate the position there and await the arrival of the 1st Gordon

Highlanders to take over. The rest pushed on rapidly to the capture of the orchard, where again there was no very great resistance, though heavy casualties occurred from a cross-fire of machine-guns.

From the orchard the battalion swung to its left as ordered, with its right directed on La Quinque Rue, and the 22nd Brigade making for a position on its right. Some men of the Scots Guards, in the excitement and confusion of battle, got separated and mixed up with the Royal Welsh Fusiliers of the 22nd Brigade, but the majority carried out their leftward swing, and the leading companies got forward to a line running north from La Quinque Rue to the Rue des Cailloux. It was extended on the right by the Royal Welsh Fusiliers of the 22nd Brigade.

Meanwhile, the Border Regiment, on the left of the Scots Guards, had been held up at a point considerably short of the north-east corner of the orchard, and consequently the left flank of the Scots Guards was exposed as it advanced eastwards, and was severely enfiladed from the German trenches on that side.

When "F" Company, under Sir F. FitzWygram, with Lieutenants Marsham-Townshend and Garforth, had reached a point south of the Rue des Cailloux, between it and La Quinque Rue, they were very heavily fired on by machine-guns, and strongly counter-attacked from an orchard on their left, as well as from their left rear. The time was still only about 5.30 a.m. About forty men of "F" fought their way out to the right, and eventually joined the Royal Welsh Fusiliers about La Quinque Rue, but, with the exception of these, the whole of "F" Co. was cut off and surrounded by the enemy. How gallantly they fought was shown by the state of the ground, where German and Scots Guards' dead lay mingled together, where they had fought the fight to its bitter end.

There is some doubt as to the exact point at which "F" Company was overwhelmed. The account given above is based on the Adjutant's diary, Major Cator's report, and a pencil note in the diary to the effect that Captain Warner indicated the spot as given above.

On the other hand, Sir F. FitzWygram's own account, written from Germany, where he was a prisoner, includes a rough sketch which represents the orchard as on the right of Prince's Road, instead of on the left as in the marked official map in the regimental records. This rough sketch represents the place where he was counter-attacked as being in the angle formed by Princes Road on the east and the Rue des Cailloux on the south. This would be very far short of the place described in the diary, and still farther short of that indicated by Captain Warner. Sir F. FitzWygram shows the counter-attacks as coming from the two sides of the angle, and the one which cut him off as the more northerly of two from Princes Road. He also says that he had got as far forward as was ordered, but had had to fall back to this point, owing to British " shorts." He was himself wounded in the arm, and was unconscious when he was picked up by the Germans.

In dealing with this matter, it must be remembered that roads which are clearly marked on the printed map might easily fail to be recognized in the battle after the fearful shelling they had had. Curiously enough, on the map is marked another orchard just behind the position indicated by Captain Warner. Is it possible that Sir F. FitzWygram confused that orchard and the one near Princes Road ? It hardly seems likely, as he distinctly says that his orchard was probably what newspaper accounts represented as the third German line. There were two German trenches only short of the Princes Road orchard.

Having destroyed " F " Co., the German counter-attack moved southwards and westwards against the advancing second and third lines of the Scots Guards, who lined out to the south from the eastern edge of the orchard which they had taken in the first rush. The fire which they opened from this line, and from the machine-guns of the battalion under Lieutenant E. Clarke, inflicted tremendous losses on the enemy, and brought his counter-attack in this direction to a standstill. The battalion was much split up at this time, men digging themselves in where they happened to stop in the retreat. Small parties of men of different regiments were now seen coming back from the direction of La Quinque Rue.   These were collected and organized in a fresh line facing generally south-east and east, with its left about the point in the German first line where the Scots Guards had broken into it at the first attack.

Meanwhile, strong German reinforcements had come up against the left of this line, which prevented, by enfilading it, any advance of the right of the line.

Captain Warner started with a reconnoitring party towards the point where " F " had been destroyed, but it was found impossible to advance over this ground, and it was only by plunging chest deep into a ditch full of water that safety was found.

The Border Regiment, which, it will be remembered, had been held up at an early period of the first attack, was now reinforced by the 1st Battalion Grenadier Guards, and the two succeeded in advancing a short way.   An attempted advance, farther to the left, by a Territorial battalion of the Royal Scots Fusiliers, failed to capture the farm from near which " F " Company had been counter-attacked.

The position above described had been reached about 5 p.m. and remained little changed till nightfall.

At 8.30 p.m. the Grenadiers and 6th Gordon Highlanders were ordered to take over the front line from the Scots Guards, the Grenadiers on the left and Gordons on the right holding the German first line from the point of entry southwards, in support.   At this time only six of the 16 officers who had gone forward with the battalion in the morning were present.   The whole of " F " Company was missing or absent, as well as one platoon of L.F.   R.F. could muster only 30 men.   The total casualties could not then be ascertained.

When the Commanding Officer and the Adjutant began, after dark, to collect the men near the orchard which had been taken in the morning, only about 300 could be got together.   Orders were then received to withdraw the battalion to the German first-line trench, which was to be held and put in a state of defence.

The night was spent in getting in the wounded, and in

turning the German trench into one facing the opposite way. Rations were got up, and every man had a meal. Later in the night there came in 37 survivors of " F " Company. These men, as has been mentioned above, succeeded in forcing a way through the German attack on " F," and reaching the Royal Welsh Fusiliers of the 22nd Brigade, to whom they attached themselves. With them they joined in the fighting of the day, with such gallantry as drew from the O.C. Royal Welsh Fusiliers a report acknowledging the valuable services they had rendered.

At daybreak on the 17th another storm from the British artillery burst upon the enemy in front of the Grenadier Guards and the Border Regiment. White flags were soon held out, and unarmed Germans with their hands up rushed out to surrender. They were Saxons, and they had a sorry time as they crossed No Man's Land ; for the British artillery was playing heavily on it, whilst the Prussians behind them deliberately fired on the wretched Saxons in an endeavour to stop the surrenders.

After the bombardment a successful attack was delivered by the 21st Brigade on the left, in which the Scots Guards had no share. Nevertheless, they were shelled all day, but luckily the shooting was high, and most of the shells pitched harmlessly behind them.

During this day the rest of the wounded were got in, the dead were buried, and it became possible to ascertain the extent to which the battalion had suffered.

Of officers ten were casualties.

Killed : 2nd-Lieutenants L. A. Jarvis and F. Marsham-Townshend.

Wounded : Captain H. C. C. Beaumont.

Missing : Captain Sir F. FitzWygram (prisoner of war, wounded), Captain C. Rivers-Bulkeley (killed), Lieutenants W. G. A. Garforth (killed), W. C. Hope (wounded), A. N. Hepbrune-Scott (wounded), D. G. Stephenson,[1] J. Mackenzie.[1]

Of other ranks C.S.M.s Burrough (R.F.), Johnson (" G " Company), and Lawton (" F " Company) were killed,

[1] The bodies of these officers were afterwards found and identified.

and altogether casualties in other ranks were 47 killed, 182 wounded, and 172 missing—total 401.

C.S.M. Johnson was shot through the head in the very act of bayoneting a German, and his body was afterwards found still grasping his rifle, with the bayonet embedded in the German's head.

A trench-mortar and many German prisoners were taken during the advance.

In the afternoon of the 17th May the battalion was shelled in its trench, but only one man was wounded.

About 9 p.m. the battalion proceeded, in darkness and rain, to dug-outs in a fort near Brigade Headquarters on the Rue du Bois. About noon on the 18th it moved to bivouacs in a field about half a mile down the Rue de l'Epinette, and at 5 p.m. returned to Hinges.

Next day (19th) it went to Busnes for rest and refitment.

At Busnes the orchards were full of blossom. The " rest " programme was simple : early morning parade, handling of arms under Sergeant-Major Moncur, a short route march or physical drill, and the men had the afternoons to themselves. " Handling of arms " was a means to an end. When men come out of action weary and unstrung, there is no better way of restoring alertness. As the war went on other methods of training were introduced, plans for teaching and " stiffening " were tried, but nothing ever was invented to improve on the old steady drill.

There, on the 27th, the whole of the 7th Division was inspected by General Joffre, the French Commander-in-Chief. In the march-past the 20th Brigade led. A draft of 250 men, under Lieutenant Wynne-Finch and 2nd-Lieutenants Balfour and Warde, arrived from England on the 28th, and on the 1st June the battalion moved to Cerise le Raux, sending, on the 2nd, " G " and L.F. Companies into second line, where Lieutenant L. Drury-Lowe was wounded.

On the 3rd the machine-guns, under Lieutenant Clarke, went up to support an attack by the 6th Gordon Highlanders, in which two machine-gunners were killed and three wounded on the 4th. The battalion moved, on the

5th, for further rest, into billets at Mt. Bernenchon. Here there was nothing to record except water sports in the canal on the 9th and 11th. On the first day the battalion beat the 6th Black Watch, of 51st Division, at water polo, and on the second there were present Sir H. Rawlinson, General Gough, and, later, H.R.H. the Prince of Wales.

On the 12th the battalion marched to Essars on the way to take over trenches next day at Givenchy from the 8th Royal Scots. Battalion Headquarters were at Windy Corner, with L.F. in reserve. The 14th was a day of heavy bombardment by both sides, which caused a loss to the Scots Guards of 8 men killed and 15 wounded. In the evening they returned to Essars.

Next day they bivouacked in Gorre Wood during an attack by the 21st Brigade opposite Givenchy, which eventually failed. The battalion then went into Corps Reserve, and was joined by 60 men from the base.[1]

On the 18th it again went into second- and third-line trenches at Le Plantin, which were very bad owing to the presence of dead Germans, from whom they had been recently captured. Nothing beyond the usual incidents of trench-warfare happened till the 28th June, when the enemy exploded a mine near Sunken Road. The battalion was ordered to occupy the crater, but this was found to be impossible, owing to its proximity to the enemy trenches, and the Scots Guards had to rest content with bombing the Germans in it by a party of bombers under Lieutenant Warde. Shelling went on till, on the 30th, the battalion went back to Busnes, the march being trying owing to the wet weather.

During Lieut.-Colonel Cator's absence on leave, from the 2nd July, the 2nd Scots Guards were temporarily commanded, first by Captain Bagot-Chester, and then by Captain E. Warner. At Busnes training of various sorts went on. On the 7th Sir Douglas Haig visited the battalion, which next day lined the roads for the arrival of Lord Kitchener.

---

[1] In Flanders in the summer of 1915 there were circulated a number of leaflets describing the places where British troops had fought in the past, or which had played some important part in military history.

The battalion continued at Busnes till the 13th, training and having some diversion in the form of a concert and a cricket match, in which " F " Company gained a bloodless victory over " G." After a few days at Calonne, the battalion took over the trenches in the neighbourhood of its great fight at Festubert, moving up to La Quinque Rue on the 21st, and stretching back to Prince's Road, where they had attacked on the 16th May.

The 22nd July was a bad day for one working party at " Tube Station," on the light railway by which supplies were brought up. An unlucky shell pitched right in the midst of the men, of whom it killed six and wounded three others.

General Capper returned to command of the 7th Division on the 22nd, and, after a period in the trenches, the battalion was back at Calonne.

On the 5th August the 2nd Gordon Highlanders held a mounted gymkhana as a farewell to the 2nd Scots Guards, with whom they had served in the 20th Brigade for nearly a year and from whom they were now about to be parted on the formation of the Guards Division. There was a dinner and concert in the evening, given to the rest of the 7th Division by the 2nd Scots Guards sergeants, and there were other exhibitions of the good feeling prevailing amongst its constituent parts. Two days later there was another contest, when Sergeant Gillies of the 2nd Gordon Highlanders undertook to wrestle any two men of the Scots Guards in an hour's actual wrestling. He threw his first man in twenty-five minutes, but just failed with his second owing to lapse of time.

On the 8th August the battalion was inspected by Major-General Capper, who, as an officer writes, made them

" a delightful farewell speech on our leaving the 7th Division, praising the troops for all they had done since the outbreak of the war. Everybody, I think, was rather touched by his speech, for all ranks regretted very much leaving the Division, which had so much esprit de corps and an undying fame, which maintained the highest standard to the end of the war, in spite of the frequent changes of the troops composing it."

After three enthusiastic cheers for the General, the battalion marched past, headed by the band of the Devonshire Battalion, who had come to relieve it. The music was taken up later by the divisional band, and by the drummers and pipers of the Gordons. As the Scots Guards marched off, the route was lined by the Gordons, Border Regiment, and others, who gave them a splendid farewell ovation.

Meanwhile, the history of the 1st Battalion from the 15th May till it also went to join the Guards Division was less eventful than that of the 2nd. Leaving Béthune on the 16th May, the battalion went into trenches at Le Rutoir, near Vermelles. In this neighbourhood, sometimes in trenches, sometimes in reserve, it remained for the rest of May. On the 31st Lieut.-Colonel the Master of Ruthven became G.S.O. to the 47th Division, and command of the battalion was taken over by Captain Sir Victor Mackenzie, till he was succeeded, on the 10th June, by Lieut.-Colonel S. H. Godman, D.S.O. The battalion was at that time in trenches near Cuinchy, ground familiar to it since the events of the preceding January. Then they were at Cambrin; from the 17th at Labeuvrière, and from the 24th at Burbure, well back from the front line. There were amusements, when out of the line, in the shape of cricket, and, despite the season, a drawn match at football with the Cameron Highlanders. The end of June saw the 1st Scots Guards at Verquin, where there was more cricket and football, and plenty of training and fatigues.

They were back again in the Le Rutoir trenches on the 6th July, enjoying the delights of German shelling, but suffering few losses. There were of course intervals of training and sports when out of trenches at Verquin, and in a Brigade Horse Show there the battalion carried off three first and two second prizes.

On the 22nd July billets were at Sailly la Bourse, and on the 1st August the battalion was in trenches south of La Bassée, whence large digging parties were sent out. Captain Cuthbert, D.S.O., was slightly wounded on the 31st July.

In this neighbourhood the 1st Battalion remained till,

8

on the 27th August, it went to Béthune and started on its march next day to join the Guards Division.

It was during this period that the Victoria Cross was gained by Lieutenant G. A. Boyd-Rochfort, for an action which is fully described in the following extract from the *London Gazette* of the 1st September 1915, giving the reasons for the award :

" George Arthur Boyd-Rochfort—Lieutenant, 1st Battalion Scots Guards—For most conspicuous bravery in the trenches between Cambrin and La Bassée on the 3rd August 1915.   At 2 a.m. a German trench-mortar bomb landed on the side of the parapet of the communication trench in which he stood, close to a small working party of his battalion.   He could easily have stepped back a few yards round the corner into perfect safety, but, shouting to his men to look out, he rushed at the bomb, seized it, and hurled it over the parapet, where it at once exploded.   There is no doubt that this splendid combination of presence of mind and courage saved the lives of many of the working party."

This chapter ends with the mention that those who had taken part in the first year of the war had made a wonderful effort, which they were proud of.   They were short of reserves, heavy artillery, gun ammunition, Stokes' mortars, Lewis' guns, light railways, barbed wire, tools and aeroplanes.

It was about this time that the effort of the munition service at home began to make itself felt, and every want in the first year began to be provided during the following years of the war.

CHAPTER VI

THE FORMATION OF THE GUARDS DIVISION

Division formed near St. Omer—Special training for Battle of Loos—Advance to reserve positions for attack.

BEFORE the Great War everyone in England was familiar with the Brigade of Guards, consisting of the Grenadier, Coldstream, and Scots Guards, with the 1st Battalion of the Irish Guards. There was then no such thing as a Guards Division such as had long existed in Continental armies, of which the most famous was the First Napoleon's Imperial Guard, with its later extensions of the Middle and Young Guard.

The idea of an English Guards Division, it appears, was started by Lord Kitchener and, according to the history of the division in the Great War, it seems probable that he intended it to become permanent. If he did so, the intention has now been abandoned and, for the present at any rate, the life of the Guards Division began and ended with its splendid record in the war.

There were, no doubt, as recorded in the history, misgivings amongst both Guardsmen and other military authorities as to the advisability of the project. Some thought that the influence of such fine battalions as those of the existing Brigade of Guards would be better distributed amongst the other divisions of the British Army, than concentrated in a single division separate from the rest. Another argument might be that divisions d'élite, such as the French Guard in the hands of Napoleon and his successors became, are a mistake, and even that they might be treated in a manner calculated to arouse envy and jealousy in the troops of the line, by being used only as a special corps, to be saved from the ordinary hardships and fighting, and only thrown in at supreme moments. So it was that Napoleon used his Old Guard, at any rate. He would keep it out of harm's way during a long day's fighting by the bulk of his army, until he was ready to produce what he called an *événement*. Then the laconic order, as at Lützen, " *la Garde au feu*," would send forward the Guard to complete the victory, the way to which had been prepared with infinite labour and perhaps heavy losses by the rest. Whatever fear may have been entertained on this score, the history of the several battalions of the British Guards Division from 1915 to 1918 shows to have been unfounded.

The Guards were never spared the untold labours and hardships which fell to the lot of every British soldier equally, were he a Regular, a Territorial or a " Service " man. Again, some thought that there would be difficulty in maintaining the former high standard of the Guards regiments if their numbers were increased, as would be necessary for the constitution of a full division according to the modern scale. It was, of course, inevitable that with the call to arms of the nation, the very highest standard, the standard which had been attained in the long training of peace times by the Guards, could not be absolutely maintained. Yet no one who follows the history of the division, or of its individual battalions, can ever feel a shadow of doubt that in all of them the traditions, discipline, and fighting qualities of the old Brigade of Guards were as nearly worked up to as possible. We have already quoted the remark of an officer of the Scots Guards in November 1914, that " the new men, although they have not quite got the discipline of the old lot, are at least wonderful, and have still the spirit of the Brigade of Guards, and their cheerfulness in all the mud and slime is marvellous."

The remark was as true till the end of the war as it was early in 1915.

The whole history of the division goes to show that, allowing for the effects of the shorter time for training in the case of men raised during the war, the relative efficiency of the battalions was fully maintained, and the discipline and esprit de corps of old times suffered no diminution.

The reason the Foot Guards retained their discipline

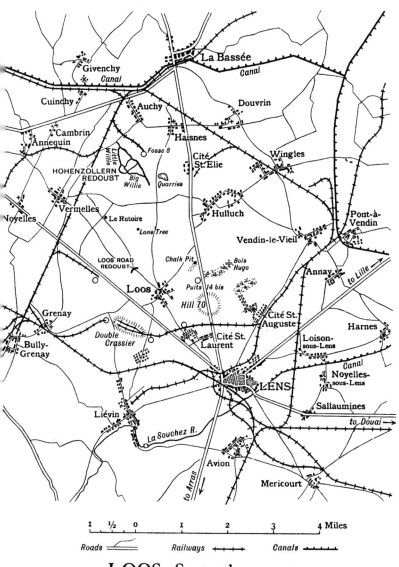

LOOS, September 1915.

※ It is notable that the small height of GIVENCHY and about two miles south of it was the only part of the front line of the Allies that never moved forward or back from October 1914 to the end of the War.

was that the recruits' training was kept on at their permanent depot at Caterham and their own Reserve Battalions from beginning to end of the war.

The number of the Guards battalions before the war was, of course, insufficient for the infantry of a division, and it was necessary to increase them. The Guards battalions already at the front in October 1914 were the 1st and 2nd Battalions Grenadier Guards, the 1st, 2nd, and 3rd Battalions Coldstream Guards, the 1st and 2nd Battalions Scots Guards, and the 1st Battalion Irish Guards. The 3rd Battalion Grenadier Guards had been kept back in London.

On the 1st March 1915 the 1st Battalion Welsh Guards had been raised and was on guard at Buckingham Palace. The new battalions raised after the decision to constitute a Guards Division were the 4th Battalion Grenadier Guards, the 4th Battalion Coldstream Guards (Pioneers), and the 2nd Battalion Irish Guards.

The Guards Division enjoyed the great advantage of a homogeneity, at any rate as regarded the infantry, which did not exist in any other division of the army. Of its twelve battalions, eight had existed before the war. The 1st Welsh Guards were raised before the division was constituted, and had already acquired the spirit and comradeship of the Guards. The other three were merely additions to already existing regiments, to which of course they at once adhered.

The old Brigade of Guards had been associated ever since the original formation of its several battalions, it had nearly always served during peace time within a limited area, and the battalions had been in constant association. Officers and men of these mostly knew one another, often intimately, and a spirit of brotherhood pervaded the whole brigade.

Line divisions in the Great War, on the other hand, were often, even generally, a collection of units which had had very little previous connexion, especially in the case of Territorial and " service " battalions.

The several battalions of a line regiment were generally split up amongst different brigades and divisions, and it was rare that a brigade contained more than one battalion of any regiment. The same may be said very often of divisions, though with the regiments which ran into very large numbers of Territorial and " service " battalions it necessarily sometimes happened that there would be two or three of them in the same division.

There was some attempt at territorializing divisions, such as the " Eastern " or the " Lancashire," but there were many which contained battalions from widely separated parts of England.

With the Guards Division it was different. Every officer and man was primarily a Guardsman, owing an allegiance not only to his own particular regiment or battalion, but also to the Guards Division.

The whole division was officered, almost without exception, even as regards its staff, by Guardsmen, and though Guards officers went to command other brigades or divisions, it was never the case that outsiders were given commands in the Guards Division.

Leaving out of consideration the very high standard of training, drill, and discipline which had always characterized the Guards, the great advantage of the spirit engendered by the traditions, associations, and intimacy of its units in the case of the Guards Division is obvious.

How strong the feeling of comradeship was between the regiments was illustrated by the strong expressions of regret recorded in the diary of the 2nd Scots Guards on the occasion of the separation of the 4th Grenadier Guards from the 3rd Guards Brigade on the formation, early in 1918, of the 4th Guards Brigade, which was to serve with another division.

The command of the new Guards Division was given to Major-General the Earl of Cavan, who had so greatly distinguished himself at the First Battle of Ypres and elsewhere. His command could only be for a brief period, until his certain promotion to higher commands. In January 1916 he was succeeded by Major-General G. P. T. Feilding, who led the Guards Division till six weeks before the conclusion of the war, when on the 11th September

Major-General T. G. Matheson succeeded him till the return home of the division.

The constitution of the Infantry Brigades [1] of the new division was as follows :

1ST BRIGADE.

Commander—Brevet Colonel (Temporary Brigadier-General) G. P. T. Feilding, D.S.O.

2nd Grenadier Guards—Brevet Lieutenant-Colonel G. D. Jeffreys.

2nd Bn. Coldstream Guards—Major (Temporary Lieut.-Colonel) P. A. Macgregor, D.S.O.

3rd Bn. Coldstream Guards—Major (Temporary Lieut.-Colonel) J. V. Campbell, D.S.O.

1st Bn. Irish Guards—Major (Temporary Lieut.-Colonel G. H. C. Madden.

2ND BRIGADE.

Commander—Lieut.-Colonel (Temporary Brigadier-General) J. Ponsonby, C.M.G., D.S.O.

3rd Bn. Grenadier Guards—Colonel N. A. L. Corry, D.S.O.

1st Bn. Coldstream Guards—Major A. G. E. Egerton.

1st Bn. Scots Guards—Major (Temporary Lieut.-Colonel) S. H. Godman, D.S.O.

2nd Bn. Irish Guards—Brevet Lieut.-Colonel Hon. L. J. Butler.

3RD BRIGADE.

Commander—Colonel (Temporary Brigadier-General) F. J. Heyworth, C.B., D.S.O.

1st Bn. Grenadier Guards—Major (Temporary Lieut.-Colonel) G. F. Trotter, D.S.O., M.V.O.

4th Bn. Grenadier Guards—Major G. C. Hamilton, D.S.O.

2nd Bn. Scots Guards—Major (Temporary Lieut.-Colonel) A. B. E. Cator, D.S.O.

1st Bn. Welsh Guards—Lieut.-Colonel W. Murray-Threipland.

It is desirable to give also the names of officers of the Scots Guards present at this time with the 1st and 2nd Battalions Scots Guards. They were :

[1] It seems unnecessary, for the purposes of this history, to give details of other arms.

1st Battalion.

Commanding—Temporary Lieut.-Colonel S. H. Godman, D.S.O.
Senior Major—Captain N. A. Orr-Ewing, D.S.O.
Adjutant—Temporary Lieutenant A. J. Thompson.
Quartermaster—Honorary Captain D. Kinlay.
Company Commander—Captain Sir V. A. F. Mackenzie, Bart., M.V.O.
Company Commander—Captain A. V. Poynter, D.S.O.
Company Commander—Captain J. H. Cuthbert, D.S.O.
Company Commander—Captain J. S. Thorpe.
Captain M. Barne.
Lieutenant H. C. Hammersley.
Lieutenant N. M. Ferguson.
Lieutenant A. M. Jones.
Temporary Lieutenant J. A. E. Drury Lowe.
2nd-Lieutenant G. S. Armstrong.
2nd-Lieutenant C. W. Mackworth-Praed.
2nd-Lieutenant G. A. Boyd-Rochfort, V.C.
2nd-Lieutenant C. E. J. Trafford.
2nd-Lieutenant D. W. Ellis.
Attached Medical Officer—Captain P. Walsh, R.A.M.C.

2nd Battalion.

Commanding—Temporary Lieut.-Colonel A. B. E. Cator, D.S.O.
Senior Major—Captain G. J. M. Bagot-Chester.
Adjutant—Lieutenant W. H. Wynne-Finch.
Quartermaster—Honorary Lieutenant T. Ross.
Company Commander—Captain W. J. M. Hill.
Company Commander—Captain A. R. Orr.
Company Commander—Captain J. A. Stirling.
Company Commander—Temporary Captain F. H. Ballantine-Dykes.
Lieutenant C. H. Seymour.
Lieutenant N. G. B. Lechmere.
Lieutenant E. S. Clarke.
2nd-Lieutenant S. H. T. Broadwood.
2nd-Lieutenant R. E. Warde.
2nd-Lieutenant Hon. C. T. Mills.
2nd-Lieutenant E. F. W. Arkwright.
2nd-Lieutenant R. L. Macdonald.
2nd-Lieutenant F. Ward.

Attached (for instruction)—2nd-Lieutenant M. W. Hocker, A.S.C.

Attached Medical Officer—Captain J. W. Houston, R.A.M.C.

Presbyterian Chaplain—Rev. Macrae, C.F.

Officers of the Scots Guards employed on the staff were Lieut.-Colonel the Master of Ruthven as G.S.O.1 of the Division, and Captain E. C. Warner, as Staff Captain, 3rd Brigade.

The area selected for the training and consolidation of the Guards Division was about Lumbres, twelve miles west of St. Omer. In this area the infantry brigades were collected as the several battalions constituting them were relieved and gathered in from the divisions to which those in France had so far belonged or arrived from England. In the case of the new 1st Guards Brigade no such collection was necessary, as the old 4th (Guards) Brigade of the 2nd Division consisted wholly of Guards battalions and merely changed its name and its division.

The Guards Division, with the 21st and 24th Divisions, constituted the new XI Corps, to the command of which Lieut.-General Haking was appointed.

The time spent in the Lumbres area was devoted not only to the consolidation of the new division, but also to special training for the coming Battle of Loos, in which the Guards Division as such was to make its debut in the field.

By the middle of September the Guards Division was in perfect order and condition. On the 16th and 17th Lord Cavan reviewed the 2nd and 3rd Guards Brigades, in which respectively were the 1st and 2nd Battalions Scots Guards. In a note on this review he said, *inter alia*:

" I was very particularly impressed with . . . the marching of the left flank company of the 1st Battalion Scots Guards . . . and with the exact timing of the handling of arms throughout both brigades."

The 2nd Battalion was the first to start on its march to join the new division. Leaving Béthune, it marched through back areas, via Mollinghem, to Helfaut, near

St. Omer, where the Guards Division was assembling. It was inspected by Lord Kitchener, on the 18th August, at St. Omer. In this neighbourhood the 2nd Battalion remained for a long time, far from the front, but very busy training, practising attacks or taking cover, and all the various activities of modern war.[1] The 1st Battalion, meanwhile, had only left Béthune on the 28th August to join the Guards Division. On arrival it was billeted at the village of Tatinghem, about three miles from St. Omer. On the 7th September the two battalions met at Tatinghem to play their annual inter-battalion football match, which was won by the 2nd, by one goal to nothing, after a closely contested game.

On the 24th September General Haking fully explained to his Divisional and Brigade Commanders the coming operations, and that evening Lord Cavan issued the following proclamation to the Guards Division :

" On the eve of the biggest battle in the world's history the General Officer Commanding Guards Division wishes his troops God-speed. He has nothing to add to the stirring words spoken by the Corps Commander this morning, but he wishes to impress upon everybody two things—first, that the fate of future generations of Englishmen hangs on this battle. Second, that great things are expected of the Guards Division. He knows that, as a Guardsman of over thirty years' service, he need say no more."

Similar conditions of training, drill, route marches, wood-cutting, and other fatigues, relieved by some amusements, prevailed whilst the new division was shaking itself together, till the 22nd September, when the 2nd Battalion started on its march back to the familiar area south of the La Bassée canal about Vermelles. They had reached Ecquedecques on the 25th, when rumours began to reach them regarding the first day of the Battle of Loos, the bombardment preceding which had been distinctly audible the day before.

---

[1] It was not till the Battle of Loos had begun that *everyone* had to learn to throw a bomb.

As they marched through Marles les Mines, the British cavalry passed the column on its way to the front. The Scots Guards had already passed two miles beyond Hallicourt, when they were ordered to billet there, and had to trudge back through the rain. They were dog tired when they at last reached their billets at 11.30 p.m. They had been on their legs off and on since 8 a.m., with a halt at Ecquedecques, most of the time in heavy rain and on roads churned up into deep mud by the traffic.

In the afternoon of the 26th the 2nd Battalion marched, via Nœux les Mines and Sailly la Bourse, to Vermelles, bivouacking at Coron du Rutoire, where they were lined up behind trenches for the night, in much discomfort from the cold wind which was blowing.

The 1st Battalion, marching with the 2nd Guards Brigade, had reached Houchain, west of Nœux les Mines, on the evening of the 25th, and on the following day joined the 2nd Guards Brigade at Sailly la Bourse.

On the 26th the British Army suffered a grievous loss in the death of General Sir Thomson Capper, the man who had commanded the 7th Division with such success at the First Battle of Ypres, and had so unstintingly recognized the great services of the 2nd Scots Guards when serving under him in the 20th Brigade.

The following appreciation of General Capper is worth reproducing. It was written by an officer of the Scots Guards two months before the General's death, and shows how he was esteemed by regimental officers serving under him :

" In 1914 he had been given command of the 7th Division, and during their assembly at Lyndhurst, in England, had taken infinite trouble over their training, which was on really sound lines, the value of which was proved when they landed on the Continent in Belgium and had to fight against great odds. He was a man with a most wonderful personality, and could always be relied on to get the best out of any man he might have to deal with. He was always very straight and fair, and if he once had made up his mind that a thing was possible, and that the cost was worth it, he would say so and carry

it out to that end.   From what one saw of him, purely
as a Regimental Officer, there was nothing that one could
really find fault with.   I know for a fact that in 1914,
during the first fighting round Ypres, if anybody wanted
to find General Capper, they had only to go where the
fighting was thickest.   Personally I attribute the whole of
the fighting esprit de corps to his wonderful individuality,
which lived afterwards.   The fall of Ypres was largely
saved by his spirit and pluck."

His brother was given the command of the Division by
the F.M. C.-in-C. beside the late General's grave.

CHAPTER VII

THE BATTLE OF LOOS

General plan of battle—Description of the ground, rain and cold—
Story of the fighting and losses.

WITH the general political and strategical considerations which led to the Battle of Loos this history of a single regiment is not concerned.

The general plan of the offensive decided on was, as concerns the British Army, an advance by the 1st Army under Sir Douglas Haig, in conjunction with the French 10th Army on its right, which was to move with its left south of the mining town of Lens and its numerous suburbs. That would leave a gap opposite Lens itself, and it was expected that the advance on both sides would compel the troops in that place either to retire promptly or to surrender.

The main French attack was to be in Champagne, and hopes were indulged in of a union of the Allied forces between Maubeuge and Valenciennes, cutting off the intervening German forces, unless they retired in time. All such hopes were destined to be disappointed.

The front of the 1st Army's advance was to stretch south from the La Bassée canal nearly to Lens. On this front the IV Corps on the right and the I on the left were to open the battle, whilst the XI Corps and the cavalry were to be held back in general reserve for employment when and where it should be found necessary in the course of the development of the attack. There was always the possibility that the Germans in Lens might try a counter-attack, either on the right of the British or the left of the French 10th Army. To be ready for the former, the reserve was considered necessary.

The right of the IV Corps was directed on the two slag heaps known as the Double Crassier south of Loos, and its left touching the southern side of the road from Vermelles to Hulluch.

The I Corps would touch the left of the IV on the last-named road, and would extend with its own left to the southern side of the La Bassée canal.

The mining village of Loos lay in a hollow about half a mile to the left of the main road as it goes south-eastwards from Vermelles to Lens, and a side road leads to it from a point in the main road about 1,000 yards south-east of where the German trenches crossed it, with the British front line about 150 yards to the west, and both running generally north and south.

On the southern side of the Loos depression ran, from west to east, a low ridge ending in the famous Hill 70, the highest contour from which it took its name, being only about 80 feet above the lowest part of Loos. Another spur, on which was No Man's Land on the main road, was of just the same height as Hill 70. The whole country was made specially defensible by the numerous mine shafts with their buildings and slag heaps.

From north to south, across the top of Hill 70, passed the road from La Bassée to Lens, and the fact that it went straight over the top, rather than make a circuit to east or west, itself shows that Hill 70 was not the marked feature that might be supposed by anyone on first hearing the name.

This road marked the line of the most important points in the action of the Guards Division in this part of the Battle of Loos.

Taking as a point from which to measure the famous Tower Bridge (two pylons connected by a girder bearing a resemblance to its namesake), the most northerly point is the Chalk Pit, 1,600 yards to the north-east, and a few yards on the west side of the La Bassée–Lens road. North-eastwards from the pit ran a wood, 500 yards in length and from 50 to 60 in breadth, known to the British as Chalk Pit Wood. Proceeding along the road towards Hill 70 for 500 yards, we find the mine shaft known as Puits 14bis, with the " Keep " on the west side of the road. The Keep was a small red house close to the Puits, on the side towards the wood. Opposite it, stretching east for 1,200 yards in different widths, was the Bois Hugo, and parallel to it, 300 yards south, another wood. The road slopes upwards all the way from Puits 14bis to the summit of Hill 70, where the Germans had an extensive redoubt just on their side of the crest.[1]

Behind Hill 70, on its eastward slope, was the Cité St. Auguste, one of the numerous mining villages or suburbs surrounding Lens, each consisting of ordinary houses, all of which had cellars which were practically ready-made dug-outs. The whole area about Puits 14bis, the Chalk Pit, and the neighbouring woods was covered with elaborate trenches and machine-gun posts, so arranged that, if they were entered by an enemy in one part, he had only begun his work, and would find it next to impossible to hold what he had gained. Most elaborate preparations had been made on the British side for this battle, which, if Lord Cavan rightly described it as the greatest so far in the world's history, was not to be compared with some of those which came later. The British artillery, up to now, had always been inferior in strength to the German ; for Loos there were collected about 600 guns of all calibres, from the 18-pdr. field-gun to the huge 15-inch " Granny," which dominated the field south of the La Bassée canal, besides another 400 yards north of it. The battle began with the infantry attack at 6.30 a.m. on the 25th September, after a bombardment which had begun four days earlier. With the events of that day we have little concern, for the Guards Division was far out of line in reserve. Early successes had carried part of the right of the British line over Hill 70, Puits 14bis, and the Chalk Pit ; but these gains were lost in the evening. The old German front line and the village of Loos were in British possession. During the following night the 21st and 24th Divisions were marching up through a pouring rain to take part in the attack of the 26th on the positions which the Germans still held between Hulluch and Hill 70. The attack of the 26th was a failure, and the enemy was still established in the neighbourhood of the Hulluch–Lens road and

[1] Map facing p. 102.

on Hill 70. The Guards Division had now to try to carry the lines before which the other divisions had failed.

The 1st Guards Brigade on the left and the 2nd on the right had been brought up in the afternoon of the 26th to the old German front line, and were now ordered to relieve the 21st and 24th Divisions on a line from about 800 yards south-west of Hulluch on the left to the northern edge of Loos. This relief was completed, after many difficulties had been overcome, by about 6 a.m. on the 27th, and patrols were sent out towards the enemy to dig themselves in whilst the morning mist continued to shroud them from view. No further move was made by these two brigades during the morning.

In the attack which was to be made in the afternoon, the 2nd and 3rd Guards Brigades were to play the leading parts. The 1st, on the left, was to support that of the 2nd, in the centre, and to form a defence for its left flank as it got forward to the Chalk Pit and Puits 14bis, which, with Hill 70 on the right, constituted the objective for the day. The last named was the objective of the 3rd Guards Brigade, on the right of the 2nd.

The attack of the 2nd Brigade, with which we must deal first, was to commence by the advance of the 2nd Irish Guards, supported by the 1st Coldstream, against the Chalk Pit and the wood south-west of it. When the Irish Guards were established there, the 1st Scots Guards would go forward to storm the Keep and Puits 14bis, in which they would be helped by the fire of the Irish Guards from the Chalk Pit and its Wood on the left, and supported by the 3rd Grenadiers, who would move into the trenches evacuated by the Scots.

Early in the morning of the 27th, the 1st Battalion Scots Guards marched into Loos, which had been taken on the 25th, and held since, under a continuous rain of German shells, of which many were gas. The battalion went into trenches north of the village, and remained there till the afternoon, still suffering from the German bombardment.

The British bombardment had been going on since noon, when at 3.40 p.m. it became intensive on the whole area about the Puits and on the nearer portion of the Bois Hugo.

Five minutes later the attack of the Irish Guards started, covered by machine-gun fire and much helped by a smoke-screen launched from the trenches occupied by the 8th Royal Berkshires, south-west of Hulluch. The Chalk Pit and the Wood were taken without much difficulty, the latter now forming a protection for the left of the Scots Guards in their final advance up the slope leading to Puits 14bis. The 1st Scots Guards started on their advance of 1,500 yards, of which the first 1,100 downhill were passed at the double under shell-fire only, which did not cause serious casualties. As they then started to move uphill they began to suffer heavily from machine-guns about the Puits and the Bois Hugo in front, and even more from the German trenches on Hill 70. The advance was led by " C " Company on the right and L.F. on the left ; R.F. was in support, and " B " in reserve. There was some confusion on the left, owing to inter-mixture of L.F. with the Irish Guards. The Scots Guards had also been joined on their right by a part of the 4th Grenadier Guards, from the 3rd Guards Brigade, under Captain Morrison. That officer had lost touch with the rest of his battalion in Loos, and, being unable to get orders, decided to go forward with the attack of the 2nd Brigade, and rejoin his own battalion later if possible. The losses of the Scots Guards as they moved up the slope were terribly heavy from the machine-gun fire above mentioned, but they persistently carried on, and gained the Puits and the Keep. By this time, however, there was left only a small portion of the Scots Guards under Captain J. H. Cuthbert, and a dozen or so of Captain Morrison's detachment of the 4th Grenadiers.

It was a great achievement, in the face of the terrible fire, to have gained the position at all ; it would have been a greater to hold it ; for the position had been so completely prepared and covered by fire by the Germans that it was almost untenable by any British who got into it. There was hand-to-hand fighting and machine-gun fire from the Bois Hugo and the slopes of Hill 70 on the right.

9

On the left, the Chalk Pit had been momentarily lost by the Irish Guards, but had been regained with the help of the 1st Coldstream.

Captain Cuthbert received a welcome reinforcement in the arrival of a platoon of the 3rd Grenadier Guards, the battalion supporting the 1st Scots Guards.

But the fire on the approach to the Puits was so intense that it was practically out of the question to send him more. At last the position about the Puits became so desperate that it was decided to evacuate it, and the Scots Guards, with a company of the 3rd Grenadiers, dug themselves in in trenches near the foot of the slope leading to the Puits. Here their left touched the right of the 2nd Irish Guards in Chalk Pit Wood, whilst the Pit itself was still held by the 1st Coldstream, on whose left again were the 2nd Coldstream Guards of the 1st Guards Brigade. Captain Morrison's 4th Grenadier Guards were at first on the right of the 1st Scots, but presently went to join the rest of their battalion in the attack on Hill 70.

It is now time to turn to the doings of the 3rd Guards Brigade, on the right of the 2nd, and to those of the 2nd Scots Guards.

After a night of shivering in a bitter cold wind in trenches at Corons de Rutoire, the 2nd Scots Guards stood to arms at 5.30 a.m. on the 27th. Even here it caught some of the " overs " from the German guns directed on the troops and batteries in front, and one corporal was killed, though no other damage was done.

It was not till 2 p.m. that orders were received for the advance on Loos by the Vermelles–Lens road. The brigade had been warned that as they passed over the crest of the spur, about where the road crossed what had been No Man's Land before the 25th, they would be fully exposed to the German artillery on Hill 70 and north of it. The whole brigade, therefore, marched in artillery formation from a point short of this.

The Vermelles–Lens road ran along the ridge south of and above Loos, and to reach that place it was, therefore, necessary to incline to the left and pass down a glacis slope intersected by the German trenches taken on the

25th, in full view of the enemy gunners. These conditions prevailed over about a mile. What might have happened to them, but for Colonel Cator's admirable arrangements for the controlling movements, halts, and extensions, was brought forcibly to the notice of the battalion. On this slope they saw the remains of the 21st Division transport which had been destroyed by shell fire on the 26th, " a horrible sight and very smelly from the dead horses " as an officer's diary fully describes it. As it was, the losses were comparatively small. This part of the movement was well described in *The Times* of 8th November 1915, thus :

" The men on reaching the ridge were met by a tornado of shrapnel fire. Nevertheless, the brigade advanced with the steadiness of men on parade, and men of other battalions who could see the manœuvre from their own trenches have spoken again and again of that wonderful advance as being one of the most glorious and impressive sights of the war, and of how they were thrilled to see those large silhouettes pressing silently and inexorably forward against the sky-line."

Loos, when it was reached, was likewise under heavy shell fire, and Lieutenant MacDonald was hit on the head by a flying brick, though that does not appear to have been counted as a wound. Gas shells added to the difficulties in Loos, the men had to put on their gas-masks and there was some confusion. It was in this that Captain Morrison and his detachment of the 4th Grenadiers got separated from the rest of the battalion, and eventually, as has been narrated in connexion with the attack of the 1st Scots Guards, took part in the storming of the Puits.

The attack of the 3rd Guards Brigade on Hill 70 had been intended to be contingent on the success of the operations of the 2nd Brigade. Brigadier-General Heyworth, commanding the 3rd, had seen the 1st Scots Guards reach the Puits, and believed that they had succeeded in taking and holding it. He, therefore, launched the attack of his own brigade about 4.45 p.m. The leading battalions were the 1st Welsh Guards on the right, and some 200 men of the 4th Grenadiers, all they had left after the separation of Captain Morrison's portion on the left.

The 2nd Scots Guards were in support, the 1st Grenadiers in reserve. The former were posted in Loos, whilst the Welsh and 4th Grenadiers went forward against the western slopes of Hill 70. Loos was still under heavy shell fire, and the Scots Guards had a very unpleasant time, especially as gas shells were still being used.

It was not till nearly 8 p.m. that it was known that the leading troops had reached the hog-backed ridge of Hill 70, and the 2nd Scots Guards were sent up to relieve them. They had suffered heavily, and when the Scots Guards reached them, they found that part of the Welsh Guards were over the crest, close in front of the German redoubt. The crest itself was untenable by either side, and every man who stood up on it was almost certain to be shot. It was decided, therefore, to entrench just below the crest on the British side. In this operation the Scots Guards were employed all night, assisted by Royal Engineers and some of the 4th Coldstream Guards (Pioneers). Lieutenant C. A. M. Cator, with one of the working parties, was slightly wounded by the explosion of a " dud " shell, which was struck by a pick. He was more fortunate than Captain Lord Petre of the 4th Coldstream, who, by the same explosion, was mortally wounded and died a few days later.

By midnight the new position had been greatly strengthened, and a wire entanglement had been erected in front of it by the Royal Engineers.

By daybreak on the 28th the 2nd Scots Guards were well dug in on the western slope, the German trenches being about 60 yards below the hog-backed crest on the other side. Many wounded had to be got in, and splendid work in doing this was performed by the stretcher bearers. The position of the battalion was now as follows :

It held the forward position on the east of Loos, with its right swung back to join the British main line. Its left flank was in the air, not joined up with the 2nd Guards Brigade, which, as we know, had been unable to hold Puits 14bis, and had had to form a line with its left in Chalk

Pit Wood. To protect this flank from being turned, it was decided to construct a redoubt there, armed with two machine-guns. But it was hardly possible to dig there above ground in daylight, in face of the German fire, and most of the day was spent in strengthening the front-line defences.

During the 28th another attack was made by the 2nd Brigade on Puits 14bis, but the attacking battalion was the 1st Coldstream Guards, and the 1st Scots remained in their trenches of the previous night, heavily shelled but not otherwise engaged. Though the objective was temporarily gained, it had to be relinquished, as on the 27th.

The companies of the 2nd Scots Guards, lying in shallow unencumbered scrapes in the face of Hill 70, watched with painful intensity the attack of the 1st Coldstream (2nd Brigade) from the Chalk Pit. The slight slope gave a view of the battle line right back north to Hulluch and beyond. They were helpless spectators of what seemed a staged show. The feeble bombardment, the gallant attack, and the groups dribbling back to the starting-place.

The 2nd Battalion Scots Guards machine-guns did what was possible to aid this attack of the 1st Coldstream Guards. During the night of the 28th-29th the 2nd Battalion, with the aid of the Royal Engineers, built the redoubt to protect its left flank.

During the 30th the German shelling did not cease. The 1st Battalion continued working at the trenches to the right of Chalk Pit Wood—150 men being relieved by Divisional Cyclists, and sent back to the trenches north of Loos, from which the attack of the 27th had started. There had been pouring rain for the last three days, and the men were miserably cold and wet, and had had no sleep for three nights when, at 1.30 a.m., the 2nd Battalion was relieved in trenches by the 22nd London Regiment. It marched back through Loos, fortunately without suffering any casualties whilst passing through the village, which was now a regular shell trap.

Billets were occupied at La Bourse. The 1st Battalion still had another day of trenches and shelling on the 30th. Just twenty-four hours after the relief of the 2nd Battalion, the 1st was replaced by two companies of the Norfolk and one of the Essex Regiment. It marched to billets at Verquinel. In the period 27th-30th September both battalions of the Scots Guards had lost heavily, especially the 1st, which had carried out the attack on Puits 14bis.

In the 1st no officer was killed, but the list of wounded was long.

Lieut.-Colonel S. H. Godman, D.S.O.; Major N. A. Orr-Ewing, D.S.O.; Captains Sir V. Mackenzie, M.V.O., A. V. Poynter, D.S.O., J. S. Thorpe; Lieutenants E. D. Mackenzie, N. M. Ferguson, A. M. Jones, H. H. Liddell-Grainger, D. H. Brand, D. W. Ellis, G. S. Dawkins.

In addition there were missing Captain J. H. Cuthbert, D.S.O., and 2nd-Lieutenant G. S. Armstrong [1]—altogether 14 officer casualties. It is hardly surprising that the 1st had to borrow from the 2nd the services of Captain J. A. Stirling and Lieutenants C. H. Seymour, E. P. Orr-Ewing, F. Ward and A. F. Purvis. Of other ranks the 1st Battalion had 27 killed, 324 wounded, and 98 missing. Total 469. The casualties of the 2nd Battalion were lighter. Lieutenant C. A. M. Cator was wounded, and of other ranks 17 were killed and 112 wounded.

After such serious losses the 1st Battalion required time to refit and recruit its numbers before returning to front trenches.[2] In the next few days it received reinforcements of two officers and 386 other ranks, and it would have been well could time have been spared for them to shake into place. But the Guards Division was still wanted, and on the 5th October the battalion was again sent up to the battle front.

General Foch's 9th French Army had now taken over

---

[1] Both recorded later as killed.

[2] About October 1st a large draft joined the 1st Scots Guards. The O.C. the R.F. Company took a census of the new men in his company. 95 per cent. were Scotsmen or of Scottish parents; but their immediate origin and their professions were the most diverse. Among them were a dock foreman from Buenos Aires, several men from " camps " on the Plate River, a mechanic from the nitrate fields, one from Yokohama, and one from Broken Hill Mine Rhodesia.

Loos, at the request of the British Commander-in-Chief, who found his line too extended for his available troops. The XI Corps had been changed in constitution. The Guards Division was still with it, but the shattered 21st and 24th Divisions had been replaced by the 12th and 46th.

During the night of the 3rd-4th October, the 1st Guards Brigade had relieved the 6th Infantry Brigade of the 2nd Division opposite the quarries west of Cité St. Elie, whilst the 3rd relieved the 5th Infantry Brigade on its right. The 2nd Guards Brigade was in reserve at Vermelles. It had been intended to resume the offensive against the quarries, but unfortunately, early in the morning of the 4th October, a German attack on the Hohenzollern Redoubt, farther north, had wrested that salient system of trenches from the 28th Division. The consequent exposure of the left flank of the troops to the south necessitated a change of plans. It was now decided to make a side-slip of the XI Corps northwards, and to interpolate the IV Corps between it and the left of the French at Loos.

Of the XI Corps the 12th Division was to take over the line from the left of the IV Corps to the right of the Guards Division, south-west of the quarries. In consequence the 3rd Guards Brigade was warned that it would be relieved, in the night of the 4th-5th October, by the 37th Infantry Brigade of the 12th Division, and would itself take over the billets of the 2nd Guards Brigade. The last-named brigade would relieve the 83rd Infantry Brigade (28th Division) on a line of 1,500 yards, the left of which was on the Vermelles–Auchy–La Bassée road, which crossed the front just north-west of the Hohenzollern Redoubt. That work, therefore, faced the left and centre of the 2nd Guards Brigade—the 1st Guards Brigade was on the left of the 2nd. These reliefs were completed well before dawn on the 5th October.

Matters remained fairly quiet on the front of the 2nd Guards Brigade during the next two days, but there was a great deal of hard work for both battalions of the Scots Guards, as well as other Guards battalions, in bringing up gas-cylinders, of which 120 were intended to be used by each brigade in a projected attack. The communication and other trenches had been so badly damaged by bombardment that the work of bringing up the cylinders was greatly hampered by their condition. On the 8th October the 3rd Grenadier Guards were holding a small salient in the British line just south of Big Willie, a trench running east and then south-east from the junction of the south and west faces of the Hohenzollern Redoubt.[1]

At 4 p.m. on the 8th October the enemy launched an infantry attack which fell heaviest on this salient. The 3rd Grenadiers were attacked from three sides, and the battalion soon lost most of its bombers, began to run short of bombs also, and was driven out of its front trench. Help came to them from bombers, led by Sergeant Brooks of the 3rd Coldstream, on the right; and the 1st Scots Guards, in support, were called on to reinforce the line. " B " and L.F. Companies were sent up, and joined the 3rd Grenadiers in the fight, and a constant supply of bombs was sent up. By 7 p.m. the lost trenches had been recovered. In this affair the losses of the two companies of the 1st Scots Guards were four men killed and six wounded.

During the attack on the trenches south of Big Willie on the afternoon of the 8th October, Brigadier-General Ponsonby, commanding the 2nd Guards Brigade, called on the 3rd Brigade for support by a battalion. The 2nd Scots Guards were ordered out for this purpose, and " F " and R.F. Companies were sent up as supports. They do not, however, appear to have been required, or to have been engaged in the action of which the story has been told in connexion with the 1st Scots Guards.

The Guards Division was relieved in front line by the 12th and 46th Divisions, in the night of the 12th-13th October. There was a sharp fight before the relief on the left of the 1st Guards Brigade, but in that neither battalion of the Scots Guards was engaged.

On the afternoon of the 13th the 12th and 46th Divisions carried out an attack on their front which failed with

[1] Map facing p. 102.

heavy losses. During it matters were at one time so critical that the 1st Grenadiers and 1st Welsh Guards of the 3rd Guards Brigade moved out ready to help if required. The 2nd Scots Guards were not called upon. So heavily had the 12th and 46th Divisions suffered in their unsuccessful attack of the 13th, that it was decided again to relieve the 46th Division by the 3rd Guards Brigade in the night of the 14th-15th, and to send the whole Guards Division into the front on the following night.

The trenches in front of the Hohenzollern Redoubt were now in an even more terrible state than when the Guards were there before. They had been almost obliterated in parts, and the communication trenches were hardly passable. Dead and wounded of both sides were scattered everywhere. The attack was to be renewed on the 17th October. Its ultimate objectives were Dump and Fosse trenches, to be followed by the Dump itself, and Fosse 8 behind it. There were, however, to be two stages, and for the first Dump and Fosse trenches were the limit. The 3rd Guards Brigade on the right was to capture the ground enclosed between the south face of the Hohenzollern Redoubt and Dump trench, whilst the 2nd Guards Brigade was to take the northern part of Little Willie and the rear of the Redoubt, the west face of which, with part of Little Willie, was already held. There were bombing attacks by the Germans on the west face during the relief, which were repulsed, and the relief was completed with difficulty.

The attack, well supported by artillery and trench-mortar fire, started at 5 a.m. on the 17th. With the attack of the 2nd Brigade on the left we need not deal, as the 1st Scots Guards do not appear to have been called up into it. In the right attack the 2nd Scots Guards took a prominent part in front, with the 4th Grenadier Guards in support. On that morning the battalion was ready by 4 a.m. Headquarters were moved forward 250 yards along the communication trench, and " G " Company was spread along it to form a chain for passing up bombs and supplies to the front.

The attack started at 5 a.m., " F " Company going south-east along " Big Willie," L.F. by a communication trench branching off to the left, and R.F. by another, reaching the German front at the same point, about 100 yards north of the junction of " Big Willie " with Dump trench.

At first nothing was heard of the attacking companies, except reiterated demands for more bombs. Then it appeared that they were having a very stiff time of it. Most of their bombers were casualties, and untrained bombers were wasting bombs, often throwing them without pulling the pins out, and getting them thrown back by the Germans.

About 6.30 a.m. Lieutenant R. Warde, in charge of the bombers, came back wounded in the leg, but returned when it had been dressed. He was soon wounded again, in the shoulder, and was brought in on a stretcher.

An attempt by Captain Orr to improve the situation by attacking over the open with " F " was stopped early, both Captain Orr and Lieutenant Lechmere being killed.

At 8 a.m. divisional orders arrived to consolidate on the ground so far gained. This consisted of about 150 yards of " Big Willie " gained by " F," and about 200 yards gained by L.F. R.F. had got forward, but found themselves in a cul-de-sac and were driven back by a German counter-attack. The rest of the day was spent in consolidating the new line.

The casualties in this attack were :

Officers : killed, Captain A. Orr ; missing, believed killed, Lieutenant N. Lechmere and Lieutenant C. W. Shelley ; wounded, Lieutenants R. Warde and E. Clarke.

Other ranks : killed, 20 ; wounded, 66 ; missing, 16.[1]

The morning of the next day was occupied, whilst the mist lasted, in bringing in the dead lying in the open. At 7 p.m. German shells knocked in a portion of the parapet on the right and buried seven men, of whom only four were rescued alive.

---

[1] This was the first estimate. The casualties in other ranks were found, later, to number 136.

There was a full moon that night, and the British front was so close to the enemy that all work in improving the defences had to be done by sapping, as the machine-gun fire prohibited work above ground. By 8.30 p.m. the battalion had been relieved by the 2nd Coldstream Guards, and went back to Sailly la Bourse. That night Lord Cavan went round all the companies and congratulated them on their recent achievements.[1] After three days for refitment and rest the 2nd Battalion again went to Vermelles on the 23rd October, and relieved the 2nd Irish Guards in Railway Reserve Trench.

Matters were quiet here, and the battalion, being relieved on the 26th, went through Béthune to billets at Cantrainne. There the battalion remained, training, route marching, and receiving instruction till they moved to Merville on the 9th November. Some small reinforcements came in, and on the 14th November the battalion was again in trenches from the Fauquissart road to Triolet, with three companies in front and R.F. in reserve in redoubts behind. These were very bad trenches, and the men had to bring up planks to floor the dug-outs.

There had been nothing special in the work of the Scots Guards battalions after the attack of the 17th October, for they had no share in the bombing attack by the 2nd Irish Guards on the 19th. They had their hands full with work at improving the devastated trenches about the Hohenzollern Redoubt. The Guards Division was relieved here by the 12th Division in the night of the 26th-27th October, and went into rest areas west and south-west of Béthune. On the 24th October Lieut.-Colonel Lord Esmé

---

[1] The following letter of appreciation, dated 18th October, was received by Colonel Cator from Lord Cavan

" I have just seen the 1st Army Commander and he asked me to convey to you and your grand men his sincere appreciation of the great effort you made yesterday. I told him no battalion had fought with greater tenacity and courage than yours did yesterday, and I very deeply deplore your losses. It is, however, our very bounden duty to get a good line for further efforts, and your task, which was intensely difficult, gave us a good start.

" Please tell the men how much their work was appreciated by me and all above me."

Gordon-Lennox took over command of the 1st Battalion, which next day went by train to Lillers, and thence into billets at Bourecq and St. Hilaire.

On the 28th it was ordered to Lillers for inspection by H.M. the King—Colonel-in-Chief of the Guards Division. On the way it was stopped and sent back, in consequence of the unfortunate accident in which His Majesty was seriously injured by his horse rearing and falling back on him. The 2nd Battalion was turned back for the same reason.

CHAPTER VIII

THE WINTER OF 1915 AND THE SPRING AND SUMMER OF 1916

In marshy ground east of Louane stream—Brigades get back for periods of rest at camps near Calais—March 16th both battalions march back into the Ypres area.

IT had now been decided not to subject the Indian Corps to another winter of trials and climate so uncongenial and injurious to them, especially the plainsmen as distinguished from the Gurkhas, Garhwalis, and some of the Pathans.

The XI Corps was to replace them in the line they now held, extending from south of Richebourg l'Avoué to east of Laventie.

As the 12th Division had replaced the Guards about the Hohenzollern Redoubt, it could not well be moved, and its place in the XI Corps was taken by the 19th Division, then in the neighbourhood of Festubert. The share of this line allotted to the Guards Division extended from the intersection of the Estaires–La Bassée road and the Rue du Bois, to Picantier on the Rue Tilleloy east of Laventie.

This section of the British front was only rivalled as the worst by such parts as some of the trenches about Ypres. The whole was marshy and liable, in winter, to inundation, and the problem of draining it, even partially, was a serious and difficult one for the Engineers. How it was dealt with does not belong to the history of an infantry regiment ; but, for those who are curious as to it, an excellent account is to be found in the *History of the Guards Division*.

The impossibility, in most parts, of digging trenches capable of occupation by troops in this water-logged country had been recognized from the first, and that recourse must be had to breastworks raised above the ground level.

These were in existence when the XI Corps took over the

front, but they were in bad condition, and, though thick at the bottom, were often not proof against rifle bullets towards the top. The amount of work which had to be done on them was appalling, and kept all battalions in front line more than fully occupied. That, too, under conditions of danger and difficulty, for the German front, with its snipers, was not far off, and large working parties collected in one place were out of the question.

The Germans here were as usual very much better off, for on their side the ground rose to the Aubers Ridge, which the British had failed to take at the battle of Neuve Chapelle. Their position gave them, not only drier quarters for their troops, but also great advantages in the matter of observation.

The circumstances of the British front necessitated a special system of defence adapted to the country.

It was unlikely that any great enterprise could be undertaken in the winter by the enemy, who had everything to lose and nothing to gain by any advance of their front likely to be made. Still, the unlikely had to be provided against, so long as it was within the limits of possibility, and if great attacks were improbable, it was still likely that there would be smaller local ones.

With any reasonable consideration for the health and the maintenance of the efficiency of the men, prolonged service in the front line was not to be thought of, and it was necessary to keep as small a garrison as was safe in the forward area.[1]

The general rule for a corps on this front was that two divisions at a time only should be employed in front, whilst the third was in Army Reserve.

For the XI Corps a somewhat different system of reliefs was adopted, on the suggestion of Lord Cavan. The southern half of the line was to be held in front by the 12th and 19th Infantry Divisions relieving one another in turn.

For the northern section the Guards Division alone would be responsible, always keeping one brigade in reserve and two in the line. By this arrangement it was

In some of these trenches, e.g. Fauquissart, there was a plague of rats.

possible never to have any battalion for more than forty-eight hours at a stretch in the line. The Guards, having had a special training at the time of the constitution of the division, could afford to do with less time for training than the other divisions. Each Guards brigade had six days out of every eighteen in Army Reserve, and when it was in line, two of its battalions were in front line, with the other two in reserve behind. The defences were in three lines. The front line of breastworks was supported by strong points behind them distributed along the Rue Tilleloy. Behind this forward line, generally on the line of the Rue Bacquerot, was another chain of posts known as the " *Croix Barbée* " system, of which Winchester post was one of the most important, and was provided with a garrison by the left front battalion of the division on duty on the right of the Guards area. These lines constituted the front system to be held at all costs. In the event of the front system giving way, there was still in rear a line of defences to fall back upon, which was not permanently occupied, but for the manning of which, in the event of its being required, provision was made by the Divisional Reserve and the 4th Coldstream Guards (Pioneers).

Needless to say, a mere passive defence of these lines was never contemplated. The Germans were to be perpetually harassed, their men killed and their nerves kept on edge by local raids. To facilitate these, lanes were cut in the enemy's wire at intervals by the artillery, and once cut were kept open and unrepaired by regular artillery and machine-gun fire. Into which of these open sores, and on what day or at what hour, poison might be injected in the form of a British raid, the Germans could never tell. Every possible encouragement was given to enterprise and the acquisition of information about the enemy's defences, the units which held them, their strength, mining operations, and many other matters of like character. The war diaries of both battalions of the Scots Guards during this period are blank as regards extensive raids.

In addition to the arrangements for defence and offence, many excellent plans for the diversion of the men when out of the front line were made in La Gorgue and Merville.

Provisions, too, were made for preservation of health, sanitation, clothing (and especially gum-boots), such as perhaps were not thought of, and certainly were not possible in the first winter of the war.

We now return to the movements of the two battalions after the relief of the Guards Division at the Hohenzollern Redoubt on the 26th-27th October.

On the 16th November the 1st Battalion took over trenches in the Duck's Bill, just north of Neuve Chapelle, from the 3rd Grenadier Guards. On the 20th till the 24th it was in billets near Merville, then at La Gorgue and in trenches east of Laventie. In this neighbourhood, and at Merville, the time was passed in and out of trenches till December 14th, when the battalion was in Brigade Reserve at Riez Bailleul.

On the 18th command of the battalion was taken temporarily by Captain J. Thorpe, on Lord Esmé Gordon-Lennox's going sick. Captain Thorpe was wounded in trenches on the 22nd, and Captain M. Barne took over temporary command.

The battalion being in trenches on Christmas Day, the men's Christmas dinner had to be postponed till the 28th, when it took place at La Gorgue, preceded by a concert. On this day Lord Esmé Gordon-Lennox resumed command. Nothing, beyond a couple of lectures, occurred till the end of 1915. The second lecture, on the 31st December, was by Major-General the Earl of Cavan on " The Great Chapter VIII," on tactics (*Field Service Regulations*).

Nothing worth noting happened to the 2nd Battalion up till Christmas Day, when the battalion was in trenches east of Laventie.

During the night of the 24th-25th December a lot of talking was heard in the enemy lines, and Germans shouted in English to our men. At dawn two German snipers began shooting, and one of them killed C.S.M. Oliver with a bullet in the head. The sergeant-major was an excellent N.C.O. and very popular with the men. Nevertheless, within ten minutes both German and British soldiers were clambering out of trenches and fraternizing in No Man's Land. News of this only reached the Battalion

Headquarters by a message from Brigade, who had heard of it from Corps Headquarters. The C.O. himself at once went off to the trenches to put a stop to the fraternization, but by the time he got there it was all over, and the men were back in trenches settled down for the day's routine. The enemy soon began shelling again, though they stopped in the afternoon and evening. They appeared, from the shouting in the trenches, to be making merry at night. Of course, as with the 1st Battalion, the men's Christmas dinner had to be postponed.

On the 26th the battalion was relieved by the 1st Welsh Guards, but returned to trenches on the 28th. They were out again on the 31st, and the officers had a cheery " Hogmanay " night dinner, followed by a concert, for which a piano was borrowed in the village, and a tune on the pipes by the pipe-major.

On the 22nd December the Guards Division lost the commander who had led it since its formation, by the promotion of the Earl of Cavan to the command of the XIV Corps. Regrets at the separation were great on both sides, but were soon afterwards modified by the announcement that the Guards Division was to be transferred to the corps commanded by their late divisional chief.

In succession to Lord Cavan the command of the Guards Division was given to Brigadier-General G. P. Feilding, now promoted to Major-General, as his predecessor had been advanced to Lieut.-General.

General Feilding had commanded the 4th (Guards) Brigade in succession to Lord Cavan, and, after the formation of the Guards Division, had commanded the 1st Guards Brigade. At the beginning of the war he had been in command of the 3rd Coldstream Guards, which he had led through the retreat from Mons, at the Battle of the Aisne, and through the great struggle of the First Battle of Ypres. As commander of the Guards Division, he was with it from December 1915 till October 1918, when there remained but a few weeks before the conclusion of the Armistice.

General Feilding's place at the head of the 1st Guards Brigade was taken by Brigadier-General C. E. Pereira, C.M.G.

10

1916

The year 1916 opened with the 1st Battalion going into trenches from La Gorgue and the 2nd marching to Merville out of the line. The early months of the year were on the whole uneventful for the Scots Guards, and we shall as usual pass rather rapidly over periods of trench warfare, stopping only to mention events of interest, or to describe specially important raids on the enemy trenches. We may as well deal with each battalion in succession for periods of a month at a time. For the 1st Battalion the whole of January 1916 was passed between Laventie or Merville and the trenches in front. Shelling of course went on on most days, but as the total casualties of the battalion from hostile action were represented by one man wounded, it was plainly not very effective. There were daily route marches when out of trenches; they were certainly the most effective means for keeping the men in good training when not otherwise employed. Football was all very well in its way, and it was played; but all could not play, whilst all could route march. Drill, too, was part of the day's work, for subalterns as well as men. Referring to the former, at least those who were now joining for the first time, an officer writes in his diary:

" It was surprising how quickly they all forgot their drill after being in the trenches for a few days. I think the real truth of it was that they never got a proper grounding at drill before they came out to France, and that it went in at one ear and out of the other. Besides, many said to themselves we are only here for the war, we will just know enough to carry us along. This was said by them, as they had not realized that without good drill and proper discipline one was not at one's maximum of usefulness.

" Provided one had the proper grounding of these two, one could be fairly certain of oneself in the crisis of a battle or at any other time."

The words were those of Lieutenant W. Wynne-Finch, then Adjutant of the 2nd Battalion. They are quoted as an

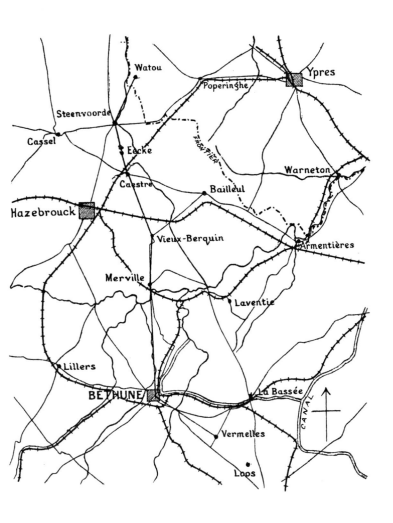

YPRES – BETHUNE, OCT. 1915.

appropriate answer to many more than the temporary officers to whom they in the first place referred.

There were, of course, the usual amusements in the form of concerts, boxing tournaments, and the like.

What has been said above applies generally to the 2nd as well as the 1st Battalion. It was at Merville in the early days of January, and the opportunity was taken, on the 2nd, for the men's deferred Christmas dinner in the afternoon, during which the regimental band played outside. In the evening the officers also had their Christmas dinner, which, like that of the men, was a great success. It was held in the Merville Hôtel de Ville, and afterwards some pipers were brought in to play. It was rather a trial for them to play on the top of a big dinner, and, when a drink of neat whisky was added, it is not surprising that the more sensitive musical ears of the audience were somewhat shocked.

The 2nd Battalion was, at first, just north of Merville, and later at Laventie, taking its turn of trenches in the same neighbourhood as the 1st. Its losses would have been as insignificant, but for one unlucky shell on the 23rd, which fell in Hougoumont House, killing four men and wounding five. February was equally uneventful for the 1st Battalion, which was at Riez Bailleul or in trenches, till the 16th, having only one casualty—Sergeant Martin [1]— killed by a stray bullet outside Battalion Headquarters on the 9th. On the 16th the 1st Battalion started to march to the Ypres area. It reached St. Jan ter Biezen, near Poperinghe, where it went into hutments on the 27th, and spent the last two days of the month there, supplying a large working party for the Elverdinghe defences on the north face of the Ypres salient. The 10th February was the 2nd Battalion's unlucky day, as a dug-out on the left of the trenches it was holding got a direct hit by a shell which killed five and wounded two men—these being the only casualties of the month. On the same day a house was set on fire by the German bombardment. Though no one was killed or wounded, there was

[1] One of the oldest pipers of the Scots Guards, killed on his way home for permanent leave from the front.

a considerable loss of material, including 18,000 rounds
of S.A.A.

The promised transfer of the Guards Division from the
XI Corps to the XIV was carried out in the middle of
February. In the XI Corps the Guards were replaced
by the 25th Division, the relief being carried through
between the 14th and 16th February. The XIV Corps, in
which the 14th Division was to be replaced by the Guards,
was at this time on the north-eastern front of the Ypres
salient, with its right not far from Hooge, and its left
touching the right of the French near Boesinghe. Its
6th Division was on the right, the 20th on the left, when
the Guards arrived to relieve the 14th, which had just gone
back into Corps Reserve about Cassel.

Whilst the division was out of line, the opportunity
was taken to give the Guards battalions in turn a short
period of change of air, recreation, and training on the
opener spaces about Calais. As will be seen, the 2nd was
the first of the two Scots Guards Battalions to make this
trip, and it went there direct, without passing through
the new area near Cassel.

On the 16th the 2nd Battalion marched from Merville
to Lestrem, where it entrained for Calais, and went to
camp three miles from that port. A heavy gale was
blowing, and most of the camp had been flattened out.
The tents had to be re-erected in severe cold before the
men could rest.

On the 13th February Lieut.-Colonel Cator had left the
battalion, on promotion to command of the 37th Infantry
Brigade. He was succeeded in command of the 2nd Scots
Guards, on the 19th by Lieut.-Colonel R. S. Tempest,
from the staff of the 3rd Guards Brigade. Captain Hon.
R. Coke had commanded temporarily during the inter-
regnum. In the camp at Calais there was rest from active
warfare, but there was vigorous practising of attacks,
especially the new bombing organization. During its
stay in the neighbourhood of Calais, the 2nd Scots Guards
had had a good share of diversions, in addition to hard
training, but they missed the crowning entertainment of
the " Great Calais First Spring Meeting," which did not

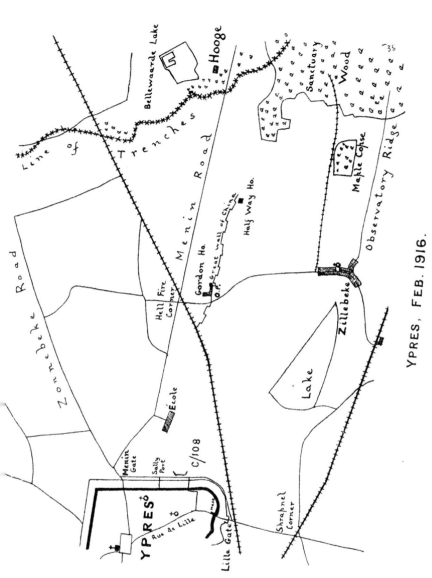

YPRES, FEB. 1916.

Facing page 134.

come off till a fortnight after they had left, when the 1st Battalion was there.

The country was covered with snow when the 2nd Battalion started to return to the front on the evening of February 24th. Fontinettes station was reached about 11 p.m., and hot soup fortified the men against the cold of the night journey. Cassel was reached at 6 a.m. on the 25th, three hours overdue. After breakfast the battalion marched to billets at Wormhoudt, where, still not in the line, it was on the 29th, busy practising bombing in trenches dug by it for the purpose. On the 1st March both battalions of the Scots Guards were in the Ypres region, the 1st at St. Jan ter Biezen, and the 2nd at Wormhoudt. On the 5th the 1st went by train from Poperinghe for its turn in the camp of Beaumarais, near Calais. It was nearly at full strength, with 19 officers and 950 other ranks. The usual exercises and training, as with the 2nd Battalion, were carried on in camp.

The 2nd Guards Brigade was responsible for the " Great Calais First Spring Meeting " held on the 12th March— its commander, Brigadier-General J. Ponsonby, acting as judge. A racecourse is generally to be found where there is a considerable collection of the British Army not actively engaged, and Calais was no exception. The course was a precarious one, for till the last moment it was uncertain whether the tide would not flatten out the steeple-chase course. Everyone who could possibly raise a mount entered it, including a sporting Irish priest of mature years, who rode his own horse. The class of animal run was no doubt very mixed, but that did not diminish the sporting character of the Meeting. If there is one thing more than others characteristic of the British officer, it is his love of a race for the sport of the thing. It used to be said of a well-known General in India, that he would run his " dhobi's " donkey rather than let a race fall through from lack of entries.

Fortunately the course held firm, and the five events on the card were run off, the 1st Scots Guards winning two of them, besides an extra match between five of the best horses.

The battalion returned by train on the 16th to Cassel, and marched to the Winnezeele area at Droglandt. On the 19th it moved to Poperinghe, and remained there till the 25th, when it went to Ypres. Next day it relieved the 2nd Battalion in trenches near Hooge, with the 1st Coldstream Guards on the right and the 1st Guards Brigade on the left. If the trenches were bad on the last front occupied, they were still worse at Ypres, and it would not be fair to attribute their condition to the neglect of the outgoing division. The conditions of ground were as bad as, or worse than, those in front of Laventie, and the German artillery was more active and had an unpleasant habit of concentrating a bombardment on a particular area and knocking front trenches, and especially communication trenches, out of all shape. This was only more or less stopped when the British artillery adopted the same tactics, and, instead of attempting to knock out the German guns, in which its success was negligible, devoted itself to giving a bad time to the unfortunate infantry in trenches, which were often no better than, and as easily knocked to pieces as, the British.

As on the Laventie front, the Guards were unremittingly employed in repairing damage and making improvements in the trenches. In this they were assisted by the Royal Engineers in improving the possibilities of machine defence by the utilization of ruined buildings, and by building concrete or steel emplacements, which were coming into fashion as the war dragged on, and the ultimate development of which took the form of the German " pill-box," which played so large a part in later events.

The 30th March was a specially bad day in the trenches which had been taken over by the 1st Scots Guards on the 26th. The German bombardment was concentrated on this area from 1.30 till 7 p.m.

The casualties for a day when there was no infantry attack by either side were extremely heavy. Lieutenant F. Ward and 2nd-Lieutenant F. T. Mann were wounded, and of other ranks 24 were killed, 47 wounded, 8 missing, and 20 were admitted to field ambulance suffering from shock. The last item conveys some idea of the severity of the enemy's fire. That night the battalion was relieved by the 3rd Grenadier Guards and returned to Ypres. The relief was very difficult, owing to continued intermittent shelling, and the circumstances of the preceding day. Stragglers were still coming in long after daybreak.

An unfortunate accidental explosion of a bomb during instruction in the 2nd Battalion on the 4th March wounded Major Baden-Powell, second in command, and five men, of whom one died of his wounds.

There were several similar accidents about this time, which were attributed to the dangerous shortening of the bursting time of the Mills grenade from five to three seconds.

On the 6th the 2nd Battalion moved two miles west of Poperinghe in a snowstorm. They had one man killed when R.F. and " F " were employed on digging near Ypres. On the 15th, when the battalion was entraining at Poperinghe for Ypres, another train ran into that which was being loaded. One sergeant was rather severely injured, and a few men were shaken. After spending most of the day in Ypres, the battalion moved, in the evening of the 16th, to front-line trenches which extended from the Ypres–Roulers railway on the right to within 50 yards of the Ypres–Zonnebeke road on the left. They took over from the 2nd West Yorkshire Regiment, and had the 4th Grenadier Guards on their right, and the 11th Essex on their left.

These trenches were in the worst state of disrepair, the parapets were so low as not to protect men walking in the trenches, and were not bullet-proof. The parados was almost non-existent, and there were no drainage arrangements.

Work was often interrupted by artillery fire, and comparatively little progress could be made in making good the trenches until, on the night of the 20th-21st the battalion, on relief by the 1st Welsh Guards, went into Ypres. It was again in these trenches from the 24th March, still vainly endeavouring to improve them, but being obliged to leave them still in bad order when relieved by the 1st Battalion in the night of the 26th-27th.   The last days of March were spent at Poperinghe.

After spending the first two days of April in Ypres, the 1st Battalion was in trenches till the 7th, with constant bombardment going on.   The 5th was a particularly bad day, on which 4 men were killed and 16 wounded, the latter including C.S.M. Clarke.

On the 8th the battalion went by train from Ypres to near Vlammertinghe, where they were out of the line, and were able to hold battalion sports on the 17th, in which the events were keenly contested by all ranks, " B " and " C " Companies being even for first place with 24 points each, against 18 for R.F. and 15 for L.F.

To show how the Ypres front had stabilized since 1914, the night relief marched through Menin-gate and the square, then by train back to Vlamertinghe.

On the 19th April the battalion was to have returned to trenches through Ypres, but the relief had to be postponed till next day, owing to the fact that the enemy had gained a footing in part of the trench held by the 2nd Battalion, and to the heavy shelling.   In the night of the 19th-20th the battalion took over from the 4th Grenadier Guards, in trenches on the Poelcappelle road, north-east of Ypres.   The rest of the month was spent between Ypres and trenches without the occurrence of anything notable, except a good deal of aerial activity, which was favoured by fine weather.

On the 7th April the 2nd Battalion took over trenches from the 1st Welsh Guards on the St. Jean road, and Captain J. Astley Corbett, Lieutenant A. Primrose, and five other ranks were wounded by shrapnel.   Either in these trenches or in Ypres, the battalion remained till the 19th April, hard at work, as usual in these low-lying trenches, repairing damage.

On the 19th April the 2nd Battalion was in trenches near Wieltje.   R.F., commanded by Captain C. J. Balfour, was in the front line, which was bombarded by the Germans from 6 a.m. till 4.45 p.m.   Many of the shells fell short, but about Wieltje itself some of them struck the trench.

At 4.45 p.m. the bombardment, which so far had been somewhat desultory, became intense, and a 5·9-inch pitched at the mouth of the dug-out in which were Captain Balfour and Lieutenants Scott and Swinton. Driven from their dug-out, the officers scattered, Captain Balfour and Lieutenant Swinton going northwards, Lieutenant Scott south. The former describes the bombardment then going on as the worst the battalion had yet suffered. It was still as heavy as ever at 6 p.m., when Captain Balfour, the trench in which he was being now a mere shambles, found that he had at hand about forty men. Amongst them they could raise only three rifles and a dozen bombs. Under these circumstances there was nothing to be done but to try to get back to the second line, to get reinforcements and then to reoccupy the front when a lull in the bombardment should render this possible.

Having got a fresh platoon from " G " Company, Captain Balfour heard that Lieutenant Scott and twenty men in groups were holding some fifty yards of broken trench, but that so far the Germans had not advanced with infantry. Lieutenant Scott, with Lieutenant Thewlis of the 1st Coldstream Guards, who had come up to reconnoitre the trenches for the coming relief, had established himself in the trench he had reached after the dug-out was rendered untenable. There he and his twenty men held on, in scattered groups, wherever it was possible to find a piece of undestroyed trench.

At dusk two platoons of " F " Company were sent up to reinforce the front.

Between 8 and 9 p.m. a patrol of about fifty Germans came forward, but, when fired on by Lieutenant Scott's party, fled back. About twenty-five of them were caught by the British guns and wiped out. Captain Balfour says that another patrol of ten got into the trenches and ran up against a single Scots Guards bomber. They shouted " Hands up," but were met with the reply " D—n all hands up," and a bomb hurled at them which drove them off. As they fled, the bomber killed five with his rifle within twenty-five yards of the trench, and another fell into the hands of the 4th Grenadiers on the right. This enabled the identification of the patrol as belonging to the 24th Regiment Bavarian Guard. It was 11 p.m. before Captain Balfour could get up again to the front line, where he found most of the trenches, including those about the dug-out from which he had been driven, almost entirely obliterated.

By this time the whole of the front line had been re-occupied, though only by detached groups, and there was a gap of fifty yards on the right between the Scots Guards and the left of the 4th Grenadiers. Several men who had been buried by shell fire were dug out, some dead and some still alive.

In the small hours of the 20th the 2nd Scots were relieved by the 1st Coldstream Guards, and went by rail from Ypres to Poperinghe, where they stayed till they moved, on the 27th, to Vlamertinghe for the rest of the month. By the time Captain Balfour and his men got to Ypres the last train had left, and they had to trudge to Poperinghe, avoiding main roads, which were heavily shelled.

The casualties in the front line on the 19th April were in R.F.: 9 killed, 17 wounded, 7 missing, whilst the attacked platoon of " G " lost 1 killed, 4 wounded, and 7 missing, and there were 5 more casualties in the rest of the battalion. The missing were probably some of those who had been buried by shell fire.

It was this affair which delayed the relief by the 1st Battalion.

May 1916 was quite uneventful for both the battalions, except for the much regretted death of Brigadier-General F. Heyworth, C.B., D.S.O., who had commanded the 3rd Guards Brigade since its constitution. He was temporarily commanding the Guards Division when he was shot through the head on his way up to the front line by an enemy sniper. At his funeral, on the 10th, the 1st Battalion was represented by an officer and four C.S.M.s, as bearers, and the pipers of the battalion. He was buried in Brandhoek Cemetery.

The whole of May was spent by the battalion in trenches

near Ypres, or in the various surrounding camps. The casualties of the month were only four other ranks killed and eleven wounded.

The month was equally uneventful for the 2nd Battalion. Naturally, as it belonged to the brigade which he commanded, it was more strongly represented than the 1st at General Heyworth's funeral. A Guard of Honour under Lieutenant Hon. A. Howard was furnished, and the funeral procession was led by the massed drummers and pipers of both battalions. General Heyworth was succeeded in command of the 3rd Guards Brigade by Brigadier-General C. E. Corkran.

The casualties of the month were even lighter than those of the 1st Battalion, amounting to only six wounded. June was a month of final preparations for the great allied offensive on the Somme, but these did not directly concern the Guards Division ; for it was to wait some time before moving to the field of the great battle.

It had not been intended to send the Guards Division back into the Ypres lines at present, but a change of plan was necessitated in June by events on the Canadian front about Sanctuary Wood and Hooge. There the Germans had begun a series of attacks on the 2nd June, which had resulted in the driving back of the Canadians for a considerable distance. After several assaults and counter-attacks, the latter had recovered some of the lost ground, but the enemy was still in possession of Hooge on the 13th June, when a call was made for a Guards Brigade to take over part of the Canadian line. For this purpose the 2nd Brigade was detached, and on the 15th-16th was sent up in lorries to Vlamertinghe, and on to trenches opposite Hooge and in Sanctuary Wood. In the latter, the 1st Scots Guards relieved the 60th Canadian Regiment. The place was in a terrible state. Everywhere were ghastly traces of the recent fighting of the Canadians, and as for trenches, they hardly existed, and what remained of them was constantly under the enemy's artillery fire. Communications had everywhere been cut, and the only means of intercourse between headquarters and the front line was by runners across the open.

The shelling, which had been going on all day on the 16th, increased after dark, and soon after midnight was so heavy on the trenches and roads leading to them, that an immediate attack was expected and artillery support was demanded by S.O.S. signal from the units right and left of the battalion. A tremendous barrage of shrapnel and H.E. shells was put down. The expected attack did not materialize, but the battalion's losses on this day were severe, owing doubtless to the very poor cover offered by the shattered trenches. Lieutenant M. N. Schiff was killed, Lieutenant Brand and 2nd-Lieutenant Mann were wounded. Of other ranks there were 15 killed and 25 wounded. It was difficult to evacuate the wounded in the morning of the 17th, owing to want of telephone communication with headquarters and the German artillery fire, which, however, was less heavy than on the 16th. This fire continued on the 18th, in the night of which day the battalion was relieved by the 3rd Grenadier Guards.

It then went to dug-outs at the " Bund " behind Zillebeke Lake, and on the 22nd to " E " camp near Vlamertinghe, where next day Lord Esmé Gordon-Lennox left command of the battalion to take up special duty at headquarters of the 4th Army. Major M. Barne took temporary command.

On the 24th there was a very successful concert, organized by the sergeants' mess, with the help of the Regimental Band. Brigadier-General Ponsonby was present.

On the 27th the 1st Battalion went into trenches at Canal Bank, north of Ypres, where they were next to French troops on their left. Here they remained under ordinary trench conditions till the end of the month.

After being at various places behind the line in the Ypres area, the 2nd Battalion returned to trenches on the north road on the 23rd June. The trenches were bad, as usual in this neighbourhood ; the work of constantly repairing them was very irksome, and the men's clothing got into a filthy condition in

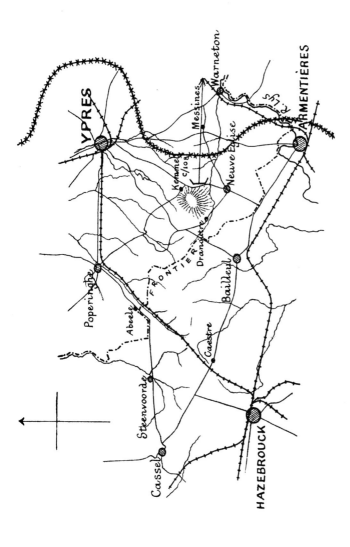

KEMMEL, JUNE 1916.

carrying it out.[1] This tour of trenches, which lasted till the 29th, was marked by casualties above the average. Twelve other ranks were killed or died of wounds, and twenty were wounded. The 1st Battalion continued the usual routine in and out of trenches near Ypres till the 17th July, when it had ten days in camp "D" at Vlamertinghe, and on the 26th was moved by train from Poperinghe to Bollezeele, twenty miles off.

[1] The trenches opposite von Kluck Farm, north of Ypres, were very heavily trench-mortared. The Germans had a light railway, which brought up supplies and occasionally a big "minnie."

CHAPTER IX

THE BATTLE OF THE SOMME

Guards Division moved to Somme area in July—Description of country and the fighting there—At end of September Guards Division moved back to rest till December 1st, when they renewed action on the Somme.

THE Guards Division was now moving southwards to the neighbourhood of the Somme battle, which had been in progress since the 1st July. At first, however, it was not to engage in the more active operations east of the river Ancre, but was to be attached to General Hubert Gough's Reserve Army, on the right bank of the Ancre, from the bend of that river opposite Beaumont Hamel, northwards to near Hébuterne. This was a comparatively quiet part at the time; for the great battle was in progress across the Ancre to the south-east, and the bend of the Ancre to the south was the pivot upon which it worked for the present, and, therefore, only to be held firmly.

At Esquelbecq, on the 26th July, the 1st Battalion entrained for Petit Houvin, near Doullens, and marched thence about ten miles to Lucheux. The march was very hot, and a good many men had to fall out, but rejoined later.

The Guards Division in this neighbourhood was in Corps Reserve to the XIV Corps. The front was held by the 6th, 25th, and 20th Divisions, in that order from right to left. The strength of the 1st Scots Guards on this day was 24 officers and 920 other ranks. For the 2nd Battalion the month of July was much the same as for the 1st, except that it was required to send a representative detachment to the review of Allied troops by the President of the French Republic on the 14th July, the national fête day. The detachment selected consisted of Lieut.-Colonel R. S. Tempest (commanding), Lieutenant W. H. Wynne-Finch (Adjutant), Lieutenant T. Ross (Quartermaster), one orderly room clerk, one orderly and two cooks, with nine other ranks. This party went by

144

train to Abbeville on the 11th. There it was in rest camp four miles from the station, where the whole of the troops representing the British Army came under the command of Colonel Tempest. On the 13th the detachment went with the rest to Paris, where it was billeted in the Caserne Pepinière, Rue St. Lazare.

On the 14th it marched to the Place des Invalides, where the whole representative detachment was drawn up in close column, with Belgian troops on its right, and Russian on its left. On the opposite side of the road were French Native Algerian troops. Unfortunately, there was heavy rain from 7.30 till 9.45 a.m. President Poincaré walked down the lines of troops and inspected them. At 10 a.m. the troops were formed, marched past the President, and then through Paris, by the Pont Alexandre III, the Champs Élysées, Place de la Concorde, Rue Royale, Boulevard Madeleine, Grands Boulevards, Porte St. Denis, and Place de la République, whence they returned in lorries to the Caserne Pepiniere. They spent the 15th sightseeing in Paris, and at 8.20 p.m. on the 16th, marched to the station, headed by a French band. Entraining at 10 p.m., they reached Abbeville next morning, and got back to Poperinghe on the 18th at 5.45 p.m.

On the 17th L.F. had casualties numbering eight, including Lieutenant J. G. Lumsden, wounded by shrapnel just after crossing the canal.

On the 20th Lieutenant P. Gold, out with a wiring party, was killed by a shot through the head, and Lieutenant A. L. Maynard also was wounded in the head. Seven more casualties were caused on the 22nd, during relief by the 1st Welsh Guards, by a 5·9-inch shell falling in the trench at the point of junction of " F " and " G " Companies.

Lieutenant Hon. A. J. P. Howard had been wounded earlier in the day by a bomb thrown by a German patrol at his wiring party. On the 28th the 2nd Battalion went to camp " D," on by train to Bollezeele, and billeted at Millam. On the 30th it marched to Cassel, and entrained for the Somme, detraining at Frevent, and marching via Lucheux to Halloy.

On the 2nd August the 1st Battalion moved up nearer to the front, to the Bois de Warnimont, near Authies, where Lieut.-Colonel S. H. Godman, on recovery from his wound, took over command on the 8th from Major M. Barne, who became second in command. Next day the battalion lined the road and cheered H.M. the King and the Prince of Wales as they motored past.

On the same day the battalion relieved the 2nd South Lancashires of the 75th Brigade in front of Auchonvillers, facing Beaumont Hamel, just west of the Ancre Valley. R.F. and L.F. Companies were in front line, " B " in support, and " C " in reserve. There was no infantry activity at this time at Beaumont Hamel, but on its first night in trenches the battalion lost 1 man killed and 8 wounded by " minenwerfer " bombs, and there was a good deal of artillery work by both sides. In the air the British were in command, and the few German aeroplanes which ventured to appear were soon driven off.

The 1st Battalion occupied these trenches alternately with the 3rd Grenadier Guards till the 16th August, when they were in the out of line post at Bertrancourt and moved to the left to Sailly aux Bois to take over trenches from the 10th K.R.R. Company at Hébuterne. Here " B " and " C " Companies were in front, with R.F. in support, and L.F. in reserve. Being relieved on the 21st by the 22nd Royal Fusiliers, the battalion marched to Bus lez Artois, south-west of Sailly aux Bois.

Here we must pause to give a general description of the country on the Somme front, which is very different from the generally low-lying marshy areas about Ypres and Loos, in which the Scots Guards had mostly operated since the race to the sea of the end of 1914. There trenches were often impracticable, and their place had to be very inadequately supplied by breastworks above ground-level. In some places the line had to consist of a very light occupation of the forward breastworks, backed by a line of forts constructed where a slight rise in the ground or a building offered facilities.

The country of the Somme and its tributary the Ancre in no way resembles this. The valleys of those rivers, it is true, are as marshy as, or even more so than, the areas above described. Both rivers spread out into valleys which are a sheet of marshes or open ponds, and in many places the stream itself is an insignificant feature compared to the confused tangle of reedy swamps and stagnant water on either side.

But once outside the immediate valley of the river, the country rises steeply on either bank of the Ancre to a rolling plateau of open chalk downs, sprinkled with villages and woods, which played a great part in the Battle of the Somme. The greater part of the battlefield may perhaps be likened to the rolling country, with many sunken roads, through which the railway from London to Southampton passes beyond Basingstoke. In these areas trenches could be dug and dug-outs constructed which might be described as luxurious by those who had been accustomed to the horrors of the trenches in Flanders. It was only in the valleys of the Somme and the Ancre that those conditions could be again encountered, and the greater part of the long-drawn-out Battle of the Somme was fought on the plateau above. The British had no fighting then in the actual valley of the Somme, and it was only when they descended on the Ancre, above the tributary valley near Beaumont, that marshy land was encountered. Even here the marshes of the Ancre, which are almost continuous between Beaumont and the junction with the Somme, cease to be bad above Grandcourt. A striking fact at this time was that there were very few isolated buildings; in fact, the villages were little more than groups of farms. There were no fences to speak of, and much larger fields than in " subdivided Flanders." Also the sunken roads through the chalk country became a very marked feature in all fighting. On August 23rd the 1st Battalion Scots Guards marched, with the rest of the 2nd Guards Brigade, from Bus lez Artois to Amplier, on its way to the scene of more active operations beyond the left bank of the Ancre. On the 24th Naours was reached, and on the 25th the battalion went by rail through Amiens to Mericourt, where it detrained and marched to Morlancourt, on the east bank of the Ancre.

11

Here it was still in the far-back areas of the battle front, which ran at this time generally from the Ancre north of Ovillers la Boisselle to Longueval, where it bent back southwards to join the left of the French attack near Hardecourt aux Bois.

At Morlancourt the battalion remained till the 9th September, busy with the training of all sorts practised when out of line.

On the 3rd September there occurred a sad accident and a very gallant action. 2nd-Lieutenant G. de L. Leach, the battalion bombing officer, was detonating bombs in the Orderly Room, when the fuse of one of them was accidentally ignited. There were two other men in the room, and Leach, realizing the danger to them, shouted a warning, and rushed to the door, carrying the bomb, and evidently intending to throw it into some bushes.

As he got out, he found several people standing about. Before he could throw the bomb where it would do no harm, it exploded. Both his hands were blown off, and he was wounded in the legs and stomach. He was taken to the hospital at Corbie as soon as possible, but died on the way. His self-sacrifice cost him his life, but saved the lives of several others. His splendid conduct was suitably acknowledged in the finding of a Court of Inquiry held that evening. Between this heroic action and that which gained the Victoria Cross for Lieutenant Boyd-Rochfort on the 3rd August 1915, the possible distinction appears to be that the latter dealt with an enemy bomb in the presence of the enemy, whilst 2nd-Lieutenant Leach held to his body to save others a British bomb not in the actual line. Had he been under fire at the time, even if the bomb had been British, he also would no doubt have been awarded the Cross.[1]

In recognition of his splendid action, a posthumous award was made of the Albert Medal in gold. According to the *History of the Guards Division*, this was the first

[1] The rules of the V.C. seem to bar its grant in such a case. Nevertheless, there is an exceptional case in the Rifle Brigade, where it was awarded for gallantry in dealing with a burning railway wagon full of explosives in Canada, in peace time.

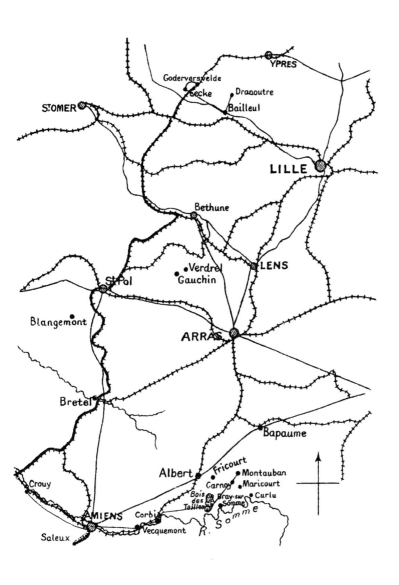

AMIENS–LILLE, AUG. 1916.

icing page 148.

instance of the award of this decoration to an officer of the Guards.

On September 9th the battalion moved six miles to Happy Valley, north of Bray-sur-Somme, where, on the 11th, orders were received to move to the front next day.

The march of the 12th was without packs or surplus kit, and led north through Carnoy, where there was a long halt. After dark the battalion moved on to Bernafay Wood, which had been in British hands since the middle of July. Battalion Headquarters were in the wood, and the 4th Grenadier Guards were relieved. The dispositions were : Headquarters with " C " and L.F. Companies in Bernafay Wood ; R.F. and " B " in support to the Irish Guards in front of it.

Meanwhile, the 2nd Battalion had followed the 1st Grenadier Guards on the 1st August to Bus lez Artois. On August 9th the battalion was visited by His Majesty the King and Sir Douglas Haig, and next day went, via Bertrancourt, to relieve the 9th Loyal North Lancashires in trenches in the support line. On the 14th it moved up to the front line in place of the 1st Welsh Guards. On the 19th it was relieved by the 24th Royal Fusiliers and returned to Bus.

Thence they followed the 1st Grenadier Guards, on the 20th to Sarton and on the 22nd to Hem. They were at Vignacourt on the 25th ; entrained and went by Amiens and Corbie to Méricourt, and marched to Ville-sur-Corbie.

There is a curious remark in the diary of the 7th September at that place. The battalion practised an attack in extended order up a ravine, and the diary says, " the attack was very badly carried out, owing to the majority of officers not knowing the primary principles of open fighting."

The remark is noteworthy as showing the narrowing effects of a long course of trench warfare, and the difficulties of passing from it to open warfare, especially for newly joined officers and men whose whole experience of war, so far, had been acquired in the peculiar form suitable to the trenches. On the 9th September the 2nd Battalion marched and bivouacked just north of Carnoy, where, in the evening, they heard the heavy bombardment in support of the British attack on Ginchy, four miles to the north-east.

The 2nd Battalion was destined to precede the 1st in its entry into the Battle of the Somme.

The XIV Corps now formed part of Sir H. Rawlinson's 4th Army. The 3rd Guards Brigade was relieving the 47th and 48th Infantry Brigades, which had suffered severely in an attack on Ginchy and the German work known as the Quadrilateral, to the east of it on the road to Morval. The 4th Grenadier Guards were to take over from the 47th Brigade on the right, the 1st Welsh Guards from the 48th on the left, south-east of Ginchy.[1] In support of these were the 1st Grenadier Guards in Bernafay Wood, whilst the 2nd Scots Guards remained in reserve north of Carnoy.

At 11.15 a.m. on the 10th September the 2nd Scots Guards received orders to send up two companies to Bernafay Wood, about two miles to the north-east of their bivouac in the old British line north of Carnoy, and at 2 p.m. the rest of the battalion was ordered up.

At 7 p.m. L.F., under Lieutenant Tyringham, and " G " Company, under Captain J. A. Stirling, were moved up to reinforce the left of the 1st Welsh Guards, who were then holding a line north and north-east of Ginchy, another two miles to the north-east. There, under the orders of the O.C. Welsh Guards, the two companies established a line and assisted in the capture of the orchard at the northern end of Ginchy, where they took over seventy prisoners. During their advance to the front line they had come under the German barrage, and suffered several casualties. Lieutenant Tyringham was knocked out by a shell, and suffered from shell-shock.

During the night R.F. Company was employed carrying up rations, etc., for the 1st Grenadier Guards, and " F " on the same service for the 4th Grenadier Guards. In R.F. Lieutenant Rutherford fell into a deep trench in the dark and injured himself.

---

[1] This was where the " sausage balloons " for observation were first seen. On August 14th, the " sausage " was shot down close to Auchon-villiers.

By the morning of the 11th the line at Ginchy had been well consolidated. " G " and L.F. Companies remained in it with the 1st Welsh Guards throughout the day. The other two companies and headquarters were in Bernafay Wood, the south-east corner of which came in for unwelcome attentions from the enemy's artillery in the afternoon. The casualties were few, thanks to the foresight of the company officers, who had moved their men into trenches in the wood. At 8.15 the part of the battalion in Bernafay Wood went up by the south-east corner of Trônes Wood to relieve the 1st Welsh Guards at Ginchy. Headquarters were in an old German dug-out on the north-east side of Guillemont, which was shared with Battalion Headquarters of the 1st Grenadier Guards, who were holding the line on the right of the 2nd Scots Guards. In going up to Ginchy there were some casualties in R.F. Company from shell fire. During the night L.F., R.F., and " G " held the front line, with " F " in reserve. The line north and north-east of Ginchy was linked up during the night by the capture of a piece of ground by Captain Stirling with " G " Company.

The comparative quiet at Ginchy on the 12th was only interrupted by the front line receiving some " shorts " from the British 9·2-inch guns. At 10.30 that night the battalion, on being relieved by the 2nd Grenadier Guards of the 2nd Guards Brigade, marched back without loss to Happy Valley.

The losses in this tour of service were one officer (Lieutenant Tyringham) shell-shocked, and Lieutenant Rutherford accidentally injured. Of other ranks 11 were killed, 12 wounded, and 6 missing.

The next push forward from Ginchy by the Guards Division, towards Lesbœufs, was fixed for the 15th. In it the 3rd Brigade was to be in Divisional Reserve, ready to reinforce the 1st or 2nd in front, or to exploit their successes. The possible rôles of the brigade were discussed at a conference at Brigade Headquarters on the 13th. It was thought that it might take one of the following forms :

(1) If the attack was completely successful, the brigade should push through Lesbœufs to the high ground south-west of Le Transloy.

(2) If the 1st and 2nd Brigades reached their objective, indicated by a blue line on the map, the 3rd would pass through to capture Lesbœufs.

(3) Merely to take over the line held by the leading brigades when exhausted by fighting.

(4) To form a defensive flank in the event of the front of the Guards Division getting forward farther than one of the division (6th and 14th) on its flanks.

At 2 p.m. on the 14th brigade orders on these lines for the next day were given out and explained to officers and N.C.O.s.

The History of the Guards Division, pp. 144–145, is at variance with Captain J. A. Stirling's notes. He was in command of "G" Company. These are his notes :

"On the night of September 10th the Company was sent up with L.F. Company to come under the orders of Colonel Murray Threipland, commanding 1st Welsh Guards. We found a sharp German barrage east of Trônes Wood, and the shelling got worse at the north end of Guillemont village, where Colonel Murray Threipland had established himself in a deep German dug-out. (Just outside this dug-out Tyringham was shell-shocked.)

"We were told that no one knew the exact position in Ginchy village, but we were to fill in a gap on the left of the 1st Grenadiers. 'G' Company in front, L.F. in support. It was a very dark night. Continuous shelling and a good deal of machine-gun fire from the east (direction of the 'Quadrilateral').

"We turned north towards Ginchy village, with a Welsh Guard guide, who seemed to have no idea of direction or where his companies were.

"On the edge of Ginchy village we met Captain Drury Lowe, with part of King's Company, G.G. He told me that the village was full of scattered German parties and no British troops, except perhaps a few wounded men of the 16th (Irish) Division.

"We decided to 'drive' the village between us. The Grenadier Guards taking the right of the Guillemont–Ginchy road, 'G' Company on the left side.

"As soon as we entered the village, the Germans began coming in and surrendering. The north border of this

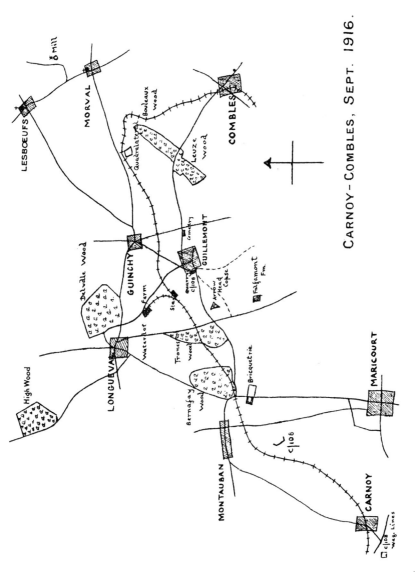

CARNOY–COMBLES, SEPT. 1916.

Facing page 152.

village was much broader than I had expected, and we could only establish posts, and our flank towards Delville Wood seemed to be in the air.

" Vanneck and I tried to ' spot ' the situation, and ran across a trench full of frightened Germans just outside, west of the village.

" When daylight came we found ourselves rather pinned to the posts, as there were German riflemen in trenches just north-east of the village, who had a good view, at short range, of any movement of our men.

" During 11th and 12th we were impartially shelled by *both* sides."

The battalion marched at 5 p.m. to Carnoy, and, after a halt of four hours there, moved at 10 p.m. to its assembly position on the east of Trônes Wood and north of the light railway which runs from Morval past Trônes Wood. The 4th Grenadier Guards were on the right, south of the railway, with the 1st Grenadier Guards supporting the 4th, and the 1st Welsh Guards supporting the 2nd Scots Guards.

Here we must return to the 1st Scots Guards, whom we left on the 13th September in Bernafay Wood. L.F. and "C" Companies were on fatigue, making headquarters for the division. The other two companies in Bernafay Wood received a very heavy shelling, which killed 2nd-Lieutenant E. Holland and 13 other ranks, whilst the wounded were Lieutenant R. J. Champion (remained on duty) and 24 other ranks.

The 14th was spent in Bernafay Wood, preparing for the attack next day. At midnight of the 14th-15th the battalion moved up to its assembly position in front of Ginchy. In order to understand the action of the two battalions of the Scots Guards on the 15th September, some account is necessary of the general scheme of the attack, by which it was hoped to reach a line running from north-east to south-west just beyond the village of Lesbœufs on the forward slope of the last ridge before reaching the road from Bapaume, via Le Transloy and Sailly Saillesel, to Péronne. As we shall see, the advance on the 15th never reached Lesbœufs, so we may leave that line out of consideration for the moment. The Guards Division on a front of two brigades, 2nd Brigade on the right, 1st on the left, was to advance north-eastwards from Ginchy to Lesbœufs. The front covered by the Guards Division was about 1,200 yards, about equally divided between the 1st and 2nd Brigades. The attack in the same general direction would be extended by the 6th Division on the right and the 14th on the left, and it was possible that these two divisions might not be able to keep in line with the Guards, especially the 6th, which had to deal with the German Quadrilateral. The formation of a defensive flank on either side was, therefore, one of the possible functions of the 3rd Guards Brigade, which was in reserve about Trônes Wood.

The first objective of the leading Guards Brigades was the Green Line as shown on the map,[1] which lay about 1,000 yards north and north-east of Ginchy, just beyond the ridge from which Lesbœufs comes into view. When this objective should be reached, the 2nd Brigade on the right would consolidate and hold on whilst the 1st mastered the Brown Line. Then both brigades would push on to the Blue Line, another 1,100 yards beyond the green. The 3rd Brigade would be available for any of the purposes laid down at the conference on the 13th September. The weather unfortunately was cold and wet on the 15th September. The troops had spent a bad night, exposed to rain and cold, and the ground in the morning was slippery and difficult to move over.

The orders for the attack by the 2nd Guards Brigade placed the 3rd Grenadier Guards on the right, with the 1st Scots Guards in support of them. On the left were the 1st Coldstream Guards, with the 2nd Irish Guards in support. On the left of the 2nd Guards Brigade was the 1st, and on the right the 6th Division. At 5.40 a.m. what the battalion diary calls the "Armoured Creepers," otherwise tanks, which were to lead the attack, were coming up, but were so heavily fired on that they came to a standstill.

For twenty minutes from 6 a.m. there was a slow fire from British "heavies," followed at 6.20 by a creeping barrage, behind which the leading battalions of the 1st and 2nd Guards Brigades advanced to the attack towards

[1] Facing p. 148.

the north-east. The attack by the 2nd Guards Brigade was to be on a front of 500 yards north-east of Ginchy. It had been found on the preceding days that any signs of activity were at once followed by a heavy German barrage on the eastern edges of Ginchy and Guillemont villages. It had been decided, therefore, to align the whole 2nd Brigade east of Ginchy, so that the barrage might not cut off the supporting from the leading battalions. As the troops started to the attack, the enemy barrage became intensive, but, save for one shell bursting among the 1st Coldstream Guards and knocking out some men, did very little harm. It was 6.20 a.m. when the whole brigade moved forward. It was believed that there was no inter-mediate line of trenches before reaching the green line, though machine-gun fire was to be expected from a German trench running north and south on the right flank of the advance.

Apparently the trench indicated was that marked on the map as running from the Triangle to the Quadrilateral. The Triangle was a German strong point just short of the green line, and near the top of the rising ground which had to be passed before reaching that line. The Quadrilateral was a German rectangular work about 1,200 yards east of Ginchy in the area of the attack of the 6th Division, for which it furnished a very tough nut to crack.

All round Ginchy the ground was a net-work of shell holes resulting from recent bombardments, and every landmark on the near side of the ridge behind which lay the first objective had been obliterated. The ground, too, was almost unknown to the brigade.

As it moved forward it soon found that the absence of intermediate lines was a myth.[1] The shell holes had been

[1] A map found later on the body of a German officer shows that these two lines were recognized as such by the enemy and are marked on their map.

The map also shows that there was a whole battalion (probably of the 14th Infantry Regiment) in these lines. The 3rd Battalion of the same regiment was in support, with two companies in the green line, and the 1st Battalion, 7th Infantry Regiment, on their left.

The report on the finding of this map remarks :

" This distribution of troops explains the comparative ease with which connected up in two lines, which had to be overcome before the main trench of the objective could be attacked. The garrison of the two lines fought to the last man, and caused heavy loss to the attacking brigade, which was increased by very heavy machine-gun fire. The right flank was exposed by the failure of the 6th Division to take the Quadrilateral.

For protection against the fire from the trench already mentioned as running north and south, the 3rd Grenadier Guards threw out a right flank guard, which moved to within 200 yards of it, and endeavoured to keep down its fire. Meanwhile, the 1st Coldstream Guards on the left of the brigade had been checked by running into the creeping barrage on its left. This caused the whole direction of the attack to swing round from north-east to north. As the attack went forward, the 1st Scots Guards were in close support of the advancing portion of the 3rd Grenadier Guards. Owing to various movements, the 1st and 2nd Brigades were a good deal mixed up on their contiguous flanks.

When the first objective was reached by the 2nd Guards Brigade, the 3rd Grenadier Guards were on the right, with a flank guard thrown back against the trench on their right. The 1st Scots Guards were in close support and had already reinforced them. On the left, touching and partly mixed up with the right of the 1st Brigade, were the 1st Coldstream Guards. The objective had been reached on the front of the 2nd Brigade, when the Germans in the Triangle had been finally disposed of. Owing to the change of direction, due to the delay of the 1st Coldstream Guards when they ran into the British barrage, all units were a good deal mixed up, and when, about 11 a.m., Lieut.-Colonel Godman of the 1st Scots Guards took over command in the first objective, he had under him a mixture of 3rd Grenadiers, 1st Coldstream Guards, 1st Scots Guards, and 2nd Irish Guards.

It was at this period of the battle that Lance-Sergeant

the green line was taken when reached, in spite of the fact that it had not been much damaged, either as to wire or the trench itself by the bombardment."

THE BATTLE OF THE SOMME

Fred McNess performed the act of gallantry which gained for him the Victoria Cross, the grounds for the conferment of which distinction are thus stated in the *London Gazette* of the 26th October 1916 :

" No. 13301 Lance-Sergeant Fred McNess, 1st Battalion Scots Guards.—For most conspicuous bravery. During a severe engagement, he led his men on with the greatest dash in face of a heavy shell and machine-gun fire. When the first line of enemy trenches was reached, it was found that the left flank was exposed and that the enemy was bombing down the trench. Sergeant McNess thereupon organized a counter-attack, and led it in person. He was very severely wounded in the neck and jaw, but went on, passing through the barrage of hostile bombs in order to bring up fresh supplies of bombs to his own men. " Finally, he established a ' block,' and continued encouraging his men and throwing bombs till utterly exhausted by loss of blood."

With the green line in their possession, and with the aid of a Scots Guards machine-gun, the 3rd Grenadiers were now able to enfilade the trench on their right and to draw their flank guard in to the front line. To understand the position, especially as concerns the 3rd Guards Brigade and the 2nd Scots Guards, it is necessary to state briefly what had been happening meanwhile with the 1st Guards Brigade. Checked at first by machine-gun fire from the sunken road of Ginchy, they had finally reached the 1st objective, which, however, was, owing to the obliteration of all guiding landmarks, at first mistaken for the brown line. The brigade was here in line with the 2nd Brigade on its right, and it now pushed on to the brown line when it had been discovered that only the green line had at first been reached.

The 2nd Guards Brigade, on the green line, proceeded to clear the German communication trenches leading back toward Lesbœufs by means of small parties of bombers followed by bayonet men, and eventually got forward about 1,500 yards from the starting point of the morning. Beyond this, after the losses already suffered, there could be no general advance, but bombing parties went out and seized some small trenches toward the blue line. One party in particular of about 120, consisting of Scots Guards under Captain Sir Iain Colquhoun, and of 3rd Grenadiers under Captain O. Lyttelton, got forward some 800 yards to a trench where they could overlook Lesbœufs. They were a little on the near side of the blue line, on the right of the Ginchy–Lesbœufs road. Reinforcements could not be sent up to them, as the brigade was not now strong enough to go forward to Lesbœufs, and it had been decided not to attempt to do so that day.

At 11 a.m. the position was this. The first objective was strongly held, as was the second, and parties were dug in in places between the second and the third at from 500 to 800 yards in front of the former. The whole of the assaulting brigades had pushed forward, but had now not the men left to warrant an attempt to take Lesbœufs and the line beyond it. It was still necessary to hold the second objective strongly, as the 6th Division on the right had failed to get forward or to take the Quadrilateral.

About 5 p.m. the advanced posts beyond the second objective were compelled to fall back by the attacks of a German battalion on both their flanks.

It was not till 9 a.m. on the 15th, two hours and forty minutes after zero hour, that the 2nd Scots Guards were ordered forward. They advanced in artillery formation, with L.F. and " G " on the right and left respectively in front line, and R.F. and " F " in second line. When they had passed the line of Waterlot Farm and Guillemont railway station, they first began to come under shell fire, and when they reached the slope of the hill between Guillemont and Ginchy it was decided to halt and dig in whilst waiting for the situation in front to be cleared up. The shelling increased at 11.30 a.m., and an officer was sent forward with a patrol to reconnoitre the position of troops on the left and to find the least exposed line of advance to the top of the hill. This advance was completed by noon with a few casualties, chiefly from the rifle fire of wounded or stray Germans left behind in shell holes.

Again the battalion dug in under cover on the near side

of the crest. Only a few casualties occurred here. About
5.30 p.m. the 2nd Scots Guards were ordered up to reinforce
the troops in front commanded by Lieut.-Colonel J.
Campbell, commanding the 3rd Coldstream Guards of the
1st Guards Brigade. The advance had scarcely begun
when both Lieut.-Colonel Tempest, commanding the
battalion, and Captain Wynne-Finch, the Adjutant, were
wounded and put out of action. The position where
reinforcements were required appeared to be incorrectly
described, and the O.C. 2nd Scots Guards himself went
forward to get a more accurate knowledge of the situation.
It appeared that the battalion would have to make an
advance of 500 yards from the crest of the hill behind which
it lay. It would be under direct observation by the Germans on the opposite rise, and the whole valley was commanded by enemy field-guns.

The first of the 2nd Scots Guards to reach the troops
under the immediate command of Colonel Campbell was
L.F. Company, commanded by Lieutenant W. A. Boyd.
When he reached that position he found that the trench
was far short of the position indicated in the original
orders issued to the battalion ; also that the trench had
so many troops in it that, in addition to them, there was
only room in it for one company of Scots Guards. As
other companies came up, they were forced either to lie
down behind the trench, or else to occupy some pieces of
trench, afterwards known as the " Switch," which ran
from the Flers line towards Lesbœufs.

Captain Thorpe, commanding R.F. Company, ordered
his men to reoccupy the Flers line for cover, and as he
was moving there he was killed.

About 5 p.m. the enemy launched a determined counter-
attack from the sunken road leading west from Lesbœufs
towards Flers.

Lieutenant Boyd now found himself, owing to the casualties among senior officers, in command of the battalion. He
formed as many men as possible along and near " Switch "
trench, so as to form a defensive flank for the left of the
1st Guards Brigade. Their fire and that of the British
Lewis guns was so effective that, though the British

casualties were also heavy, the losses of the counter-attack were so severe that it melted away. By the defeat of this counter-attack, the advanced parties of the 1st Guards Brigade were saved from a movement which threatened to envelop their left.

It was while organizing the defence against this counter-attack that Lieutenant D. Chapman was killed. The Medical Officer, Captain G. Walker, R.A.M.C., rendered conspicuous service in helping to reorganize the battalion and get touch between the companies after the first advance when, owing to the loss of senior officers, there was some confusion.

After the repulse of the counter-attack, a bombing post was made at the eastern end of " Switch " trench, and the battalion remained in this position during the night of the 15th, and until relieved by the 59th Brigade of the 20th Division.

In the first line the battalion found themselves in a " deep " German line, and the men were astounded at the security our enemies had attained.

Colonel Campbell, when a few days later he met Captain J. A. Stirling, then temporarily commanding the 2nd Scots Guards, told him that Lieutenant Boyd had handled the position with ability. The Lewis-gun teams had rendered specially good service during the counter-attack.

Captain the Hon. R. Coke, who had been left behind with others as a reserve of officers in case of heavy casualties, was called up to take command of the battalion, but he also was wounded on his way up.

Two more officers from the reserve came up, Lieutenant E. T. M. McDougal to act as adjutant, and Lieutenant D. J. Bethell to command R.F. Co., vice Captain Thorpe, killed.

The battalion was now attached to the 1st Guards Brigade, and remained so on the 16th, when an attack by the 1st Grenadiers and 1st Welsh Guards was held up. That night (16th) the 3rd Guards Brigade was relieved by the 59th Brigade, and the 2nd Battalion Scots Guards went back to Carnoy. The 1st Battalion also, after being in trenches on the 16th, when the 18th Brigade passed through to attack, were relieved the same night, and went back to the Citadel in Happy Valley. Both battalions had suffered heavily on the 15th.

1st Battalion.

Officers : killed, Lieutenants L. Norman and E. P. Orr-Ewing ; 2nd-Lieutenant W. Martindale.

Wounded : Captains H. C. E. Ross and H. W. Bayly ; Lieutenant D. S. Barclay ; 2nd-Lieutenants E. Miller, V. S. Daniell, W. L. E. Childers, and R. V. Powell.

Other ranks : killed, 36 ; wounded, 179 ; missing, 63.

2nd Battalion.

Officers : killed, Captain J. S. Thorpe, M.C., and Lieutenant D. A. J. Chapman.

Wounded : Lieut.-Colonel R. S. Tempest ; Captain and Adjutant W. Wynne-Finch ; Captain the Hon. R. Coke ; Lieutenant R. E. Fuller-Maitland ; 2nd-Lieutenants G. S. Dawkins, L. F. C. Murdoch, and E. A. Wodehouse.

Other ranks : killed or died of wounds, 14 ; wounded, 118 ; missing 23.

The 1st Battalion was refitting and resting at the Citadel when, on the 19th September, it was ordered to move up nearer the line, in view of another projected attack. It marched to Carnoy on the 20th, having received on that day and the day before two large drafts aggregating 412 other ranks and 4 officers. This raised its strength again (including 2 officers and 18 other ranks attached) to 24 officers and 955 other ranks present, besides 4 officers and 103 other ranks detached. At Carnoy orders were received, on the 24th, to move up to Trônes Wood next day. Before starting, each man was supplied with 4 hand grenades and 100 extra rounds of rifle ammunition ; ground flares and sky rockets were also taken. However, the battalion, after going to Trônes Wood, returned later in the day to Carnoy. That evening R.F. Company was told off to carry for the 3rd Brigade, and went up into the line. Meanwhile, the 2nd Battalion had been doing its rest and refitment at Carnoy, where it received reinforcements of 3 officers and 250 other ranks from Base and the Guards

Entrenching Battalion. Captain Thorpe was buried, with the full pipe band, in the military cemetery at Carnoy on the 17th.

On the 20th September the 3rd Brigade had orders to relieve the 59th Brigade (20th Division). It was shelled while forming up, but had no casualties. The going being very bad, the relief was not completed till 4 a.m. on the 21st. Battalion Headquarters were in the Flers line. The 4th Grenadier Guards, who were on the left, shared Battalion Headquarters with the 2nd Scots Guards on whose right were the 3rd Coldstream Guards. Lesbœufs, before which the attack on the 15th September had stopped, was still untaken, and the line in front of it had not been materially advanced since the two battalions of the Scots Guards had left it. The most important change had been the capture of the Quadrilateral, which had held up the 6th Division on the 15th.

The 3rd Guards Brigade was now in position near the scene of its recent operations in the Flers line, some distance behind the front line.

The fresh attack now to be made was originally ordered for the 23rd, but, on the 21st, was postponed till the 25th on account of bad weather.

The 2nd Battalion, therefore, remained where it was on the 22nd, or rather half of it did ; for " F " and R.F. Companies were relieved by two companies of the 1st Welsh Guards, and sent back for forty-eight hours to Trônes Wood, the other two remaining in the Flers line.

At 2 p.m. on the 23rd began the bombardment preparatory to the attack on Lesbœufs two days later. Only a few casualties resulted from the German reply on this day, and during the following night work was carried out on the communication trench leading from Flers line to the front. The companies in Trônes Wood were not exempt from German shells, which fell there also. They were joined on the night of the 23rd by Battalion Headquarters.

On the 24th " G " and " F " Companies relieved the Welsh Guards, who had taken over from " F " and R.F. in front line when they were sent to Trônes Wood. At

the same time the two last-named companies came up
from Trônes Wood and occupied a trench 50 yards in
rear of the left half battalion. In bringing up " F "
Company to this line, 2nd-Lieutenant C. F. H. Fenner
was killed when he was on the top of the new communication trench, which was being shelled by the enemy.

His place in command of the company was taken by
2nd-Lieutenant the Hon. A. N. A. Vanneck. Lieutenant
the Hon. V. A. Cochrane-Baillie took command of L.F.
in place of Lieutenant P. Wallace, who had gone sick.

The 25th September was the day fixed for the Guards
to finish up the job which they had so well begun ten days
earlier, but had been unable to complete then, largely
owing to the failure of the divisions on their right and left
to get forward, and to the consequent exposure of both
flanks. This time they were to get forward to the ridge
beyond Lesbœufs.

The 1st Guards Brigade, on the right of the division,
was to attack Lesbœufs itself, the boundary between it
and the 6th Division on its right passing along the Ginchy–
Lesbœufs road and through the centre of the latter village.
The 3rd Guards Brigade, on the left of the 1st, was to deal
with the trenches north of Lesbœufs.

The 2nd Guards Brigade was to act as reserve to the
others, with two battalions in Trônes Wood and two at
Carnoy, which were respectively, as the crow flies, about
2½ and 5 miles in rear. This time the objectives were
again designated the Green, the Brown and the Blue Lines.

The first objective, the Green Line, was about 300 yards
in advance of the front on the right boundary of the
division, increasing to about 900 on the left, thus involving
a partial change of direction of the front of the division as
it advanced, and giving the 3rd Brigade a longer distance
to pass than the 1st.

The second objective, the Brown Line, ran along the
western outskirts of Lesbœufs, and then along the
Gueudecourt road.

In this case, the distance between the objectives was
less on the left than on the right. The final objective was
just beyond Lesbœufs and on to Gueudecourt.

12

The advance was to be simply from one objective to the next behind a creeping barrage. A standing barrage would be put down by half the available guns on the first objective, and to lift later as the creeping barrage reached successive stages, on to the second and third objectives. The creeping barrage, starting at zero hour 100 yards in front of the infantry, and moving 50 yards every minute, would become stationary when it was 200 yards beyond the Green Line. At one hour after zero it would move forward as before to beyond the Brown Line, and an hour later to beyond the final objective on the left of the attacking brigades.

On the right of the Guards Division the 6th was to take Morval, and beyond it the 5th Division would operate, in combination with the French, to cut off Combles. On the left of the 3rd Guards Brigade the 21st Division of the XV Corps was to capture Gueudecourt.

Zero hour was fixed for 12.35 p.m. on the 25th, when the creeping barrage started and the infantry went over the top. The weather, unlike that of the 15th, was fine and dry, which facilitated movements.

The dispositions for the Guards Division were, 1st Guards Brigade, on the right, to attack Lesbœufs in front ; 3rd Guards Brigade, on the left, to attack the trenches north-west and north of Lesbœufs, that is on the (German) right flank.

The 2nd Guards Brigade was on this day to be in support, with two battalions in Trônes Wood and two at Carnoy. It will be observed that this was by no means a close support. Trônes Wood was 4,200 yards as the crow flies behind the front, and Carnoy about the same distance further. The 1st Battalion Scots Guards took little part in this day's fighting, in which the 2nd was heavily engaged.

The 3rd Guards Brigade had on its right the 1st, on its left the right of the 21st Division. The dispositions within the 3rd Brigade were, on the right the 2nd Battalion Scots Guards touching the 1st Irish Guards, the left battalion of the 1st Brigade. On the left the 4th Battalion Grenadier Guards.

Each of these leading battalions had two companies in

GUARDS DIVISION
Operations, Sept. 15, 1916

FLERS

Assembly Trenches of 2nd & 1st }
Guards Brigades .... } ——————

1st Objective .... — — — —

2nd   „   .... —·—·—·—

3rd   „   .... •••••••••••

4th   „   xxxxxxxx

Trenches .... ⌇⌇⌇⌇⌇⌇

Germans on Left Flank }
before attack .... } ♦♦♦♦♦♦♦♦

Left flank of
14th Div.
(XV Corps)

Delville
Wood

— Scale —

Yds 1000   500   0   1000 Yds

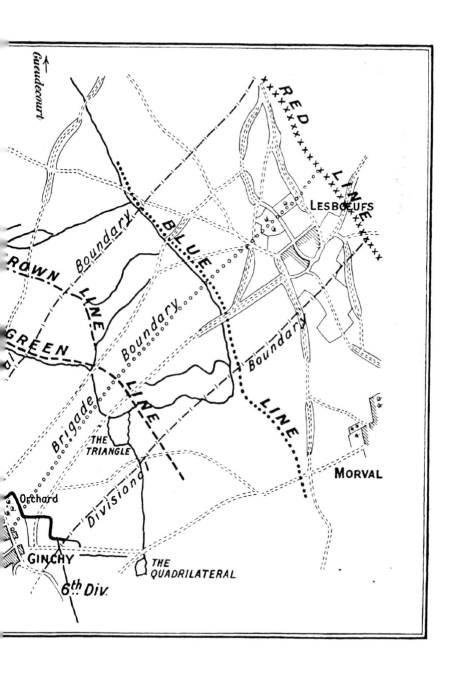

the front line, called the " X " line, and two in support, 100 yards behind, in the " Y " line. In the 2nd Scots Guards L.F. was on the right in front, supported by R.F. ; " G " on the left was supported by " F."

The 1st Battalion Grenadier Guards was in support of the leading battalions, about 100 yards behind their second line, in line " Z."

The 4th Battalion of the 3rd Brigade (1st Welsh Guards) was in reserve in the Flers line.

The 2nd Scots Guards were to advance in four lines. The first wave was to consist of two companies in extended order on a frontage of two platoons, the other two platoons of these companies to follow in similar formation 50 yards in rear. The third and fourth lines, constituting the second wave, would be similarly formed by the two supporting companies. There would be 100 yards interval between waves. The attack was towards the north-east, and the scheme provided that at zero (12.35 p.m.) the two leading battalions should capture the German front line, about 400 yards from the starting point, immediately reform and advance to capture and consolidate the second objective, which was the sunken road running from Lesbœufs past the windmill, north of the village, and thence towards Gueudecourt, about 700 yards beyond the first objective. Touch was to be kept with the 21st Division by the 4th Grenadier Guards, and with the 1st Guards Brigade by the 2nd Scots Guards. This line was to be consolidated, and, should the 21st Division be held up, a defensive flank was to be formed on the left, facing north.

When this second line had been secured, the 1st Grenadier Guards would pass through the leading battalions to the capture of the next objective, east of another sunken road to Gueudecourt. Every man in the attack carried a shovel in addition to his ordinary " fighting order." Companies had a fighting strength of about 150, but there were only 13 officers available, inclusive of 3 at Battalion Headquarters.

As the 2nd Scots Guards went over the parapet, 2nd-Lieutenant H. L. Knollys was wounded, but carried on. Little trouble was found with the first German line on the right, the occupants of which surrendered as the right half battalion entered it. The left half, and still more the 4th Grenadier Guards on its left, were partially held up by a German strong point in Bow trench on the left, and got forward more slowly than the right. However, the companies reformed, and the whole of the leading battalions of the 3rd Guards Brigade gained the German first line without great difficulty. The distance to this first line was about 400 yards. On the left of the 4th Grenadier Guards, who, as well as " G " Company, 2nd Scots Guards, had suffered many casualties from the strong point, the enemy held on in the northern trenches, and the right brigade of the 21st Division was unable to get forward. So far the right half battalion of the 2nd Scots Guards had suffered little. They were in close touch with the 1st Irish Guards (1st Brigade) on their right. The creeping barrage restarted at 1.30, and the Scots Guards now got forward to the sunken road and began digging in. This second advance was over a space of 700 yards. About 100 yards before the sunken road was reached, the battalion was held up for a minute by running into the British barrage, and by the German barrage. The road was not held by the enemy. A great part of the day's casualties occurred during digging in at it. The left half battalion and the 4th Grenadiers came up more slowly, as their left was now exposed by the failure of the 21st Division to get forward.

The German bombardment of the sunken road was very heavy, and the British casualties began to be serious.

Here 2nd-Lieutenant Knollys was wounded a second time. Sergeant MacLean, just recovered from a recent wound, greatly distinguished himself by his coolness in a very critical half-hour.

The advance of the 1st Grenadier Guards through the leading battalions had been delayed by the German barrage. When their King's Company did come through, detachments, both of the 2nd Scots and the 4th Grenadier Guards, pushed on behind them to take up better positions short of the third objective. As has already been stated, the holding up of the 21st Division had resulted in exposing the left flank of the 3rd Guards Brigade, an exposure which increased in depth as the latter brigade got forward.

When the 1st Grenadier Guards were on the third objective, the 4th Grenadiers were forming a defensive flank on the left, facing north over a space of 1,000 yards. To strengthen this flank, the 1st Welsh Guards came up from reserve, and the remains of the 2nd Scots Guards, being now reinforced by R.F. of the 1st Scots Guards under Lieutenant R. Abercromby, moved forward and entrenched, facing north and east between the two sunken roads. Here the battalion, assisted by the 55th Company Royal Engineers, consolidated strong points and were reinforced by machine-guns. The ground was easy to dig, and fair cover was soon made. Before 9 p.m. mules and transport of the 2nd Scots Guards had carried water and a spare ration right up to the front line held by the brigade, where they were distributed to all the battalions.

The battalion reached all their objectives up to time, but found 4th Grenadier Guards held up. They took the trench which was holding them up, but the next division could not get on, and so by 3 p.m. the battalion had a mile or more of exposed flank looking due north. V. Cochrane-Baillie had found a dug-out as Company Headquarters east of the Brown Line, and from the rising ground near it they could see parties of Germans bolting out of Gueudecourt and Transloy. The cavalry were in vain called for, though they were supposed to be close up.

At 7.30 a.m. on the 26th a tank attacked the strong point which had given so much trouble to the 21st Division, and forced its occupants to surrender. About 100 came and surrendered on the approach of the tank. The encircling movement north of Gueudecourt had not progressed sufficiently at this time to enable the defenders of the area to be captured. Large numbers of Germans were seen and fired at as they escaped north-eastwards towards Beaulencourt.

Gueudecourt was now captured by the 21st Division on the left of the Guards.

After dark on the 26th the three remaining companies of the 1st Scots Guards took over the trenches held by the 2nd Battalion and their own R.F. Company, which latter remained there with them. The 2nd Battalion went back to Trônes Wood, where Lieut.-Colonel Orr-Ewing, on return from England, resumed command.

The losses of the 2nd Battalion on the 25th September were :

Officers killed : 2nd-Lieutenants C. F. H. Fenner and A. F. Chapman.
Wounded : 2nd-Lieutenant H. L. Knollys.
Other ranks : killed, 40 ; wounded, 199 ; missing, 88.

The 1st Battalion, presumably R.F. Company only, lost 1 man killed and 4 wounded.

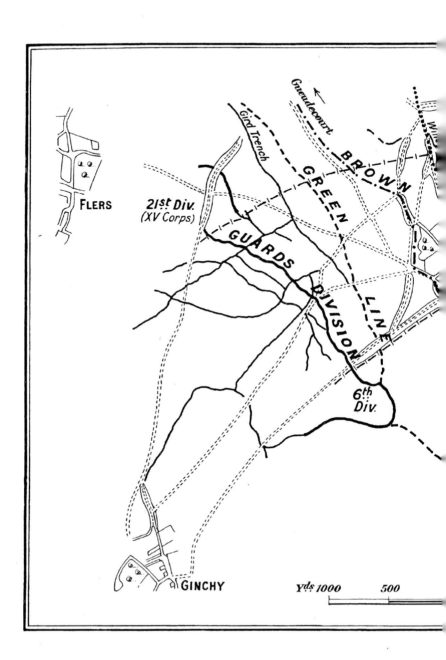

FLERS

Gird Trench

Greudecourt

BROWN

GREEN

21st Div.
(XV Corps)

GUARDS

DIVISION

LINE

6th
Div.

GINCHY

Yds 1000   500

GUARDS DIVISION
OPERATIONS, SEPT. 25, 1916

le Transloy

Rainy Trench

LESBŒUFS

LINE

MORVAL

British Line before attack ———
1st Objective .... – – – –
2nd „ .... —·—·—
3rd „ .... •••••••••
Divisional Boundaries .... —ı—ı—
Trenches ....

— *Scale* —

1000

2000 Yds

CHAPTER X

Terribly wet weather—In March Germans falling back on the Hindenburg Line.

AFTER the capture of Lesbœufs and Gueudecourt at the end of September 1916, there was little further advance by the British on this part of the Somme battlefield, and the two battalions of the Scots Guards had a comparatively quiet time, without serious fighting and with few losses. It remains, therefore, only to record quite briefly the movements of the two battalions.

The 1st was in line beyond Lesbœufs till the 30th September, when it was relieved by the 8th Middlesex and moved back to a camp on the Fricourt–Carnoy road, where it remained till the 2nd October. It then marched to near Dernancourt, entrained there, and proceeded via Amiens to Airaine, whence it marched to billets at Warlus.

On the 5th the Adjutant went to the brigade as Staff-Captain, and his place was taken by Lieutenant H. L. N. Dundas.

There was a long stay at Warlus, during which the usual training, instruction, and route marches were carried on, and there were distributions of medal ribbons and honours recently gained. Spare time was filled by amusements of various kinds. In the daytime a good deal of football was played. On October 14th the battalion football team went to Vergies to play the 2nd Battalion, the latter winning. That evening there was a regimental dinner for officers at 1st Battalion Headquarters, at which many Scots Guards officers who were at the front were present. Battalion sports were held on the 20th, followed by a cinematograph show in the evening, and next day the sergeants were victorious in a football match against the officers. An accident occurred on the 26th, when Lance-Corporal W. Dorans was killed during instruction in the use of the Lewis gun.

On the 1st November the whole of the Guards Division was assembled near Belloy-St. Leonard for inspection by H.R.H. the Duke of Connaught. The weather, which had been far from irreproachable during much of the time at Warlus, was fortunately very fine for the inspection, though the rain came down again soon after it.

The battalion football team was badly defeated on the 4th November by the 3rd Grenadier Guards in the 2nd Guards Brigade Football League, but on the same day the tug-of-war was won in the 2nd Battalion Gymkhana, as well as first prize for the best horse.

On the whole, a busy but not unpleasant time was spent at Warlus during the seven weeks which came to a close on the 10th November with orders to go to the front again.

The movements of the 2nd Battalion during the same period were similar.

After remaining at Trônes Wood till the 29th September, the battalion was in camp just south of Fricourt on the 30th, and on the 1st October marched about 5 miles, then went about 30 by motor to Avesnes, and marched 2½ more to billets at Vergies.[1] At this time the Guards Division was temporarily attached to the X Corps.

What has been said about the doings of the 1st Battalion at Warlus applies generally to those of the 2nd at Vergies. On October 18th Lieutenant the Hon. R. Coke, D.S.O., became Adjutant of the battalion in place of Lieutenant E. T. M. MacDougal, who had acted since the 5th.

There was a big brigade field-day on the 20th. The inspection by H.R.H. the Duke of Connaught on the 1st November has already been mentioned. H.R.H. gave a separate address to the Officers, N.C.O.s, and men of the Guards Division who had received decorations in the war, and the 3rd Brigade was complimented on its marching past.

The battalion diary of this period is rather dry, and does

---

[1] The battalion went back to rest south of the Somme, past "Awaine," where Edward III spent the night in 1346, and was nearly trapped by the French armies congregating from Amiens and Normandy. He crossed a ford at Blanche Tache next day (St. Bartholomew's Day), and fought the Battle of Crécy three days after.

not condescend to mention such things as entertainments or sports, but we know from that of the 1st that the 2nd had their football and gymkhana, and no doubt other amusements, as in the case of the 1st. On the 10th the battalion marched off till they met motor-buses, which conveyed them to Treux, whence they marched to the sandpits at Méaulte. On the 11th they were back in the familiar Trônes Wood. Next day the Guards Division relieved the 17th in trenches. The 2nd Scots Guards relieved the Duke of Wellington's and Manchester battalions in reserve trenches. On that day the 1st Battalion reached Bure in French motor-buses from Warlus, and marched to Méaulte. On the 12th it went to camp " H," on the Carnoy–Montauban road, and took over huts from the 10th West Yorks. Here it remained till the 18th, when it moved to " D " camp.

In the afternoon of the 19th, R.F. and " B " Companies went into trenches in front of Lesbœufs, in relief of the 1st Welsh Guards, whilst " C " and L.F. returned to camp " H." The Welsh Guards had relieved the 2nd Battalion on the 15th. The latter had, during its short period in trenches, lost 7 killed and 21 wounded. It had gone back, on relief, to camp " F," Montauban, where it was accommodated in a very muddy camp, partly in huts and partly under canvas. It remained here till it moved back to the sandpits at Méaulte on the 20th. The 1st Battalion, when it relieved the Welsh Guards on the 19th, had some losses, apparently in the course of the relief. 2nd-Lieut. A. Mervyn Jones and Lieutenant W. E. D. Shortt were wounded, 2 men were killed, 5 wounded, and 1 missing. On the next day 2 men were killed and 4 wounded, and on the same day the wounded airman of a British aeroplane, forced to descend in No Man's Land opposite the battalion, was carried off by the enemy.

The 1st Battalion was back again in " H " camp on the 21st November, till the 3rd December, when R.F. went into dug-outs short of Leuze Wood, Headquarters to dug-outs on the Bouleaux Wood–Combles road, and the rest into dug-outs round Bouleaux Wood. Here, next day, the 1st Battalion relieved the 2nd in front trenches, with three companies in front (L.F. on right, " B " centre, " C " left), and R.F. in reserve in dug-outs near Combles.

The 2nd Battalion had left " A " camp at the Méaulte sandpits on the 26th November for " B " camp, which consisted of French huts. These are described as very comfortable, with a mattress for each man and a stove in each hut—a welcome change after the tents at camp " A." On the 1st December the battalion had moved forward to Maltzhorn Farm, and on the 2nd relieved the French troops who had hitherto held the trenches here. The British right was at this time being extended southwards to relieve the French of part of the front they had hitherto held.

The arrangement of the companies was, as later in the case of the 1st Battalion, three (R.F., " F," and " G ") in front and L.F. north-east of Combles in support.

When the 1st Battalion took over on the 3rd December, the 2nd went back to Bouleaux Wood.

The winter of 1916 on the Somme front was characterized by very bad weather, rain, snow, frost, and thaw alternating. It is true that a great part of this area was undulating, and that drainage of the higher land was very much easier than in the water-logged parts of Flanders, but in the Somme area the mud was of a peculiar consistency and depth, and in the low-lying valleys conditions were not so very much better than in Flanders. The surface of the country was everywhere pitted by the shells of both sides in the fighting which had extended over the months succeeding the 1st July.

Roads and other landmarks had been obliterated, and it was difficult to find the way over the shell-torn surface which intervened between the rear and the front lines. The distances were often long, and there were few communication trenches available. Sometimes it happened that part of a battalion, or even of a company, might find itself on a slope in comparative comfort in deep, well-drained trenches, whilst the rest, down in the valley, were little better off than they would have been near Givenchy or Ypres. There were cases where men literally had to be dug out of the clinging, chalky mud in which they had got embedded, and the consequences of straying into a shell-hole or crater might be fatal. All this had to be remedied as far as possible by the troops in occupation, and they were kept more than busy with fatigues. Even the rest camps, when reached, were often far from the pleasant relief which their name promised, and, as in the case of camp " F," were often muddy areas in which the huts were built, or perhaps only tents were to be found. The whole of December was spent under these unpleasant circumstances, to the accompaniment of frequent hostile bombardments, which, however, were not followed by infantry activity, which was practically precluded by the conditions of weather and ground on both sides. Casualties were generally small, and what there were were almost entirely caused by artillery fire.

The 2nd Battalion had obtained permission from the Brigadier to wear patches of red, blue, and white dicing, like that worn in peace time on the forage caps of the Scots Guards, and it is noted in the battalion diary of the 8th December, that officers and warrant officers started wearing it on their steel helmets. Christmas Day saw the 2nd Battalion in trenches. They had fraternized freely with the enemy on the first, and to a certain extent on the second, Christmas Day of the War. On this third Christmas Day there were no demonstrations of friendliness on either side. On the contrary, there was a smart bombardment of the German trenches by the British artillery, the reply to which resulted in the death of two men of the 2nd Scots Guards.

In the evening of the last day of the year a German deserter came over to the 2nd Battalion, saying the enemy's front was badly knocked in and the dug-outs had collapsed. Nevertheless, he was wearing a good waterproof, which had kept him quite dry.

Conditions in January 1917 were very similar to those of the close of 1916. On the 3rd the 1st Battalion was sent by rail to Corbie, a real back area where German bombardments could only be heard, not felt. Here the time was mainly occupied in cleaning up clothing, checking deficiencies in kit and equipment, and generally smartening up after a long period of trenches, support, or reserve. The fighting-strength of the battalion about this time was 711. On the 7th the battalion had a concert and cinema display at the Grand Cinema of Corbie, which is quite a large town. The regimental band of the Welsh Guards played during this afternoon's entertainment. Next day Major-General Feilding, G.O.C. Guards Division, presented medal ribbons to those of the 2nd Brigade whose names appeared in the New Year's list.

Each battalion of the brigade was represented by one company of 100 other ranks selected from the pick of all the companies of each to form a composite company. At this parade Lieutenant and Adjutant E. D. Mackenzie received the D.S.O., which had also been awarded to Captain M. Barne, who was absent on leave. C.S.M. W. Hopkins received the D.C.M.

On the 9th the 1st Scots Guards were taken in buses to camp "X" near Maurepas, a couple of miles south-west of Combles, and considerably to the right of their old position at Lesbœufs. Combles had been, in the early days of the Somme battle, in the left sector of the French front. The British line had now been extended to the right to relieve the French IX Corps. When the 1st Battalion relieved the 2nd Middlesex on the 10th January, R.F. in first line held eleven posts on the east of the Péronne–Bapaume road, facing the great wood of St. Pierre Vaast and close up to the German line on the edge of that wood. "B" Company was in support, and "C" and L.F. in reserve at Priez Farm west of Rancourt. This was one of the higher and drier positions of the line. The weather was characterized by snow, sleet, and rain till the 13th, when the battalion again returned to Maurepas on relief. The accommodation there was in tents and dug-outs, and the camp was very muddy. There was plenty of work to be done by working parties in improving it. The bad weather culminated on the 17th, when the battalion had returned to the line, in a heavy snowstorm, after which the 18th dawned on a dead white landscape.

So far the 1st Battalion had been busy trying to improve their trenches, and there was no advantage in stirring up the wasps' nest in the opposing German trenches, or drawing fire which would hamper the working parties. The necessity for quiet had ceased by the 18th January when, with a chivalry or a sense of humour which was equally wanting on the German side, Headquarters of the 2nd Guards Brigade thought fit to give notice that there would be an end to the temporary informal truce from rifle fire on the British side. A notice was drawn up " Warning ! all Germans exposing themselves after daylight to-morrow, January 19th, will be shot." The notice was duly served by the 1st Scots Guards outside the German wire on a German officer, to whom it was translated, and who promised to communicate it to his neighbourhood. The circumstances of the delivery of the notice suffice to show that there really had been some sort of tacit understanding about not shooting.[1]

There had been no such understanding about shell fire, and the 19th was rather a bad day for the 1st Battalion, as Lieutenant W. L. Greenlees and C.S.M. Hopkins were wounded, whilst one man was killed and three were wounded by a shell near the headquarters of the front company (" C ") when on their way to Priez Farm. With this exception, matters were generally quiet, and casualties were few during the rest of January. The period was spent between Maurepas and the front near St. Pierre Vaast Wood till the 28th, when the battalion moved from Maurepas by rail from near Carnoy to Méricourt l'Abbé, on the river Ancre below Albert.

On the 24th Lieut.-Colonel Godman had gone to command the brigade, and Lieutenant E. D. Mackenzie took over temporary command of the battalion, his place as Adjutant being filled by Lieutenant H. L. N. Dundas.

Almost the whole of the civil inhabitants having left Méricourt, there was no difficulty about finding quarters, which, however, turned out generally to be cold and uncomfortable, owing to their stone or earthen floors.

The 2nd Battalion began the year at Bouleaux Wood, whence they moved, on the 2nd January, to Bronfay Farm, and on the 3rd to Méricourt l'Abbé. Here they were till the 9th, a period corresponding to that spent by

[1] This incident is not recorded in the war diary of the 1st Scots Guards.

the 1st at Corbie. Méricourt being a smaller place than Corbie, the 2nd Battalion did not apparently have quite such a good time as their comrades of the 1st. The distribution of New Year Honours by the G.O.C. Guards Division took place in circumstances similar to those at Corbie on the 9th January. Fifteen men received the Military Medal, and one the D.C.M. On this day " R.F." first started wearing the new red and white shoulder badges. The next few days were occupied with work on the Billon Farm Camp, south of Carnoy, and on the 18th the battalion went forward to Priez Farm with three companies, L.F. being left behind at Maurepas. At Priez Farm there was much work to be done at improving the camp, burying telegraph and telephone cables, and putting in the new semicircular iron dug-outs, for which receptacles resembling gun emplacements were prepared. The country being now covered with snow, working parties were very much " in evidence " to any German aeroplane which might come over. They did not do so with impunity, as one was seen by the 1st Battalion to fall in flames as the result of a direct hit— a somewhat unusual occurrence. Another activity consisted in tunnelling operations to provide shell-proof cover for troops. On the 22nd the Germans took to shelling the road near Priez Farm. Two unfortunate salvoes of " Whizz Bangs," coming over in the middle of relief by the 1st Grenadier Guards, wounded five of the Scots Guards, of whom one died of his wounds. On this relief being completed, the battalion returned to Billon Farm. As an example of what the men were liable to, we may quote the entry in the diary of the 25th January :

" Baths allotted to the battalion. Water frozen, so only clean clothes available, without baths." The midwinter Serpentine bather might regard this as a disappointment, but tastes differ. Three days later it was too cold for out-door Sunday services, so the Presbyterian Chaplain visited the men in huts, whilst the English Church and Roman Catholics held their services in huts.

There was nothing notable in trenches in the latter part of January. The 1st Battalion continued at Méricourt l'Abbé till the 13th February, without the occurrence of anything remarkable. On that day it went forward as far as Billon Farm camp. At Méricourt the new box-respirator had been served out and tested, with very satisfactory results. Each officer and man spent a certain time wearing it in a gas-charged hut, and the fact that no evil consequences were experienced, gave a feeling of confidence in its efficacy. Mustard gas had not yet made its appearance.

On the 16th February German aeroplanes succeeded in hitting a neighbouring shell-dump, the contents of which continued exploding all day, causing box-respirators to be worn in case of accidents from gas. On the 20th the battalion received a notable access, not only to its corps of officers, but also to its cricket team, by the arrival of Lieutenant F. T. Mann, now the Middlesex cricket captain.

On the 23rd " B " Company went to Maurepas, whilst the rest went on tó Priez Farm. Here Lieutenant H. L. N. Dundas, the battalion bombing officer, was promoted to brigade bombing officer, his place in the battalion being taken by Lieutenant J. M. Cobbold. Cable laying and tunnelling work still employed fatigue parties.

A good Divisional Soup Kitchen was established, which supplied soup at regular hours in the evening to all companies, and also at any hour to returning fatigue parties. On the 25th news arrived of the evacuation by the enemy of positions on the 5th Army front, and the battalion was warned to be ready to move forward at short notice, in the event of similar evacuation on its front. Nothing definite, however, happened before the end of the month, when the 1st Scots Guards were again at Maurepas.

In February the 2nd Battalion had, on the whole, a rougher time than the 1st. On the 1st Lieutenant Hon. A. J. P. Howard was wounded in trenches ; 1 man was killed and 5 were wounded. The thermometer was down to within 4° of zero on the 3rd at Maurepas.

Again, on the 8th, when the Germans retaliated for a barrage put down for an attack by a battalion of the 17th Division on the left, 5 Scots Guards were killed and 7

wounded.   On the 11th the left half battalion, with details
from " F " and R.F., went by train and march to Ville-
sur-Ancre, whilst the right half temporarily relieved the
1st Battalion for fatigues near Trônes Wood, staying there
till the 16th, when it rejoined the left half.   At Ville-sur-
Ancre the battalion played two football matches.   In the
first (17th February) it beat the 4th Grenadier Guards
(3—0), and in the second (24th February) the 1st Grenadier
Guards were beaten (4—0).

The battalion was inspected on the 22nd by the Divisional
Commander, and on the 23rd by the French General
Lyautey, at that time Minister of War, the former being
entirely satisfied.

An unfortunate accident occurred on the 25th, when
C.S.M. Hayes, D.C.M., was accidentally killed on the
brigade bombing ground.   He had gone out to France with
the battalion, and had been nearly two years with the
bombing company.

February ended with the 2nd Battalion at Priez Farm,
less one company (R.F.) detached, as usual, to Maurepas.

January and February had been comparatively uneventful months, but March was to be livelier ; for the German
withdrawal to the Hindenburg line had begun, and was
to be followed up closely.

On March 11th the 1st Scots Guards were again in
trenches in the old locality facing St. Pierre Vaast Wood.
They now had " C " and " B " respectively in the right and
left front line, each of them occupying eleven posts—
R.F. was in right, L.F. in left reserve.

There was always much to be done in improving positions,
and in the changing circumstances it was possible to
employ the reserve companies on fatigue, supervised by the
Royal Engineers.

The weather was still bad, and snow fell at intervals.
The battalion was backwards and forwards between
trenches and Maurepas or Priez Farm, without anything
specially notable till it went into trenches in relief of the
3rd Grenadier Guards on the 11th.   The order now was
R.F. and L.F. in right and left front line respectively, with
" C " and " B " in the corresponding reserve positions.

The night of the 13th-14th was destined to be one of important raids. Rumours had been rife that the enemy on the Guards Division front was evacuating his positions and retiring. This could only be confirmed by raids into the enemy trenches, in which the capture of prisoners might be hoped for. The first operation was undertaken about 8 p.m. on the 13th, when Lieutenant Brodie, Corporal Waddell, and two men sallied forth to ascertain the weakest place in the German wire for the raiders to attack. The point being selected without the discovery of the party, Lieutenant Brodie with the two men returned to No. 8 post, marking his line by unrolling and laying a tape as he went. Corporal Waddell was left at the selected post to cut the wire.

At 10.45 p.m. Lieutenant Brodie went out again with 24 other ranks, following the tape till they came to the gap which Waddell had succeeded in making practicable. Passing through the opening, the party extended over a front of about 100 yards to advance on the enemy's line. Brodie went with the left section, and presently saw three German sentries in a forward sap. He and his section attempted to cut them off, but in the deep mud it was impossible to approach them unobserved. Bombs were thrown at the Germans, of whom two were killed. The third German also threw bombs, which wounded Brodie, his sergeant, and five men. The whole party then withdrew by the route by which they had come. Lieutenant Brodie appeared to be clearly right in reporting that this part of the German trench was not strongly, if at all, occupied ; for all the noise of the exploding bombs drew no rifle fire from it. The next party went out at 1.45 a.m., consisting of 1 N.C.O. and 6 men. They left the right-hand post of the battalion front, and moved southwards along a sap towards a German listening-post, which was reported to exist in this direction. On reaching it, it was found empty but showing signs of recent occupation. This party also withdrew.

The last patrol started from Post No. 10. Lieutenant Brand and six other ranks constituted it. Their objective was the capture of a machine-gun, the location of which

13

had been reported. Unlike the other parties, Brand's found the enemy in his direction very much on the *qui vive*, and considerable rifle fire was heard from the post. Thereupon the party turned south along the German wire, hoping to meet a patrol. None, however, was to be seen, and the party returned to the British line. The reconnaissance had been a failure in so far as no prisoner was captured, but it had at least served to confirm the suspicions that the enemy was relaxing his hold on his line.

On the 14th Major Barne took command of the battalion, on Lieut.-Colonel Godman going to hospital.

On that day Lieutenant Brand went over to the enemy's line, which he found to be unoccupied, and walked the whole way down the front of St. Pierre Vaast Wood. The result of the reconnaissance, when reported to Brigade Headquarters, elicited orders for the battalion to occupy the German front at dusk, this being the first move forward on the corps front. Lieutenant Brand received the Military Cross for his reconnaissance.[1]

That night, after the German trench had been occupied, strong patrols penetrated 500 yards into St. Pierre Vaast Wood without meeting a German.

The advance in pursuit of the retiring enemy commenced in earnest next day at 7 a.m., when " B " and " C " Companies moved forward, under Captain Sir I. Colquhoun, with the 2nd Irish Guards on their left and the 8th Division on the right. L.F. took over the old British front, and R.F. remained in the reserve trenches. By dusk on the 15th the leading companies had pushed forward to a line 300 yards in front of the old line on the left, and 600 yards on the right. The advance through the wood was necessarily cautious. The battalion was reinforced in the support line by the loan of No. 1 Company, 3rd Grenadier Guards, placed under the orders of Major Barne. That company and R.F. of the Scots Guards laid a " duck-board "

---

[1] Cf. *History of the Guards Division*, vol. i, p. 205, third note. The time of Lieutenant Brand's visit to the German trench is given in the battalion diary as " about 3 p.m." If Lieutenant Cropper of the artillery was in the trench at 2 p.m., he must have been the first to visit it. As stated, there is no mention in the diary of anyone accompanying Lieutenant Brand.

after dark across the old No Man's Land and up to the
leading companies, which took up an outpost position.
The enemy's shelling that night fell short of the outpost
line. The whole of the north-east portion of the great
wood was occupied during the 16th March, and when
" B " and " C " Companies were relieved by the 3rd
Grenadier Guards they and Battalion Headquarters returned to Priez Farm. The other two companies were
separated, L.F. remaining in the old British front trench
under orders of the O.C. 3rd Grenadier Guards, whilst
R.F. was sent to act as reserve for the 2nd Irish Guards.
R.F. rejoined the battalion next evening, but L.F. remained
with the 3rd Grenadier Guards till the evening of March
19th, when it rejoined the others at camp " B " at Combles,
to which they had marched that day. It was still cold
and rainy, and on the 20th snow alternated with rain, both
being driven by a strong north-east wind. At Combles
the battalion remained till, on the 24th, it was unexpectedly
marched to Cléry-sur-Somme, where, owing to its having
recently been part of the battle line, the only accommodation was in tents, which the men had to pitch on the slope
of the bank of the Somme.

As Wellington in 1810 fell back before Masséna on the
lines of Torres Vedras, so now the Germans were deliberately
falling back to the great defensive position of the Hindenburg line, which they had prepared with infinite skill and
care in rear. Thence they hoped to issue in due course
as Wellington issued from Torres Vedras. Again, as
Wellington in his retreat to Torres Vedras had done his best
to clear the country he was leaving of all supplies and con-
veniences for the enemy, so the Germans now endeavoured
to hamper the advance of the British and to render the
new country into which they were marching as inhospitable
and difficult as possible. But they were more ruthless
than Wellington, and had better means at their command.
As they fell back, the whole country-side was devastated,
the villages burnt, the bridges blown up, trees felled across
the roads, and the roads themselves, as well as railways,
rendered temporarily impassable by the explosion of mines,
which left everywhere great craters fatal to all traffic.

The difference between them and Wellington was that the latter, retiring through an allied country, was bound to show what consideration was possible to its inhabitants, and to rely largely, and often in vain, on their devotion to the common cause in sacrificing their own immediate personal interests. The Germans, on the other hand, were in a hostile and hated country, towards whose inhabitants they need not, and did not, show the slightest consideration, and whom they were prepared to remove wholesale to other parts.

For the British, as they went forward, it was absolutely necessary to build up and repair the ruined communications with their rear. This entailed road and railway repairs, clearing of obstructions, and of the " booby traps " and delayed-action mines, in the setting of which the Germans displayed a fiendish ingenuity.

One of the most important reconstruction works was that of the railway from the rear towards Péronne by the north bank of the Somme, which below that place flows from east to west. This work, and indeed all reparation work in this neighbourhood, was rendered more than ever difficult and laborious by the rapid thaw which had succeeded a long frost and turned the face of the land into a sea of mud. The Guards were honourably distinguished by their splendid work in this class, and it was about this time that General Feilding thought it right to remind regimental officers that it was an old-established custom for officers in the Guards, under such circumstances, to take off their coats and turn to with their men at the pick and shovel. The existence of such a custom is probably news to a good many of the public, to whom it cannot be too well known.

The battalion worked so well and quickly as to elicit a complimentary letter on their performance from the O.C. Canadian Railway troops, just ahead of whom they were working.

They remained at Cléry till the end of March.

The 2nd Battalion was still busy burying cables at Priez Farm for the first three days of March, when it moved to Maurepas, and on the 6th to Frégicourt, with two

companies at Haie Wood and one each at Combles and
Frégicourt. It was still under German artillery fire, and
lost one killed and two wounded on this day, and two
wounded on the 7th.

In the evening of March 8th, after a heavy snow-storm
in the morning, the 2nd Battalion relieved the 1st Welsh
Guards in trenches facing east, just north of Sailly Saillisel
and east of the Péronne–Bapaume road. Though there
were no casualties during the relief, the battalion lost one
man killed and nine wounded during the night.

The companies were posted thus : " G " on the right
was in Palz trench in front and Potsdam Right trench
behind it. R.F. had two platoons in Potsdam Left,
supported by two of L.F. in Cheese Support. The other
two platoons of L.F. were in Switch trench, which ran
back from the right of Potsdam Right. L.F. Company
headquarters, " F," and the other two platoons of R.F.
were behind Switch and Potsdam Right trenches—rather
a complicated arrangement.

Snow on the 9th was followed by a thaw on the 10th,
which made Palz trench untenable, and matters grew
worse on the next two days, when a continuous downpour
of rain soon caused the unreveted trenches to fall in.
Palz trench had to be evacuated, except for one post, where
the 2nd Scots Guards were relieved, at night on the 12th,
by the 2nd Coldstream Guards. Captain H. B. Clarke,
R.A.M.C., attached 2nd Scots Guards, was killed on the
duck-boards on his way out of trenches. The other losses
of the battalion during their four days in this position
were heavy, amounting to 12 killed and 85 wounded.

Another unfortunate incident occurred on the 15th,
when Private Creig of R.F. was accidentally shot by
a comrade. On March 17th there were impromptu battalion sports, and battalion dinner in the evening, during
which the Grenadier Guards band played. Lieut.-Colonel
N. A. Orr-Ewing, D.S.O., was created Chevalier of the
Military Order of Savoy. Next day there was another
football match, in which the officers were beaten by the
sergeants after a good game.

The weather was still cold, but dry, when the battalion

marched to Maurepas on the 19th. Thence it went once
more to Priez Farm. On the 22nd Brigadier-General
Corkran left the brigade, to the regret of all. The command
was taken over by Lord Henry Seymour, D.S.O.

The next few days were spent at Bronfay and Cléry,
where railway work continued, and Captain C. A. M. Cator
temporarily took command of the battalion during Lieut.-
Colonel Orr-Ewing's absence on leave. On the last day
of March the weather began to improve, though there
had been snow as recently as the 26th. The 1st Battalion
was also at Cléry on the 1st April. On the 2nd Captain
Sir I. Colquhoun took temporary command of the 1st
Battalion, when Colonel Godman went on leave, Major
Barne being away on special work at the time.

Railway work continued and the weather again became
bad, with snow on the 4th and on later days. Nothing
of any note occurred during the battalion's long stay at
Cléry up to the 25th April, or on the remaining days of
the month spent at Rocquigny. At the end of the month
the battalion had a strength of 21 officers and 833 other
ranks present, besides 2 officers on leave, and 4 officers and
174 others detached.

For the 2nd Battalion April was equally uninteresting.
After being at Cléry till the 12th, it was at Cartigny [1] for
the rest of the month, training, and playing football in
leisure hours. On the 29th the battalion football team succeeded in breaking the record of the 3rd Cyclist Battalion,
who till then had been undefeated for eighteen months.
As a curious example of the various ways in which dis-
tractions were provided for the men, it is recorded that
there was a competition for a prize offered by the C.O. for
the best garden in camp. The men were so keen on this
that every tent had its garden. May again was a quiet
month for both battalions. The 1st was at Rocquigny
on railway work till the 11th, when it went to Cléry for
training. On the 3rd Lieut.-Colonel B. H. S. Romilly,
D.S.O., arrived and took over command of the battalion.

---

[1] III Corps H.Q. were in the château. The Corps was commanded by
Lieut.-General Sir W. P. Pulteney, who had commanded a battalion of
Scots Guards during most of the Boer War.

On the 10th, as the result of a brigade conference, it was decided to attach to Battalion Headquarters, in addition to the existing establishment, (*a*) the Assistant Adjutant (Lieutenant W. E. D. Shortt); (*b*) the Signalling Officer (Lieutenant B. W. Duncan); (*c*) the Intelligence Officer; and the duties of each were laid down. On the 15th May the 2nd Guards Brigade was reviewed at Curlu by H.M. the King of the Belgians, the Grenadier Guards band playing at the saluting point.

With the advent of May the term of service of the Guards Division on the Somme front was drawing to an end.

During the latter two-thirds of April and the first days of May, General Allenby, with the 3rd Army, had been engaged just north of the Somme area in the series of offensive movements constituting the Battle of Arras. It had not fallen to the lot of the Guards to take any part in those operations which had ended on the 4th May.

The French, meanwhile, had failed in the great operations on the Aisne by which General Nivelle had hoped to decide the war.

For reasons which do not concern the history of a regiment, it was now decided to undertake the next offensive by the British in the northern area, so familiar to most of the Guards battalions, and in particular to the Scots Guards, earlier in the war. Its move to this area involved the transfer of the XIV Corps from the 4th Army to the 2nd, commanded by General Sir Herbert Plumer.

CHAPTER XI

Preparing for Ypres—Reconnaissances—"Mats" being made for crossing wet places—Steady advance.

THE First and Second Battles of Ypres had been defensive battles on the part of the Allies, the third was to be offensive, and the Guards Division was destined to play a great part in it.

On the 18th May the 1st Scots Guards moved to Ville-sur-Ancre, where they remained till the 30th, preparing for the move northwards. On the night of the 30th they entrained at Heilly, detrained next morning at Arques on the outskirts of St. Omer, and marched two and a half miles with the rest of the 2nd Guards Brigade to War-drecques. R.F. Company had been left behind for the moment, but followed by train from Heilly in the night of the 31st.

During May Captain Sir Iain Colquhoun left the battalion to take command of the 2/4th Leicestershire Regiment.

The 2nd Battalion Scots Guards, which was at Cartigny on the 1st May, marched ten miles to Curlu on the 2nd, returned to Cartigny on the 6th, and remained there till the 18th.

On the 13th battalion sports were held in beautiful weather, in the presence of Lieut.-General Sir W. Pulteney, the Army Commander, and other high officers. They were a great success. Scarcely were the sports finished when a terrific, though short, storm broke on the camp, blowing down fifteen tents and blocking the road by washing down the bank at the side of it. The battalion went to Bronfay Farm for a night on the 18th, and next day to Corbie till the 30th, on the night of which day it, like the 1st Battalion, entrained for the St. Omer district, and went into billets at Brandinghem, five miles south-east of the town.

At the beginning of June the 1st Battalion had an effective strength of 27 officers and 1,010 other ranks, which at the end of the month stood at 31 officers and 1,053 others, figures which indicate that the time of serious fighting had not yet been reached during the month. The offensive had begun on the 7th June with the capture of the Messines–Wytschaete ridge, but, though the Guards infantry were warned to be in readiness, they were not called up then.

At Wardrecques, far in the back area, training continued vigorously till the 8th June. On the 7th the two battalions held joint aquatic sports in the canal near Wardrecques. On the 9th the 1st Battalion went to the Zudansques area for special musketry and other exercises, returning to Wardrecques on the 10th. On one of their route marches from this place the C.O. 1st Cameron Highlanders sent his pipe band to play the battalion through the village of Zuytpeene, where his battalion was quartered. June 12th, when the battalion marched by Wormhondt to St. Jan ter Biezen, was an intensely hot day, and the march, though not very long, was extremely trying. Here, in camp " M," on the Watou–Poperinghe road, an unwelcome visit was paid by a number of German aeroplanes, none of which was brought down by the heavy anti-aircraft artillery fire opened on them. That afternoon the battalion moved off to relieve the 17th Royal Welsh Fusiliers in the Boesinghe area.

Battalion Headquarters were at Bleuet Farm, about a mile and a half west of the Yser Canal, on the Elverdinghe–Boesinghe road, a low-lying area which at this time of year had not quite the same objectionable features as in winter. L.F. was in support, and the others at neighbouring farms which are only shown on trench maps. There was much aerial activity in the fine weather prevailing, and there was occasional heavy shelling of Spinney Wood on the right, which the enemy evidently suspected to be the site of a British battery.

The battalion, being relieved on the 17th, went back to Roussol Farm and the Elverdinghe defences. In this neighbourhood it had one man killed and four wounded by shells. On the 22nd it was sent up to relieve the 2nd

Irish Guards in front line of the Boesinghe sector, with
L.F. in front line on the right, " C " on the left, " B " and
R.F. in immediate and more distant support respectively.
The enemy shelling here was heavy in the day and inter-
mittent at night.

We must interrupt the narrative here for a moment to
explain what is meant by " mats," of which a good deal
will have to be said in the course of the coming actions.

One of the troubles of this front, where the British were
separated from the enemy by the Yser Canal, was the
difficulty of crossing that obstacle, as a necessary preliminary to an offensive movement or a raid.

The same difficulty was likely to occur farther on in
the marshy streams which would have to be passed. The
bed of the canal was of such deep sticky mud that any man
attempting to ford it when the water was low enough was
almost certain to be held firm by sticking in the mud. Light
bridges, founded on broad bases of empty oil tins, were
stored in chambers constructed on the near side of the
canal bank, but for the purposes of raids recourse was had
to " mats," which were strips of strong canvas about three
feet wide, of a length rather greater than the breadth of the
canal. The canvas was backed by wire netting and battens
of wood at short intervals. It was found by experiment
that these mats when rolled up could be easily carried, and
could be unrolled by a couple of men as they moved across
the canal. Moreover, it was found that the breadth of
the surface prevented the mat from sinking far in the
mud, even when walked upon. A rope hand-rail carried
by the men served to mark the position of the mat as it
was laid.

A raid was now projected, and an officer's patrol under
Lieutenant Duncan sent out to the canal to reconnoitre
obtained the following information :

(a) The canal could be crossed on a " mat " extended
from side to side.

(b) Dense undergrowth prevented anyone on the canal
bank being seen from the trenches.

(c) The enemy's wire, like the British, was easy to pass
through.

(*d*) That the enemy's front trench was almost empty. This was confirmed on the 24th by another patrol under 2nd-Lieutenant Hon. A. M. Kinnaird.

The projected raid was carried out at 12.45 a.m. on the 25th by No. 10 platoon of " C " Company, less one section, under Lieutenant C. A. E. Mahomed, which had remained behind at Roussol Farm practising for the raid and was now brought up.

The locality on which the raid was to be directed was the enemy's front trench known as " Baboon " trench, just beyond the farther bank of the Yser Canal, north-west of the Bois des Crapouillets. An elaborate operation order was issued for it by Colonel Romilly, and the objectives laid down were :

(1) Reconnaissance of the Yper Lea stream running parallel to and beyond the canal.

(2) Capture of prisoners.

(3) Testing of mats as a means of crossing the canal.

The three sections of No. 10 Platoon had a strength of about ten men each. The two on the flanks were commanded by sergeants, the centre one by Lieutenant Mahomed himself. Two men from each were to be left to guard the " mat " when the section had passed. On reaching the trench the centre section (forcibly called the " Cut-throat Section ") would remain in it and kill or capture any Germans found there. The outer or reconnaissance sections would each leave four men facing inwards and outwards in the trench. There would remain in each flank section four men and a sergeant, who would move forward to the Yper Lea, and then turn inwards along it till they reached the centre, where they would recross the trench and return by their own " mat," picking up the guards left to block the trench and guard the " mat." The centre section would retire after the flank sections had recrossed the canal.

Arrangements were also made to support the raid by trench-mortar fire directed on Baboon Support trench, 400 yards beyond the canal, and, if necessary, dealing with any enemy machine-guns which might interfere with the laying of the " mats " and the crossing. The whole affair worked exactly according to plan, so there is no need to describe further. The centre section had no opportunity of exercising its " cut-throat " functions, for not a single German was seen. The crossing of the canal was effected without difficulty, the men working in pairs. There was a little confusion on the right, owing to a Stokes mortar shell bursting short, which led the right section to believe they were being attacked, and to begin bombing the trench. This was soon set right, and the raiders, having accomplished their mission, except as regards taking prisoners, which was not their fault, got back just after 2 a.m. without loss to themselves or the four Royal Engineers who accompanied them. Much useful information as to the position beyond the canal was acquired. Lieutenant Mahomed brought specially to notice the good conduct of Sergeants McAulay and Leitch. Of the former, who apparently got his D.C.M. for this affair, we shall hear again at Cambrai.

After this the battalion was at Cardoen Farm, west of Elverdinghe. At this time the enemy were doing a good deal of shelling of the roads in order to interrupt traffic, rendering them specially dangerous.

At the end of the month the battalion was at de Wippe Cabaret camp, waiting for orders to go into the back area. The 1st Battalion meanwhile was occupied for the greater part of July in intensive training for their part in the coming Third Battle of Ypres, which lasted from the 31st July 1917 till the 10th November.

At no previous period of the war does the training for a forthcoming offensive appear to have been so complete and systematic as on this occasion. For it the 1st Scots Guards went to Herzeele on the 2nd July. The sector in which they were to be employed was that which they had just left, namely, the Yser Canal north of Ypres, and one of the principal objects of the training was to accustom the men to the conditions likely to prevail there in the near future, and to perfect the details of the arrangements for driving the enemy from the strong positions he held on his side of the canal.

For this purpose the afternoon of July 3rd was employed

in digging practice trenches, as nearly as possible reproducing those which would have to be attacked. This
work could only be completed on the 4th. The 5th was
set aside for brigade training in anticipation of the visit
of H.M. the King next day, when it was intended to show
him a sham attack by the Brigade on these prepared
trenches. His Majesty duly witnessed this on the 6th,
but there was more to be done before commanders were
satisfied that the preparations were perfect. The attack
was again practised next day, the pipers and drummers
being now utilized to mark the line of movement of the
barrage which would have to be followed in the real attack.
" The men," says the diary, " are gradually perfecting
the several parts they will play in the coming offensive
operations. Units are working in perfect unison, and the
leaders are realizing what is expected of them. The
formation adopted is that laid down in the latest Manuals,
i.e. *Training of Divisions for Offensive Action* and *Training
of Platoons for Offensive Action.*" Nevertheless, this was
by no means the last practice of the attack before it actually
took place.

At this time Captain E. D. Mackenzie, D.S.O., the
Adjutant, was called to understudy the Staff-Captain of
the brigade, and his duties were taken over by Lieutenant
W. E. D. Shortt.

On the 13th the 1st Scots Guards were definitely told
that their sphere of operations was to be in the area north
of Poperinghe, and on the 14th they moved up to the
" Forest Area," where, tents being few, most of the battalion had to bivouac among the trees and undergrowth
which, in the prevailing great heat, was anything but a
hardship. In this area there was a model of the Yser
Canal in the neighbourhood of Boesinghe. It was in the
south-east part of the camp, and on it the companies were
able to practise crossing. More models of the enemy's
lines had also been constructed for attack practice.

On the 17th July carrying parties going out in the
evening were caught in the German gas-shell barrage, and
twenty-seven other ranks had to go to hospital suffering
from the effects. Fortunately, none were serious cases.

The box-respirator gave no protection against mustard gas, which the Germans were now using, and which raised blisters and caused ulcers on parts of the body exposed to it. In most cases, however, a few days' treatment in hospital sufficed for a cure.

Fire control, box-respirator drill, and rapid loading were other subjects of practice.

On the 21st the battalion was moved forward to the Roussol Farm area, west of Elverdinghe, where the enemy was still at his old occupation of shelling the roads. Here the battalion was billeted in farm house and in bivouacs. Large working parties were employed in the line, and on the 22nd 2nd-Lieutenant J. F. Smyth, who was with the carrying parties, was killed by a shell.

Platoons 15 and 16 of L.F. Company were now practising for an intended raid. The rest of the battalion was kept busy with fatigues at all hours of the day. The billets, being in view of the German observation balloons, were frequently shelled, and many men had to be sent to Field Ambulance suffering from the effects of mustard-gas shells. The battalion expected to be sent into front line on the 25th July, and was armed and equipped as arranged for the forthcoming operations, but the movement was countermanded, and the battalion moved back to the camp evacuated by the 1st Irish Guards (1st Guards Brigade).

This camp was badly bombed by aeroplanes on the night of the 27th, but the most severe casualties among men and horses occurred at the north end of the camp, and did not fall upon the 1st Scots Guards.

There was final practising of the attack on the model trenches on the 28th.

Having brought the 1st Battalion to the eve of its entry into the operations of the Third Battle of Ypres, we may bring the 2nd Battalion movements up to the same date before commencing to describe those operations.

When the 2nd Battalion reached the St. Omer area at Bandinghem on 31st May 1917, it remained there till 16th June, when it marched to Moringhem, and on the 18th moved by motor-bus to Herzeele, where model trenches were dug, and the 3rd Guards Brigade practised attacks on them as has already been described in the case of the 1st Battalion and the 2nd Brigade.

The XIV Corps constructed a large model in sand of the area covering the whole corps frontage to a depth of more than a mile. The scale was sufficiently large to show all details, which were corrected daily according to aeroplane reports. A platform was built round the model, so that opportunity was given to all ranks to study it.

This opportunity was greatly appreciated, especially by N.C.O.s, who were able to gain far more information from it than from ordinary maps.

June was an uneventful month, and on the 1st July the battalion moved to camp in the woods near Coppernoller-hoek, in the Proven area.

On the 4th July serious casualties occurred. Lieutenant F. R. Pretyman and 15 other ranks were killed, and 9 other ranks wounded whilst on fatigue. The work at this time was generally near Elverdinghe, the four miles' march to which started after dusk. It consisted chiefly in carrying up ammunition and material to the front, laying buried cable lines, etc. It was frequently interrupted by shell fire, and was costly in deaths and wounds. Altogether in this way the battalion lost, between the 1st and the 23rd July, 1 officer killed and about 50 other ranks killed or wounded.

The attack beyond the canal, which was originally proposed for the 25th July, was postponed for various reasons till the 31st, and it was decided to give a rest out of line to the two Guards brigades (2nd and 3rd) which were to lead the advance on that day. The 1st Guards Brigade was, therefore, ordered to occupy the front on the 26th, and to cover the whole of it with the 3rd Coldstream Guards. Accordingly, part of that battalion relieved the 2nd Scots Guards in the afternoon of the 26th, and the latter went back into reserve area after having had, as shown by the casualties above given, a very bad time from the German bombardment. At this time information collected from various sources induced General Feilding to believe that the enemy had abandoned, or at least only held lightly, his trenches in the immediate neighbourhood of the Yser Canal, and that it was feasible to cross and establish a line covered by an outpost line beyond the canal, as far as Baboon Support trench, which would greatly facilitate the earlier operations on the 31st July.

Accordingly, patrols of the 3rd Coldstream Guards were sent across the canal on the afternoon of the 27th.

The front trenches were found to be unoccupied, and the patrols got forward without any serious opposition to a line starting on the left just short of Bois Farm on the eastern edge of Wood 14. Thence it ran south-east to cross the Ypres–Staden railway about 400 or 500 yards beyond the canal. The right was there thrown back as a flank guard to Canal Support trench. At first another flank guard had to be maintained on the left, but this was able to be withdrawn later, as the French on the left, who had temporarily retired, again came into line. The 3rd and 4th Coldstream Guards worked hard at improving the defences of this line, and though there was considerable German shelling to hamper them, there was no infantry counter-attack, and an invaluable bridge-head was established to cover the crossing of the canal on the 31st.

On Sunday, the 28th, the Officer Commanding the 2nd Scots Guards went, with his company commanders and transport officer, to reconnoitre Voynier Farm, the point of assembly for the attack on the 31st. This farm lay about 500 yards on the near side of the Yser Canal, just south of the Elverdinghe–Boesinghe road.

On the 23rd Lieutenants W. E. Ferryman, A. R. W. Menzies, J. V. T. W. T. Perowne, and Captain A. L. Maynard, and on the 24th Lieutenant Hon. V. A. C. Harbord, all went to hospital gassed. On the 23rd of other ranks 4 were killed, 12 wounded, and 120 sent to hospital gassed. On the 24th 8 were wounded and 10 gassed. On the 25th 2 more were killed, 8 wounded, and 2 gassed.

At 12.5 a.m. on the latter day a raid was carried out across the canal on Baboon trench by the 2nd Scots Guards, whilst similar raids were made by the Coldstream Guards on its right and the French on its left. This raid was for the purpose of gathering information as to the German trenches and strength beyond the Yser Canal, and especially to report on the Yper Lea stream running parallel to and beyond the canal. It was commanded by Lieutenant Hon. G. W. Elliot, was very successful, and returned without loss. It was found that the German front line had been rendered untenable by the British bombardment and was almost unrecognizable. The enemy had withdrawn from it to positions 500 yards in rear of the canal. The Yper Lea appeared to be a much less formidable obstacle than had been supposed, and was almost dry. When the 2nd Battalion had gone up into front line on the 23rd July, the divisional front extended from the French right, on the outskirts of Boesinghe, for about 1,500 yards to a point about 500 yards south of the bridge which had carried the Ypres–Staden railway across the canal. The boundary between the 2nd Scots Guards on the left and the Coldstream Guards (2nd Brigade) on the right, passed south of Boesinghe Château. Each battalion was on a front of one company. In the Scots Guards, R.F. was in front ; " F " in support close to Boesinghe Château on what was called " Y " line ; " G " was in reserve in " X " line, 500 yards behind the canal, with two platoons another 500 yards back. L.F. was in second reserve near the transport line. Battalion Headquarters in Boesinghe Château.

The 1st Battalion Scots Guards was the first of the two to come into action in the opening of the attack on the 31st July, and must be first dealt with.

On the afternoon of the 29th " C " and L.F. Companies took over from the 2nd Coldstream Guards on the canal bank and in the outpost gained on the 27th. The left was marked by the southern side of the Ypres–Staden railway, where the battalion was in touch with the 2nd Irish Guards on its left and the 38th Division on its right. During the relief both banks of the canal and the approaches to it were heavily shelled by the enemy, and the dug-out in which was Lieut.-Colonel Romilly, commanding the battalion, was blown in by a 5·9-inch shell and had to be evacuated. Colonel Romilly, suffering from shell-shock, was compelled to go to hospital, and command of the 1st Battalion was taken over by Captain H. C. E. Rosss D.S.O., who, on the testimony of the G.O.C. 2nd Guard,

14

Brigade, acted throughout the battle with marked success. He nearly lost his chance when Major Stirling arrived to take command; but the latter was required to act as liaison officer with the French on the left of the 3rd Guards Brigade. Lieutenant F. T. Mann, who had been sent back to Herzeele with Lieutenants Trappes-Lomax, R. N. Macdonald, and Hon. J. A. Burns, and 78 other ranks as reinforcement reserves, came up as second in command.

When " C " and L.F. took over, the former was on the right, the latter on the left, each with two platoons in the outposts and two behind. Bridges on the canal were limited to three petrol-tin ones, and generally communications with Brigade Headquarters were difficult.

R.F. and " B " had been left, meanwhile, in camp in the Forest area.

A detachment of " G " Company was specially trained with a company of the 201st French Infantry Regiment (1st French Division), so that the attack could be well locked up. This combined plan worked very well.

Patrols sent out 200 yards beyond the outpost line in the night of the 29th-30th reported no signs of enemy snipers or machine-guns, and the same was the case on the afternoon of the 30th. At 6.30 that evening R.F. and " B " moved up from Forest area, the former going into the " X " line and the latter into the " Y " line on the south of the canal, and sending up to reconnoitre the bridges and forming-up places. At 9.30 these companies moved up again to the positions from which they were to advance as the first and second waves in the attack. By 10.30 the whole battalion was in position beyond the canal and across the Yper Lea. The companies were posted as follows :

R.F. (Lieutenant W. D. Hope) on the right, and " B " (Lieutenant R. H. Dalrymple) on the left in front line.

In the second line, " C " (Captain W. P. A. Bradshaw) on the right, and L.F. (Lieutenant J. M. Cobbold) on the left. The " moppers up " from the 1st Coldstream Guards formed in rear of the second wave. Liaison with the 113th Brigade on the right was close, but on the left, owing to the arrangement of the front to facilitate maintenance of direction, the Scots Guards were some distance behind the right of the 2nd Irish Guards. The machine-guns were behind the fourth wave. The general scheme of the attack by the Guards Division was for the 2nd Brigade to lead on the right, with the 3rd on its left and the 113th Brigade (38th Division) on its right. The leading battalions of the 2nd Guards Brigade were to be the 1st Scots Guards on the right and the 2nd Irish Guards on its left. The 1st Guards Brigade was in reserve.

The area assigned to the battalion started with its left on the railway and right touching the left of the 16th Royal Welsh Fusiliers, the left battalion of the 113th Brigade. The battalion front was about 400 yards. The area then moved forward diagonally across the railway till, at a point about 300 yards east of the north-east corner of Artillery Wood, the railway (exclusive) became the right-hand boundary, and continued so during the rest of the advance.

There had originally been four objectives, but owing to circumstances already described, the first no longer existed, and we may now call the first the Blue Line, running north-west from the railway, about 800 yards from its crossing the canal.

The second objective was the Black Line, more or less parallel to the first and about 600 yards on. The Blue and Black Lines converged towards the left, and on the left boundary of the Guards Division were only about 400 yards apart.

The third objective, the Green Line, beyond which the operations of the 2nd Guards Brigade were not to extend, was yet another 1,100 yards farther on.

At the Black Line the Scots Guards were to stop whilst the 3rd Grenadier Guards passed through them to the capture of the Green Line. The only function of the Scots Guards beyond the Black Line was to send four platoons in rear of the 3rd Grenadiers to construct two strong points on a line intermediate between the Black and the Green Lines. These platoons were also to hold the Green Mill Line between the Blue and Black Lines. The attack of the battalion was to be in four waves at intervals of 100 yards, the first two being formed by R.F. and " B," the third and fourth by " C " and " F." Two platoons of the 1st Coldstream Guards were told off to " mop up " for the Scots.

About the time the Scots Guards got into position on the night of the 30th July, the divisional artillery fire was increased in volume, and gas shells were used against the German batteries. This continued till the creeping barrage began at 3.50 a.m. on the 31st.

The 1st Scots Guards started forward at zero + 8 minutes, when the first wave of the 38th Division had got up into line with their right.

In support of the leading battalions the 3rd Grenadiers were on the right, behind the 1st Scots Guards, and the 1st Coldstream Guards on the left, behind the 2nd Irish Guards. They did not cross the canal till after the advance of the leading battalions had made some progress. The advance was covered by a machine-gun barrage. The German barrage was put down on the banks of the canal, where the ground was so soft that the casualties caused by it at the commencement were comparatively small. It remained there, so that, as the Scots Guards advanced, it fell mostly behind them. The British barrage left out about 400 yards opposite the Scots Guards left, and consequently many German snipers and machine-guns were able to do much damage from that area as the battalion advanced.

It was towards 5 a.m. when the Blue Line was in the hands of the Scots Guards. It had been found to be only lightly held, and was taken without difficulty by the first two waves, who at once began consolidating. They had with them the battalion snipers under Lieutenant B. W. Duncan, and were followed by one of the two " mopping up " platoons of the 1st Coldstream Guards, and by the third and fourth waves. It was during this consolidation of the Blue Line that the heaviest casualties of the day occurred, from the fire of German snipers, and machine guns in concrete emplacements in Artillery Wood on the left, and Big Clump beyond the railway on the right.

Lieutenants C. A. E. Mahomed and E. A. C. Lloyd were both shot dead, and Lieutenant W. D. Hope was severely wounded in the head. A determined rush presently cleared out the two troublesome posts on the flanks. Captain Bradshaw now found himself the only unwounded officer in " C " and L.F. supporting companies, which he reorganized and led forward about 5.20 a.m., passing through the first two waves to lead the advance on the Black Line. In this stage, again, there was severe opposition and serious loss. It was occasioned by snipers and machine-guns hidden in Hey Wood on the left, as the others had been hidden in Artillery Wood. Casualties were also caused by the fire of German riflemen ensconced in shell-holes in front of the Black Line trench. Nevertheless, between 6 and 7 a.m. the Scots Guards and the Irish Guards on their left had occupied the Black Line. A good number of prisoners had been taken, together with twelve machine-guns and a trench-mortar.

The supporting battalions of the brigade (3rd Grenadiers on the right, 1st Coldstream Guards on the left), now came through the Black Line and passed on to the attack of the Green Line, which was reached, in the face of a good deal of opposition, by both battalions about 8 a.m.

Meanwhile, the 1st Scots Guards sent forward the four platoons as ordered to construct the two strong points intermediate between the Black and the Green Lines. The rest of the battalion remained completing consolidation of the line they had taken till 1.30 p.m., when the whole battalion was withdrawn and sent back into reserve at Roussol Farm. Losses had been expected to be heavy on this day ; for the positions to be taken were known to be difficult of access and to be considered by the enemy to be almost impregnable. The battalion diary says they were not beyond expectation, but they were certainly heavy. Between the 29th and 31st, which included losses due to the German artillery before the actual attack, they were :

Officers killed : Lieutenants C. A. E. Mahomed and E. A. C. Lloyd.
Wounded : Lieutenants (Acting-Captains) J. M. Cobbold

and W. D. Hope ; Lieutenants G. M. Cooper, C. R. Finnis, J. K. Edwards, and G. Johns.

Other ranks, by companies :

	Killed	Wounded	Missing
R.F.	9	54	2
"B"	7	44	4
"C"	12	55	2
L.F.	14	54	5
Total	42	207	13

For the 2nd Battalion the battle of the 31st July 1917 was a day of less severe trial and smaller losses than it was for the 1st.

On the 30th, at 9.30 p.m., the battalion marched to the forming-up position, with the exception of 80 men of L.F. Company employed on carrying, who had already gone up. As we know, the 3rd Guards Brigade was to take up the line on the immediate left of the 2nd, and what has been said of the boundaries of the latter serves to indicate the right boundary of the 3rd Brigade. Battalion Headquarters were located at Boesinghe Château, and it is stated that the night of the 30th was a singularly quiet one there, no shells falling near the château. Headquarters of the 4th Grenadier Guards were already established there. There were no casualties in forming up.

The attack of the 3rd Brigade was to be led by the 1st Welsh Guards on the right and the 1st Grenadier Guards on the left. On the right of the 3rd Brigade was the 2nd Guards Brigade, on the left the 1st French Division, of which the 201st Regiment immediately adjoined the left of the 2nd Scots Guards. To it, as liaison officer, was attached Major J. A. Stirling.

The part to be played in the 3rd Guards Brigade by the 4th Grenadier Guards on the right, and the 2nd Scots Guards on the left of the support line, was similar to that assigned in the 2nd Brigade to the 3rd Grenadiers and the 1st Coldstream Guards ; that is, they were to pass through the leading battalions of the brigade when the latter had established themselves on the Black Line, and to proceed to the capture of the Green Line. There was a Dotted

Green Line beyond, which was to be taken by the 1st Guards Brigade, the reserve brigade of the Guards Division on this day.

As already stated, the interval to be passed by the 3rd Guards Brigade between the Blue and the Black Lines was considerably less than in the case of the 2nd Guards Brigade, owing to the convergence of the lines towards the left.

It was, therefore, not till zero + 38 minutes, that the 1st Grenadiers and 1st Welsh Guards started to master successively the Blue and Black Lines, at the latter of which they were to stop. The barrage preceding them was in three belts. The nearest to their front was of 18-pdr. shrapnel, beyond that was a barrage of 4·5-inch high explosive shells, and in front of that again one of heavy shells.

The 2nd Scots Guards began to close up to the canal at zero + 38 minutes, and moving slowly forward over it had reached, by about 6 a.m., Wood No. 15, some 1,200 yards beyond it. So far it had had an easy time. A few shells fell near the canal, and a few more later near Wood 15, but the battalion had encountered nothing that could be described as a barrage. In fact, the enemy appears to have concentrated his efforts more upon the sector of the 2nd than on that of the 3rd Guards Brigade. Before 7 a.m. the battalion was formed up behind the Black Line, which had been carried by the leading battalions of the brigade. Half an hour later it went through, with the 4th Grenadier Guards on its right, to the capture of the Green Line. Battalion Headquarters had already moved up to the northern edge of Wood 15. The formation for the advance was R.F. Company on the right and " F " on the left, each in two waves at intervals of about 100 yards. " G " followed in rear to "mop up." L.F. had two platoons employed in carrying. The other two were with Headquarters. R.F. was commanded by Captain C. A. M. Cator, " F " by Lieutenant Hon. V. A. W. B. Cochrane-Baillie, " G " by Lieutenant E. Knollys, and L.F. by Lieutenant E. S. Ambler, with Lieutenant F. W. Priaulx in charge of the carrying party

The British artillery fire is described as being so " devastating " that the enemy were able to put up little or no resistance between the Black and the Green Lines, the latter of which was successfully reached. The only temporary check to the Scots Guards was shortly after the advance began, when some trouble was experienced on the left from the fire of a machine-gun at Major's Farm. A platoon of " G " was sent up to reinforce the second wave, and the line was soon able to move on.

The French, on the left, had been held up for a time by a single machine-gun at Colonel's Farm, which had caused them severe casualties. Eventually the enemy evacuated the farm, and the French were able to move up to the Green Line, where they touched " F " Company's left, which had been temporarily exposed by the holding up of the French.

In the advance the 2nd Scots Guards had taken about fifty prisoners and two field guns near Major's Farm. The prisoners had to be, for the most part, sent back through the French, as the battalion was too weak to furnish escorts.[1]

Other captures included two " minenwerfer," a machine-gun, a complete listening set, a complete store of medical equipment, and a large quantity of rifles, ammunition, etc. No great number of Germans were killed in the open, except at Major's Farm. A great many who failed to escape had been bombed in their dug-outs in Wood 15 by the Welsh Guards. In one dug-out alone there were twenty dead. The concrete blockhouses, from which the enemy generally fled as the British approached, were undamaged and capable of obstinate defence had the Germans held better. As it was, they furnished admirable cover for the British troops.

At the Green Line the 2nd Scots Guards were assisted in consolidating by 100 men lent by the Welsh Guards. Battalion Headquarters were moved forward to Saules Farm. The day's casualties in the battalion indicate the rather feeble nature of the German defence.

---

[1] It will be remembered that they had suffered very heavily from gas shells about the 23rd-26th July.

The only officer casualties were Captain C. A. M. Cator, M.C., and Lieutenant C. H. L. F. M. T. Chamberlayne, wounded, the latter whilst doing liaison work with the French—one warrant officer, Drill-Sergeant G. W. Dewar, was wounded.

Of other ranks 10 were killed and the wounded were 49, of whom 35 were walking cases.

The 1st Guards Brigade went through the 2nd and 3rd at the Green Line about 10 a.m. and occupied the Dotted Green Line, which ran due east and west from the Green Line on its left to a point beyond the Steenbeek about 1,000 yards in front of the Green Line.

The rest of the 31st July was uneventful for the 2nd Scots Guards till the evening, when they were relieved by the 4th Grenadier Guards without molestation, and marched back to bivouacs near Decouck's Farm, between Elverdinghe and Roussol Farm.

It rained heavily during the 1st August, when the 1st Battalion was getting a little much needed rest after the battle of the previous day, and in compiling lists of deficiencies in equipment, etc., and casualties.

Next day Major M. Barne, D.S.O., who had been in ambulance for some days past, rejoined and took over command of the battalion from Captain Ross. It was now but a skeleton of a battalion ; for its fighting strength was only 12 officers and 260 other ranks when, at 4.30 p.m., it was ordered back to trenches to relieve the 1st Irish Guards of the 1st Guards Brigade in support at the Green Line, the front line, as we know, being on the Dotted Green Line. " C " Company was left behind in the Blue Line, and Battalion Headquarters were stationed at Garde Barrière House, north of Pilckem. The assumption of positions was rendered difficult by the enemy's barrage.

In the night of 3rd-4th August the battalion was again moved forward to relieve the 1st Irish Guards on the Dotted Green Line. The Irish Guards had had a platoon on the left beyond the Steenbeek, but the Scots Guards were ordered to keep the whole of their left front company (R.F.) in the hither side of the stream. Battalion Headquarters were in Captain's Farm, the battalion now being on the left of the 2nd Guards Brigade. Heavy enemy artillery fire continued, and caused it a loss of 3 men killed and 22 wounded on the 3rd, and 1 killed and 1 wounded on the 4th.

On the latter day the 1st Scots Guards were relieved by the 2nd, and entrained at Elverdinghe for Purbrook Camp, near Proven, where they arrived in the early morning of the 5th. Here they remained for some time resting, training, and refitting. After the battle of the 31st July the 2nd Battalion had remained at Decouck's Farm till sent up, as just mentioned, to replace the 1st in the front line on the Steenbeek. The trenches here were very wet and muddy after the recent heavy rain, and the German shelling continued. Captain's Farm, where 2nd Battalion Headquarters had replaced those of the 1st Battalion, received a special share of the enemy gunners' attentions.

The rain ceased on the 6th, which was warm and fine after the cold and wet which had of late made these trenches so particularly unpleasant. That night the battalion was relieved by the 1st Grenadier Guards and followed the 1st Battalion to the neighbourhood of Proven in Privett Camp. In the relief Lieutenant Hon. G. W. E. Elliot received wounds of which he died later. The battalion's casualties between the 4th and the 6th August had amounted to 9 killed, 19 wounded, and 3 missing. Both battalions remained in their respective camps near Proven, far behind the line, occupied as usual in such positions till the 21st August.

The following are the only occurrences worth noticing as outside the usual routine. On the 6th Lieut.-Colonel Tempest, D.S.O., and Major Romer arrived, and took over, as C.O. and second in command respectively, the 1st Battalion.

On the 7th August letters were received from the Commanders of the Corps, Division, and Brigade, congratulating and complimenting the 1st Battalion on its action on the 31st July. These were read out on parade.

On the 8th the 1st Battalion was visited by the Army Commander, Sir Hubert Gough, commanding the 5th

Army, who inspected all officers who had been engaged, and one sergeant of each company. He congratulated them on their magnificent bearing in the recent battle, and on the good work done by the battalion. He did the same for the 2nd Battalion, and presented medal ribbons to those who had gained them.

On the 9th a large working party of the 1st Battalion was sent up to the front. It comprised a Major and 5 other officers, with 250 other ranks. Lieutenant Cobbold, who was with it, was wounded. On this day Lieutenant H. L. N. Dundas, who had been acting as Bombing Officer at Brigade Headquarters, returned to the battalion and took over command of L.F. The reinforcement of 2 officers and 76 others, who had been left at the corps camp before the battle of the 31st July, also rejoined.

On the 10th, when Lieut.-Colonel Tempest went temporarily to command the brigade, Major Romer replaced him in command of the 1st Battalion.

There was a football match between the two battalions on the 14th August, notwithstanding the rather inappropriate season and temperature.

On the 19th the 1st Battalion went by rail to Elverdinghe and marched to Burke's Farm.

The 2nd Battalion remained where it was. On the 25th the 3rd Guards Brigade was inspected by the French General Anthoine, who presented French decorations awarded to officers and men of the XIV Corps. The brigade, commanded by Lieut.-Colonel N. A. Orr-Ewing, D.S.O., marched past and advanced in review order. Major J. A. Stirling, M.C., was in command of the 2nd Scots Guards.

On 27th August the 2nd Battalion moved up and took over the left sector of the 29th Division front from one battalion and portions of two others of the 87th Brigade. Meanwhile, the 1st Battalion had been employed on road making near Bleuet Farm from the 19th to the 21st. During this it was several times bombed by enemy aeroplanes, and two men were wounded. On the 21st it went back by train from Elverdinghe to Proven, and on by march to Piccadilly Camp, where it remained till the 27th, and then marched to Caribou hutment camp.   It was there till the end of the month.

The 2nd Battalion finished the month of August in the front trenches.   The front was now some 1,800 yards beyond the Steenbeek, which had marked the limit of the advance on the 31st July.   The extreme front consisted of a line of posts beyond the Broembeek, which, like the Steenbeek, was an extremely variable obstacle.   In dry weather in the summer it was a mere ditch marking the lowest line between two so-called ridges, which themselves were in reality only small undulations of this flat country. When, however, there was heavy rain, as there so often was in the course of these operations, the ditch got filled to overflowing its banks, which had everywhere been broken down by the shells of both sides.   By this overflow the adjoining land was turned into a marsh dotted in every direction by the shell holes which, as the water filled them, formed deep ponds, in many of which it was quite easy for the incautious passenger to get drowned, especially when moving at night.   There was a particularly bad bit of this sort towards the left boundary of the Guards Division, in front of Ney Wood, which was on the rise beyond.

In order to prepare the way for the next stage in the advance in this direction, it was desirable to push the line forward some 250 yards to the crest of the ridge beyond the Broembeek, which was still held by the enemy.

On the left of the 2nd Battalion front there stood on the gentle upward slope a copse known as Ney Copse.   The French had been much in this part, and had left a remembrance of the fact in the fancy names they had bestowed on localities.   Besides Ney Copse and Wood, there are such names as Mondovi, Champaubert, Montmirail Farm, Lannes Farm, and Craonne Farm, all recalling victories of Napoleon or the names of his generals.

The north-east corner of Ney Copse was about the position to be acquired, and it was seized and consolidated by the 2nd Scots Guards, but the crest to the east was still held by the Germans, who, on it, were interposed between the left of the battalion and the 4th Grenadier Guards on their right. The posts in Ney Copse were consolidated by the Scots Guards, but apparently Ney Wood, 300 yards east of Ney Copse, was held by the enemy. No details of this affair are forthcoming.

The losses incurred in this operation, and during the occupation of trenches from the 27th to the 31st August, amounted to 7 other ranks killed and 31 wounded.

On the 1st September, when the 1st Battalion was still at Caribou Camp, Lieut.-Colonel Tempest was given the command of the 43rd Infantry Brigade, and Major M. Romer succeeded him in command of the 1st Battalion Scots Guards.

The battalion continued at Caribou Camp till the 5th September without incident, beyond a football match with the 3rd Grenadier Guards. On the afternoon of the 5th it marched to Harrow Camp, where there was work on the improvement of dug-outs and shelters. In the evening of the 6th a working party of 400 was sent up to the front, where it had 1 man killed and 4 wounded. These working parties at the front were continued on subsequent days, 4 men being wounded on the 7th, 5 on the 9th (one mortally), and 2 on the 10th. Next day, when company commanders went up to reconnoitre the part of the line to be taken over, Lieutenant F. T. Mann and Lieutenant R. D. Smith-Cunninghame were wounded, though neither of them seriously. An air-raid on the 12th, and slight shelling of the camp, resulted in no casualties to the battalion.

On the 13th, in the evening, the battalion went up to relieve the 1st Irish Guards in the line and had 6 men wounded in doing so.

On the 14th the battalion was in trenches south of the Broembeek, with R.F. Company on the right resting its right on the Staen railway. " C " was in the centre, and L.F. on the left, with " B " in support.

In the early morning and evening enemy aircraft were active, firing at the posts with machine-guns, and there was the usual shelling of normal violence.

In the evening Lieutenant D. Mackinnon with twenty other ranks of R.F. patrolled along the railway nearly up to the Broembeek. Here they located an enemy post, from which they were fired on with machine-guns and bombs. They returned with one casualty.

Next day some slight alterations in the line were successfully carried out, and a standing patrol was formed by 2nd-Lieutenant I. D. Erskine and twenty men at Ney Cross Roads, in order to prevent the enemy from maintaining a post at the bridge over the Broembeek. Next day the whole of the XIV Corps was barraged by the German artillery, apparently in preparation for local attacks, but the prompt reply by the British guns nipped in the bud any such movement. That evening 2nd-Lieutenant Erskine's patrol was again placed at Ney Cross Roads, whilst Lieutenant D. Mackinnon again patrolled along the Staden railway rather farther than before. They had to withdraw under heavy fire from an enemy strong-point beyond the Broembeek. Reorganizing, the party returned, bombed the strong-point, and forced its occupants to retire. They then patrolled towards the north-east and returned along the Broembeek.

In the night of the 17th-18th the 1st Scots Guards were relieved by the 3rd Grenadier Guards and returned by platoons to Bught Camp.

An unfortunate accident had occurred in the morning of the 17th in the transport lines. A British airman, finding himself forced to land, got rid of a live bomb by throwing it overboard. It exploded in the transport lines, killing 1 man and wounding 4 others, as well as Major Barne, D.S.O.,[1] who died of his wounds next day. He had only returned from leave in England on the previous day. His funeral at Mendringhem cemetery, Proven, was attended by such of the officers as could be spared, as well as by the C.O. and the pipers and drummers of the 2nd Battalion. On the 20th the 1st Battalion moved by train from Elverdinghe to Piccadilly Camp, near Proven.

[1] Major M. Barne, D.S.O., rejoined the Scots Guards from the Suffolk Yeomanry in the spring of 1915. In the autumn of 1915, during the Loos fighting, he was temporarily in command of the 1st Battalion, and on several other occasions, between then and 1917, acted as C.O. He was an officer who saw more continuous service with the 1st Battalion than any other, and he will be deeply missed. He had not an enemy in the world, and was held in affectionate regard by all ranks.

Two men had been killed and one wounded by shells at Bught Camp or on the way to Elverdinghe. During the stay at Piccadilly Camp the usual training went on, with occasional fatigue parties sent to the front.

On the 29th the battalion moved to a new camp at Herzeele. At this time there were actually with the battalion 21 officers and 840 other ranks.

The 2nd Battalion was in the Forest area for the first twelve days of September. On the 11th a competition for the best platoon in drill and turn out was won by R.F., with " F " Company second, and L.F. third. The three best turned-out men were adjudged to be Private W. Jones (L.F.), Private W. T. Kane (R.F.), and Private Grant (L.F.).

On the 12th the battalion moved up to Abblingley Camp, Zonnerbloom, near Elverdinghe, where it supplied fatigue parties for laying tram lines, making tracks, burying cables, and improvements in the camp. One of these parties of 100 men under Captain W. H. G. Ewart, was shelled in the night of the 16th with gas shells. One man was killed and two were gassed.

The brigade and division commanders visited the camp on the 19th, and a football match that afternoon resulted in a victory for the battalion over the 1st Grenadiers.

The succeeding days were spent at Privett Camp, Proven, and Herzeele, and on the 29th the 2nd Battalion replaced the 1st at Piccadilly Camp, where they again had a football success against the 11th K.R.R.C. The month of October was to be distinguished by the continuation of the advance across the Broembeek, in which both battalions had a share.

The 1st Battalion remained at Herzeele from the 1st to the 6th, practising attacks and being instructed, with the aid of a sand model of the scene of the approaching operations. At Herzeele, whence the battalion moved to Piccadilly Camp on the 6th, there were left all details which were not to take part in the operations. They were under the command of Sir V. Mackenzie.

CHAPTER XII

THE THIRD BATTLE OF YPRES (*continued*)

Both battalions to Ypres front again—Terrible mud and shell-holes
—Mid-October both battalions out of line again.

MEANWHILE, the 2nd Battalion was at Proven from the 1st to the 4th October, continuing its victorious career at football [1] in the intervals of training. On the afternoon of the 5th it entrained at Proven for the front. Its fighting strength was 32 men per platoon, and 3 officers per company, in all 12 officers and 832 other ranks.

The rest went to Herzeele to join Sir V. Mackenzie's details of the 1st Battalion, as part of the Divisional Reinforcement Battalion.

Detraining at Elverdinghe at 6 p.m., the battalion marched by platoons to their old positions in the Broembeek line. Only R.F. Company was left behind in the Elverdinghe area as reserve. That night the battalion relieved the 1st Border Regiment, and the companies were placed with " F " in the right front sector and L.F. on its left ; " G " was in support ; Battalion Headquarters at Widjendrift ; L.F. and " G " Headquarters at Montmirail Farm ; and those of " F " at Cannes Farm. The 6th was a quiet day till the evening, when a German aeroplane, flying very low, fired on the left platoon with a machine-gun, but caused no casualties.

In the night of the 6th-7th a patrol under a N.C.O. was sent out by each front line company to ascertain if any Germans still remained on the near side of the Broembeek. They went right up to it, but found none of the enemy.

The 7th was quiet, and that night the 2nd Battalion, being relieved by the 1st Scots and the 2nd Irish Guards of the 2nd Brigade, went back to Wellington Camp, Elverdinghe. There was much hard work on roads in the

[1] There were three Association internationals in the team.

forward area, under orders of the C.R.E., XIV Corps. The workers were constantly shelled, and had a number of casualties, among them Lieutenant R. J. Daniels, wounded on the 9th.

The 1st Battalion left Piccadilly Camp on the afternoon of the 7th October, after being supplied with extra equipment in the morning, and at night relieved the 2nd Battalion as stated above.

After dark on the 8th the companies moved into the assembly positions for the attack next morning. The assembly was completed by 1 a.m. on the 9th, when the companies were in the following positions : L.F. and " C " in front line, with their right about 500 yards from the railway on a front of about the same length. R.F. and " B " were in support. Of the conditions under which these positions were taken up, Colonel Romer wrote a few days later :

" The state of the ground was indescribable ; water and bog and shell holes everywhere, and it seemed impossible on Monday night that the companies could get formed up in their proper formations and ready to start off with the barrage at 5.20. Also, all this time it was pouring with rain. However, it was no use fussing, and at 5.20 the barrage started and the shaking of the ground was extraordinary."

On the left of the 1st Scots Guards were the 2nd Irish Guards ; on the right the 2nd Coldstream Guards.

The supporting battalions were formed in the area between Cannes Farm, Montmirail Farm, and the Wijdendrift–Langemarck road. Of these, the 3rd Grenadier Guards were in rear of the 1st Scots, the 1st Coldstream Guards behind the 2nd Irish. The orders were for the two leading companies of the Scots and Irish Guards to capture the first objective, where the two supporting companies of each would pass through them and take the second objective.

This first objective was just beyond the road from Lannes Farm, in the French area, to Grunterzale Farm near the right boundary of the 2nd Guards Brigade area. To reach

15

it the Broembeek had to be crossed almost at the start, indeed the British advanced posts were now beyond it in Ney Wood. The stream was reported to vary in breadth from 8 to 20 feet, and the marsh south of Ney Wood has already been mentioned. Moreover, the stream was blocked about Lannes Farm, which tended to bank it up to the east (up-stream) when, as now, there was heavy rain.

The only crossings were a brick bridge partially destroyed at Ney Copse in the area of the 1st Guards Brigade, and a culvert just below Ney Wood, which also had been destroyed. The second objective was a line 800 yards beyond the first. The third was farther on towards the Houthulst Forest, but was beyond the limit of the 1st Scots Guards operations for the day.

The supporting battalions of the brigade would not cross the Broembeek till the first objective had fallen. They would then pass through the leading battalions at the second to capture the third objective. Colonel Romer writes, in the letter already quoted, " The whole attack went off just as if it had been done at Aldershot. Every officer and man was splendid, and it could not have been a more brilliant success."

The barrage started at 5.20 a.m., followed by the infantry. The Broembeek had to be crossed almost at once by bridges and " mats," which were necessary here, though the 1st Brigade, higher up, could do without them. Colonel Romer had the unpleasant experience of falling into the stream or one of the shell-hole ponds on its near side.

The advance of the leading companies to the first objective met with but little opposition, except at Ney Wood, on the left of the Scots Guards, where a machine-gun came into action, but was quickly suppressed by rifle fire.

The first objective was reached up to scheduled time, and during the pause of forty minutes there, R.F. and " B " Companies passed through L.F. and " C," and formed up behind the barrage. They again met with little opposition in the capture of the second objective.

Here the supporting battalions, which had been following slowly, went through the leaders, the 3rd Grenadier Guards passing through the 1st Scots Guards, and the 1st Coldstream through the 2nd Irish Guards. They, too, formed up under the barrage and advanced to the third objective. The 1st Coldstream Guards on the left had trouble with a strong point on their left, which they eventually took, its garrison of forty Germans surrendering, with the exception of the officer, who refused and was bayoneted. The 3rd Grenadiers, who passed through the 1st Scots, reached the objective, as did the left of the 1st Guards Brigade. As, however, the 29th Division on their right were behind, it was necessary for the right of the brigade to be bent back from the objective to near Cairo House as a defensive flank.

Consolidation had been at once commenced by the Scots Guards on the second objective, beyond which they were not to go, and by 3 p.m. they were well dug in. Colonel Romer says that " all that afternoon they gave us the most infernal shelling with great big stuff."

About 5.30 p.m. the enemy counter-attacked the left of the Coldstream Guards, where it joined the right of the French, but, thanks to a prompt reply by the artillery to the S.O.S. sent up, the attack was stopped before it got within 400 yards of the line. Another attack later in the evening was stopped even shorter.

2nd-Lieutenant D. Mackinnon, of the 1st Scots Guards, was killed after the second objective was reached. Captain C. W. Hammerton, Lieutenant R. N. Macdonald, and 2nd-Lieutenant I. D. Erskine were wounded. Of other ranks the losses in the period 8th-10th October were 31 killed, 141 wounded, and 2 missing.

Between 7 and 8 a.m. on the 10th about fifty Germans were seen retiring from shell holes near Houthulst trench. The left machine-gun of the 1st Scots Guards got on to them and inflicted heavy casualties.

During the night of the 9th-10th, L.F. and " C " Companies and Battalion Headquarters were relieved and went back to Dulwich Camp, where they rested till evening, and then moved up to a camp in Wood 15, with headquarters in Saules Farm, whilst R.F. and " B " Companies, on relief in the second objective on the 9th, withdrew to the camp in Wood 15. There the 11th and 12th were spent in resting and improving the camp.

In the afternoon of the 11th Saules Farm was heavily shelled, Lieutenant W. E. D. Shortt being killed and Captain H. C. E. Ross and Lieutenant B. W. Duncan and Lieutenant Drummond wounded, as well as 1 man killed and 3 wounded. Headquarters then moved from Saules Farm to Wood 15.

On the afternoon of the 13th the battalion, on relief by the 2nd Irish Guards, went back to Dulwich Camp.

It was now the turn of the 2nd Battalion to take a hand in the fighting beyond the Broembeek. On the night of the 10th October they moved up from Wellington Camp, Elverdinghe, in support of the 3rd Guards Brigade, the rest of which was now holding the whole divisional front on the new line gained by the 1st and 2nd Brigades on the 9th. Two platoons of R.F. Company were attached to the 1st Grenadier Guards, with the object of maintaining touch between that battalion and the left of the 17th Division, which had not got so far forward as the Guards by 500 yards. The two platoons were to form a defensive flank here, and link up with the 17th Division, which had taken the place of the 29th on the right of the Guards.

The rest of the battalion was thus disposed as reserve in the attack next day by the 3rd Guards Brigade. The remaining two platoons of R.F., under Captain Hon. A. J. P. Howard, took up a position south-west of Vee Bend, where they had a fine field of fire in the event of an enemy counter-attack penetrating the gap between the right of the 1st Grenadiers and the left of the 17th Division. " G " Company, under Lieutenant E. Knollys, M.C., was posted about the east end of Ney Wood, ready to support the leading battalions of the brigade if required. L. F. and " F " were between Captain's and Fourche Farms, about 700 yards short of the Steenbeek; Battalion Headquarters being at Fourche Farm.

R.F. reached its position unharmed, but " G " ran into a heavy German barrage before reaching the Broem-

beek. By it 2nd-Lieutenant J. A. D. Milne, 2nd-Lieu-
tenant G. M. Oliver, the acting Sergeant-Major, and some
N.C.O.s and men were wounded. Shortly after they
reached their position, another barrage of H.E. and
mustard gas was encountered, which lasted some time,
and during the night the whole neighbourhood was shelled
with H.E. and gas. Captain Hon. A. J. P. Howard and
Lieutenant E. Knollys, M.C., were gassed, and there were
about eighty other casualties, mostly gas cases. This
ceased as an organized bombardment when the attack
began at 3.25 a.m. on the 12th. Lieutenant Knollys had
been replaced in command of "G" Co. by Lieutenant D. J.
Bethell. During the 12th nothing special happened to the
main part of the battalion, which had only a few casualties
from shells. The battalion stretcher bearers acted with
those of the 1st Grenadiers in clearing the field during the
night of the 12th-13th.

On the morning of the 13th Lieutenant D. J. Bethell
sent in to say that the mustard gas of the night of the 11th-
12th was hanging badly about the organized shell holes
in which were "G" Company in Ney Wood, and many
men were consequently suffering from gas in the form of
blisters. With the approval of the G.O.C. 3rd Brigade,
the company was withdrawn to the near bank of the Broembeek.

We must now relate the doings of the two detached
platoons of R.F., attached, as above stated, to the 1st
Grenadiers to try to get in touch with the 17th Division.

On the night of the 11th the two platoons, under orders
of the O.C. 1st Grenadier Guards, were posted about 300
yards in rear of Egypt House, and had taken up their
position by midnight. Their orders were to follow the
first wave of the Grenadiers at a distance of about 70
yards.

At 5.25 a.m. on the 12th, the two platoons advanced as
ordered to Egypt House, just behind which there was a
heavy German barrage. They then moved forward again
to a position behind Angle Point, where they got into
shell holes.

At 5.55 German snipers were very active, and killed or

wounded several men. At 6.15 a.m. one of them killed
2nd-Lieutenant H. W. Green, in command of the two
platoons and the only officer with them. The command
passed to Lance-Sergeant A. L. Ingram. Shortly after
8 a.m. an order was received from the O.C. 1st Grenadier
Guards to report position, and to keep Aden House, beyond
the right boundary of the Guards Division area, under
constant fire. The next order was at 11.30, to consolidate
the position at Angle Corner. Here the two platoons
remained till, at 5.30 p.m., 2nd-Lieutenant Byng of the 1st
Grenadiers arrived on the scene, saying the two platoons
were to take some emplacements in front of them, after
first ascertaining by a patrol whether they were strongly
held. Corporal Green, with Privates Grant and Simpson,
went out for the purpose. They returned, reporting that
there did not appear to be many Germans, and that they
thought the emplacements might easily be taken.

2nd-Lieutenant Byng then went out himself with his
orderly and the same three men, when some Germans were
killed by rifle fire or bombs. Private Grant and the orderly
were wounded. An attack with trench-mortar support
was then prepared, but was stopped by order from the 1st
Grenadier Guards, which said that a counter-attack was
expected next morning; therefore the proposed attack
was countermanded, and the platoons were ordered to
connect themselves with the right of the Grenadier Guards
by trenches. Communication with the right of the 17th
Division was not obtained on the 12th October. This
is attributed by the *History of the Guards Division* to failure
on the part of the observer of the contact aeroplane to
notice that the left of the 17th Division had moved too
much to the right and had reached its objective at a point
which left a gap between it and the right of the 1st Grenadiers. The expected counter-attack had not come off
at 6 a.m. on the 13th, when Private Grant, who had been
wounded as already stated, was seen waving his helmet
as a signal to advance. Though badly wounded, he had
ascertained that the Germans had retired before making
his signal.

The platoons then advanced, and found themselves in a

position with two earthen emplacements and a concrete dug-out. In this new position they were shelled and sniped during the day.

A patrol of Corporal Hill and three men was sent out to ascertain the whereabouts of the 17th Division and also whether Aden House was occupied by the enemy. They found the house was not held, but were unable to get into touch with the 17th Division, evidently for the same reason as has been given above, for the failure to gain contact on the 12th. Corporal Hill was wounded and one man was killed by snipers. A stretcher bearer was also killed when attending to a wounded man in the open.

The platoons were relieved at 11.45 p.m. on the 12th and rejoined their battalion. The weather had been bad throughout these operations.

In the evening of the 13th the whole battalion was relieved, and went back without mishap to Rugby Camp, Elverdinghe. The casualties in this tour of service in the front had been :

Officers killed : 2nd-Lieutenants J. A. D. Milne and H. W. Green.
Wounded : Lieutenant G. M. Oliver and 2nd-Lieutenant C. Fellowes.
Other ranks : not stated.

The 1st Battalion had arrived at Dulwich Camp on the 13th October in heavy rain. Next day was fine, but there was a rain of bombs from German aeroplanes.

Five of them were dropped on the camp, with the serious result of 6 men killed and 12 wounded.

On the 17th the battalion moved to Piccadilly Camp, where it was congratulated by the C.O. on parade on its recent fighting.

Next day they went by train to billets at Houle, near St. Omer, where, on the 21st, they were visited by H.R.H. the Duke of Connaught. He was received with three cheers by the companies drawn up in single file on either side of the road. Officers and all N.C.O.s above the rank of sergeant, as well as all N.C.O.s and men who had received decorations in the war, or been mentioned in despatches, or in reports on the recent fighting, were inspected separately by H.R.H. on L.F. parade ground. The Scots Guards band played in the afternoon on the parade ground.

On the 25th the Guards Division was inspected by the Commander-in-Chief, Sir Douglas Haig.

On the 27th the battalion gained a victory at football over the Guards Divisional Supply Column.

On the 29th it paraded at 9.30 a.m., when the C.O. pinned ribbons on nineteen men who had been awarded the Military Medal. It was at Houle till the end of October.

The 2nd Battalion was more fortunate than the 1st in the aeroplane bombing about Elverdinghe, their only casualties being three men wounded in a coffee bar at Bleuet Farm. On the 15th October the battalion went to " H " Camp for the night, and next day to Plurendon Camp, Proven. Here they were joined by 2nd-Lieutenant H. L. Knollys, M.C., and Lieutenants Sir A. F. Slade and C. Fairbairn, who had been with Corps Reserve at Herzeele. On the 20th they went by train to the village of Holque, near St. Omer.

Here, on the 21st, they were visited and inspected by H.R.H. the Duke of Connaught, in the same way as the 1st Battalion. The inspection by, and presentations to, H.R.H. were in a field just outside the village. The battalion was also present at the inspection of the Guards Division by Sir Douglas Haig on the 25th. For the rest of October it was training about Helque, a country ill-suited for the purpose, owing to the numerous canals and broad ditches by which it was intersected.

Four of the battalion football team had been gassed in the recent operations. However, their places were easily filled, and the team was able to beat the Ordnance Depot, the R.A.O.D., and a team from the 3rd Belgian Army in the last days of October, and to win a return match with the Belgians on the 1st November.

The 1st Battalion was still at Houle on the 1st November, when the Military Cross was awarded to Lieutenants L. N. Dundas and B. W. Duncan, and the D.C.M. to Acting-

THE THIRD BATTLE OF YPRES   219

C.S.M. T. Brownlow of " C " and Acting-Sergeant A. Gordon of " F " Company.

A Brigade Rifle Meeting was held on the 5th, and on the 6th the Croix de Guerre was presented to 2nd-Lieutenant C. A. A. Robertson. There were battalion sports on the 8th, when " B " Company carried off the Company Cup, and was again successful in the Inter-Platoon Shooting Competition next day. On the 10th the battalion marched to billets at Inghem, on the 11th to Laires, and on the 12th to Bryas, north of St. Pol, where it was split up in the neighbourhood, owing to shortage of accommodation.

Meanwhile, the 2nd Battalion continued at Holque in the first week of November, taking part in a Brigade Cross Country race, which was won by the 4th Grenadier Guards. There was a Boxing Competition on the 3rd, in which the battalion won the heavy-weight competition open to the brigade, and two special contests.

On the 6th the Guards Division was to have been inspected by General Anthoine, commanding the 1st French Army, who was afterwards to present French decorations gained by the division in the recent operations. The weather was so bad that all were dismissed from parade except the recipients of decorations. On the 7th the battalion won the Divisional Football Cup in a match against the 2nd Irish Guards.

On the 9th it commenced its march southwards. It was at Inghem on the 9th, at Laires on the 10th, and at Maisnel St. Pol from the 11th till the 16th. The sixteen-mile march to this last place was in very bad weather, and was very trying.

CHAPTER XIII

THE BATTLE OF CAMBRAI

November 17th both battalions moved toward Cambrai, where tanks were to be used for the first time—2nd Battalion at Bourlon Wood—1st Battalion near Fontaine—Advance of Germans—1st Battalion at Plouich—2nd Battalion in reserve—Both battalions to rest-quarters.

THE idea of the Battle of Cambrai in which the Guards were now to take part was nothing new. It had been considered in the secrecy of G.H.Q. for months previously to November 1917, and the area had been selected for various reasons, one of them being that the rolling country was suitable for the action of tanks, which it was proposed to employ in large numbers. The Battle of the Somme had been preceded by a tremendous bombardment of many days, which was more or less of a danger signal to the enemy and directed his attention to the threatened front. Cambrai was to be a surprise attack, and for its success depended largely on the maintenance of secrecy till the last moment. There was to be no preliminary bombardment, and the wire cutting and suppression of enemy posts which fell to the artillery in 1916 was now to be done by the tanks. What finally cast the die in favour of undertaking the operation so late in the season was the Italian disaster at Caporetto, and the necessity for doing everything possible to prevent the Germans reinforcing the Austrians on that front.

Every precaution was taken to keep the secret, and it was so well kept that the enemy was undoubtedly taken completely by surprise when the attack broke out. Amongst other instance of the care which was taken to keep him in the dark till the last moment, it may be mentioned that when the attacking troops were sent into front line, twenty-four hours before the advance, the outposts were still left in the occupation of the relieved regiments, so

that, in the event of a raid, the change might not be discovered by the capture of an outpost.

In the back areas the same care was taken, and though
use was made of models of the Cambrai front for training
purposes, they disclosed nothing as to where the area of
attack was to be.

All sorts of rumours were spread amongst the men who
were moving towards the battle area as to their ultimate
destination. We know from the *History of the Irish Guards*
that they believed they were going to Italy, and the diary
of a line battalion states that its men were ready to go
anywhere, including Ostend or Italy.

The diaries of the Scots Guards disclose no inkling as
to the destination ; for officers, as well as men, were kept
completely in the dark. When it became necessary that
Corps and Divisional Commanders should be told, they
were still sworn to the maintenance of the most complete
secrecy till the very last moment.

The Guards Division was not to take part in the first
break through, but it was required to exploit the initial
success which was anticipated. It was for this reason
that the division began to march southwards to its concentration area about St. Pol, twenty miles west of Arras,
and more than forty from Cambrai.

As has been stated, the 1st Battalion Scots Guards, with
the 2nd Guards Brigade, was at Bryas on the 12th, and the
2nd Battalion, with the 3rd Guards Brigade, at Maisnil
St. Pol on the 11th.

From these places the march continued for the 1st
Battalion on the 17th November to Maizières, on the 18th
to Grand Rullecourt, and on the 19th to Courcelle le
Comte. Here they were under orders to be ready to move
at two hours' notice, for the 20th was to be the day of the
great attack. The 2nd Battalion also began to move
forward on the 17th, when it reached Grand Rullecourt ;
on the 18th it was at Berles aux Bois, and on the 19th at
Achiet le Petit, three miles south of the 1st Battalion,
and with like orders as to readiness to move.

Notwithstanding these orders, it was not till 6.80 a.m.
on the 22nd that the 2nd Battalion was sent off by buses

to Rocquigny, which was reached at 9 a.m. Here it was about four miles north-east of the scene of its fighting at Lesbœufs in the Battle of the Somme. Thence it marched on the 23rd to Beaumetz lez Cambrai, rested there a few hours, and then proceeded to support trenches at Flesquières, where the 6th Battalion Black Watch was relieved.

The 1st Battalion had also received orders late on the 22nd to march next morning to Lebucquière, a little west of Beaumetz, where they arrived at 10.30 a.m., and where we will leave them for the moment whilst we follow the fortunes of the 2nd Battalion, which was the first to come into action in the Battle of Cambrai. When the 2nd Scots Guards took over from the 6th Black Watch in what they called " support " trenches, they were really in what had been the Hindenburg Support Line, which, with the main Hindenburg Line, had been broken through in the first rush of the attack of the previous days. Flesquières stands near the top of the northern slope of a spur known as the Flesquières Ridge, which runs out from the high ground to the west towards Noyelles sur l'Escaut, where it ends at the river Scheldt (Escaut). From the north side of the ridge minor spurs project northwards, gradually sloping down to the dead straight line of the Bapaume–Cambrai road. North of that road, about Fontaine Notre Dame and west of that village, the country rises again towards the north, especially through the great Bourlon Wood, which lies spread like a blanket over the hog-backed hill on which it is planted. The village of Bourlon lies on the north-western edge of the wood. The Flesquières Ridge and Bourlon Wood were the two vital parts of the battlefield which had been intended to extend well beyond the Scheldt, and to include the high ground beyond it and east of Cambrai. Had the Bourlon Wood been taken, and also the Flesquières Ridge and the ground beyond the Scheldt, the whole Hindenburg Line north of Quéant-Pronville would have been turned, and great possibilities of forcing the abandonment of that line would have been before the attacking 3rd Army.

But, though the advance had progressed rapidly on the 20th November, it had been held up for a time at Flesquières ; the Scheldt bridge at Masnières had broken down and rendered impossible the passage of the tanks, on which great reliance had been placed for the operations beyond the river.

Finally, the advance against Bourlon Wood had failed, and on the 21st there were no British troops in the wood, though the line extended round Fontaine Notre Dame on the Bapaume–Cambrai road beyond it. But it did not take in La Folie Wood, and was only across the Scheldt at the bend about Masnières.

Since the 21st there had been much fierce fighting in Bourlon Wood with the enemy as he recovered from the first surprise which had disorganized his troops on the spot. His reinforcements were rapidly coming up. Fontaine Notre Dame had been lost to a strong German counter-attack on the 51st Division, who were unable to recapture it. The 40th Division, on the left of the 51st, had striven to gain the Bourlon Wood and the village beyond it.

Into the latter they had penetrated, but were unable to remain there, and in the night of the 23rd-24th November, were only holding with difficulty the south-western part of the wood, on the highest portions of which the enemy was established in a commanding position.

The 1st Guards Brigade on the right and the 3rd on the left were ordered to relieve the 51st Division during the night of the 23rd-24th ; but that division had no information of this arrangement, and was itself preparing for internal reliefs when it got its first information of the intended relief of the whole division.

The Guards Brigades had had a long, trying march, from Rocquigny to Beaumetz, and on to Flesquières in the case of the 3rd ; and to make matters still worse, the information they had received as to the positions of the 51st Division was either defective or incorrect. The difficulties of the relief, in the dark, in a strange country, can therefore be easily imagined.

When day broke on the 24th the 1st Guards Brigade found themselves stretched out on a line from south-east of Cautery on the right north-westwards to the south-east of Bourlon Wood. The 3rd Guards Brigade was in support at Flesquières, with the 2nd Scots Guards south-west of La Justice.

During this day the 2nd Guards Brigade and the 1st Scots Guards moved up to Ribecourt, on the south side of the Flesquières Ridge, where they also were in the Hindenburg support trenches.

On the left of the 1st Guards Brigade the 40th Division, commanded by Major-General J. Ponsonby, formerly commanding the 2nd Guards Brigade, was still holding on in the south-western lower portion of Bourlon Wood.

For the Guards the 24th passed quietly, save for intermittent shelling; but it was different on the front of the 40th Division, which was twice counter-attacked, and was now almost exhausted by its long fight in the wood. To enable it to maintain its position, the 3rd Guards Brigade was placed under the command of General Ponsonby, and the 2nd Scots Guards were sent up to support the 119th Brigade, the right-hand brigade of the 40th Division. The 2nd Scots Guards were in scattered dug-outs between Flesquières and La Justice.

At 8.30 p.m. an urgent message reached Major Stirling from the 119th Brigade saying that the position in the wood was most critical, and asking for immediate support. The greater part of Bourlon Wood was lost, and Major Stirling was directed to put himself in communication with Lieut.-Colonel Benzie, commanding the forward area at Anneux Chapelle. When Major Stirling reached Anneux with the battalion, he found that Lieut.-Colonel Benzie knew but little of the precise position of affairs in the wood. Orders and information would be received from Lieut.-Colonel Plunkett commanding the troops in the wood, who was to be found at a point in the wood south of the main cross-ride running east and west.

The battalion, with one section 3rd Guards Brigade Machine-gun Company, at once moved off. By 10 p.m. it was at Anneux, with the advanced Headquarters in Bourlon Wood before 11 p.m. It was a very dark night, and the units in the wood had become very much mixed up. German patrols and machine-guns were holding the highest part of the wood, and the latter were firing down the ride which runs from north to south through the centre of the wood.

It was the intention of Lieut.-Colonel Plunkett, commanding the British troops in the wood, that the 2nd Scots Guards should occupy the high ground in the northeast portion of it, getting into touch on their left with British troops who were wrongly believed to be in Bourlon village. Colonel Plunkett's troops consisted of scattered and exhausted parties from the South Wales Borderers, East Yorks, King's Own, Argyll and Sutherland Highlanders, and 15th Hussars. He had only one field officer to control them, and he was wounded shortly after the 2nd Scots Guards arrived.

In order to clear up the situation regarding Bourlon village, a patrol was sent out under 2nd-Lieutenant J. R. Hamilton. The whole of this patrol was either killed or wounded. 2nd-Lieutenant Hamilton himself was wounded. More patrols, organized by Lieutenant P. Purcell Gilpin, were more successful, and succeeded in proving that the Germans, not the British, were still in full possession of the village of Bourlon.

The battalion now took up a line through the centre of the wood, with its right on the eastern margin and extending north-westwards. R.F., " F," and " G " Companies were in front line, L.F. in support.

In the centre of the wood just north of the cross-ride, running east and west, is a cup-shaped depression, the lips of which Major Stirling had ascertained to be strongly held by numerous German machine-guns. He also found that there were practically no British troops north of the cross-ride. On this east and west ride the battalion took up a position till it was light enough to push forward patrols. These, after a good deal of fighting, occupied a position from the sunken road in continuation on the right to points somewhat north of the east and west ride.

Major Stirling was able to report that the Germans appeared to have at least one man to the yard in every strong position extending south-east from the cross roads on the central ride about 150 yards north of where it crossed the east and west ride. The machine-guns were in prepared emplacements in the line, and more German machine-guns were active in the south of Bourlon village.

It was about noon on the 23rd that Colonel Plunkett received orders that the whole wood must be cleared at any cost. When it had been cleared, the Scots Guards were to hold a semicircular line from the sunken road on the right, continuing the east and west ride towards Fontaine Notre Dame, round the north-eastern part of the wood to the eastern extremity of Bourlon village. The 2nd Scots Guards had a frontage of attack of 750 yards, extending to 1,250 as they reached the north-east edge of the wood. Major Stirling decided to make good the central cross roads, and to try to work northward from the sunken road. A group of machine-guns would cover the inevitable gap between the two wings. It was necessary to keep one company in reserve near the centre of the wood. The attack commenced at 2 p.m., when the cross roads on the left, north of the east to west ride, were made good and held. The company on the right ran into the main enemy line, and lost all its officers and sergeants. It had very heavy casualties and was held up, in spite of being reinforced by one platoon from the support company. The attack had been unsupported by either artillery or trench-mortars. It was made by " F " Company. In it Lieutenant A. R. W. Menzies, commanding " F," was killed, and Lieutenant G. Hamilton mortally wounded. Sergeant R. Malcolm also was killed. When it had dug in, the company had to repulse a German counter-attack.

The troops on the left of the Scots Guards in the west of the wood could make no progress, so the battalion, unable for this reason to go forward with its left, established itself on a line extending from the cross roads on the north and south ride on the left, to a line north of the sunken road on the right.

This position denied to the enemy the advantages of observation from the highest part of the wood. Here the battalion held on until, during the night of the 25th-26th, it was relieved in the line by the 186th Infantry Brigade of the 62nd Division. It was then withdrawn to the south-central part of the wood. It was supporting the right sector with the 4th Grenadier Guards on its left in support of the left sector in the wood. Here it was replaced, in the night of the 26th-27th, by the 2nd Irish Guards of the 2nd Guards Brigade, and went back to Flesquières. The casualties of the battalion in Bourlon Wood were :

Officers killed or died of wounds : Lieutenant A. R. W. Menzies ; Lieutenant G. Hamilton.
Wounded : Captain Hon. A. J. P. Howard ; 2nd-Lieutenant J. R. Hamilton.
Other ranks : 17 killed, 65 wounded, 9 missing.

In concluding this account of the action of the 2nd Battalion in Bourlon Wood, we must quote the following appreciation of its work extracted from a letter addressed by Major-General Ponsonby, commanding 40th Division, to the Major-General Commanding Guards Division on the 29th November :

" I wish to express, on behalf of my Division, my sincere thanks for the support given us on the 24th and 25th November by the Battalions of the Guards Division placed at my disposal for the defence of Bourlon Wood, namely, the 2nd Bn. Scots Guards and the 4th Bn. Grenadier Guards.

" I would like to bring to notice particularly the 2nd Bn. Scots Guards, who throughout the period prevented the enemy from breaking through the right flank of the position, and assisted in repelling at least two of the enemy's counter-attacks.

" I enclose extracts from the reports of the Brigadier-General Commanding 119th Infantry Brigade :

" ' The 2nd Bn. Scots Guards reinforced the firing line, which had become very thin, early in the morning of 25th November, and remained in action till they came under the orders of the 186th Infantry Brigade on the night of 26th-27th November.

" ' All ranks behaved with the utmost gallantry, and,

16

assisted to repel two German counter-attacks at least, in addition to continual enemy pressure.

"'They inspired all with great confidence. . . .

"'To the above-mentioned units I wish to express my gratitude.'"

We now return to the action of the 2nd Guards Brigade and the 1st Battalion Scots Guards.

On the afternoon of the 25th November Headquarters of the Guards Division were warned that it would probably be required very shortly to attack Fontaine Notre Dame, the large village lying across the Bapaume–Cambrai road south-east of Bourlon Wood. The village was, so far, untouched by artillery fire, and G.O.C. Guards Division requested a bombardment by the corps artillery before his infantry attacked.

The bombardment, on the morning of the 26th, was inadequate ; the artillery available being only two field batteries and one section of 6-in. howitzers.

It was not till the afternoon of the 26th that it was finally decided that the Guards Division should attack Fontaine next day, whilst the 62nd Division on the left, which had now relieved the sorely tried 40th Division, carried the rest of Bourlon Wood and the village of Bourlon. The 2nd Guards Brigade was still in reserve at Ribécourt, when it received orders to relieve the 1st Brigade in the night of the 26th-27th in front line, preparatory to executing the attack on Fontaine.

The attack was to be carried out by three battalions advancing on Fontaine from the west. The fourth battalion, the 1st Scots Guards, were to hold the right of the line, sending one company and a machine-gun forward by a sunken road which leads from the north-east end of Cantaing to the western part of Fontaine, and to hold the road as a protection for the right flank of the attack. This was not to be done till the battalions on the left had reached the first objective, a line running from south to north through Fontaine past the church, and thence across the railway west of the station to bend back round the north side of Bourlon Wood.

The second objective was the railway station and the

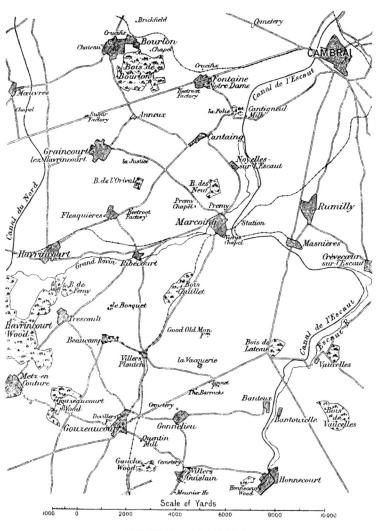

BATTLE of CAMBRAI
November 20th 1917.

eastern part of Fontaine. When this was taken, an out-post line was to be thrown out round the village on its north, east, and south-east sides.

The 1st Scots Guards had a good deal of difficulty in relieving the 1st Irish Guards in the night of the 26th-27th November, as snow was falling during a great part of the time. The attack on the 27th was to follow almost in continuation of the relief. When the relief was completed, the 1st Scots Guards' line touched with its left the right of the 3rd Grenadiers, continuing their front south-eastwards, and then bending eastwards to the sunken Cantaing–Fontaine road, and on to the northern end of Cantaing.

L.F. was on the left, " C " Company in the centre, and " B " on the right in front line, with R.F. in support. The 2nd Brigade had the 1st Scots Guards, 3rd Grenadiers, 1st Coldstream, and 2nd Irish Guards in that order from right to left. As a support, the 1st Welsh Guards (3rd Brigade) had been attached to the 2nd Brigade.

By the time the attack of the three battalions on the left started, at 6.20 a.m. on the 27th, the snow of the night had changed to a drizzling cold rain. The infantry advance was preceded by a creeping barrage moving forward at a uniform pace of 100 yards per minute. A further protec-tion was afforded to its right by a heavy standing barrage on La Folie Wood, which lay on the right flank of the Scots Guards, and was still full of German machine-guns. This barrage also covered all approaches to Fontaine on the German side. Fourteen tanks had been ordered to cross the starting line at zero hour, but they were late, and the infantry did not wait for them.

Shortly before 7 a.m. it appeared that the attacking battalions of the 2nd Guards Brigade, on the left of the 1st Scots, had reached the first objective, where the barrage was to pause for half an hour. The time had arrived for the Scots Guards to send up " C " Company, which had been detailed for the advance, by the sunken road from Cantaing to Fontaine. A reconnaissance by Lieut.-Colonel Sir V. Mackenzie and Lieutenant the Hon. A. Kinnaird, during a snowstorm in the preceding night, had ascertained that for the first fifty yards from Cantaing this road was not sunken and sloped upwards. For that distance it was absolutely without cover against the German artillery and the numerous machine-guns in La Folie Wood. It was, however, believed that this space could be crossed by crawling without serious loss. This was fairly correct as regards La Folie, but not so as regards fire from the southern part of Fontaine. Of course it might be supposed that this latter fire would no longer exist once the 3rd Grenadiers had reached the first objective. But the battalions attacking Fontaine had already suffered heavily in a village which, as has been mentioned, had not been seriously damaged by artillery fire. Consequently those battalions had been too weak to clear the houses systematically, and when they were on the first objective they had left behind them a hornet's nest of snipers and machine-gun posts.

As " C " Company of the 1st Scots Guards moved towards the south side of Fontaine, it met a destructive fire which caused many casualties. Lieutenant the Hon. A. Kinnaird was wounded in the leg first, and as he turned half round, was again hit in the back. He was dragged back about 400 yards by Sergeant J. McAulay to a dug-out, where he died. The other two officers (Lieutenants A. M. Scott and Hon. J. A. Burns) were less seriously wounded, but were put out of action, and command of the company passed to Sergeant John McAulay, who had already gained the D.C.M. on the 25th June in Lieutenant Mahomed's raid. Patrols sent out by " C," which had not got farther than about 150 yards south of the outskirts of Fontaine, failed to get into touch with the 3rd Grenadier Guards, and the Germans organized a counter-attack on the exposed left flank of the company. This was beaten off by Sergeant McAulay and his men, and some fifty of the enemy were killed.

About 9.30 a.m. a message came back to Sir V. Mackenzie from " C " Company asking for reinforcements to enable them to hold on. At the same time, a message from the officer commanding " B " Company explained the situation. Two platoons of R.F. were sent up, and thanks to the skilful guiding of Private Freeman, they joined the remains

of " C " without incident and remained with them till relieved in the following night. At the same time, Lieutenant
Dalrymple, commanding " B " Company on the right,
was ordered to take command of " C " in addition to his
own. At dusk orders were received from brigade for all
battalions to withdraw to their jumping off positions.
This was done in good order and without further loss.
That night the other three battalions of the 2nd Brigade,
which had suffered terrible losses in the attack, were
relieved by battalions of the 1st and 3rd Brigades, but the
1st Scots Guards were left where they were till the night
of the 28th-29th.

The 1st Scots Guards had naturally suffered less than
the others, as they had had only a company and a half
engaged in the actual attack. Remembering this, their
losses were proportionately very heavy. They were :

Officers killed : Lieutenant Hon. A. M. Kinnaird, M.C.
Wounded : Lieutenants A. M. Scott, Hon. J. A. Burns,
and 2nd-Lieutenant W. G. Horton.
Other ranks : 15 killed, 47 wounded, 5 wounded and
missing, and 6 missing.

Sir V. Mackenzie speaks very highly of the conduct on
this day of 2nd-Lieutenant Horton (" B " Company), who
himself brought about a dozen men to safety from an
exposed position and also carried a Lewis gun up to a
position on the left and placed it there, being wounded
in both wrists whilst doing so. He also commends the
guidance of Private Freeman (runner of " C " Company),
which enabled the two platoons of R.F. to get across
half a mile of exposed ground without losing a man.
Lieutenant Dalrymple and Lieutenants Stewart and Scott
are also praised. Stewart located a German machine-
gun and organized a bombing party against it, but could
not quite reach it. He also carried back a wounded man
at dusk from within 10 yards of a German post.

But the hero of the day was undoubtedly Sergeant
McAulay. Of him Sir V. Mackenzie wrote :

" He took command of the company after all his officers
had been hit, cheered and encouraged them, brought back

Arthur (Kinnaird) and many wounded men from positions of danger, beat back a counter-attack, killed several Germans, and was altogether splendid. I am recommending him for a V.C., but they are hard to get."

The recommendation was duly accepted in the following terms in the *London Gazette* of the 11th January 1918 :

" No. 10053 Sergeant John McAulay, D.C.M., 1st Bn. Scots Guards. For conspicuous bravery and initiative in attack. When all his officers had become casualties, Sergeant McAulay assumed command of the company, and, under shell and machine-gun fire, successfully held and consolidated the objective gained. He reorganized the company, cheered on and encouraged his men, and, under heavy fire at close quarters, showed utter disregard of danger.

" Noticing a counter-attack developing on his exposed left flank, he successfully repulsed it by the skilful and bold use of machine-guns, aided by two men only, causing heavy enemy casualties.

"Sergeant McAulay also carried his company commander, who was mortally wounded, a long distance to a place of safety under very heavy fire ; twice he was knocked down by the concussion of a bursting shell, but nothing daunted, he continued on his way until his objective was achieved, killing two of the enemy who endeavoured to intercept him. Throughout the day this very gallant Non-Commissioned Officer displayed the highest courage, tactical skill, and coolness under exceptionally trying circumstances."

McAulay, originally a miner, had abandoned that employment and taken service in the Glasgow police, from which he joined the Scots Guards. In the police he had distinguished himself not only as an efficient P.C., but also as a heavy-weight boxer.

With the failure of the attack on Bourlon Wood and Fontaine Notre Dame on the 27th November, it may be considered that the Battle of Cambrai ended as far as the British offensive is concerned. The failure to take those vital positions, combined with the breakdown of the proposed occupation of the heights south-east and east of

Cambrai, and the insufficiency of troops available to renew the attempts, sounded the death-knell of all hopes of cutting off or compelling the retreat of the German troops on the line from Quéant–Pronville northwards. But, as it was, the surprise attack of the 20th November had resulted in the British driving a deep wedge on a considerable front into the German defence.

The Hindenburg Line and its support had been mastered from the Scheldt about Banteux on the right to north of the Bapaume–Cambrai road on the left, a length of about eight miles as the crow flies.

No one could suppose that the German High Command would submit tamely to the loss of this area, which they had lost, as has been admitted, owing to the efficiency of the British surprise.

They had, as a matter of fact, set to work at once to bring up reinforcements, to prepare for a great counter-attack to fall upon both flanks of the new British salient, and to cut off the troops at its head before they could effect their retreat.

The effects of the reinforcements had already been felt in the attacks on Bourlon Wood and Fontaine, when successes gained by the Guards had to be abandoned from sheer weakness of numerical strength and want of driving power from behind in the shape of supporting troops.

The counter-attack was bound to come, but how soon it might fall does not appear to have been appreciated. When, therefore, it began with the utmost fury on the 30th November, it was almost as great a surprise for the British as their attack of ten days earlier had been for the enemy. When the German troops poured up into Bourlon Wood and over the ridge to the west of it they were unexpected, but the British troops were awake and ready, and the left flank of the salient held firm. On the right flank it was different, and the British line gave way. The accounts of hundreds of British troops streaming to the rear, unarmed and in disorder, and those of whole battalions destroyed by the sudden attack show how complete the surprise had been.

It may safely be said that to the inimitable steadiness

and discipline of the Guards, coming up from reserve, the avoidance of a terrible disaster was solely due.

The 1st Battalion Scots Guards remained at Cantaing during the day of the 28th till, at about 8 p.m., it was relieved by a battalion of the South Staffordshire Regiment. It marched back to its old quarters in the Hindenburg support line about Ribécourt.

In the afternoon of the 29th the three brigades of the Guards Division were concentrated thus :

1st Brigade, Metz-en-Coûture.
2nd Brigade, Ruyaulcourt and Bertincourt, respectively, about 4,000 and 6,000 yards to the west.
3rd Brigade, Trescault, about 3,500 yards north by east of Metz-en-Coûture.

It was not till 6 p.m. that all units had reached their billets. Those of the 1st Scots Guards were in Bertincourt, the farthest point back from the front of the 1st and 3rd Brigades, and in the great fighting of the next day or two, the 2nd Brigade being in reserve to the other two, the 1st Scots Guards took no active part. It was never called farther forward than Queen's Cross, a mile in rear of Gouzeaucourt. At 8 a.m. on the 30th Guards Divisional Headquarters received a wire to the effect that the enemy were attacking in force, and the division was to be prepared to move at a moment's notice. Presently it was rumoured that the Germans had broken through and had taken Villers Plouich and Gonnelieu. At 10 a.m., under orders from the IV Corps, the 1st Brigade was ordered to Hendecourt, about 4,500 yards a little east of south from Metz-en-Coûture, the 2nd and 3rd Brigades being at the same time ordered to replace the 1st about Metz-en-Coûture. Twenty minutes later IV Corps wired that the enemy had taken Gonnelieu and Villers Guislain. The Guards Division was to be under the orders of the VI Corps.

The 1st Brigade was then ordered to Gouzeaucourt, instead of Hendecourt, and to hold the ridge beyond it (Quentin Ridge) running south-west from Gonnelieu towards Revelon. The 3rd Brigade was to come up on

the right of the 1st, the 2nd Brigade on the right of the
3rd about Revelon. At 11 a.m. the Guards Division was
transferred again, this time to be under orders of the III
Corps instead of the VI.

Between noon and 1 p.m. information was received that
the enemy had captured the line Villers Plouich–Gouzeaucourt, and fresh orders were issued to the Guards Brigades.
The 2nd Scots Guards, leading the 3rd Brigade, had
already got nearly to Dessart Wood, when the march of
the brigade was changed to the north-east, so as to bring
it on to the left flank of the 1st Guards Brigade attacking
Gouzeaucourt. The 2nd Guards Brigade was ordered to
Queen's Cross, about a mile in rear of Gouzeaucourt.

Officers of the Guards Division, riding forward to reconnoitre towards the Villers Plouich-Gouzeaucourt line, met
several hundred officers and men of other units streaming
back in disorder, often without arms or equipment. No
attempt was being made to stop the rout.

The 3rd Brigade was to act vigorously, and not to wait
for the arrival of the 325th Brigade, R.F.A., which could
not be up for a little while.

At 3 p.m. the 1st Guards Brigade reported their recapture
of Gouzeaucourt, and that they were consolidating a line
just east of it, farther advance being stopped by machine-
gun and artillery fire at close range from the Quentin
Ridge.

The 3rd Guards Brigade had now been ordered to pro-
long the left of the 1st from towards Villers Plouich.
Moving in artillery formation between Havrincourt and
Gouzeaucourt Woods, it gained the prescribed line with
the 4th Grenadier Guards on the right touching the left
of the 1st Guards Brigade, whilst the 2nd Scots Guards
on the left touched with its left the right of the 59th
Division. The 1st Welsh Guards were in support, the
1st Grenadiers in reserve. The time was about 4.30, the
close of the short last day of November.

Of the Scots Guards R.F. Company was on the right
in front, " G " in the centre, and L.F. on the left in
trenches north and east of Villers Plouich, which had been
evacuated by the enemy when Gouzeaucourt fell to the

1st Guards Brigade. " F " was in reserve near Beaucamp. Patrols sent out towards La Vacquerie found parties of the 12th and 20th Divisions still holding trenches between Villers Plouich and La Vacquerie.

The casualties in the 2nd Scots Guards had not been heavy on this day—5 killed, 5 missing, and 17 wounded. The brunt of the fighting had fallen on the 1st Brigade in taking Gouzeaucourt, before the 3rd was up in line.

At 10.30 p.m. the Guards Division received orders to attack, in conjunction with the cavalry on its right, the line Gonnelieu–Gauche Wood–Villers Hill Ridge, which included Quentin Ridge. The attack next morning was to be supported by tanks, and zero hour was to be arranged with the cavalry. The hour was fixed for 6.30 a.m. on the 1st December. The 1st Guards Brigade was to lead on the right, the 3rd on the left. The boundary between the two brigades ran from the south central part of Gouzeau-court along the north-west slope of Quentin Ridge. The infantry were to be preceded by tanks, and a heavy barrage was to be put down on Twenty-two Ravine south of Gonnelieu.

The 2nd Guards Brigade was again in Divisional Reserve at Gouzeaucourt Wood.

The night of the 30th November-1st December was fine and cold and quiet. The 20th Division was to attack first during the night, and the Guards only to do so in the event of its failure, which was reported towards 3 a.m. With the attack of the 1st Guards Brigade we need not deal in detail. Gauche Wood was reached about 7 a.m. and, after repulsing two counter-attacks on its right, the brigade conquered Quentin Ridge and consolidated a line extending along it to the eastern edge of Gauche Wood.

The 2nd Scots Guards remained in reserve during the attack on Gonnelieu and the German positions on the ridge west of it. R.F. Company was sent up to keep touch with the 1st Grenadier Guards when they moved into position on the right.

It was intended that the 183rd Infantry Brigade should relieve the 2nd Scots Guards that night, and that the latter should take over the line from the 4th Grenadiers, who had suffered heavily in the attack, and now, having been reinforced by two companies of the 1st Grenadiers, were holding a line just west of Gonnelieu. The 183rd Brigade, however, was not up in time for the reliefs to take place that night, and consequently both the 4th Grenadier and the 2nd Scots Guards remained where they were during the 2nd. Only " F " Company of the latter was moved into line, the other three relieving the 4th Grenadier Guards in the night of the 2nd-3rd December. In this position R.F., " G," and L.F. were in front and " F " in support.

Next night the 3rd Guards Brigade was relieved by the 1st, the 2nd Scots Guards being relieved by the 1st Irish Guards, and returned to bivouacs near Metz-en-Coûture. On the 4th the battalion was in Gouzeaucourt, whence, at 10 p.m., it marched to Etricourt, and went by train next morning to Beaumetz les Loges, five miles south-west of Arras. A few words only are required regarding the 1st Battalion during the battle about Gouzeaucourt and Gonnelieu. The 2nd Brigade, as already mentioned, was in reserve on the 30th, the 1st Scots Guards being at Bertincourt. Vague reports of German attacks reached them in the early morning, and they were placed under orders to be ready to move at a moment's notice. About 11 a.m. orders came to move to Gouzeaucourt, and they were off within twenty minutes. At the wood they camped as best they could in the open, and remained there the whole day. In consequence of the success of the attack of the 1st Guards Brigade, it was not necessary to call in the assistance of the 1st Scots Guards, who, after remaining at Gouzeaucourt Wood during the night of the 30th November-1st December, were sent up at 5.30 p.m. on the latter day to take the place of the 3rd Coldstream Guards of the 1st Brigade in the line in front of Gouzeaucourt village. It was a bitterly cold and wet night. The position of the battalion was on a line extending from the edge of Gauche Wood on the right northwards in front of Quentin Mill and along the Quentin Ridge till it joined the right of the 3rd Grenadier Guards.

In this position the battalion remained during the 2nd

and 3rd December, in clear frosty weather. They were heavily shelled at times, but their casualties were only nine men wounded. On the 4th, on relief by the 4th South African Infantry, they marched back to Gouzeaucourt Wood. At 5.45 p.m. on the 5th they were ordered to march to billets at Fins, but on the way were told that, owing to Fins being constantly shelled, they were to go to Etricourt. They were delayed for four hours next morning at Etricourt station, owing to the line having been blown up, but finally entrained about noon and reached Beaumetz les Loges at 8 p.m. Thence they marched to Simancourt, where they were accommodated in Nissen huts. Here they remained behind the line till the close of 1917. There were no events of note during the month. On the 14th December there was special work in making the Nissen huts safer against bombs from the air, where activity on the part of the Germans was anticipated. The protection consisted of an earth and sandbag bank three and a half feet high, which, on the face of it, does not seem a very effective one. However, it was apparently recognized that protection against a direct hit from above was impossible, and that if a bomb exploded anywhere near the hut, the bank would save the lower part from being pierced by fragments, and men sleeping would be safe.

On Christmas Day the men had a good dinner, and the officers of the battalion dined together at night. The weather being snowy was seasonable. On the 26th the sergeants had their Christmas dinner and a concert. On the 30th the C.O. and Company Commanders went by bus to inspect the portion of the line to be taken over shortly.

The 2nd Battalion had reached Beaumetz les Loges at midnight of the 5th-6th December, and next morning marched to Barly, two miles west of the 1st Battalion's quarters at Simancourt. Here they remained till the 10th, when they marched into Arras, where they, as well as the 1st Welsh Guards, were quartered in the Prison. Battalion parades are said to have been impracticable, though the reason is not stated in the diary, but a certain amount of company drill and arm drill was got through, and a good deal of musketry on very good ranges. On the 13th Lieutenant R. L. Macdonald, whom we have hitherto known in the 1st Battalion, was transferred to the 2nd.

From the military point of view, the period from the 11th to the 31st December was entirely uneventful. The weather was very cold, with, on some days, as much as thirty degrees of frost; and football was played with vigour until the ground got too hard for it. The battalion's victories on the football ground were over the 2nd Seaforth Highlanders (1—0), Gordon Highlanders (2—0), 1st Irish Guards (2—0), in the Guards Division Competition.

The 2nd Battalion was still in Arras on the 31st December 1917.

CHAPTER XIV

THE EARLY MONTHS OF 1918 AND THE GERMAN
OFFENSIVE IN THE SPRING

March: German attack on 5th Army farther south—Both battalions in and out of trenches near Arras.

1918, the last year of the war, opened quietly with no presage of the great events which were to take place in March, when the Germans began their last desperate endeavour to force a decision in their favour, or of the more decisive events of the summer and autumn which ended in their total defeat. Bernhardi had written that in Germany's next war the issue would be " Weltmacht oder Niedergang." He believed no doubt in the former, but it was the latter that was to be the end.

On the 1st January the 1st Battalion Scots Guards left Simancourt after a quiet New Year's Eve, and marched to Arras, where they took over the quarters of the Welsh Guards, who, as well as the 2nd Scots Guards, had just gone out to the front. Next day the 1st Battalion relieved the 9th Black Watch in support trenches south of Fampoux and Lancer Lane. Fampoux itself is on the north bank of the Scarpe, the valley of which river hereabouts closely resembles the valleys of the Somme and the Lower Ancre. There is the same mixture of open ponds and marshes, with the stream itself forming a much less marked feature. On either side of the valley is a rolling open country, similar to that above the Ancre and the right bank of the Somme, though the general level of the country is not so high above the river as that about Albert, and the undulations are perhaps rather gentler.

The 1st Battalion was now in the undulating country on the right bank of the Scarpe, in a neighbourhood which had been the scene of much desperate fighting in the Battle of Arras in the spring of 1917. In that battle, however, the Guards Division had played no part, and the country was strange to them.

It was still freezing hard when the 1st Scots Guards took over from the 9th Black Watch. There was no difficulty in the relief, and the front was remarkably quiet at this time. On the 5th the battalion relieved the 3rd Canadians, holding front-line trenches both north and south of the Scarpe about Rœux, the next village on the north bank 2,500 yards east of Fampoux. A few trench-mortar bombs were all the disturbance on the 6th, and on the 7th it thawed rapidly all day, but froze again at night. Again there was but little enemy artillery activity, and again the frost continued, which must have been a satisfaction after the utter discomfort of the thaw.

January 9th was quiet, and that evening the battalion was relieved by the 2nd Coldstream Guards and went back by rail to Arras. Owing to a truck being derailed, it was late in reaching the town. The quietude of this tour of trench work may be gauged by the fact that one man killed was the only casualty during it. Even he is said in the diary to have been " very unluckily " killed.

The trenches had been generally comfortable, with good dug-outs. The battalion was back in the Arras Prison, which is said to have been " very comfortable," and, as the thaw began again on the 10th, it was lucky to be out of trenches. On the afternoon of the 13th Sergeant McAulay was presented by the Divisional Commander with the V.C. ribbon, which he had gained at Fontaine Notre Dame on the 27th November 1917.

When the battalion relieved the 1st Grenadier Guards in the Right Reserve Battalion sector in the night of the 16th-17th, they had to set to work reveting and cleaning up the trenches which had been damaged by the thaw. The battalion went up in place of the 3rd Grenadier Guards in right front trenches on the 21st. Things were still very quiet during this tour of front trenches, save for an occasional outbreak of trench-mortar fire. Only one man was killed during this time, and there were no cases of trench feet. On the 25th the 1st Scots Guards went back to reserve trenches, on relief by the 3rd Grenadier Guards. They were again in front from the 29th January to the end of the month.

The 2nd Battalion had a distinctly worse month of January than the 1st. On the 1st January they relieved the K.O.S.B. on the Gavrelle–Rœux line, north of the Scarpe, for a tour of duty of eighteen days, of which ten were in front line and eight in reserve. They took turns with the 1st Welsh Guards. Here the results of the thaw were most disastrous. It appeared that the battalion's predecessors had been most energetic in digging thirty-six miles of trenches on the front of 5,000 yards now occupied by the Guards Division. But the trenches had not been reveted, and consequently during the first twenty-four hours of thaw two of the main communication trenches and the whole of the front line absolutely disappeared. When, therefore, the battalion went into reserve on the 15th, the relief took eleven hours, owing to the men being completely stuck in the mud. So bad were things that, on the 16th, the front line was evacuated, save for weak sentry groups, whilst the support line on higher ground was strongly held.

The defence was now organized thus. The front or outpost line north of the Scarpe was comparatively weakly held by troops whose function was to break the first violence of an attack, retiring on the main line of resistance behind them where the great contest would be. In rear of this again was the reserve line, where the reserves would be concentrated, and on which the troops of the first and second lines would fall back only in the last resort.

On the night of the 11th-12th, when the battalion went into reserve, it was very heavily gas-shelled at 2 a.m. Practically the whole Headquarters Staff was affected by gas.

Otherwise the line was generally quiet till the night of the 18th-19th, when the tour ended in relief by the 1st Irish Guards. During it the casualties had been 1 man killed, 2 died of wounds, 5 wounded, and 20 gassed.

After eight days in Divisional Reserve at Arras, devoted to general cleaning up, inspection of arms and clothing, and various training exercises, two companies were sent to relieve the 2nd Coldstream Guards in the night of the

26th-27th. One of these was attached for work to the
1st Welsh, and one to the 1st Grenadier Guards holding
the line. The rest of the battalion remained in Arras.
In the night of the 30th-31st, the whole 2nd Battalion
relieved the 1st Welsh Guards in the right sector. Three
companies were in line and the fourth in support.

The 1st Scots Guards were in front trenches on the 1st
February, when they were relieved by the 2nd Coldstream
Guards, and returned to Arras for the usual rest and cleaning
up. They had had a quiet four days in front, save for
occasional shelling, the casualties resulting from which
were 1 man killed, 1 wounded, and 3 slightly gassed.
They were again in front, in relief of the 2nd Irish Guards,
on the 5th February. The relief was delayed by the expectation of gas shelling. Three companies were in front
line, with R.F. in reserve. From the 6th to the 9th the
weather was fine and the line quiet, the only casualty
being one man wounded, and another on the 10th, when
the battalion returned to the intermediate position at
Northumberland Avenue, on being relieved by the 1st
Coldstream Guards. Here they were busy from the 11th
to the 14th, cleaning up and repairing trenches and sal-
vaging material. On the amount of these duties performed, the battalion was congratulated by the Brigadier-
General.

They went back to Arras on the 15th, this time to the
Levis Barracks, instead of the Prison.

On the 19th the officers and sergeants attended a rather
unusual lecture by the Divisional Commander on the
expected German offensive. He pointed out that the
enemy might be expected to employ underhand means,
distributing pamphlets, sending out secret agents, and when
he did advance doing so behind a screen of civilians or
Germans disguised as such. All ranks were warned to be
on the look out for such tricks. On the 20th the battalion
relieved the 3rd Grenadier Guards in the front line, which,
though quiet at first, began to show signs of returning
activity of trench-mortars and artillery. Patrols were
sent out to examine the enemy wire and No Man's Land.
On the morning of the 21st No. 43 Post (" C " Company)

17

captured four Germans, one of whom died. The capture was important, as it showed that there had been a divisional relief of Prussian troops by the 5th Bavarian Division. When the battalion was relieved on the 25th by the 1st Coldstream Guards and sent back to Northumberland Avenue, its only casualty had been one man wounded. In the night of the 26th-27th February the 1st Coldstream Guards carried out a very successful raid, in which twelve prisoners were taken. The 1st Scots Guards were not actually engaged in this raid, but they did a good deal of the preliminary patrol and reconnaissance work for it. It is stated that the enemy *moral* was low, that some of the prisoners were crying, and that many Germans were killed owing to their being literally unable, through fright, to leave the trenches. It will be remembered that these were Bavarians who had replaced Prussians, the latter being probably removed elsewhere for the coming offensive.

The 2nd Scots Guards spent the first week of February in front line, improving trenches and having a generally quiet time, till they were relieved in the night of the 7th-8th by the 1st Grenadier Guards, and went to replace the 9th Gordon Highlanders at Gordon Camp, which they found very comfortable. Here they won the Divisional Football Cup, beating the 3rd Coldstream Guards by five goals to nothing.

On the 9th there was a farewell dinner to the 4th Grenadier Guards, who were now leaving to become a unit in the 4th Guards Brigade, part of the 31st Division. The two battalions had always been great friends, and an otherwise pleasant evening was only marred by regrets at parting. Early in February, for reasons into which we need not enter, British Infantry Brigades on the western front were reorganized on the basis of three, instead of four, battalions, as hitherto. In the case of Brigades of the Line this was generally done by the disbandment of one battalion of the New Army, and its absorption into other depleted battalions of its own regiment.

With the Guards Division a different course was taken, as all its battalions were regulars, and there were no

" service " battalions available for breaking up. From each of the existing three Guards Brigades one battalion was taken, and the three so collected were formed into the 4th Guards Brigade, which, however, was detached from the Guards Division and became a brigade of the 31st Division. In this way the 1st Guards Brigade lost the 3rd Coldstream Guards, the 2nd lost the 2nd Irish Guards, and the 3rd lost the 4th Grenadier Guards. Captain E. D. Mackenzie of the Scots Guards became Staff-Captain of the 4th Guards Brigade, but otherwise the Scots Guards history has no special interest in that of the 4th Guards Brigade.

Next day the battalion went up into line for one day, returning to Gordon Camp on the 12th, when relieved by the 1st Welsh Guards.

From the night of the 13th-14th to that of the 18th-19th, the battalion was again in support line, out night and day on fatigues, but fortunately with very good weather and no casualties. Headquarters were on the Arras–Douai railway. The battalion moved up to front line on the night of the 18th-19th, to relieve the 1st Grenadier Guards. Again the time was quiet, and much work was done in improving and reveting the trenches and putting up wire. The only casualties were in " G " Company, when a trench-mortar bomb killed one man and wounded three.

The 1st Welsh Guards came up on the night of the 22nd-23rd, and the 2nd Scots Guards went back by train to Baudimont Barracks, Arras. From the 23rd to the 26th they were in reserve, and then moved up to support, when they had five men wounded (one mortally) on the 27th.

March 1918 on the Arras front came in like a lamb but, unlike the proverbial weather, it went out like a lion from the point of view of the war ; for the great German offensive began on the 21st, though its full fury fell on the 5th Army farther south. Still it fell heavily also on the 3rd Army, commanded by General Sir Julian Byng. Here it failed to attain the great temporary success which attended its desperate attack on the right of the British line, where it touched the left of the French. The 1st Scots Guards were in the intermediate position on the 1st March, and returned to Gordon Camp on the 2nd, when Lieut.-Colonel Romer rejoined from leave.

Here resting, cleaning up, and training were the order of the day, and there were special fatigues for burying cables on the 5th. On the 4th it had been ordered that each company should have a special wiring party, of one N.C.O. and twelve men, to be exempted as far as possible from other fatigues and kept solely for wiring when in line.

On the 7th the battalion went up direct from Gordon Camp to relieve the 3rd Grenadier Guards in line. From the 8th to the 12th during this tour the German trench-mortars were active, especially against the front posts, where " C " Company had two men buried alive, and unable to be dug out in time to save them, on the 11th. There was not much shelling, but everyone was expecting an early enemy offensive. Unfulfilled prophecies had predicted it for the 13th.

When the battalion was relieved in the night of the 12th-13th by the 3rd Coldstream Guards, the relief was delayed as the light railway had been damaged by shells, and the relieving battalion had to march up. The 1st Scots Guards relieved the 3rd Grenadiers in intermediate line. German aeroplanes were active during the next few days, and two men were wounded by their bombs. The excitement over the expected offensive began to subside.

On the 17th the battalion, on relief by the 3rd Coldstream Guards, marched to Brigade Reserve at St. Laurent-Blangy, an eastern suburb of Arras. L.F. Company was left behind in the intermediate line, under the direct orders of the Brigade Commander, in case of the commencement of the offensive.

On the 19th the 1st Scots Guards went to their old quarters in the Arras Prison, where they were next day on the eve of the German attack.

The movements of the 2nd Scots Guards during the days of March up to the 20th were as follows :

On the 1st they relieved the 1st Grenadier Guards in line ; snow turned to rain on the 4th. The tour was quiet, with very few casualties till the 6th, when, on relief

by the 1st Welsh Guards, the battalion went into Arras.
A gas bombardment was just coming on as they left the
front. In the night of the 11th-12th they went to Fampoux
by buses, and into support lines. Next day, in expectation
of the German offensive, L.F. and " G " Companies
were under the tactical command of the O.C. 1st Grenadier
Guards. During the next few days the British artillery
barraged the German front line, and the enemy guns
replied, causing some casualties in L.F. Company
on the 15th.

In the night of the 15th-16th the battalion relieved the
1st Grenadier Guards in the front trenches. At this time
the German offensive was expected at any moment, and
in preparation for it the front line of trenches was abandoned
as a serious line of defence, and the companies stood to
in the second as the line of resistance. The weather was
splendid, and the line quiet till the 19th, when rain began.
That night the 2nd Scots Guards were relieved by the
2nd Duke of Wellington's Regiment of the 4th Division,
and went back to billets at Berneville, five miles south-
west of Arras, where they were cleaning up and resting on
the 20th.

The first great German offensive of 1918 opened on the
21st March on a front of between fifty and sixty miles on
the Somme and Arras fronts, against the British 5th and
3rd Armies and the right of the 1st. On this front were
arrayed seventy-three German divisions in all, against
thirty-four British infantry and three cavalry divisions,
of which at first only twenty-two infantry divisions were
in line. The 3rd Army had eight infantry divisions in
line, and the Guards and six other divisions in reserve.

Notes repeatedly mention the system of caves at Rœux,
which were the pivot of defence north of the Scarpe. The
machine-gun strong-posts organized over this strong
Ancre front during February and the first half of March
were certainly of great assistance to the 4th Division
when the attack actually was delivered.

The heaviest attack, and the most spectacular and
alarming in its success, was that delivered on the salient
held by the 5th and the right of the 3rd Army, the objective

being the driving of a wedge between the British armies and the French on their right, and the forcing of the former back on the sea and away from their allies. Farther north the force of the onslaught grew less as it approached the hinge on the right of the 1st Army, on which the Germans hoped to swing open the door.

Nevertheless, it was absolutely necessary for the enemy to press that part of the line, and to prevent succour reaching the hard-pressed British right from it. There were certain, therefore, to be heavy attacks even on the left of the 3rd and the right of the 1st Army, especially as the great salient was driven in and had to fall back into the line to the north.

The troops employed by the Germans in this part appear to have been of quality inferior to those used farther south ; for capture of prisoners in raids had indicated the introduction of at least one Bavarian brigade, and most of the prisoners captured in one raid were described as young boys of poor *moral*, or men called up from civil work from which they could ill be spared save for a great emergency.

On the 21st March the Guards were the division in reserve of the XVII Corps, of which the 15th Division and 3rd Division held the front line. On this part of the front there was no attack by the enemy on the 21st, but there was a very heavy one on the VI Corps, which held the line to the right of the XVII.

The first intimation received by the 1st Battalion Scots Guards was the commencement of a long-range bombardment of Arras, a thing which had hitherto been unknown since the Guards Division arrived on this front. The shells began falling in Arras at 5 a.m.

By 11 a.m. the division was under orders to be ready to move at two hours' notice. At 5.15 p.m. orders reached the 2nd Guards Brigade to move at once, and an hour later it was on its way to Mercatel, three and a half miles south by east of Arras, the 1st Scots Guards leading. Near Mercatel they went into a camp, the neighbourhood of which was bombed by German aeroplanes. The battalion had no cookers or officers' kits, which had gone astray and did not come up till next morning.

The 2nd Battalion Scots Guards was still left at Berneville, which lies, in a straight line, some six miles west by
north of Mercatel. They were kept in readiness to move,
and at 1.15 p.m. on the 22nd they also were ordered to
Mercatel by bus.

Meanwhile, at 6 a.m. on the 22nd, the C.O. and Company
Commanders of the 1st Scots Guards had gone to reconnoitre the third system of defence just east of Boyelles,
a couple of miles from Mercatel on the Bapaume road.
This defensive system, in the latitude of Mercatel, ran
from the west side of Wancourt, past the west of Henin-sur-
Cojeul, passed 800 yards to the east of Boiry Becquerelles,
and then turned south-eastwards round the east of St.
Leger.

It was found to consist of two lines of trenches, but only
" spit-locked." [1] It was believed that the battalion might
be ordered to occupy it.

At this time the 34th Division (VI Corps) was still
holding the second defensive system about the Henin
Ridge to the east of Boyelles.

At 1 p.m. the battalion was ordered to occupy at once
this third line from opposite Boyelles on the right (south)
to opposite Boiry-Becquerelles on the left. They were
off within ten minutes and occupied the trenches, with R.F.,
" B " and " C " Companies in front line, and L.F. in
support. They at once set to work deepening and improving the trenches. With them were mixed up many
men of different units of the 34th Division, which had
already been withdrawn from the Henin Ridge and the
second line of defences, leaving nothing now between the
Guards and the advancing, and so far victorious, enemy.
Much shelling ensued, but no infantry attack. A move
into the third-line defences had been ordered in consequence of the announcement of the presence of German
infantry on the ridge between Croisilles and Henin.

When the 3rd Guards Brigade reached Mercatel in the
afternoon of the 22nd, they remained there in the quarters
previously occupied by the 2nd Brigade, and it was only

[1] i.e. only marked out by the removal of a narrow line of turf or surface
soil.

at 1.15 p.m. on the 23rd that the 2nd Scots Guards were ordered into the line with the 1st Battalion. The 2nd came in in the night on the left of the 1st Battalion, which side-slipped to the right to make room for it, and at the same time reduced the length of its own line by keeping only R.F. and " B " Companies in front line, with L.F. and " C " in support. During the 23rd the 1st Battalion saw small parties of the enemy continually crossing their front about 500 yards off, and managed to kill a good number of them, themselves losing only two men wounded. Patrols were kept constantly out and on the move during the night of the 23rd-24th. The headquarters of the two Scots Guards Battalions were now close together. The left of the 1st Battalion touched the right of the 2nd in the line. The Guards Division now had in front line its 2nd Brigade on the right, and 3rd on the left, with the 1st in reserve. On the left of the 3rd Guards Brigade the 3rd Division carried on the line northwards ; on the right of the 2nd Guards Brigade was the 31st Division, with the 40th beyond it.

During the 24th the enemy showed no signs of a disposition to attack the Boiry–Boyelles line, but a great deal of movement was visible on the Henin Ridge.

Troops of various brigades, and even divisions, were falling back rapidly on the right of the 1st Battalion. They halted in the line for a few hours, and then continued falling back, leaving the West Yorks Battalion on the right of the 1st Scots Guards. That battalion had five casualties from shell fire during the day, and its headquarters were ordered to withdraw to a sunken road in rear, where they shared a few dug-outs with the 3rd Grenadier Guards, who were then in reserve.

The 2nd Battalion dug in busily during the 24th, and rendered their position a very strong one. The enemy had been sending out stray patrols, which were fired on and driven back. That evening the 2nd Battalion was relieved by the 1st Welsh Guards, and retired to the " Army Line," 500 yards in rear. This line ran past the eastern sides of Mercatel, Boisleux St. Marc, Hamelincourt, and thence by Mory Copse, north of the village of the same name.

On the 25th the position of the 1st Scots Guards remained
unchanged, but the 3rd Grenadier Guards now moved up
to the front on its right. That morning Lieutenant L. N.
Murphy and four other ranks were slightly wounded.
Then the enemy crossed the battalions' front to attack the
3rd Grenadier Guards. Both battalions had what the
Scots Guards diary calls " a good shoot " and the attack
on the Grenadiers was completely repulsed. Again on this
day much movement was seen amongst the enemy 800
or 900 yards away, and Lewis gunners and snipers plied
their weapons vigorously, causing, as was clearly seen,
numerous casualties to the enemy. The German shelling
increased, and one shell unfortunately landed on the dug-
out occupied by the battalion orderlies, of whom 1 was
killed and 3 and a signaller wounded. In the line
3 other ranks were killed and 11 wounded. During the
day attacks on the right of the 31st Division compelled it
also to retire, thus exposing the right flank of the 2nd
Guards Brigade. Consequently, during the night of the
25th-26th the 2nd and 3rd Guards Brigades were ordered
to fall back to the " Army Line." The withdrawal of the
1st Scots Guards was made by sections at intervals of two
minutes, and was completed without a single casualty.
Two companies left outposts 700 yards in front of the new
line, each consisting of about two sections and a Lewis-
gun team under an officer. The 2nd Scots Guards had
remained in support during the 25th, but, when the withdrawal took place at night, they stood fast and became the
front line. The withdrawal in the night was closely
followed up by the Germans, who were seen within two
hours of the occupation of the new line. " B " Company
outpost of the 1st Battalion, under Lieutenant Renwick,
saw many of the enemy at daybreak. Their Lewis gun
fired seven drums of cartridges at small parties and inflicted considerable losses on them. That morning Lieutenant C. C. Nainby-Luxmore was slightly wounded, and
Lieutenant J. C. I. McConnel was shell-shocked. The
day was quiet on the whole, though many small parties
of the enemy were seen. All four companies of the 1st
Battalion were in line, in the order from right to left,

L.F., " C," R.F., " B." Lieutenant Maclay was slightly wounded, but remained at duty. Of other ranks, 2 were killed and 8 wounded. In the ensuing night the 1st Battalion Scots Guards was relieved by the 1st Irish Guards, and sent to huts at a sugar factory 200 yards east of Boiry St. Rictude, and west of the Arras–Amiens railway.

During the day the 2nd Scots Guards, when they had become front line in consequence of the retirement of the previous night, came into line again on the left of the 1st, and the two battalions shared headquarters.

The 2nd Battalion was in touch again with the enemy by 5 a.m. on the 26th, after the withdrawal to the " Army Line." They had posts pushed out as far as Boyelles and Boiry Becquerelles, but these were forced to retire fighting before the strong advance of the Germans from Henin Ridge. Many large bodies of the enemy were seen in that direction, and the battalion diary complains that the artillery on this day failed to take advantage of many excellent targets presented to them.

The new quarters of the 1st Battalion at the sugar factory were so heavily shelled on the 27th March that it went to ground in a neighbouring trench, and even then it had 4 other ranks killed and 6 wounded.

The 2nd Battalion, too, had a bad time in the morning of the 27th from artillery. Its headquarters were blown in, but fortunately without casualties. At noon the German barrage lifted, and was followed by a rather feeble infantry attack on the front held by R.F. and " F " Companies, which was easily repulsed. Headquarters had to move back 200 yards and dig in on the railway, in consequence of what had happened in the morning.

On the 28th March the position of the 1st Scots Guards remained unchanged, except that L.F. was sent up to support the 3rd Grenadier Guards, who were attacked. Shelling was still heavy, killing 1 man and wounding 4. On this day Captain E. C. T. Warner, D.S.O., M.C., joined the battalion as second in command, but remained with the transport. In the night of the 28th-29th the 1st Battalion relieved the 3rd Grenadiers in front line. On that day perhaps the 2nd Battalion rather regretted its complaints of the day before with reference to inadequate artillery support ; for, when the Germans replied after a severe bombardment of their position by the British, their fire caused severe losses to R.F. and " F " Companies. The enemy attacked on both flanks, but apparently not the battalion itself. The attack on the right was no doubt that on the 3rd Grenadiers, to support whom L.F. Company of the 1st Battalion was sent up as stated above. Both the C.O. and Adjutant of the 2nd Battalion were so worn out by this time that they had to go down for forty-eight hours' rest, leaving Major J. A. Stirling in temporary command.

On the 29th March, in the morning, Lieutenant D. H. Brand, M.C., of the 1st Battalion, was killed, and was buried later near Battalion Headquarters. Though the day is described as " quiet," 11 men also were wounded. The enemy was seen to be busy digging in about 1,000 yards in front of the British. The 2nd Battalion also was shelled all day, and at night, being relieved by the 1st Grenadier Guards, went into support line at Boisleux au Mont, on the Amiens–Arras railway where the branch line to Cambrai turns off eastwards. On the left of the battalion the Canadians took the place of the 3rd Division.

The last two days of March were quiet for both battalions of the Scots Guards, though shelling cost the 1st a loss of 2 men killed and 11 wounded between the two days. There had been a heavy attack on the 30th on the front of the 1st Welsh and 3rd Grenadier Guards in front, as well as on the 1st Brigade on the right and the Canadians on the left of the Guards Division. All had been repulsed with very heavy losses among the enemy, who had about reached the end of their tether in this direction. The Scots Guards were not required to aid in these fights.

CHAPTER XV

German attack stabilized—Heavy fighting about Arras—Back to rest—
To the front again—U.S.A. troops attached to Foot Guards for instruction.

THE German offensive on this part of the line had been
stabilized by this time, and the British retirement had
reached its farthest point towards the west. It had
probably never been meant or attempted to make a breach
in the line here. The great enemy effort was nearer to
the junction of the British right with the French left,
but it was essential to its success that the troops of the
3rd Army should be " fixed," and prevented from sending
help to its own right and the sorely pressed 5th Army
beyond it.

On the 1st April the 1st Scots Guards were relieved at
night by the 1st Coldstream Guards. One man was
wounded during the relief.

" B " and " C " Companies proceeded to their old
quarters at the sugar factory east of Boiry St. Rictude,
whilst headquarters with R.F. and L.F. moved to
hutments at Blaireville, three miles to the north-west.

The leaving of half the battalion close up to the front
was clearly a precautionary measure in case of renewed
German attacks.

The last nine days had been very strenuous for both
battalions, which, though never suffering really heavy loss
on any single day, had been losing officers and men on
each, the total amounting to a large number.

The 1st Battalion had lost up to the 1st April :

Officers killed : Lieutenant D. H. Brand, M.C. (29th
March).

Wounded : Lieutenants L. N. Murphy (25th March),
C. C. Nainby-Luxmore (26th), J. C. I. McConnel (shell-
shock 26th), Maclay (26th).

Other ranks : killed, 13 ; wounded, 60.

The casualties of the 2nd Battalion were heavier :

Officers wounded : Lieutenants A. H. Williams (during bombardment of Arras when acting as Traffic Officer, Guards Division), W. H. Widdowson (26th March), I. S. Miller (27th), R. L. Macdonald (28th).

Other ranks are not stated separately for this period, but between the 22nd March and the 15th April there were 34 killed, 149 wounded, and 5 missing, and it may be assumed that most of these were in the period in question. The losses of the 1st Battalion in other ranks in the same period were 20 killed and 83 wounded.

Even the half of the 1st Battalion at Blaireville was not exempt from occasional German shells, which killed 1 man and wounded 6 on the 2nd April. The other two companies at the sugar factory, being close up, got more shelling. On the 3rd April they lost 2nd-Lieutenant J. W. H. Gow, and 4 other ranks wounded and 1 killed. That night the whole battalion went into front line to relieve the 3rd Grenadier Guards. Rain on the 4th made conditions in trenches very miserable, and, the C.O. being ill, Captain E. C. T. Warner, D.S.O., M.C., was in temporary command.

When it cleared up on the 5th, artillery and aerial activity increased and 5 men were wounded. On the 6th a " minenwerfer " bomb fell on a post garrisoned by R.F. Company, killing 5 men and severely wounding another. The battalion was relieved on that day by the 1st Coldstream Guards. The main roads were at this time being so heavily shelled that it was necessary to follow side roads as " B " and " C " Companies went back to Blaireville, leaving R.F. and L.F. this time to remain in the more advanced position. The two latter companies found themselves in trenches knee-deep in water, and, as it rained heavily in the night, the discomforts of the position increased.

The battalion again relieved the 3rd Grenadier Guards in line on the 9th. The 10th was quiet, but Lieutenant E. Maclay was wounded in the head by a sniper, and died next day in the Canadian Stationary Hospital No. 3.

The weather cleared up again on the 11th,[1] and on the 12th arrangements were begun for the contemplated relief of the Guards Division on the 14th-15th. Whether the relief would come off, however, seemed doubtful, as there was during the evening and night heavy shelling on spaces between the companies and Battalion Headquarters, and between the latter and Brigade Headquarters. This, with the continual breaking of telephone wires, seemed to point to systematic attempts to cut communications before a projected attack. The inference, however, seems to have been unwarranted, for there was no attack up to the 14th, when the 1st K.R.R.C. (2nd Division) came up by buses and relieved the battalion. There was some delay in the relief, owing to three buses full of men, relieving R.F. Company, temporarily going astray. The relief was safely accomplished, and the 1st Scots went by buses from Ransart to La Cauchie, well out of the line near the Arras–Doullens railway.

The 2nd Scots Guards, from the 1st to the 15th April, took turns with the other two battalions of the 3rd Guards Brigade, the 1st Grenadier and 1st Welsh Guards, in occupying the front line, support, or reserve trenches. The routine was four days for each battalion in line, followed by two in reserve at Blaireville. During the last-named periods the men had baths and a little rest. The line was generally fairly quiet, but intermittent shelling continued throughout the time. There was particularly heavy shelling from the 4th April to the 6th, the day on which the Germans far to the right began their last effort to break through at the junction of the British and French armies south of the Somme.

The 2nd Battalion was relieved twenty-four hours after the 1st, when in the night of the 15th-16th, the 2nd Battalion South Staffordshire Regiment of the 2nd Division took over from them without difficulty, and they went by

---

[1] The German offensive on the Lys opened on the 9th April, and on the 11th the 4th Guards Brigade went, as part of the 31st Division, to render distinguished service on that front. That, however, is of course a matter outside the scope of this history.

bus to Barly, four miles north of the 1st Battalion's station at La Cauchie.

They found Barly very crowded, and all ranks were far from comfortable there.

The 1st Battalion also had indifferent billets at La Cauchie, but even they were a welcome change after the hard time the battalion had recently spent in the line. After one day of complete rest, refitting, reorganization, and training went on from the 17th April.

There was still uncertainty as to the German intentions, and from the 20th April onwards one company always held itself in readiness to move at a moment's notice from 7 a.m. till ordered to stand down. The idea was that, in the event of an approaching attack, this company should go forward at once as a covering outpost for the assembly of the brigade in its defensive position. The way to the intended outpost position was carefully reconnoitred, so that there might be no chance of any delay in an emergency. Fortunately the emergency never arose.

Beyond an inter-company rifle competition on the 24th, which was won by R.F., there is nothing to record till on that day orders were received to again move into the line on the 25th, when the Guards were to relieve the 32nd Division then holding it.

The 2nd Battalion had had an equally uneventful time at Barly from the 16th to the 25th April, when it relieved the 2nd Battalion Manchester Regiment (96th Infantry Brigade) at the same time as the 1st Battalion took over from the 2nd K.O.Y.L.I.

At this time the 1st Battalion, having received a draft of 225 other ranks on the 22nd, was above strength. After providing for the standard of 25 other ranks per platoon for the line, there remained over more than 400 details to be left behind. These went to St. Amand under Captain Warner. The surplus personnel was now ordered not to be sent to the Reinforcement Battalion, but to be left separate for each unit, an arrangement which was regarded as more satisfactory by the battalion.

The Guards Division was now occupying the Bucquoy–Ayette system of trenches to the right (south-west) of its recent position about Boisleux. There had been several changes in commands during April. Early in the month Brigadier-General Lord Henry Seymour gave up command of the 3rd Guards Brigade, which he had held since the 21st March 1917. Lieut.-Colonel N. A. Orr-Ewing, of the 2nd Scots Guards, succeeded temporarily to the command, till it was taken over by Brigadier-General G. B. S. Follett. That officer had been commanding the 2nd Brigade during the absence, in consequence of gassing, of Brigadier-General Sergison-Brooke since the 23rd March. General Follett commanded the 3rd Guards Brigade till he was killed on the 27th September 1918.

The 1st Scots Guards were in reserve till the night of the 27th–28th April, when they relieved the 3rd Grenadier Guards in the line, the arrangement for this tour of service being, for each battalion, six days in the line and three in reserve. R.F. and L.F. were in front line, " B " in support, " C " in reserve, with an inter-company change in the middle of the period (30th), when the two flank companies made over the front to the others. The line was quiet and the shelling only slight.

The 2nd Guards Brigade was throughout the month of May the left brigade of the Guards Division, and the brigade system of reliefs was for each battalion in turn to spend six days in the left front sector of the brigade front, then three days in reserve about two miles in rear, then six days in the right front sector, and so on. The trenches occupied were from a point east of Ayette on the right to the outskirts of Moyenneville.

At this time the 1st Battalion was strong both in officers and other ranks, and, with a standard requirement for the line of only 3 officers and 100 other ranks per company, a complete relief every eight or nine days was possible. It ceased to be so soon when companies were raised to 150 other ranks and officer casualties had become numerous.

When in front there were nightly patrols, and a very successful one was carried out on the night of the 2nd May by part of " B " Company. It so happened that Lieutenant S. Renwick had gone to hospital that day with trench fever, and there was no officer left with " B " to command a patrol. Lieutenant B. W. Duncan, M.C., then volunteered to take out the patrol, the object of which was to get an identification of the opposite unit. The party consisted of a N.C.O. and seven men of " B " Company and two battalion snipers—Sergeant Robertson, D.C.M., and Private Dack, D.C.M.

Lieutenant Duncan divided his party into two and proceeded to encircle a point from which a Very light had been seen to go up. The post was rushed, at least seven Germans were killed, and three prisoners were taken, one of them wounded. For this exploit Lieutenant Duncan received a bar to his M.C.

On the 3rd May the 1st Battalion was relieved by the 1st Coldstream Guards, and went for its three days in Brigade Reserve, relieving the 3rd Grenadier Guards in the right front on the 6th. The reliefs continued throughout the month according to the roster given above.

About the 9th it was supposed that an attack was coming, and patrols were sent out every night to listen for sounds indicating an enemy evacuation. One night there was an unusual noise in the German lines, but it turned out to be nothing more than divisional relief.

In the morning of the 13th 2nd-Lieutenant C. A. A. Robertson, the Assistant Adjutant, was wounded by a shell as he passed through the village of Adinfer. Lieutenant H. L. Graham took over his duties.

On the night of the 17th-18th there was some fighting when Lieutenant E. R. Coats went out on patrol with seven men of the L.F. Company. When they were about 200 yards out from the front line, they were fired on by an enemy post. As they retired, three of the men were wounded and Lieutenant Coats[1] and two men were missing.

As soon as he heard of this, Lieutenant Dundas took out a corporal and two men to look for the missing. When they reached the place where Lieutenant Coats had encountered the enemy, they also were at once fired on. Lieutenant Dundas and the corporal were both wounded, and the search party had to come in unsuccessful.

[1] Afterwards recorded as killed.

18

Altogether this night cost the battalion 1 officer wounded, 1 missing, and of other ranks 6 wounded, 1 wounded and missing, and 1 missing.

Shelling was especially heavy between the 21st and 24th May, when the battalion lost 8 men killed and 12 wounded. On the 29th 2nd-Lieutenant A. Bence Trower, who had only joined the battalion a week before, was killed by a sniper. On the last day of the month the 1st Battalion was in reserve at Rabbit Wood.

For the 2nd Scots Guards the month of May was much the same as for the 1st Battalion.

Reliefs in the 3rd Brigade differed somewhat from those in the 2nd. The tours of duty were four days in front and two in reserve. Two battalions were always in front line and one in reserve. In reserve exchanges of personnel were carried out, generally about 5 officers and 120 other ranks on each occasion. The relieved men went back to details at Warlincourt, about eight miles in rear. Up till the 15th the line was held by companies of a strength of 3 officers and 100 men each, and, owing to the strength of the battalion at the time, there were nearly as many details as men in line, and much training was possible. After that date, when company strength in line was increased by 50 per cent. it was different. On the 11th Lieutenant E. S. Ambler was killed in very tragic circumstances. He had gone out on patrol and, losing his way, approached one of the posts of his own battalion from the front. As he had two orderlies in line with him, he was mistaken by the post, to whom no blame can be attached, for an enemy patrol, was fired on and killed.

The increase in the company strength on the 15th was due to apprehension of an enemy attack. The artillery activity at this time was great on both sides, the enemy paying special attention to headquarters of the battalion in reserve. Here Lieutenant M. A. J. Malcolm was wounded on the 17th when standing in an exposed trench just outside Battalion Headquarters. The night of the 19th was a disastrous one. At this time, as with the 1st Battalion, listening posts were being sent out nightly to try to detect signs of enemy concentration for attack.

The night was one of bright moonlight, in which two patrols of the 2nd Battalion were detected by the enemy and fired on with machine-guns.

In one patrol 2nd-Lieutenants Hunter-Blair and Fernihough were wounded, with three men; and one man was missing. 2nd-Lieutenant Chamberlain, commanding the other patrol, was hit in the head before he had got beyond the British wire, and died on the way to the dressing-station.

On the 21st Lieut.-Colonel N. A. Orr-Ewing, who had commanded the battalion since the 25th September 1916, was appointed to the command of the 45th Infantry Brigade, 15th Division, and made over the battalion to Major J. A. Stirling, who held it till the return home of the battalion in 1919. On the same day one man was killed and three wounded by a bomb dropped on one of the posts by an enemy aeroplane. On the 26th the front post held by R.F. was heavily fired on by trench-mortars, and then about twenty of the enemy attempted to rush it. The occupants remained quiet till the raiders were close up to the wire, when they opened drum fire with Lewis guns. The enemy were driven off, but if they had any killed or wounded, they succeeded in carrying them off, for none were found by a search party later. There was a good deal of sickness during the month, as is shown by 109 admissions to hospital during it. The epidemic of " Spanish influenza," which became much worse in June, had just begun.

Other casualties were heavy for a month in which there was no general attack on either side. They were:

Officers: killed 2, wounded 3, missing 1.
Other ranks: killed 7, wounded 64, missing 1.

Much work was done during May in deepening trenches, connecting up posts, and strengthening wire.

The 1st Battalion went, on the 3rd June, from reserve into line, in relief of the 3rd Grenadier Guards on the left front sector, R.F. Company on the right, L.F. left, " B " support, and " C " reserve.

June 4th was one of the battalion's bad days. The

Germans, since its last tour in front, had brought up a heavy trench-mortar with which, in the morning of the 4th, they began to bombard the Headquarters of the two front companies, which were together in a bank. They were apparently getting their range, for the morning bombardment did not last long and was far from accurate. By it 2nd-Lieutenant P. H. Broughton-Adderley was slightly wounded, but remained on duty.

By evening the mortar seemed to have been adjusted, and commenced a much more accurate and intense fire. Lieutenant R. E. Holmes and 1 man were killed, and Lieutenant D. R. Brodie and 11 other ranks wounded. Lieutenant B. W. Duncan then took command of L.F., and later both he and 2nd-Lieutenant G. P. D. Wallis were wounded by a shell. This trench-mortar had to be silenced, and a heavy British retaliation was successful in preventing its again making itself felt during the battalion's tour of front-line service.

In the night of the 7th-8th the 1st Battalion, on relief by the 2nd H.L.I. of the 2nd Division, went back in buses to La Cauchie, where they had been in April, and which they found had been much improved in the interval as regards billets. A good parade ground, range, and assault course, and the nature of the surrounding country, made the place a good centre for training. Mornings here were devoted to training, and afternoons to sports and games. There was a very successful Battalion Sports Meeting on the 19th, in which " B " was the most successful of the companies. On the 23rd the Brigade Sports were held, and the 1st Scots Guards ended up with an aggregate of 42 marks against 13 for the 3rd Grenadiers, and 8 for the 1st Coldstream Guards. An inter-company drill competition on the 25th between the best platoons from each company was won by L.F., " C " being 2nd, and " B " 3rd.

For several weeks past there had been a number of cases of " Spanish influenza," from which in the last week of June almost every officer and many other ranks suffered. 2nd-Lieutenant A. R. Broughton-Adderley had to go down for this reason, and Captain C. W. Hammerton on account of neurasthenia.

The 2nd Battalion was in the Ayette–Ablainzeville trenches on the 7th June, about to be relieved by the 1st Royal Berkshires that night. The relief was carried out without incident, and the battalion went by light railway from Brigade Headquarters at Monchy au Bois to Gouy, and thence by march to rest billets at Sombrin. The billets were good, but there were not the same facilities for training as those enjoyed by the 1st Battalion at La Cauchie. The adjutancy was taken over on the 11th June by Lieut. the Hon. V. A. Cochrane-Baillie, M.C. On that day the 2nd Battalion football team was once more victorious, in a match against the Lanarkshire and Ayrshire Yeomanry. After that, till the 20th, little could be done, as practically the whole battalion was being inoculated against influenza. In the Divisional Horse Show on the 22nd, the battalion won the Cooker competition, and was 2nd and 3rd in two other competitions. It had little success in the Brigade Sports on the 25th. There was a boxing competition on the 28th and 29th.

On the 30th the Battalion Sports were held with success, and H.R.H. the Duke of Connaught witnessed some of the events.

The training during the month had been principally in musketry and open warfare, besides drill and physical exercises. The battalion was not above taking hints, as is shown by the statement that a more practical system of training scouts, observers, and patrols was begun, as a result of discussions with the principal raiding officer of the 2nd Canadian Division.

It was not till the 6th July that the Guards Division returned to the front, after its month of rest in the back areas. At 8.45 p.m. the 1st Scots Guards started from La Cauchie by train, and relieved the 2nd K.O.Y.L.I. as support battalion in the right sub-sector of the divisional front, which was the same as that occupied in April. The 2nd Guards Brigade was on the right, 1st in the centre, and 3rd on the left.

Battalion details were at Bailleulmont with the transport, but moved later to camp near La Cauchie. Nothing of note happened here, except the wounding of two men on the 8th. Work went on at improving trenches. The battalion was back again in reserve in the old German line from the 10th to the 14th, on which night it relieved the 1st Coldstream Guards in front line, with R.F. as outpost company, " B " and L.F. as right and left supports, and " C " in reserve. During this tour, which lasted till the night of the 18th-19th, the only casualties from the occasional shelling were one man killed and three wounded on the 16th.

It had now been decided to work the reliefs in terms of six instead of four days, so the battalion went into support for six days from the 19th. There was a bad gas shelling on the 22nd, which resulted in 27 men having to be evacuated suffering from it. Company strength in front was at this time 140 other ranks, and details were only just sufficient to supply reinforcements.

Nothing of note happened during the rest of July. The month was equally uneventful for the 2nd Battalion, which was in reserve at Blaireville on the 6th, when the 8rd Guards Brigade went into line. They had moved there most of the way by rail. Details were at Berles au Bois. On the 9th Captain H. C. E. Ross, D.S.O., joined from Italy, as second in command to Lieut.-Colonel Stirling. A football match on the 16th, against the 1st Canadian M.R., their next-door neighbours in the line, was won by the battalion.

On the 24th about 100 Americans were attached to the battalion, and these were followed on the 28th by six platoons of the 3rd Battalion, 320th Regiment, 80th American Division, sent for instruction. This necessitated considerable changes in the disposition of the battalion. The arrangement decided on was for each American platoon in turn to be given a sector of the front line. A senior sergeant of the Scots Guards was attached as adviser to each platoon. The battalion company commander in the sector took command, and the second in command of the American battalion remained at Battalion Headquarters. Mixed patrols of Americans and Scots Guards were sent out, and British officers and N.C.O.s went over the whole front and support lines with American parties.

Special attention was paid to the training of the American guides and runners. The American Transport Officers and a proportion of the " Mess Sergeants " (*Anglice* Company Quartermaster Sergeants) were attached to the battalion transport with three American limbers. The arrangements for serving the line with rations were explained to them, and practical hints were given.

The officers were from all over the U.S.A. The C.O., a Baltimore lawyer, is described by Lieut.-Colonel J. A. Stirling as " a very nice chap." The men were all from a Pennsylvania mining district, and included many nationalities and a babel of tongues. Their principal scout was an enormous Russian. They were all tremendously keen, and discipline seemed good. But supply was very indifferent. The Q.M.G.'s supply department was hopeless, though all expected efficiency from that country of organization.

The supply was so badly organized that, on certainly one occasion, troops sent up into the line for purpose of attack received no food for over two days and had to be brought out again to be fed.

On the night of the 80th-31st the battalion was relieved by the 1st Grenadier Guards, with whom the attached Americans were left in the line to continue their instruction. The casualties of the month were, in other ranks only, 5 killed and 31 wounded. Three American sergeants were gassed, the same being the case with some of the battalion's wounded. This was probably in the gas shelling of the 22nd by which the 1st Battalion suffered.

On the 1st August the 1st Battalion, who had had Americans of the 3rd/320th Regiment attached to them as the 2nd had, received a new lot from the 2nd Battalion of the 320th. The battalion diary does not give details of the system of training the Americans, but it no doubt did not differ materially from the other battalion's methods.

During the night of the 1st-2nd August, a patrol under 2nd-Lieutenant Hope, in conjunction with a brigade patrol under Captain Spencer Churchill, discovered some Germans in Observation trench. They made off at once, and the patrols were unable to catch any of them for purposes of identification. In consequence of this, a standing patrol, under Lieutenant G. V. Thomson, was sent out just before dawn on the 3rd August to Observation trench, with orders to wait there all day in the hope of catching some of the Germans if they returned. The hope was disappointed, as none were seen.

During the 3rd a British aeroplane dropped a bomb by mistake on a sunken road occupied by British troops. One man of the 1st Scots Guards was killed by it, and six were wounded, as well as one American and one man of the 1st Irish Guards.

That night the enemy tried to raid two posts held by Americans under the command of Sergeants Nicol and Dougal of the Scots Guards. The attempt was a complete failure, the raiders being driven off by fire before they reached the posts, the garrisons of which suffered no loss. They left by the British wire a rifle, a N.C.O.'s cap, and some bombs. The enemy expressed his disgust at the failure by a specially heavy bombardment next day, which wounded two men. When the battalion was in reserve on the 15th, it was relieved by the 2nd/320th American Regiment, and marched back to comfortable billets at Bavincourt. There were unusual luxuries here; the men had a good cinema and recreation rooms, and the officers the best officers' club they had yet come across. From the 18th to the 20th August preparations were being made for the British final offensive, which had already begun farther south. The attack was practised at La Bazèque, and especially the advance in conjunction with tanks. All necessary stores and equipment having been drawn, the battalion moved in buses as far as midway, where it stopped for tea and rum.

Here the 2nd Battalion must be brought up to the same point in its history, on the eve of the advance to the Battle of the Hundred Days and the final collapse of the Central Powers.

On August 1st the 2nd Battalion went back from the line into reserve at Blaireville, where, on the 2nd, the Divisional Commander addressed the officers on the

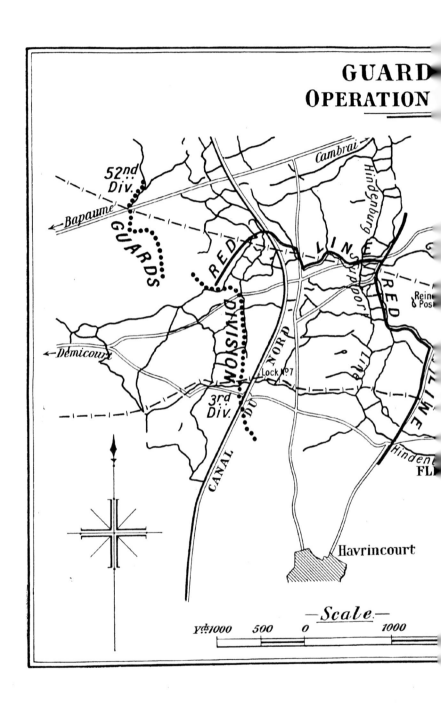

GUARD
OPERATION

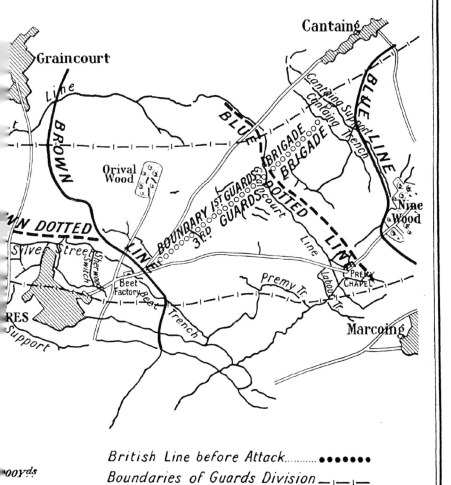

Anneux

Cantaing

Graincourt

BLUE LINE

Cantaing Support Tr.

Cantaing Trench

BROWN

Line

Orival Wood

BRIGADE

1ST GUARDS

BOUNDARY

3ᴿᴰ GUARDS

BRIGADE

BLUE DOTTED LINE

Nine Wood

ᴺ DOTTED LINE

Silver Street

Sherwood Switch

scourt Line

Labour Tr.

PREMY CHAPEL

Beet Factory

Beet Trench

Premy Tr.

RES

Support

Marcoing

British Line before Attack .... ●●●●●●●

Boundaries of Guards Division ─ ┆ ─ ┆ ─

ₒₒYᵈˢ

subject of trench discipline and antiquated methods of handling men.

The six days in reserve were made as easy as possible, and there were none but necessary and ordinary fatigues. When the battalion moved up into support in front of Blaireville on the 5th, the strong point near the station was found to be occupied by Americans, and L.F. had to go into the Blaireville caves instead.

Large search parties for salvage and solder were sent out here. As the 3rd/320th Americans relieved the Welsh Guards in front line, the 2nd Scots Guards had ten days at Blaireville, doing a great deal of musketry training, and it was not till the night of the 15th-16th that the battalion relieved the Americans in front line near Boisleux au Mont. Next night a raiding party went out to the enemy trenches under 2nd-Lieutenant E. M. M. Balfour and 2nd-Lieutenant R. A. Brand.

This raid had been practised for ten days by a picked party, armed with bayonets, trench knives, and with blackened faces; all up-to-date with the modern " frightfulness.

Their objective was the German line south of the railway embankment near Boyelles station. They were completely successful, capturing 1 wounded man, killing 2 more of the enemy, and wounding 1. Amongst much useful information obtained, it was ascertained that the railway formed an inter-regimental boundary. The party had no casualties.

Another raid at the same time, on Marc trench, was not so successful. The enemy here was on the alert, and the party had to retire just as the last strand of wire was being cut. In the night of the 19th-20th the battalion, being relieved by the 1st Grenadier Guards, went into support. There was no reserve battalion in the 3rd Brigade at this juncture, as the 1st Welsh Guards had been temporarily moved to support of the 1st Guards Brigade. The next night the Welsh Guards returned and relieved the 2nd Scots Guards, who went into reserve. By that time the attack had begun on the right.

CHAPTER XVI

THE COMMENCEMENT OF THE FINAL ADVANCE

Guards Division advances to close to Nord Canal on the Bapaume–Cambrai road.

THE final British offensive, which was destined to come to an end only with the signature of the Armistice on the 11th November 1918, began on the 8th August with the advance of Sir H. Rawlinson's 4th Army south of the Somme east of Amiens. It was assisted by attacks north of the river, and by the close of the 12th August vast progress had been made in freeing Amiens from the menace and the liability to bombardment, from which it had suffered ever since the great German offensive of March and April 1918 had been stabilized within nine miles of the city. The enemy's front had been forced back twelve miles, and he had lost in prisoners alone 22,000 men, besides more than 400 guns.

By this date German reinforcements had been gathered, and the resistance was growing more serious. It was time to strike a blow elsewhere, and Sir Douglas Haig fixed upon the 3rd Army as the next to move forward towards Bapaume, and turn the old Somme defences from the north. The main attack by the 3rd Army and the left of the 4th was fixed for the 23rd August, but two days before the great operation commenced it was desirable to gain as a starting point the line of the railway from Albert to Arras north of the Ancre. That railway was known to be strongly held by the enemy, and after the end of the German offensive of March it had remained in his hands from a point a couple of miles south of Boisleux au Mont right down to Albert.

The village of Moyenneville lay just west of the railway line, which passed between that village and Hamelincourt. The task of capturing Moyenneville and reaching the railway on the 21st August was assigned to the 2nd Guards Brigade, which owed to this its removal from the front line on the 16th August, in order to give it time to rest and prepare for the coming operations. Of the reason for its withdrawal, the brigade generally was of course not informed ; indeed, in the interests of secrecy it was encouraged to believe in the approach of a German and not a British offensive.

The 2nd Guards Brigade was to attack on the 21st August on the right of the division, its own right touching the left of the 99th Brigade, 2nd Division. Of the three battalions of the 2nd Guards Brigade, the 1st Scots Guards were on the right, the Coldstream Guards on the left, and the 3rd Grenadier Guards in reserve.

At 12.30 a.m. on the 21st the 1st Scots Guards moved up to their assembly positions,which were north-east of Ayette. The final objective of the 2nd Guards Brigade was the enemy positions in Moyenneville and to the south-east of that village, and the line of the railway north and south of it. The boundary between the left of the Scots Guards and the right of the 1st Coldstream Guards ran a little south of east past the south-west corner of Moyenneville. The capture of the village itself, therefore, fell to the Coldstream Guards, whilst the first objective of the Scots Guards was Moyblain trench running south by west from the west side of Moyenneville. The boundary between the Scots Guards and the 99th Brigade on their right ran parallel to the battalion's northern boundary, at a distance of about 1,000 yards, and started from the northern houses of Ayette.

The Scots Guards had R.F. (right) and " B " (left) Companies in front line, with " C " and L.F. in support, whilst the Coldstream Guards had three companies in front and one in support. The two leading Scots Guards companies were about 300 yards in front of the then existing outpost line, and two strong patrols were out as covering parties.

Companies were all in their positions by 3.45 a.m., more than an hour before zero, which was fixed for 4.55.

There was only one casualty during the assembly, though it was hampered by enemy gas shelling, which necessitated the constant wearing of gas masks.

Eight tanks had been assigned to precede the advance of the Scots Guards, and it had been arranged that each leading company should have three of them in front and one in reserve. As a matter of fact, only one tank turned up in time to precede R.F. Company.

At 4.55 the companies advanced in diamond formation, in a dense mist, which made it difficult to maintain direction.

The barrage moved forward from the first objective at 5.20 a.m. to the second, which was a line running south by west from Moyenneville, about 900 yards beyond Moyblain trench. On reaching the second objective the Scots Guards were to stop and consolidate the position, and also take over from the 1st Coldstream Guards the Moyenneville trench round the south-west corner of the village. The reserve battalion (3rd Grenadiers) was to pass through them to the third objective, a line parallel to the second and nearly a mile east of it.

Of the two leading companies, " B " on the left went straight through to the second objective without a check, but R.F. encountered somewhat stronger resistance, mainly from machine-gun nests, some of which were troublesome. However, all these were surrounded and captured, their crews being either taken prisoners or killed. There was, too, fairly heavy enemy shelling, which, however, caused few casualties. There was some intermixture of companies owing to the mist, but they were sorted out by good leadership, and the whole battalion was on the second objective up to time, and was busy consolidating when the 3rd Grenadier Guards passed through shortly afterwards to the third objective, the railway, which also was taken by the reserve battalion, though they had more difficulties and lost more heavily than the 1st Scots Guards. That evening the railway was held from opposite Moyenneville southwards to the left of the 3rd Division. Besides killing a number of Germans, the battalion on this day took over 100 prisoners, about 70 machine-guns, and other material.

During the day the consolidation of the second objective was completed, and the 1st Scots Guards remained there through the following night and the day of the 22nd.

The casualties in the fighting of the day were not very heavy :

Officers : wounded 2.
Other ranks : killed 5, wounded 43, missing 2.

The success of the day is attributed in the battalion diary to (*a*) skilful leadership by officers and N.C.O.s under exceptional difficulties. (*b*) The gallantry and determination of all ranks.

During the night of the 21st-22nd the 1st Scots Guards remained where they were, but some advance was made by the other two battalions of the 2nd Brigade. The 1st Coldstream Guards pushed forward outposts about 500 yards towards the western outskirts of Hamelincourt, whilst the 3rd Grenadiers also advanced posts east of Hamel Work.

The 1st Guards Brigade on the left of the 2nd had patrols of the 1st Irish Guards in Hamel Switch trench, where it ran north of Hamelincourt. A German counter-attack in the early morning of the 22nd was driven off without much difficulty.

At 5 p.m. on the 22nd the 1st Scots Guards received verbal orders (confirmed in writing later) for the continuation of the attack on the 23rd. The battalion was to capture Hamelincourt and the enemy defences of Hamel Switch to the east and north-east of the village. They were to form a defensive flank from the right in Hamel Switch, facing south-east and extending past the south of Hamelincourt to connect with the left of the 3rd Grenadier Guards about 500 yards south of the village. On the left of the 1st Scots Guards the 56th Division would attack and join up with their left north-east of Hamelincourt. The total front of the battalion would be about 2,000 yards.

The assembly posts were, for L.F. Company on the left in front, from a sunken road crossing the railway north-east of Hamelincourt on the left to the Cojeul river on the right. " C " to be right front company south-west of the village, " B " to support L.F., and R.F. in close support of " C." Companies to move off in diamond formation in rear of their reserve tanks, with three platoons in front and one in support. L.F. was to go straight through to its final objective, leaving " B " 100 yards in rear to clear up any posts left in Hamelincourt and then to consolidate the trench west of the village. " C " Company, like L.F., would pass south of Hamelincourt straight to its objective in Hamel Switch. Of R.F. two platoons would follow " C," pass through the 3rd Grenadier Guards about Hamel Work, and form the defensive flank between the right of " C " and the left of the 3rd Grenadiers about Hamel Work. The other two platoons to remain near their assembly point in reserve, ready to act on the right if required.

Eight tanks were allotted to the battalion, of which three were to proceed each leading company, and one to be in reserve with it.

At 1.30 a.m. on the 23rd August the companies began moving to assembly positions. There was some gas shelling, which caused a few casualties. At 2.30 a.m. the enemy put down a heavy gas-shell barrage on the valley east of Moyenneville. Assembly positions were reached by 4 a.m. Each leading company was formed with three platoons in front and one in support, and the whole advanced in diamond formation.

At that hour the 3rd Grenadier Guards attacked, drawing down a heavy barrage on the railway, which lasted for two hours and caused many casualties in the Scots Guards.

By zero hour (4.55 a.m. for the Scots Guards) only three of the eight tanks had arrived, and they were all with L.F. Company, which duly started its attack, followed into the village by two platoons of " B." The attack encountered heavy machine-gun fire, which it is complained the tanks gave but little help in overcoming. L.F. and the two platoons of " B," however, advanced, and, by the skilful use of ground and covering fire, succeeded in clearing the village of machine-gun nests. L.F. pushed on beyond and reached its final objective by 7.15 a.m., accompanied by only one tank. In the village many machine-guns were taken, and many Germans were killed. " B," in clearing up, captured three more machine-guns in Hamelincourt. Meanwhile, " C " and R.F. Companies on the right had waited for their tanks, of which at last only one arrived at 6 a.m. With this they then advanced and reached their final objective without serious resistance from the enemy. This was no doubt largely due to the capture of the village on their left. In connexion with this delayed advance, Sir V. Mackenzie, in a subsequent report, suggested the necessity, in future attacks, of laying down clearly what was to be done if, as had already happened more than once, tanks were late. In such circumstances it was difficult for infantry to know whether to wait for the tanks or implicitly to obey the order fixing the hour of advance. The case became specially difficult where, as at Hamelincourt, only one part of a long line had received its tanks. On this occasion the delay was clearly justified in the case of " C " and R.F.; for the operation order No. 212 said : " there will be no synchronization, as the infantry have to follow the tanks."

By 8 a.m. the Scots Guards had gained the whole of their objectives, which they started consolidating. A heavy barrage on the railway and Hamelincourt did not seriously interfere with this, though it caused some casualties in L.F. When completed, the battalion was in touch with the 3rd Grenadiers on its right and the 56th Division on its left. About 11 a.m. the 1st Coldstream Guards passed through the right of the 1st Scots Guards, moving eastwards towards St. Leger, and reaching a line west of that village, with their right 500 yards south-west of Judas Farm, a further advance of about 2,000 yards beyond the 3,000 already gained by the 1st Scots Guards.

At 2 p.m. " B," then west of Hamelincourt, was ordered to move to Judas Farm, where the right of the Coldstream Guards then was. Thence it was to form a line facing south and running back to Hamel Switch, a little west of where it is crossed by the Arras–Bapaume road.

At the same time R.F. was ordered, from its position south of Hamelincourt, to occupy Hamel Switch from the right of " B " Co. southwards to the Sensée river. Battalion Headquarters were placed at 3.30 p.m. at Hamel Work, south-west of the village. Meanwhile, the 1st Grenadier

Guards were reported to be attacking Jewel trench and Mory Switch, with orders to get into touch with R.F. at the Sensée river. They captured Mory trench, but there was still a gap between their left and R.F. when that company and " B " were in their prescribed positions at 6.30 p.m. " C " Co. and R.F. remained in their positions in Hamel Switch, 500 yards east of Hamelincourt. These positions remained practically unchanged till 10 p.m., when the 1st Welsh Guards of the 3rd Brigade began to arrive to relieve the 1st Scots Guards. The relief was carried through without difficulty, and the battalion went back to Ayette and Douchy in the early hours of August 24th. During the operations of the last three days the battalion had advanced about three miles, and had captured Hamelincourt and the trenches east of it. Besides killing many Germans, it had taken about 400 prisoners, over 200 machine-guns, and four heavy trench-mortars. In the three days the losses of the battalion were :

Officers : wounded (none killed), 6—of whom only 5 are recorded : Lieutenant Boyd, Lieutenant T. B. Trappes-Lomax, Lieutenant G. V. Thomson ; 2nd-Lieutenant M. Dalison and 2nd-Lieutenant W. H. Stewart.

Other ranks : killed 25, wounded 125, gassed 61, missing 3.

When we last parted from the 2nd Scots Guards they were in reserve at Blaireville, where they were relieved on the 21st August by a battalion of the 56th Division and moved to reserve trenches south of Ransart, which brought them into the area of the next division. They took no part in the attack on Moyenneville on the 21st, and all they knew at the time was that the 3rd Guards Brigade would sooner or later be brought up to carry on the advance which had been so well begun by the 2nd.

It was 10 a.m. on the 23rd when an urgent order was received for the battalion to move to a concentration point east of Ayette. Starting an hour and a half later, the battalion passed through Adinfer Wood and Douchy lez Ayette to the position indicated. Here they remained till 8 p.m., when orders were received to relieve the 3rd Grenadier Guards of the 2nd Brigade in support. During the night they took over positions in the embankment of the railway which branches off from the Boisleux–Cambrai line to run southwards to Bapaume. They were also in Hamerville trench, running south-east from Hamel Work.

The operation orders for the next day required the 3rd Guards Brigade to attack with all three battalions in line on a front of about 3,000 yards.

The 1st Grenadier Guards were to be on the right, the 2nd Scots Guards in the centre, and 1st Welsh Guards on the left. The village of St. Leger was still in the enemy's hands. The front attained by the 2nd Guards Brigade started on the left from the junction with the right of the 56th Division north of Judas Farm, past which it ran south through that farm to the junction of Judas trench and Mory Switch, which latter it then followed to a point north-west of Mory Copse. St. Leger had got to be taken, and it was considered advisable not to attack it frontally, but, by encircling it on the north and south, to compel its evacuation. The attack was to be carried out in a series of bounds by the 1st Welsh Guards on the north and the 2nd Scots Guards on the south. Four stages were laid down for the Scots Guards, of which the first ended at the St. Leger Reserve and Banks Reserve trenches, well to the east of the village. As this first stage even was not completed on the 24th, it is unnecessary to describe those beyond it. On the right of the Scots Guards, the 1st Grenadiers took up the task of capturing the southern portion of Banks trench and going on to Banks Reserve. In the positions in which they relieved the 3rd Grenadiers, the 2nd Scots Guards were behind the front of the battalions on their right, in which direction the attack was to start, and they, therefore, had to move up to that line before zero hour, which was fixed for 7 a.m. on the 25th. When the companies had moved up, R.F. was on the right in the southern portion of Judas trench to its junction with Mory Switch. L.F. was in close support of R.F.; "G" in support about Jewel trench, and "F" in reserve between the light railway and the Boyelles–Ervillers road.

19

Operation orders were fully explained to company commanders, especially as to direction and frontage, but the lines of approach and forming up positions were largely left to their discretion. Colonel Stirling, who himself wrote the narrative of operations, thinks that this resulted in the avoidance of preventable casualties, since the Germans shelled, at intervals between 4 a.m. and 7 a.m. likely forming up places which the companies, unrestricted by hard-and-fast orders, were able to avoid. He gives as an instance both sides of the Ervillers–Hamelincourt road, which came under heavy fire, and were consequently avoided as forming-up places when this was observed.

About 8.50 a.m. R.F. Company reported that it was in position touching the left of the Grenadiers. The advance headquarters of Grenadier and Scots Guards were together behind the junction of Mory Switch and Judas trenches. The C.O. of the Grenadiers was already, before zero, anxious for his right flank, as he understood the 2nd Division did not intend moving forward beyond Mory village. German machine-guns were in great strength in the valley running north-east and south-west in the line Mory Copse–Banks Copse, and would threaten the Grenadiers' right as they exposed it by advancing without a corresponding advance of the 2nd Division. Colonel Stirling thereupon ordered his support company (L.F. under Lieutenant P. P. Gilpin, M.C.) to keep in close touch with the Grenadiers, so as to be able to reinforce them if they were over-extended, owing to the exposure of their right.

At zero and soon after both British and German artillery were barraging the valley of the Sensée, in which St Leger lies, mostly on the south bank of the stream. Later the Germans turned their guns on to the plateau on the right bank about Hally Avenue and the sunken road running into St. Leger from the south (Crucifix Road).

The advance progressed well at first, and by 7.45 R.F. Company was east of Crucifix Copse. Over 100 prisoners had been sent in already. In this position R.F. had been brought to a standstill by machine-gun fire in front from Banks trench, and on their left front from St. Leger Wood on the east side of the village.

On the right of the Scots Guards the 1st Grenadiers were also now held up in their advance, by Hally Avenue, by intense machine-gun fire from their right front.

The enemy were in great strength in the bush and scrub on the east and south-east of St. Leger.

Colonel Stirling, therefore, ordered " G " Company to work through the southern part of the village, to try to get in touch with the Welsh Guards of the northern attack, and to reach a point some 700 yards east of the farther houses of St. Leger, which would turn the whole line of the German defences in his front. The British Field Artillery was following up splendidly, but at this time Colonel Stirling was unable to get into communication with its Forward Observation Officers. During the rest of the morning the three leading companies of the Scots Guards (R.F., " F," and " G ") were striving to work round the German positions, crawling where the nature of the ground permitted, and compelling the enemy to maintain a continuous fire from the machine-guns which constituted the greater part of their defence. Indeed, it was reported that there appeared to be no German infantry left on the ground except machine-gunners.

Many of these machine-guns were rushed, or their crews gradually shot down, though with heavy losses to the attackers. The casualties were specially severe amongst the hedges to the south-east of the village.

It was about noon when Major Bailey, commanding the 1st Grenadier Guards, was wounded, and command of his battalion was taken over by Colonel Stirling of the 2nd Scots Guards, who held it till he was relieved in the evening by the arrival of Lieut.-Colonel Lord Gort.

It will be remembered that Colonel Stirling had already sent Lieutenant Gilpin with L.F. of the Scots Guards to be ready to support the Grenadiers if the threat to their right flank should cause them to be extended beyond their strength. Two platoons of that company were now sent to support the struggle in Hally Avenue, still 500 yards or more short of Banks trench.

The reserve platoons of the Grenadiers had to be taken back to Iscariot Work, on the west side of Mory Switch, as in their more forward position they had found themselves in the zone of the British artillery fire.

During the whole of the afternoon progress was barred by the storm of machine-gun fire which at once burst out upon the slightest attempt to advance east from Hally Avenue or Mory Switch south of its junction with the Avenue. The fire came from Mory Copse, Camouflage Copse, Hally Copse, and Banks Copse. That night, after inter-company reliefs, the 2nd Scots Guards stood thus : " F " and " G " Companies were along and a little to the east of the sunken road about Crucifix Copse, with a post in the southern part of St. Leger.

The support company was dug in north of Hally Avenue, and the reserve company in Mory Switch and the bank of the road from Ervillers to St. Leger.

No tanks had accompanied the attacks of the 24th, but in the evening a section came up to assist in the renewed attack next day. Their officers did some reconnaissance of the ground before dark, and it was decided that three tanks were to act with the 1st Grenadiers eastwards from north of Mory Copse. Two more were to move towards Hally Copse, whence they would work east to Banks Copse, clearing the trenches beyond the south of St. Leger Reserve and the north of Banks trench. Two more tanks were to pass through the south of St. Leger and clear St. Leger Wood, so as to enable the Welsh Guards to get forward to beyond St. Leger Reserve. It was still dark at 4.30 on the 25th, and half an hour later a ground mist like that of the day before obscured the view.

Of the tanks assigned to the northern and central parts of the attack, the Scots Guards saw only one, which appeared to have mistaken them for the enemy. Another had apparently cleared the Germans out of Hally Copse.

Again the battalion was unable to establish itself in Banks trench, though there was hand-to-hand fighting in the scrub and the hedges south-east of St. Leger, where it had been so heavy on the 24th. It appears clear that the Germans had brought back other infantry to back up their machine-guns, and a counter-attack was attempted about 9 a.m. towards the sunken road south of Crucifix Copse. The morning mist had now lifted, and the Germans encountered such a fire of artillery, rifles, and Lewis guns that their attack melted away before it could get home.

In the afternoon at least a regiment of German infantry was reported to be crossing the British front from left to right towards the south-west. It appeared that they were about to make a counter-attack, about 4 p.m., towards Mory Copse, on the junction of the Guards with the 62nd Division, which had now replaced the 2nd on the right. The attack was met by such a storm of fire from every gun, rifle, and machine-gun available that it collapsed. During this affair L.F. of the Scots Guards pushed a platoon into Hally Copse, with a post in advance of it in gun-pits south-east of the copse. At dusk a German post was rushed and occupied about the bend in the sunken road, 400 yards north-east of Hally Copse. A line of posts was then established running thence to Crucifix Copse, and then curving eastwards to the left of the Welsh Guards on the railway north of St. Leger Wood. During the night the 2nd Scots Guards were relieved by three companies of the 2nd Grenadier Guards (1st Brigade), and marched back to the old British line west of Moyenneville. The casualties of the battalion in these operations of the 24th-25th were :

Officers killed : 2nd-Lieutenant E. M. M. Balfour, M.C.
Wounded : Lieutenant W. A. A. Leslie, M.C. ; 2nd-Lieutenant E. R. Newbigging.
Other ranks : 16 killed, 94 wounded.

These losses had not been compensated for by any marked success, and the breaking of the formidable barrier east and south of St. Leger was still a problem for the succeeding days. Its solution fell to the lot of the 1st Guards Brigade, and in it neither battalion of the Scots Guards was engaged. A heavy day's fighting on the 27th August again failed to dislodge the Germans from their strong position east and south of St. Leger, but on the 28th they were beginning to fall back, and when the 1st Guards Brigade was relieved that night by the 3rd Division, the British front was about Croisilles and nearly up to Vraucourt.

When the 1st Battalion got back to the reserve position near Ransart, in the afternoon of the 24th August, it had a couple of days clearing up there, and on the 27th moved to Hameau Switch, north of Adinfer, where the German prisoners were useful in making comfortable quarters for them. The battalion was still there on the 1st September, training and awaiting orders to move forward again. These sent it forward to east of Hamelincourt in the morning, and on in the afternoon to l'Homme Mort in Banks trench, a point which had only been reached by the British line on the evening of the 27th August. By the 2nd September the 3rd Division was on an irregular line running generally from north-east to south-west from a point north of Lagnicourt, which village was still in enemy hands. So irregular was the line, and so ill-suited by its irregularities for a simultaneous advance, that it had to be straightened out before the attack, even at the expense of some withdrawal in parts.

When the 1st Scots Guards reached l'Homme Mort, at 7.30 p.m. on the 2nd September, they received orders that the 2nd Guards Brigade was to take Lagnicourt next morning. The battalion was to be on the left, with the 3rd Grenadier Guards on its right and the 1st Coldstream Guards in reserve. The 1st Scots Guards started at 1 a.m. for its assembly positions, which were behind the light railway running along the depression just north of Vraucourt and south of Noreuil. It was disposed with R.F. on the right, " B " Company on the left, with " C " supporting R.F., and L.F. in reserve. Later, L.F. moved up to support " B." On the left of the 1st Scots Guards were the 1st Welsh Guards of the 3rd Guards Brigade, with the 2nd Scots Guards beyond them, and on the right the 3rd Grenadier Guards ; beyond them was the 99th Brigade of the 2nd Division.

Zero hour was 5.20 a.m. on the 3rd September, and a quarter of an hour before that the battalion had crossed the light railway and moved up close to the line on which the barrage was to open. The advance met with only slight resistance, a fact which gave rise to some suspicion as to whether it might not be an indication of a German trap. However, there was none, and all that the quiet meant was that the enemy intended to make his real resistance in the famous Hindenburg Line, which had been broken through in the Battle of Cambrai, but which, with practically all the gains of the Battle of the Somme in 1916, had been again lost in the great German offensive of March-April 1918. By 7 a.m. on the 3rd September the 1st Scots Guards were already on their objective and busy consolidating it. Presently they were ordered to feel forward as far as the old British line, which had marked the front from the last month of 1917 till it was driven in on the 21st March. This line was reached without difficulty by the companies, in the same order as before and preceded by strong patrols. Battalion Headquarters had moved up to Lagnicourt, and then on to a position about a mile north-west of Louverval. The battalion had advanced five miles in the day, capturing 35 prisoners, 4 field-guns, some machine-guns, and much miscellaneous material. Though the resistance is said to have been slight, the battalion had not escaped unscathed. Lieutenant H. G. B. Drummond, M.C., was killed, and of other ranks there were 5 killed, 27 wounded, and 1 missing.

In this position the battalion remained till the night of the 5th-6th.

Meanwhile, the 2nd Battalion, with the 3rd Guards Brigade, had also been engaged on the 3rd September, the 1st Guards Brigade being in reserve on that day. The 2nd Battalion, practising attacks at Ransart on the 1st September, had been dispatched at 8 a.m. on the 2nd to the 2nd Brigade concentration area south of Croisilles, passing by Douchy, Ayette, and Moyenneville. At 3 a.m. on the 3rd came orders for the battalion to pass through the Northumberland Fusiliers of the 3rd Division, who were still in front line north of Noreuil. Thence they were to attack due east. The 2nd Battalion Scots Guards was the left front battalion of the 3rd Guards Brigade. On its left was the 52nd Division, on its right the 1st Welsh Guards of its own brigade, beyond which were the 1st

Scots Guards and the rest of the 2nd Guards Brigade. The third battalion of the 3rd Guards Brigade, the 1st Grenadiers, was in reserve.

The attack met, at first, with even less resistance than that of the 1st Battalion ; for the enemy had fallen back, and only a few of his stragglers were picked up as prisoners. That he was becoming demoralized was shown by the material gathered up by the battalion, which included 1 8-inch howitzer, 3 4·1-inch high-velocity guns, 7 field-guns, and some machine-guns.

The battalion was only about 3,000 yards short of the Canal du Nord, east of Mœuvres, when the Germans began to show signs of making a stand. Here the machine-gun fire became heavy and a line was consolidated. " F " and L.F. Companies, which had led the early advance, were now relieved in front by the other two. Here Lieutenant P. R. Borrett was wounded, and here the battalion stopped for the night.

The advance had, so far, been parallel to the Hindenburg Line, which, hereabouts, ran from west to east till it turned about 1,000 yards before reaching the Canal du Nord. At that point it turned southwards, and the canal, under construction at that time, formed part of the front line of the great trench system of defence. When the advance continued in the morning of the 4th September, the Welsh Guards were still on the right of the 2nd Scots Guards. On their left was now the Drake Battalion of the 63rd (Naval) Division, which had side-slipped into this position.

The 2nd Scots Guards moved forward with their left on the Hindenburg Line for about 2,500 yards to its southward bend. They passed south of Tadpole Copse. At this point, 1,000 yards short of the Canal du Nord, the advance was held up by machine-gun fire from in front and from the right flank. In the latter direction the Welsh Guards had also been stopped by machine-guns. It was not till evening that the front was established from posts south-west of Mœuvres to the left of the Welsh Guards. Here the 2nd Scots Guards remained during the night of the 4th September, under machine-gun and artillery fire. The German resistance had been growing more strenuous, and it was evident they intended holding the Hindenburg Line where it coincided with that of the Canal du Nord. They had already abandoned the former as far east as the point where it turns south. The first stage of the Scots Guards' advance had been as far as a point south of Tadpole Copse.

During the 5th the 2nd Battalion remained in this position, but extended to the left so as to include the whole of the front of Mœuvres.[1]

The total casualties on the 4th and 5th September in the 2nd Battalion were, Captain C. R. Jones wounded, and of other ranks 2 killed and 20 wounded, a plain indication of the generally feeble resistance incurred.

In the night of the 5th-6th the 3rd Guards Brigade was relieved in front by the 2nd, the 1st Scots Guards taking over from its own 2nd Battalion, which marched back into support in trenches on the Lagnicourt–Doignies road, where for the following days, till the 11th, they had a quiet time improving the position and salving captured material. Colonel Stirling having been slightly gassed, went on special leave, temporary command of the battalion being assumed by Captain H. C. E. Ross. It will be remembered that the 1st Scots Guards had stopped on the 3rd September a mile to the north-west of Louverval. It was from here that they marched north-eastwards to relieve the 2nd Battalion in the night of the 5th-6th. That battalion was then holding the western outskirts of Mœuvres. On the right of the 1st Battalion the 3rd Grenadiers had relieved the Welsh Guards, and the Naval Division was still on the left. The relief was a troublesome one, owing not only to enemy fire, but also to the state of the ground after a heavy thunderstorm. In this new position " C " Co. on the right and L.F. on the left were the front companies, with " B " in support and R.F. in reserve. These positions were maintained during the 6th, and that night L.F. (right) and " B " moved into front

---

[1] See *History of the Guards Division in the Great War.* This does not appear to agree with the diary of the 2nd Scots Guards, according to which it would seem that the battalion was relieved in the night of the 4th-5th, not of the 5th-6th.

line, with R.F. and " C " in support. The night was disturbed by two German raiding parties, of which the first was driven off by " B " about 9 p.m., and the second by L.F. at 1 a.m. on the 7th. In the night of the 7th-8th the 2nd Irish Guards replaced the 1st Scots, who went into bivouacs just west of Lagnicourt, where they remained training till the 18th September.

Major-General T. G. Matheson, C.B., had taken over command of the Guards Division from General Feilding[1] on the 11th September, and he now paid his first visit to the 1st Scots Guards on the 13th. Lieutenant W. V. d'A. Rutherford was reported wounded on the 14th, probably by one of the shells which were still persistently directed on Louverval Wood.

During this period the battalion was in the line of resistance, the organization of which was completed on the 6th September as a precaution against a new German offensive, which, even then, was thought to be within the bounds of possibility.

Owing to its position at the time in this line, the 1st Battalion and the rest of the 2nd Guards Brigade took no part in the battle of Havrincourt on the 12th September. That battle was fought by the VIth Corps in pursuance of the organized attack which Sir Douglas Haig saw to be necessary before the final operation against the main German line of resistance on the Canal du Nord. The only functions of the infantry of the 3rd Guards Brigade in this battle were the guarding of the left flank of the 2nd Division, and the possible, though hardly probable, establishment of bridge-heads beyond the canal.

An attack on the still untaken part of Mœuvres was to be made by the 57th Division on the 11th. That division, therefore, relieved the 1st Irish Guards facing Mœuvres during the night of the 9th-10th. In the evening of the 11th the 2nd Division began pushing forward on the right of the 2nd Guards Brigade, whilst the 170th

---

[1] General Feilding had been appointed to command the London District in succession to Sir Francis Lloyd. He had commanded the Guards Division since January 1916, and his departure was universally regretted in the Division.

Infantry Brigade of the 57th Division on its left partly conquered Mœuvres. Later in the night the 3rd Guards Brigade came up to relieve the 1st. The relief by the 2nd Scots Guards on the left of the brigade was completed easily, though the 1st Grenadiers on their right had a more difficult time. The 2nd Scots Guards took the place of the 2nd Grenadiers about where they had themselves consolidated south of Mœuvres on the 5th September, but they took over ground extending rather farther south than that held by the battalion relieved.

The 2nd Division, on the 12th, took Trescault and Havrincourt, their left being safeguarded by the 3rd Guards Brigade. Of that brigade the right battalion (1st Grenadier Guards) had some fighting, but the 2nd Scots Guards, separated by them from the left of the 2nd Division, had none. 2nd-Lieutenant L. B. Maby was killed whilst going round the front line on the 12th. When the 57th Division had got its posts out to the east of Mœuvres there were many German counter-attacks on them, which necessitated great vigilance on the part of the left front company of the 2nd Scots Guards. The night of the 13th-14th was a bad one, as R.F. Company was heavily gassed. The victims were Lieutenant Hon. V. A. Harbord, 2nd-Lieutenant Studholme, and about sixty other ranks. The next two days were quiet, and in the night of 15th-16th the battalion, on relief by the 1st Welsh Guards, went back to support trenches near Brigade Headquarters.

After two days here the 1st Irish Guards (1st Guards Brigade) relieved the 2nd Scots Guards, who went back, on the night of the 17th, to billets west of Lagnicourt.

The 2nd Guards Brigade was now coming again into front line, and in the night of the 17th-18th the 1st Scots took over from the 1st Coldstream Guards of the 3rd Guards Brigade. " B " Company was in right front, L.F. centre, and " C " left, with R.F. in reserve. The 2nd Coldstream Guards were on the left and the 2nd Royal Scots (3rd Division) on the right. On the Scots Guards' front they held only the western bank of the canal.

To the right the 3rd Division were across the canal. The front held by the Guards Division at this time was divided into two sectors by the Cambrai–Bapaume road, one brigade holding each sector, with the third in reserve. Each brigade had one battalion in front, one in support, and one in reserve. The Guards' front, therefore, was two battalions with a depth of three. There were constant patrols out on the canal to look out for symptoms of a counter-attack, such as was made successfully on the 57th Division at Mœuvres, and again with temporary success on the 3rd Division.

On the 21st the 3rd Guards Brigade relieved the 2nd, whose turn it was to go into reserve at Lagnicourt. The 1st Scots were relieved by the 1st Welsh Guards. At Lagnicourt they were engaged in special practice for the attack of the canal, which they had become well acquainted with during their recent time on it. Their diary describes the canal as it was on the front which they had held from the 17th to the 21st, that is as right battalion of the brigade holding the southern sector, and, therefore, some distance south of the Bapaume–Cambrai road. The canal was under construction at the beginning of the war, and of course remained so and was dry. Its width here was about 120 feet, with perpendicular revetments of brick on either side about 15 feet high and quite unscalable without ladders, except where it happened that damage from shelling had made hand and foothold.

The attack was practised near Lagnicourt with such detail that the companies worked in the order already decided on for the real attack. In front were to be R.F. on the right, and " C " on the left, with L.F. as support, and " B " in reserve.

The 1st Battalion was west of Lagnicourt from the 21st to the 26th September.[1]

The 2nd Battalion was there from the 17th to the 26th. In the night of the 26th-27th September the brigades of

<hr/>

[1] *The History of the Guards Division in the Great War* (Vol. II, p. 162) says the 2nd Guards Brigade took over the whole of the Guards Division ront on the night of the 22nd-23rd, but the diary of the 1st Scots Guards says the battalion moved up on the 26th.

the Guards Division and the two battalions of the Scots Guards were thus posted.

The 2nd Brigade held the whole of the front line extending from the Bapaume–Cambrai road on the north to a little south-west of Lock No. 7 on the Canal du Nord— a length of about 2,500 yards. The brigade was to be the first in action next day, the other two passing through it at stated periods of the attack.

The right battalion of this brigade was the 1st Scots Guards, which had marched that evening from west of Lagnicourt by Boursies and Demicourt to its assembly positions. These were in Alban and Hunt Avenues, two trenches of the Hindenburg front line, and extended over a front of about 1,000 yards, of which a full four-fifths were north of the latitude of Lock 7. In the centre of the brigade front were the 1st Coldstream Guards, with the 3rd Grenadiers on the left.

The 1st Guards Brigade, the next in order to come into action, was concentrated, behind the 2nd, east of Louverval. The 3rd Guards Brigade, the last of the Division to pass to the front, concentrated north-west of Boursies on the left rear of the 2nd.

CHAPTER XVII

THE PASSAGE OF THE CANAL DU NORD AND OF THE SELLE

Advance made by miles instead of yards.

THE operation to be begun on the 27th was the passage of the Canal du Nord and the capture of the Hindenburg Support Line, which crossed the canal about Mœuvres and then turned south beyond it. There were also some parts of the front Hindenburg Line on the west of the canal which were still in German hands. The operation may be likened to the later stages of a nineteenth-century siege of a fortress. The Canal du Nord represented the dry ditch, the Hindenburg Support the ramparts. Other lines encountered beyond that resembled the improvised retrenchments made by the defenders of the fortress. The breaking of the Hindenburg Support Line was an operation of supreme importance, and when accomplished could well be looked upon as the beginning of the end.

The preparations for this great object were commensurate with its importance. There had been no undue haste, and the way had been gradually prepared by such actions as that at Havrincourt on the 12th, and by the constant patrols. Those troops who had hitherto been strangers to this area had had opportunites of acquiring a knowledge of it when in front line. To others, including both battalions of the Scots Guards, who had taken a hand in the Battle of Cambrai in November-December 1917, it was familiar.

All available topographical information as to both sides of the line had been supplied to the commanders of units. Though accounts of the Canal du Nord as an obstacle had varied to some extent, all were agreed that scaling ladders, if not absolutely necessary, would at least be of the utmost value to the leading battalions, to whom would fall the first passage of the canal, and to those who had to follow them over it at a later stage. Ladders, therefore, were provided by the Royal Engineers for the 1st Scots Guards and the other leading battalions. Beyond the canal the ground sloped upwards, and the first battalions to reach the eastern bank must expect to be met by a fierce fire of all sorts as they topped it. For the subsequent passage of troops in support of the leading divisions, and of ammunition and supplies, bridges had been constructed as near as possible to the front. They were in pieces for transport, and the fitting together of the pieces had been assiduously practised by those who would have to carry out the work on the day of the great attack. The troops, as we know from the record of the 1st Scots Guards, had been practised in reserve positions in the details of the advance as planned, and each company knew exactly the part it had to play when the practice attacks were translated into reality. Finally, operation orders had been drawn up in great detail, and in the case of the Guards Division, General Matheson, its commander, had personally explained them at a conference of officers, and satisfied himself that all were thoroughly up in their job.

The plan of operations, in so far as the Guards Division is concerned, will be best understood by the map on which the several objectives are marked.

It was certainly complicated, and without a map would be difficult to explain clearly. Maps of course had been supplied to officers concerned. On the right of the Guards Division was the 3rd, on its left the 52nd. The area of the operations of the Guards was marked off from the divisions on either side by lines running due east and not materially varying as to the distance between them. Across them runs at right angles the " Blue Line " marking the final objective, and passing, within the Guards' area, from a point a little south of Cantaing, past the western edge of the Bois des Neuf (*Anglice* " Wood of Nine ") to a point north of Marcoing. That final objective was for the 3rd Guards Brigade only, and its instructions were, when it reached the line, to wait for the arrival of troops of the 2nd Division, who were to carry on the advance from the Blue Line. Whilst doing so, patrols were to be pushed out towards the canal and the river Scheldt. All that sounds simple enough ; but it was in the earlier stages that the plan was complicated.

The 2nd Brigade headed the Guards Division on this day, and the 1st Coldstream Guards in the centre of it were to push farthest forward into the salient of the Red Line, which in shape will perhaps remind the reader, as it does the writer, of the outline of a Vauban horn-work, with its ravelin in front of the curtain between the two bastions. As the Coldstream Guards advanced to the curtain and the ravelin, the 3rd Grenadiers would attack northwards and clear the trenches north of the Demicourt–Graincourt road on both sides of the Canal du Nord, thus forming a defensive flank on the left of the Coldstream Guards till the 52nd Division came up into line.

On the right of the Coldstream Guards the 1st Scots Guards were to perform a part analogous to that of the Grenadiers on the left. The Red Line being attained, the 2nd Guards Brigade would consolidate. One hour and fifty minutes after zero, that is at 7.10 a.m., the 1st Guards Brigade would pass through the right of the 2nd (the 1st Scots Guards) to capture the Brown Dotted Line and so much of the Brown Line as lay to the south of it. On its right it would be in touch with the 3rd Division operating through Ribécourt, which had to be taken by it. The left of the 1st Guards Brigade would then swing forward in co-operation with the attack of the 52nd Division on Graincourt,[1] until the whole of the Brown Line was occupied. With the actual operations of the 1st Guards Brigade, as it included neither of the Scots Guards battalions, we are not concerned in detail.

The time for the intervention of the 3rd Guards Brigade and the 2nd Scots Guards was fixed at three hours and forty-five minutes after zero, that is at 9.5 a.m. At that hour the 3rd Brigade would pass through the 2nd, bestriding the road to Prémy Capelle, with its right on the southern boundary of the Guards Divisional area, and its left, as shown on the map, touching the right of the 1st Guards Brigade as it moved forward from the Brown to the Blue

[1] Map facing p. 270.

Line. It may be remembered that about a year before this was the attack of the 2nd Guards Brigade on Fontaine Notre Dame, in the same neighbourhood. That attack had ended in failure, this one was to have a very different result.

At 4.30 a.m. on the 27th a heavy German barrage on the assembly positions of the 2nd Guards Brigade interfered with that operation and caused some casualties in the 1st Scots Guards. Nevertheless, the advance began punctually at 5.20 behind a very intense and accurate creeping barrage. The Canal du Nord was reached, and with the aid of the scaling ladders was crossed with less difficulty perhaps than had been expected. The order of the companies was, as we know from their practice attacks at Lagnicourt, R.F. on the right and " C " on the left in front line, L.F. in support, and " B " in reserve.

It was beyond the canal, in the maze of trenches constituting the Hindenburg Support Line, that the enemy was encountered in force and put up the most stubborn resistance. This, however, was gradually overcome, and the time-table was worked up to with clockwork punctuality. At 7 a.m. the two leading companies of the 1st Scots Guards were on their final objective, the Red Line, forming a right defensive flank along the Havrincourt–Graincourt road, L.F. in close support, was mopping up the trenches which had been passed, and " B " in reserve was still 300 yards west of the Hindenburg Support.

Again, in absolute accordance with the time-table, the 1st Guards Brigade began to pass through the 2nd at 7.6 a.m. The Germans had a very strong position in Graincourt, and machine-gun fire continued to be heavy on the 1st and 2nd Brigades till about 3 p.m., when it was apparently diverted to meet the attack of the 52nd Division from the west. On the first objective the operations of the 1st Scots Guards ended for the day. At 7.30 p.m. they were ordered back to Boursies, which they reached at midnight. They had captured about 300 prisoners, 2 field-guns, 1 howitzer, 90 machine-guns, and 2 heavy trench-mortars. On the whole, their losses in this great achievement were not so heavy as might have been anticipated.

20

They were :

Officers killed : Lieutenant H. L. N. Dundas, M.C. and Bar, and 2nd-Lieutenant H. de B. Cordes.
Wounded : Lieutenant H. S. Marsham-Townshend ; 2nd-Lieutenants R. G. Barker, R. G. M. Eden, and W. G. Dean.
Other ranks : killed 31, wounded 69, missing 7.

The 2nd Scots Guards were west of Louverval when, at 4.45 a.m. on the 27th September, they started eastwards to take their share in the capture by the 3rd Guards Brigade of the Dotted Blue Line (Graincourt line) and the Blue Line (Containg trench).

The 1st Grenadier Guards were leading on the right of the brigade, the 2nd Scots Guards on the left, and the Welsh Guards in reserve behind the right. The battalion's line of march was south of Louverval, across the Bapaume–Cambrai road to Demicourt, and thence to a point on the Canal du Nord, 500 yards north of Lock 7, which was reached at 7.20 a.m., the time appointed for crossing. Beyond the canal progress was delayed by the machine-gun fire from the left. Owing to this, and the fear of a counter-attack from that direction, the 2nd Scots Guards never got farther forward than Shingler Street on the left flank of the 2nd Grenadier Guards (1st Guards Brigade), who were holding Silver Street trench just north of Flesquières. During the afternoon it was able to do considerable execution on the enemy, as he retreated from Graincourt, with machine-guns and a field-gun captured from him.

The left of the 1st Guards Brigade had been unable to advance on the northern part of the Brown Line, owing to the enemy being still in Graincourt. It was only when that place and the Graincourt line east of it fell to the 52nd Division on the left, about 4.30 p.m., that the 1st Guards Brigade could swing its left forward as ordered.

About 10 a.m. the 3rd Guards Brigade had the misfortune to lose its commander, Brigadier-General Follett, who was mortally wounded by a machine-gun and died at the dressing-station. He had commanded the brigade for just four months.

The 2nd Scots Guards, being on the left of the 3rd Brigade, were left where they were, whilst the 1st Grenadier and the Welsh Guards went forward on the way to Prémy Capelle. The Scots Guards had been compelled, so long as Graincourt was untaken, to be prepared to meet a possible counter-attack from that direction. The part played by the 2nd Battalion in this day's fighting was a comparatively small one, and their losses were proportionately light. 2nd-Lieutenant E. R. Newbigging was wounded, 3 other ranks were killed, 11 wounded, and 1 missing.

During the night of the 27th-28th the 2nd Division passed through the Guards Division and relieved it in the front towards the St. Quentin Canal and the Scheldt. The 2nd Scots Guards were then withdrawn to the eastern bank of the Canal du Nord, where they remained till the end of September.

Major E. T. C. Warner took over command of the battalion from Major H. E. Ross, on the latter's appointment to second in command of the Reserve Battalion Scots Guards.

For the next few days the whole of the Guards Division was resting, refitting, and training in rear. The 1st Battalion was at Boursies from 28th September till 7th October. In addition to reorganization it had to do a great deal of road making, a necessary accompaniment of a victorious advance, which left but little time for training. On the 1st October the battalion was temporarily reorganized on the basis of three platoons per company, instead of four.

The 2nd Battalion remained on the east bank of the Canal du Nord from the 28th September till the 8th October. Evidently the bed of the canal itself was looked upon as a particularly safe place, as it was selected for holding a Church of Scotland Parade on the 6th October.

By the 7th October the British front had passed well to the east, and stretched, in the line of advance of the Guards Division, from Douai in the north, nearly southwards through the western outskirts of Cambrai, to the eastern side of St. Quentin. The German positions west of the St. Quentin Canal and the Scheldt had all been conquered, and the river had been passed everywhere above Cambrai. The 4th and 3rd Armies were now to advance east and north-east on a seventeen-mile front, extending from near St. Quentin almost to Cambrai. At dusk on October 7th the 1st Scots Guards left their quarters at Boursies, and marched over country roads rendered very slippery and unpleasant by recent rain to trenches just east of Flesquières. Next day the 2nd Guards Brigade concentrated beyond the Scheldt, about two miles short of Rumilly. The 3rd Guards Brigade being in reserve for the moment, the 2nd Battalion Scots Guards did not leave the bank of the Canal du Nord till the afternoon of the 8th October, when it marched to a position south-west of Flesquières for the night, passing on, on the 9th, to another post north of the Marcoing–Masnières road. They were still west of the St. Quentin Canal.

Meanwhile, the 2nd Guards Brigade marched, in the night of the 8th-9th, to its forming-up positions for the attack on the latter day. In that fight the brigade was formed up with the 3rd Grenadier Guards on the right front and the 1st Coldstream Guards on the left. The 1st Scots Guards, in reserve, were dug in just east of Rumilly. The 1st Guards Brigade was attacking on the right of the 2nd. On the right of the Guards Division the line was prolonged by the IV Corps, on the left by the XVII Corps. The movement was directed north-eastwards towards the river Selle north and south of St. Python.

When the leading battalions of the 2nd Brigade had been gone two hours from zero, the 1st Scots Guards followed them by stages. By the time the Grenadier and Coldstream Guards had reached the Cambrai–Le Cateau road, about noon, the Scots Guards were on the Cambrai–St. Quentin road, some 3,000 yards in rear. About 5 p.m. L.F. and " B " Companies moved forward to trenches just east of Wambaix Copse, 1,000 yards short of the road. The rest of the battalion remained at the railway. The battalion had little or no fighting and no casualties on this day.

On the 10th it was the turn of the 1st Scots Guards to go into front line on the left of the 1st Irish Guards, the corresponding battalion in reserve of the 1st Brigade on the 9th. The line marked by the leading battalions on the night of the 9th was just east of the Cambrai–Le Cateau road. At 5 a.m. on the 10th the 1st Scots Guards moved forward through the 1st Coldstream and 3rd Grenadier Guards, of which the latter now became the supporting and the former the reserve battalion. The Scots Guards were formed with three companies in front, " B " on the right, " C " in the centre, and L.F. on the left; R.F. in support.

The method of advance was as follows : the three leading companies each pushed forward a strong patrol, under an officer, to make four successive " bounds " forward. As each " bound " was made good, the rest of the company closed up to the patrol and consolidated the position gained.

Carnières was taken unopposed by L.F. at 6.30 a.m. The company, it is stated by Lieutenant Swinton, was then a good mile in front of the troops on either flank. It was only when the ridge beyond that village was reached that the enemy was seen. The final objective was the high ground 1,500 yards west of St. Hilaire. This was reached against only very slight opposition. On the way the villages of Carnières and Boussières had been captured. There had been a temporary hold up by machine-gun fire on the ridge south of Avesnes. When the position on the final objective had been consolidated, the battalion was ordered to see if it was possible to push east of St. Hilaire. This was done after dark, apparently without opposition except shelling. The advance to this line was made, in the same way as that during the day, by pushing out a strong patrol, following it up from stage to stage, and consolidating each as it was reached.

The Irish Guards on the right had reached the high ground east of Quièvy by 10 p.m. The losses of the 1st Scots Guards on this day were insignificant, being only Lieutenant Priaulx and three other ranks wounded. At this small cost the battalion had advanced four miles, and captured about fifteen prisoners, also taking three villages—Carnières, Boussières, and St. Hilaire.

The line held late at night by the 1st and 2nd Guards Brigades started from a little short of Fontaine au Tertre Farm, on the right of the 1st Irish Guards, to east of St. Hilaire, whence it bent back on the left of the 1st Scots Guards to gain touch with the right of the XVII Corps west of St. Vaast. The New Zealanders on the left of the IV Corps were in touch with the right of the 1st Irish Guards.

It was clear that the German resistance was fast weakening, and that their *moral* was, as reported by prisoners, sinking rapidly.

They were already carrying out propaganda operations by spreading reports that the Germans were about to ask for an armistice. General Matheson feared that this propaganda might take another form in the shape of attempts at fraternization between the troops in lines, such as had occurred on the first two Christmas Days of the war. He accordingly issued orders warning all against anything of the sort, and saying that all the German authorities really wanted was to obtain time for the organization of a last line of defence in their own country, when they should be finally driven, as they were being, from France and Belgium. The 11th October was fixed for the 3rd Guards Brigade to come into first line, in place of the 1st and 2nd. The 2nd Scots Guards had been moved up to the Seranvillers–Estournel area on the 10th October, but, owing to the rapid advance of the other brigades, there was still a long distance to be covered in order to reach the assembly positions west of St. Vaast, and a start had to be made in the very early hours of the 11th.

Lieut.-Colonel J. A. Stirling had rejoined the 2nd Scots Guards on the 10th, and resumed command for what were to be the final operations of the war.

The battalion passed through the 2nd Brigade in the early morning of the 11th. The 3rd Brigade, having to cover the whole front of the Guards Division, was to attack in a line of all three battalions—1st Grenadiers on the right, 2nd Scots Guards in the centre, and 1st Welsh Guards on the left. The line of the first objective was on the heights about 2,000 yards east of the Erclin stream, starting from 500 yards north-east of St. Vaast, which village was to the left of the Scots Guards' front and came within the sphere of the Welsh Guards. It was still untaken. The final objective, the attainment of which entailed the passage of the river Selle, was a line starting in the north from Maison Blanche on the Solesmes–Valenciennes road north-east of Haussy and running a little east of south to cross the railway about midway between Solesmes and Vertain. To each battalion was attached one field battery and one section of machine-guns.

The 2nd Scots Guards deployed at 5 a.m. with " G " and R.F. Companies in front on the right and left respectively, " F " in support, and L.F. in reserve.

The village of St. Hilaire had already been cleared of the enemy by the 2nd Brigade. The Germans were holding the first objective.

In the darkness during the previous night's march the right of the Scots Guards had lost touch with the left of the 1st Grenadiers, whose right was directed on the orchard of Fontaine au Tertre. The line of the first objective was reached without much difficulty by the Scots Guards. On their right the Grenadiers had more difficulty, and on their left the Welsh Guards were held up at St. Vaast by machine-gun fire from St. Aubert on their left flank. The line of the first objective having been consolidated, the advance to the valley of the Selle commenced against severe fire from machine-guns. Owing to the holding up of the Welsh Guards at St. Vaast, it was necessary to connect up with them by a defensive flank on the left formed by R.F.

The fire from beyond the railway in front was so fierce that the Scots Guards were finally obliged to stop when their right had reached the heights north of the Fontaine au Tertre orchard, where it regained touch with the left of the 1st Grenadiers. The latter had gained possession of the orchard, and had even got one company as far forward as Gourlain Chapel on the left bank of the Selle.

Throughout the day the whole front of the 3rd Guards

Brigade was under heavy machine-gun and rifle fire, with intermittent blasts of shelling. The field battery under Lieutenant Chadwick, moving parallel to the reserve company, found a good position to cover the front, though it had few chances of direct observation. The fighting was heaviest on the left flank of the Scots Guards, where 2nd-Lieutenant Hon. P. C. Kinnaird with one platoon succeeded in turning the enemy's position in the deep railway cutting. The attached section of machine-guns had also kept in close touch with the battalion.

On this line the advance was held up for the night of the 11th-12th October.

During that night the Scots Guards sent out four fighting patrols to locate the enemy's positions. The two first went out from " G " and R.F. Companies, under 2nd-Lieutenants G. Buchanan and M. M. Johnson before the inter-company relief. They located some machine-gun posts.

At 2 a.m. on the 12th L.F. relieved " G " Company and " F " relieved R.F. in front line. Shortly after this relief two more patrols went out, under Lieutenant G. Pocock and 2nd-Lieutenant H. Kindersley. The result of the reconnaissance showed that the enemy was still holding the St. Aubert–Solesmes railway in force, and at present showed no signs of an intention to retire. The front of the Scots Guards was facing east, with its left bent back to meet the right of the Welsh Guards, who had not succeeded in getting forward beyond St. Vaast. The 24th Division troops, on the left of the Welsh Guards, were not up in line, and until they began to come up, further advance was out of the question. The Welsh Guards themselves had to form a defensive flank to join up with the right of the 24th Division still farther back.

In the early morning of the 12th October the Germans opposed to the 24th Division on the left of the Guards Division began retiring and were seen making their way to Haussy.

The Guards, under orders of General Matheson issued on the previous evening, stood fast, as it was clear that there was an organized German defence in their front.

About 2 p.m. the enemy appearing to have withdrawn from the railway, the Welsh and Scots Guards moved forward till the latter were established on the heights overlooking the Selle valley from Arbre de la Femme southwards to beyond the St. Vaast–St. Python road, where a line of resistance was consolidated and patrols were pushed forward to the Haussy–St. Python railway. The advance had been covered by the fire of the field battery in a hollow north of the Fontaine au Tertre orchard, and by the machine-gun section attached to the battalion. The enemy was reported in force east of the Selle. Here the movement stopped for the day, during the rest of which the battalion was under shell fire.

The 1st Grenadiers, on the right, had established posts on the railway from Gourlain Chapel nearly to St. Python.

At midnight the support company (R.F.) of the 2nd Scots Guards passed forward between the leading companies, captured an enemy post on the railway, and advanced patrols into the northern part of St. Python, taking some prisoners and reaching the left bank of the Selle. Immediately after this the right front company (L.F.) seized the junction of the railways from St. Aubert and Haussy just outside St. Python, and got into the western part of that village. Both these operations met with considerable resistance in the pitch dark, when they were carried out.

The part of St. Python on the right bank of the Selle and the slopes towards Haussy were strongly held by enemy machine-guns well concealed, whilst trench-mortars in houses on the St. Python–Solesmes road bombarded the Haussy–St. Python railway. The ground on the western side of the Selle valley was so exposed that movement there in daylight was difficult. By 6.30 a.m. on the 13th October the 2nd Scots Guards had three platoons north of St. Python and two south and west. The bridge carrying the main road across the Selle in the village had been blown up. The rest of the battalion was partly on the Haussy–St. Python railway, and partly on the heights in rear, where it had passed the night of the 11th-12th.

All crossings of the river had been destroyed, and in places the debris of bridges and houses had so dammed the stream as to create pools of an average width of thirty feet and a depth of three to the muddy bottom. The banks were grassy and sloping.

The day of the 13th October was spent mainly in clearing the part of St. Python west of the river, and attempting to get across the latter. In this operation cavalry (Oxfordshire Hussars) joined, as well as cyclists, but they were eventually obliged to withdraw.

The clearing of St. Python was rendered specially difficult, not only by numerous posts, but also by the presence of many civilian inhabitants who had not left it when the German front was still far to the west, and were now mixed up with the enemy and got in the way.

The northern part of the village was gradually cleared by Captain Green and 2nd-Lieutenant Buchanan, with Sergeant Proud, D.C.M., and a platoon of " F " Company.

The southern portion was dealt with by 2nd-Lieutenant Brand of L.F., with 2nd-Lieutenant H. K. M. Kindersley, who had hand-to-hand fighting in the south-west part. About 2.30 p.m. one platoon was actually driven out by shelling, but by evening L.F. had cleared the whole village on the near bank of the Selle, though not without loss. On this day Corporal (Lance-Sergeant) H. B. Wood, M.M., of L.F., gained the V.C. for his gallant leading of his platoon. It will be remembered that Wood was one of the party with Sergeant Burke who escaped capture by the Germans near Ghent in October 1914. The actions for which he was now awarded the Cross are detailed in the following extract from the *London Gazette* of the 14th December 1918.

" 16444 Corporal (Lance-Sergeant) Harry Blanshard Wood, M.M., 2nd Bn. Scots Guards. For most conspicuous bravery and devotion to duty during operations at the village of St. Python, France, on the 13th October 1918.

" The advance was desperately opposed by machine-guns, and the streets were raked by fire. His platoon sergeant was killed and command of the leading platoon fell to him. The task of the company was to clear the western side of the village, and secure the crossing of the river Selle. Command of the ruined bridge had to be gained, though the space in front of it was commanded by snipers. Corporal Wood boldly carried a large brick out into the open space, lay down behind it, and fired continually at these snipers, ordering his men to work across, while he covered them by his fire. This he continued to do under heavy and well-aimed fire, until the whole of his party had reached the objective point.

" He showed complete disregard for his personal safety, and his leadership throughout the day was of the highest order. Later he drove off repeated enemy counterattacks against his position.

" His gallant conduct and initiative shown contributed largely to the success of the day's operations."

It was found impossible during the day to acquire a bridge-head beyond the river, but R.E. bridges were brought forward ready to be thrown at night across the river below the village. In the evening the enemy's fighting slackened, owing to his heavy losses from the fire of the artillery and Vickers guns on the westward heights. Detachments had been seen during the afternoon moving out of St. Python towards the north and north-east, and these had offered excellent targets. One party in particular, of over thirty Germans, had been seen trying to get away up the slopes beyond the river. The howitzers got on to these with shrapnel and accounted for all but eight. The presence of French civilians in the village has already been mentioned. The German, after the manner of his kind, made use of this to endeavour to save his own skin by disguising himself as one of these unfortunate people. In one case a man, apparently a French civilian, was pointed out by a genuine Frenchman as a German soldier. Before he could be shot by Sergeant Spiers, the German succeeded in shooting both his denouncer and Corporal Lindekvist of L.F., Scots Guards.

That night the 2nd Scots Guards were relieved by the 3rd Grenadier Guards of the 2nd Brigade, and were back in billets at St. Hilaire by 3 a.m. on the 14th. The casualties of the battalion during this tour of front-line service were :

Officers killed : Lieutenant W. E. Ferryman.
Wounded : Captain C. H. Seymour and 2nd-Lieutenant Hon. P. C. Kinnaird.
Other ranks : 14 killed and 57 wounded (2 of these accidentally).

The German defence of the line of the Selle was very strenuous, and the passage was not destined to be effected by the Guards Division for some days yet. When the 3rd Grenadier Guards relieved the 2nd Scots in the night of the 13th-14th October, the 1st Scots Guards relieved the Welsh Guards on the left, with R.F. in front, " C " and L.F. in support, and " B " in reserve.

The day of the 14th passed fairly quietly, and during the ensuing night the whole of R.F. went forward, crossed the Selle and consolidated a position about east of Arbre de la Femme. In this they were counter-attacked at 5 a.m., but drove off their assailants. This attack was renewed at 7.30 a.m., when the Germans got machine-guns into some houses farther north and enfiladed the company, the casualties in which were heavy. 2nd-Lieutenant P. H. Broughton-Adderley, M.C., commanding it, received wounds to which he succumbed next day. Thirteen other ranks were killed, the same number were wounded, and three were missing. The company was then withdrawn, and that night, after being shelled all day, the battalion was relieved by the 1st Coldstream Guards of the 2nd Brigade, and returned to St. Vaast. It returned to the front line on the 18th, when it relieved the 3rd Grenadier Guards on the right, posting " B " Company in St. Python village, " C " in support, and the two flank companies in reserve. " C " had strong patrols out in the night towards the crossings of the Selle, and there was continued German shelling during the 18th, fortunately without casualties. In the night of the 18th-19th the 1st and 3rd Guards Brigades passed through the 2nd to the final attack and passage of the Selle.

Whilst both battalions of the Scots Guards were out

of the line on the 16th an attack had been made on Haussy by the right of the 24th Division, aided by some of the Coldstream Guards. The village was taken, but lost again to a vigorous counter-attack by the enemy.

On the 17th the 2nd Scots Guards had moved from St. Hilaire to Boussières, and remained there till the evening of the 19th, when they moved again to the front with the 3rd and 1st Brigades for the final attack on the line of the Selle. At Boussières the attack had been practised by moonlight, over distances corresponding to those to be covered in the coming battle. The great difficulty was found to be in keeping direction, and Lieutenant Edmunds, M.C., commanding No. 10 Platoon, " G " Company, went specially to arrange with the 8th Gloucestershire Regiment (19th Division) for proper liaison on the left boundary of the VI Corps.

This was to be a combined attack by the VI Corps and the troops on both its flanks. On the other hand, the front of the Guards Division, though consisting of two brigades, was to be shortened on its southern side by the whole length of St. Python, the 62nd Division on the right extending its left to include the village. The front of the Guards Division was thus reduced to the space between the southern edge of Haussy and the northern of St. Python.

The 2nd Scots Guards, marching from Boussières to St. Hilaire on the 19th, started again at 12.45 a.m. on the 20th, in pouring rain, for the assembly positions about the cross roads just short of Arbre de la Femme.

The 3rd Brigade was on the left of the divisional front, with the 1st on its right. In the front of the 3rd Brigade were the 1st Grenadier Guards, who were to capture the first objective, a line running south from the eastern edge of Haussy along the more easterly of the two Haussy–Solesmes roads to the dividing line between the Guards and the 62nd Division on the St. Python–Vertain road.

Of the two battalions in second line, the 2nd Scots Guards were on the left, the 1st Welsh Guards on the right. " F " and " G " Companies were in the front line of the battalion, with L.F. in support and R.F. in reserve, followed by headquarters.

The advance began at 2 a.m. on the 20th October. The leading battalions of both brigades crossed the Selle without difficulty on bridges prepared by the Royal Engineers and the Pioneer Battalion of the Coldstream Guards.[1]

Beyond the river the Scots Guards were in touch with the 8th Gloucesters on their left.

The 1st Grenadiers experienced very little opposition in reaching the first objective, which they did well up to scheduled time, following behind a creeping barrage. It was about 3.15 a.m. when the Scots Guards passed forward from the first objective to the capture of the second, a line parallel to the first and about half-way between it and Vertain. " F " Company was leading on the right and " G " on the left when, at 4.20 a.m., the British barrage ceased. At that time the Welsh Guards, on the right of the Scots, were out of touch, and both battalions encountered considerable machine-gun fire. Communication with Brigade Headquarters was difficult, owing to the ground mist and an unexplained failure of the wireless. There was, therefore, delay in getting a renewal of the artillery support. The enemy appeared to be numerous on the left towards Maison Blanche, but by 5 a.m. " G " Company, in unison with the 8th Gloucesters on its left, had cleared Maison Blanche, taking some prisoners, had passed the Solesmes–Valenciennes road, and were sending out patrols beyond the Harpies stream towards Rieux Farm, where there was a ford.

At 5.50 a.m. " F " Company on the right had passed beyond the second objective, capturing half the garrison of Haussy Châlet, with their machine-guns and two trench-mortars. The other half of the garrison, trying to escape, came under heavy fire from the Welsh Guards,

---

[1] It appears from *The Grenadiers in the Great War* (vol. iii, p. 156) that there were complaints of the insufficiency of the bridges. These complaints are not echoed in the diary of the 2nd Scots Guards, which says, " bridges over the Selle were crossed without delay." Of course, however, this refers to a period after the passage of the Grenadiers.

who were now up, and all were either killed or taken prisoners.

" F " and " G " now set to work at making a line of resistance posts at from 100 to 200 yards east of the Solesmes–Valenciennes road. In this line each company kept two platoons ; of the other two, one was in support and one in outposts about 500 yards north-east of the line. The support company (L.F.) faced north-east, well dug in on a line 400 yards west of the road, whilst the reserve company (R.F.) remained with Battalion Headquarters on the first objective at the south-east corner of Haussy.

There was heavy machine-gun fire in the morning from the direction of Vertain, and a desultory fire all day from the farther side of the Harpies.

Whilst patrolling with his platoon towards Vertain, 2nd-Lieutenant J. H. Fletcher was killed and his platoon sergeant wounded.

There was shelling of the new front line all day, the German guns paying special attention to two farms on the main road, and using gas shells against them. These were occupied by Company Headquarters.

The Scots Guards, as well as the battalions on their flanks, were ordered to send one company each to establish a line close to the Harpies river. Accordingly, L.F. passed forward from support, and dug in on the forward slope leading down to the Harpies and about 200 yards short of it. Patrols sent forward reported the stream to be everywhere only from one to two feet deep with a firm bottom, and, therefore, easily passable for infantry. The farther bank was steep.

The casualties from fire during the day of the 20th were not heavy, thanks to good digging in and taking advantage of small local ground features.

The shelling was so heavy as far back as Battalion Headquarters on the edge of the Haussy, that they had to move to the Brewery in the evening.

After dark the 1st Grenadiers took over the brigade front line, and the 2nd Scots Guards moved back, R.F. and " F " Companies to the first objective, and the other two to the Brewery Headquarters. During the 21st the battalion remained in support, and, on relief by troops of the 2nd Division, moved during the following night to billets at St. Vaast.

Its casualties during these last operations had been:

Officers killed: 2nd-Lieutenant J. H. Fletcher.
Wounded: Rev. Mr. Middleton.
Other ranks: 1 killed, 29 wounded.

These were remarkably small proportionately to the considerable successes gained.

CHAPTER XVIII

THE passage of the Selle was followed by a period of inactivity for both battalions whilst the Guards Division was out of the line. It was not till the 2nd November that the Division again went up for what was to be its final tour of fighting in the Great War.

The intervening days were spent in the area west of the Selle, where the devastation to which the Guards had been accustomed for so many months was, comparatively speaking, non-existent. The area had been far behind the fighting line, and the German retreat had latterly been so rapid that there was little time for them to carry out the systematic destruction of private property which had marked their retreat to the Hindenburg Line in 1917. Nor had the civil population by any means completely vanished, as had been the case before. Billets, therefore, were generally comfortable to an extent long unknown to the British. The time was occupied in the usual training, drill, and musketry, relieved by football and other amusements.

The 1st Battalion passed the time between St. Hilaire, Boussières, St. Python, and Capelle, at which latter they were on the 3rd November. They were inspected on the 29th October at St. Hilaire by Major-General Matheson, who expressed his satisfaction with the turn-out and smartness of all ranks. Otherwise nothing notable occurred.

The 2nd Battalion spent a similar time at St. Vaast, where they had their inspection by the Divisional Commander on the day preceding that of the 1st Battalion. It is noted that influenza again gave trouble at the end of October, chiefly among the transport. It was fatal in the case of Sergeant Black, but his was the only death.

21 307

The 2nd Battalion started its forward movement again when it marched, on the 2nd November, to Escarmain. On the 3rd the 1st Battalion was at Capelle, the 2nd at Escarmain, both ready for the fresh attack next day.

The general position in this part of the British front was this. On the 1st November Valenciennes, on the left, had been taken, and the line established two miles beyond the river Rhonelle. Thence it ran a little east of south through the western outskirts of Le Quesnoy, past the western edge of the Forest of Mormal and south-east of Le Cateau. The 1st Scots Guards were now close to the country which some of them, alas ! but few, remembered from the latter days of August 1914.

The front on which the Guards Division was to advance was a little north of Le Quesnoy about Villers Pol, at which place it changed its previous north-easterly direction to due east, aiming at its ultimate objective, the fortress of Maubeuge, round which it will be remembered the 1st Scots Guards marched in August 1914, at the beginning of the retreat from Mons.

On the 2nd November the Guards Division had started to take over the front from the 2nd Division on the left of the VI Corps front. The Guards front at first was a very restricted one of only about a mile just west of Villers Pol. It was to widen out as the wheel half-right was made at that place. This narrow front was held on the 3rd November by the 2nd Guards Brigade with the 1st Coldstream Guards on the right, and by the 1st Guards Brigade with the 2nd Coldstream Guards on the left. From this line to Maubeuge was a distance of about fourteen miles, but the fortress was indicated as the ultimate objective. As is remarked in the *History of the Guards Division* :

" Commanders and their staffs now calculated the movements of their troops in miles, not in yards. The enemy was no longer of much account. The only matters which seriously troubled the staff were the maintenance of communications and the supply of food and ammunition to the fighting troops. In their retreat the Germans displayed their usual thoroughness in the art of destruction ; bridges and culverts were everywhere broken down or ruined, and there were craters of varying dimensions along the roads."

The scheme eventually adopted for the advance to Maubeuge was for the 1st and 2nd Guards Brigades to gain about half the distance on the 4th November. On the 5th the 3rd Guards Brigade would pass through the others and carry on to Maubeuge.

On the evening of the 3rd November the 1st Coldstream Guards had forced their way through Villers Pol and on to the heights beyond, troops of the XVII Corps had got forward to the Jenlain–Le Quesnoy road on the left of the Guards. Zero hour on the 4th November was at 6 a.m., and the first objective of the Guards was the Jenlain–Le Quesnoy road on a front which, after the change of direction, was to widen out as the advance progressed.

The 1st Scots Guards left Capelle at 5 a.m. on the 4th, marching through Villers Pol to the concentration area of the 2nd Guards Brigade. The order of the brigade was the 3rd Grenadier Guards in front, 1st Scots Guards in support, as they passed forward through the 1st Coldstream. In the 1st Scots Guards L.F. and " C " Companies were in front, " B " in support, R.F. in reserve.

The morning was foggy, after rain in the night, and the roads were congested, conditions which delayed to some extent the movement of the Scots Guards. The action of the 2nd Guards Brigade began with the capture of the first objective, the Jenlain–Le Quesnoy road, after some fighting. Here the 3rd Grenadiers, followed by the 1st Scots Guards in support, passed through the 1st Coldstream, and the former attacked at about 9.30 a.m. The anticipations of a very feeble resistance by the Germans had been too optimistic ; for the Grenadiers were held up for some time by machine-gun fire, and it soon began to be clear that Maubeuge was not going to be reached on the 5th. By dusk on the 4th the front of the Guards Division had only reached a line including Preux au Sart and extending to west of Gommignies, machine-guns in which checked further progress. The advance was less than half the length contemplated. In the evening L.F. and "C" Companies of the 1st Scots Guards moved forward to keep touch with the Grenadiers. Though the battalion was not called into front line of this day, their casualties from shell fire and snipers left behind had amounted to 3 men killed and 30 wounded. Battalion Headquarters had been all day at the crossing of the Le Quesnoy-Wargnies le Petit and the Villers Pol–Frasnoy roads, where they were heavily shelled in the morning, but had no losses. The country hereabouts was close and enclosed by hedges, which facilitated greatly the machine-gun defence on which the enemy now so largely relied.

In the early morning of the 5th November the 3rd Guards Brigade passed through the 1st and 2nd to carry on the attack, with its first objectives on a line about 300 yards beyond that reached by the other brigades on the 4th.

The 2nd Scots Guards formed up on the left, east of the Rhonelle, with the 1st Grenadiers on their right and the Welsh Guards in Brigade Reserve.

They were in battle formation by zero hour (6 a.m.), with R.F. on the right, L.F. on the left, "F" Company in support, and "G" in reserve. Forty minutes later they had passed the first objective beyond Preux au Sart without seeing an enemy. Connection with the Grenadiers on the right, which had been temporarily lost, was here regained by R.F. The advance continued without incurring serious resistance through Anfroipret, which was taken, though there was some slight opposition by machine-guns in the cemetery of the village. The Germans were still retiring, and at 9 a.m. the battalion, with tanks in front, was approaching Bermeries under slight machine-gun and trench-mortar fire. It was difficult to locate the enemy in Bermeries, and the advance made little progress up to 12.30, when the village was still occupied by German machine-guns. The tanks in front of the leading companies assisted in locating and overcoming them. About 1.30 p.m. there was a sharp fight between No. 4 Platoon of R.F. and some German machine-gunners. The battalion's Lewis guns did specially good service in overcoming these Germans, of whom 9 were killed and 8 wounded and taken. The platoon lost 8 men wounded. The fourth objective, beyond Bermeries, was taken throughout its length. On it there was a good deal of enemy machine-gun fire from the railway on the right and from the direction of Buvignies in front—Bermeries and Anfroipret, villages in rear, suffered from German "heavies."

During the night of the 5th-6th November Brigadier-General C. P. Heywood, commanding 3rd Guards Brigade, was wounded, and Lieut.-Colonel J. A. Stirling went to replace him, leaving Captain S. J. Green, M.C., in command of the 2nd Scots Guards.

The Germans were still in the neighbourhood of Buvignies, and an attack was planned for dawn on the 6th to take the village and beyond it to Louvignies.

In this advance the 1st Grenadiers were still in the front on the right, but the Scots Guards had now gone into support, and the Welsh Guards had taken their place in front on the left. The Grenadiers moved forward at 6 a.m., the Welsh Guards not till a little later, as the 24th Division on the left was not yet up. The Welsh Guards occupied Buvignies without difficulty, and eventually reached the Bavai–Pont-sur-Sambre road with their outposts. Their left flank was thrown back and joined the 2nd Scots Guards, who had already dug in at a small stream half a mile west of Bavai, and formed a flank guard connecting the left of the brigade with the right of the 24th Division, which was still not up to the line reached by the Guards. In this affair Private Thomson of L.F. had the sad distinction to be the last man lost by the battalion before the Armistice.

During the afternoon "F" Company had been placed at the disposal of the 1st Grenadier Guards attacking northeast of Buvignies, in case of their requiring assistance. However, none was necessary, and the company was not engaged.

Early on the 7th the 2nd Guards Brigade passed through the 3rd to continue the attack. To the 2nd Scots Guards of the 3rd Brigade fell the task of guarding the left flank of the 2nd Brigade westwards from the railway junction south of Bavai, the 24th Division being still not up. Later in the day the 2nd Battalion went back to Bermeries to reorganize.

The 1st Battalion, when the 3rd Brigade had passed through them on the 5th November, had been sent forward to Anfroipret, but before reaching it was stopped and sent into billets at Gommignies. It rained hard all the 6th, which made it very uncomfortable, and also difficult for the movement of troops, especially for guns.

In the afternoon of the 6th officers were sent to reconnoitre the route to Mecquignies and to ascertain the disposition of the 1st Grenadiers (3rd Brigade) in the front line with reference to the attack to be made next morning.

At 2.30 a.m. on the 7th the Scots Guards moved up to the assembly positions east of Mecquignies, where the 2nd Brigade was drawn up with the 3rd Grenadiers on the left, the 1st Coldstream Guards in the centre, and the 1st Scots Guards on the right, with the 62nd Division beyond them.

When the advance started at 6 a.m. under a small barrage, the enemy was found to have retreated already, and the second objective was reached without opposition by 9.15 a.m. In the afternoon the advance was continued, and La Longueville railway station and the road south of it were occupied. The village of La Longueville itself was still held by the enemy, but it was ascertained, from a prisoner captured by a patrol of " B " Company, that it was to be evacuated in the night. The casualties of this day were only two wounded.

On the 8th the 2nd Brigade's battle order was rearranged on a two battalion front : 1st Scots Guards on the right, 1st Coldstream Guards on the left, and 3rd Grenadier Guards in support. The boundary between the 1st Scots Guards and the 1st Coldstream left the village of La Longueville to be dealt with by the latter.

The Scots Guards assembled south-west of the village under unfortunate circumstances, for three shells burst amongst R.F. during the assembly, and caused over twenty casualties. R.F. was on the right, L.F. on the left, " B " and " C " Companies in support.

The first two objectives were passed without difficulty, but in front of the third, the road running south-east from La Longueville, the battalion was held up for a time by machine-guns. R.F. established themselves on this objective by 2 p.m., but L.F. and the Coldstream Guards on the left were both stopped short of it by machine-guns established in the school of Longueville, on the south of the village on the Maubeuge road, and on the heights north of that road.

At 5.30 p.m. L.F. and the Coldstream Guards started again under a moderate barrage for the third objective, which they now reached without opposition a quarter of an hour after the enemy had retired from it on their front. In this operation the Coldstream Guards captured a German battalion orderly on whom were found orders showing that the enemy were retreating immediately on Rouveroi, just over the Belgian frontier north-east of Maubeuge. A rearguard of one company of this man's battalion (2nd Bn. 86th Reserve Infantry Regiment) was at all costs to stop the British advance to this new position during the 8th and the night after it. Patrols of the Scots Guards were at once sent out to the Maubeuge–Mons railway. At 11.30 p.m. the 3rd Grenadier Guards passed forward through the 1st Scots Guards, and were the first British troops to enter Maubeuge at 3 a.m. on the 9th November.

The 1st Guards Brigade passed through later and entrenched themselves beyond the fortress unopposed.

During the 8th November the 1st Scots Guards ended their fighting career in the war with unfortunately heavy losses, largely owing to the three shells which had done so much damage in R.F. during the assembly. One man was killed, but 47 were wounded and 2 missing. The 1st Battalion spent the 9th November at the hamlet of Les Mottes, between La Longueville and Maubeuge, entering the latter place with the 2nd Guards Brigade on the 10th, and being quartered in barracks. They were there next day at 11 a.m., when the Armistice, ending all fighting on this front, came into force.

In a letter to General Feilding, dated the 9th November,

General Matheson thus summarizes the recent achievements of the Guards Division :

" Since September 12th we have advanced 72 kilometres, out of which the Guards Division have fought for and made good 55 kilometres. The remaining 17 were made good by other divisions in this Corps. Not bad, is it ? "

The 2nd Battalion had gone to rest at Boursies on the afternoon of the 7th. On the 9th it marched with the 3rd Brigade to La Longueville, accompanied by the pipers and was everywhere enthusiastically received by the civil population, now freed at last from more than four years of German domination. On the 10th they marched to the Croix Misnil, a suburb of Maubeuge, where they were on the 11th at the time of the Armistice.

The recapture of Maubeuge was an appropriate conclusion to the operations of the war, for in some ways it had played a notable part in the early days. Though it could make no lengthened defence, such as that of Genoa in 1800, it held out long enough to detain the arrival of the besieging German troops on the Aisne, an arrival which, had it occurred a few days earlier than it actually did, might have had a great and adverse influence on the course of the battle on the Chemin des Dames.

Though it refers to the Guards Division generally, and not specially to the Scots Guards, the letter addressed to the Division by its Commander on the 11th November may appropriately be reproduced in this place. It admirably summarizes the achievements of the division since its entry upon the scenes of the final overthrow of the German military power.

11th November 1918.

To the Guards Division

" By your capture on the 9th of Maubeuge, the ancient strong place of the Low Countries, you have brought to a victorious conclusion a period of many weeks of almost incessant fighting, in which your determination and discipline have overcome the most formidable obstacles. Between the valley of the Cojeul from which you had launched the advance on August 21st to the great fortress which you entered on the 9th, you have stormed and carried a succession of ridges of great natural strength, and several canals or streams. Of the former the strongest were in my opinion the ridges south of St. Léger and Croisilles, and the high ground at Flesquières. Of the latter the two most formidable were the Canal du Nord and the River Selle.

" Out of the 81 days which have elapsed since August 21st, the Guards Division has been a total of 54 days in the firing line. Of those 54 days, 29 have been days of strenuous fighting and in which you beat back and wore down a skilful, tenacious and desperate foe. The conditions in which you fought were always hard and latterly most severe. The mined area through which you first advanced contained no cover of any kind. Latterly, since you have fought your way back into an area of still standing villages and farms, cover has been plentiful out of the line, but troops in action have been severely tried by cold, rain, and wind. In spite of these obstacles you have pressed your advantage without respite, and you have won the important goal on which the Guards Division was finally directed last week. This achievement speaks eloquently of your valour, your endurance, and your willing discipline.

" During the period of the advance the artillery of the division has been in action longer than any other arm, and has been called upon to face much hardship and hard work. It has had to fire difficult barrages at short notice, and has often come under heavy artillery and machine-gun fire in pushing up in close support of the firing line. I have nothing but praise for the co-operation of Artillery Brigade Commanders with Guards Brigadiers ; their energy, quick grasp of situations, and promptness to act have been of constant service during the advance. During the whole period the Forward Observation Officers have also shown a fine spirit in getting forward for their work, and have frequently sent back early information of great value on the dispositions of the enemy and the progress of our troops. For all this I wish to convey my warmest thanks to Brigadier-General Wilson, his Brigade and Battery Commanders, and all ranks.

" Conditions of the advance have called for all the skill and endurance which the Field Companies, R.E., and the 4th Battalion Coldstream Guards (Pioneers) could put forth. They have faced and overcome great difficulties, often under fire, often under the handicap of darkness and bad weather, often under the strain of work for long hours at a stretch. I consider that the speed and precision with which they carried out the bridging of the River Selle reflects the greatest credit on Lieut.-Colonel Lees, the Field Company Commanders, and all ranks engaged. Their success on that occasion was only one striking example of the high level of their work. The struggle to restore destroyed communications has been particularly severe during the past week, and they have acquitted themselves in a manner of which I think that they have every reason to be proud. The strain upon the Divisional Signal Company has also been very great. They, too, have had great difficulties to surmount, long hours of work and little rest. They have risen well to the occasion, and I congratulate Major Ryan and all ranks on their success. But for the determination shown by the Royal Engineers in overcoming the peculiar difficulties of a rapid advance in bad weather, over natural and artificial obstacles of all sorts, the division could never have reached Maubeuge last week.

" Nothing in the record of the Brigade of Guards is finer than the performance of the three Guards Brigades of this division since August 21st. From Moyenneville to Maubeuge they have advanced a distance of almost 50 miles. In the first week of this advance, from August 21st to 28th, in the face of very heavy fighting, they went forward a distance of 5½ miles. In the second phase, from September 3rd to 27th, during which they stormed the deep ditch of the Canal du Nord, broke through the Hindenburg System, and won the Flesquières Ridge, they penetrated into the enemy's lines a further distance of 11½ miles. In the third phase, from October 9th to 22nd, at the end of which they forced the crossings of the River Selle, they advanced a distance of 14 miles. And in their final advance, against still tenacious opposition, and in constant rain and cold, they drove the enemy back a distance of 19 miles before they reached their final goal, Maubeuge.

" This record speaks for itself. It has not been achieved without the loss of many comrades, amongst whom the heaviest is that of Brigadier-General G. B. S. Follett,

M.V.O., D.S.O., Coldstream Guards, Commanding the 3rd Brigade, who was killed in action at the Canal du Nord. To him, to the Commanders of the 1st and 2nd Guards Brigades—Brigadier-General de Crespigny and Brigadier-General Brooke, and to his successor in the Command of the 3rd Guards Brigade, Brigadier-General Heywood, who was wounded last week, I owe the warmest appreciation and gratitude. They, their staffs, and their troops have added a distinguished page to the history of the Brigade of Guards, and I wish to express my thanks to them and to all their officers, non-commissioned officers, and men.

The difficulties faced by other troops have also beset the work of the R.A.M.C., who, under the able command of Colonel Fawcus, have not allowed them to reduce in any degree their high standard of efficiency and zeal. They have also hampered the Army Service Corps and all the Administrative Services, but by one and all they have been cheerfully met and successfully overcome.

Finally, I wish to thank my own Staff for their untiring work since the beginning of the advance. They have been responsible for the co-ordination of plans, which is essential to success. The task has at times been very difficult, for the strain has throughout been great. I am deeply grateful for their industry and forethought, which have well deserved this great result.

" I am even prouder to have the honour to command the Guards Division to-day than I was when I first came to it two months ago. No troops have served their King and Country more devotedly, in hard times as in soft ; no troops have done more to win the prize which is announced to-day, the victorious cessation of hostilities and the promise of a justly rewarding peace."

(*Signed*) T. G. MATHESON,
MAJOR-GENERAL,
Commanding Guards Division.

In London the Armistice was accompanied by frantic demonstrations recalling those on the occasion of the relief of Mafeking. At the front, amongst the men who had achieved the great victory after more than four years of strenuous fighting and sufferings of every description, the end was received with calm and dignity. There were no demonstrations, no shouting, no " Mafficking," as befitted an army which owes as much almost to its discipline as to its courage and endurance. Celebrations of course there were, but of a solemn and dignified character, in addition to the usual concerts, lectures, etc., which had formed a feature throughout when the Scots Guards were in back areas ; but the subject of at least one lecture was demobilization—not war.

Both battalions of the Scots Guards were busily employed smartening up and getting rid of all signs of the trenches and other warlike activities, and in a marvellously short time the British Guardsman, save for his steel helmet, was the smart, well-groomed man of the summer of 1914, in place of the grimy, war-stained warrior of that of 1918.

On the 14th November there was a High Mass of Thanksgiving in the Maubeuge Collegiate Church, at which the Guards Division was represented by its Commander and his Brigadiers, with most of the officers, and even the chaplains of different denominations, the Roman Catholic soldiers, and the band of the Coldstream Guards.

Later in the day the division was presented by the Mayor with a French flag in commemoration of the liberation of Maubeuge, a compliment which was returned by the presentation of a silver cup by General Matheson to the municipality.[1]

On the 16th the Division held its own Thanksgiving Service in the barrack square.

All was now ready for the march through Belgium to the Rhine. The 4th Guards Brigade had ceased to exist, and its battalions reached Maubeuge in the evening of the 17th November to rejoin the brigades from which they had been separated in February 1918. That meant the return to the 2nd Guards Brigade of the 2nd Irish Guards and to the 3rd Brigade of the 4th Grenadier Guards. The coming march, over disorganized communications and through the Belgian Ardennes, promised to be anything but an easy one in the winter weather, a fact of which General Matheson warned his division.

---

[1] The cup, pending its manufacture, was only nominally represented by a document, and the flag was only provisional till a proper one could be made.

Those battalions which had colours[1] had of course left them at home under the general orders which had been in force since about 1880.

General Matheson decided that they should not be carried on the march, at any rate till the German frontier was passed.

For the march General Matheson constituted four groups of the division, the first three being headed respectively by the 1st, 2nd, and 3rd Guards Brigades.

The march started from Maubeuge on the 18th November, in the morning towards 9 o'clock, the early hours of battle days being no longer necessary. The whole division marched past General Matheson and the French Governor of Maubeuge.

The order of march of the 2nd Brigade was 3rd Grenadiers, 1st Coldstream, 1st Scots, 2nd Irish Guards. The last named had rejoined on the previous day from the late 4th Guards Brigade.

1ST BATTALION SCOTS GUARDS

On November 10th the 1st Battalion left Lesmottes and marched into Maubeuge. On the next day hostilities ceased. The battalion remained at Maubeuge till November 18th, when the march to Germany started. The first billet was Grand Reng, which is mentioned in the first chapter of this volume as the place the 1st Battalion billeted at on August 22nd, 1914. One of the inhabitants still had a Scots Guards cap star which had been left there at that time.

The battalion reached Charleroi on November 20th, and was enthusiastically received by the inhabitants. Two of the companies were billeted in a building which had been a German Hospital, but the residue of operations had been so badly disposed of that the troops were quickly moved elsewhere.

A Coldstream Sergeant here reported to Sir Victor Mackenzie, O.C.Bn. He was a 1914 prisoner, and was

---

[1] The following battalions, dating from the war, had as yet never received colours : 4th Grenadier Guards ; 4th Coldstream Guards (Pioneers) ; 2nd Irish Guards : 4th Battalion Machine-Gun Regiment.

terribly emaciated and weak, and could scarcely crawl. This naturally caused much indignation among the men at the brutal treatment this N.C.O. and probably many others had received as prisoners. During the march to Charleroi bands of released British prisoners were frequently met.

The battalion remained at Charleroi till on the 24th it continued its march towards Germany by stages of 12 to 20 miles, sometimes halting for a day or two. At Courrière some of the officers took part in a wild boar shoot, and killed four. Then on through Barvan, Chevron, and Ennal.

On December 12th the battalion crossed the German frontier over the river Arnel. The Corps Commander there took the salute, the regimental march being played. Thence on to Recht, where the Germans were on the whole inclined to be friendly to the troops. On the following day the battalion moved on to Butgenbach, and entrained at Weywert for Cologne. The 2nd Brigade was the only one which entrained, troops being urgently required at their destination. Detraining at Ehrenfeld Station at midnight, the battalion marched through the town to the Pioneer Barracks, where it remained during its stay. They were quite good barracks, little accommodation for officers, but they managed to commandeer comfortable quarters close by.

After the feeling of exultation at the occupation of Cologne had worn off life became monotonous. The chief duties were guarding various bridges, and marching through the streets of the town, which was obviously not to the liking of the Germans. All officials had to salute British officers, and occasionally the battalion returned to barracks escorting twenty or more Germans who had failed to salute the C.O. They had to march in rear of the battalion under an escort with fixed bayonets, but after a good telling off were soon allowed to go.

Demobilization started on December 28th, and about 150 men, chiefly miners and policemen, went home the following day. Otherwise the routine of barracks went on much as it does at home ; the men were not allowed to associate with Germans, and certainly showed no inclination to do so.

The Christmas dinner and the sergeants' annual Hogmanay and concert were a great success. On January 1st the officers of both Battalions had a cheerful dinner together in Cologne.

On January 7th the Colours arrived, escorted by Lieutenants M. Tennant and Solly and three sergeants.

On January 22nd the battalion went for a trip on the s.s. *Hindenburg*, the largest paddle-steamer of Cologne, as far as Königswinter, had dinner on board and enjoyed their day out. A week later the 2nd Battalion marched over to the 1st Battalion barracks and spent the day with their comrades. An inter-battalion football match took place, and after a very even game the 1st Battalion won by 2 to 1.

On February 26th the battalion left Cologne and entrained for Dunkirk, reaching there two days later. On March 2nd they left on board the *Menominer*, and arrived at Tilbury Docks that morning and at St. Pancras at midday.

The Major-General Commanding London District, Colonel Smith Neill, and many other officers were there to meet them. An enormous crowd gathered and gave the troops a splendid ovation through the streets. On arrival at Wellington Barracks, F.M. H.R.H. the Duke of Connaught welcomed the battalion home in person.

The battalion took part in the Victory March through London, passing their Majesties at Buckingham Palace, a large number of demobilized men rejoining them for the day.

2ND BATTALION SCOTS GUARDS

On November 10th the 2nd Battalion marched to Croix Mesnil, a suburb of Maubeuge, and went into rest billets. The following day the battalion received the news of the Armistice. Then followed some days of training for the march into Germany, and lectures were given by Captain Williams to all ranks on the subject of demobilization.

On Sunday, November 16th, a Thanksgiving under the

auspices of the Anglican and Presbyterian Denominations took place in the Barrack Square, Maubeuge. Twenty-five per cent. of each unit, led by the pipes and drums, were present at the ceremony.

Two days later the march towards Cologne started " by easy roads " (meaning short distances), as did Cardinal Wolsey on his journey to Leicester.

Binche, where the first fighting of Great Britain took place by the advanced cavalry in August 1914, was the first point touched by the battalion on their march towards Cologne.

To put the whole march as concisely as possible, the battalion marched by second-class roads and small villages and crossed the German frontier a short distance south of Aix-la-Chapelle, where they marched past Brigadier-General J. Campbell, V.C., C.M.G., D.S.O., Commanding 3rd Guards Brigade, their pipers playing the regimental march as they passed him.

On to Cologne, the troops still followed such bad roads that once their transport had to make a detour by side roads to reach the billets. This was the day the battalion made their longest and most tiring march of all.

Into the city—with its extremely ugly cathedral—the battalion marched past the distinguished officer mentioned a few lines back, to the same traditional air. He complimented them on their smart appearance and good march discipline.

During the period of waiting in and about Cologne, the battalion was kept occupied and interested by football, lectures, route marching, baths, practising for receiving the Colours, swimming, musketry, etc.

On January 7th the Colours arrived from England, and the battalion was drawn up in the Remigius Square to receive them.

After this some days were spent collecting all German war material found in the Ehrenfels district and conveying it to a dump in the town.

On March 6th the battalion left Cologne, in horse-boxes and trucks, for Dunkirk. Landing at Tilbury Docks, Wimbledon was reached four days later, where they were

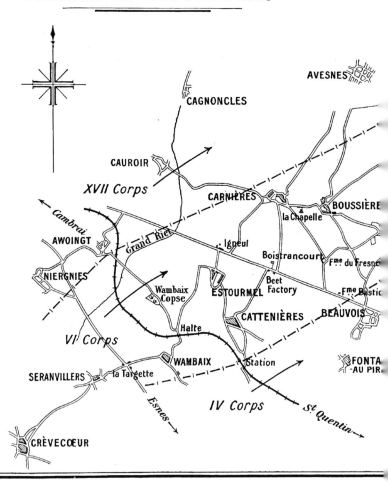

GUARDS DIVISION
OPERATIONS OCTOBER 1918

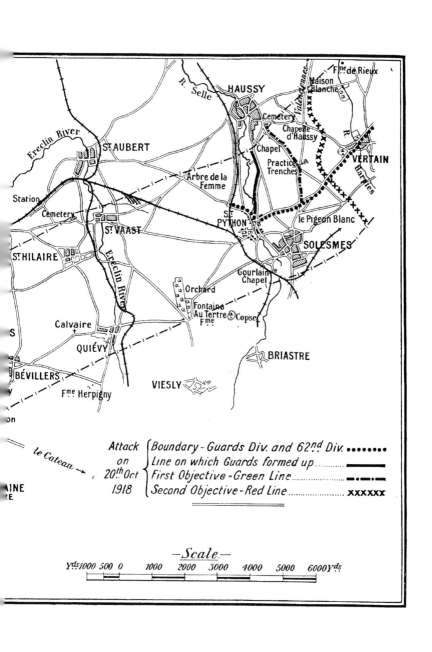

Attack on 20th Oct 1918

Boundary - Guards Div. and 62nd Div. ········

Line on which Guards formed up ▄▄▄▄▄

First Objective - Green Line ▄·▄·▄·▄

Second Objective - Red Line ✗✗✗✗✗✗

—Scale.—

Yds 1000 500 0   1000   2000   3000   4000   5000   6000 Yds

received by the Mayor, Aldermen, and Councillors, who presented an address, to which Lieut.-Colonel Stirling made a suitable reply.

The battalion marched, under triumphal arches, to billets in houses on the outskirts of the Common. A fortnight later they settled down in the camp, and demobilization started. The battalion dwindled to a very small number, but when recruiting started, and when the Victory March took place on March 22nd, the battalion had again reached a reasonable strength.

CHAPTER XIX

On the outbreak of war, Reserve Battalions of the Brigade of Guards were formed to take the men from the Regular Battalions who were under age or unfit, reservists who were surplus to the requirements of the Regular Battalions, recruits passing out of the Depot, and sick and wounded men from the battalions on active service.

The 3rd Reserve Battalion, Brigade of Guards, was formed at South Kensington on 6/8/14 to take the men of those categories of the Scots Guards and Irish Guards—each Regiment forming two companies. Colonel W. C. G. McGrigor, Scots Guards, was Commanding Officer, and Captain G. C. D. Gordon, Scots Guards, Adjutant.

On 17/8/14 all officers and men of the Scots Guards in the 3rd Guards Reserve Battalion moved to Chelsea Barracks, and on 18/8/14 were formed into the 3rd Battalion Scots Guards (4 Companies), Colonel W. C. G. McGrigor commanding, and Captain G. C. D. Gordon, Adjutant. On 31/8/14 the battalion moved to Sandown Park, Esher, and on 2/10/14 to Wellington Barracks, London, where it remained until disbanded in 1919.

On 22/10/14 the battalion was designated " 3rd (Reserve) Battalion Scots Guards," and received from H.M. the King, the Colours of the 3rd Battalion Scots Guards, which was disbanded in 1906.

The following Officers Commanded the battalion :

18/8/14–23/9/14. Colonel W. C. G. McGrigor.
24/9/14–17/6/15. Lieut.-Colonel S. H. Godman, D.S.O.
18/6/15–23/10/15. Major (afterwards Temporary Lieut.-Colonel) Lord E. Gordon-Lennox, M.V.O.
24/10/15–1/12/15. Major M. Romer.
2/12/15–29/12/15. Lieut.-Colonel S. H. Godman, D.S.O.
30/12/15–23/9/16. Major (afterwards Lieut.-Colonel) N. A. Orr-Ewing, D.S.O.

24/9/16–11/4/17. Major (Brevet Lieut.-Colonel) B. H. S. Romilly, D.S.O.

12/4/17–4/5/17. Major Sir V. A. F. Mackenzie, Bart., D.S.O., M.V.O.

5/5/17–1/8/17. Lieut.-Colonel R. S. Tempest, D.S.O.

2/8/17–29/9/17. Major Sir V. A. F. Mackenzie, Bart., D.S.O., M.V.O.

30/9/17–14/10/17. Captain (afterwards Temporary Major) J. D. P. Astley-Corbett (Temporary).

15/10/17–18/2/18. Lieut.-Colonel B. H. S. Romilly, D.S.O.

19/2/18–23/9/18. Major (Temporary Lieut.-Colonel) the Earl of Stair.

24/9/18 until disbandment. Major (afterwards Lieut.-Colonel) M. Romer.

The following Officers were Adjutant :

18/8/14–17/12/14. Captain G. C. D. Gordon.

18/12/14–7/1/15. Captain Sir V. A. F. Mackenzie, Bart., M.V.O.

8/1/15–1/1/16. Captain M. Romer.

25/10/15–1/12/15. Captain G. H. Loder, A/Adjutant, while Major M. Romer commanded battalion.

2/1/16–31/5/16. Lieutenant E. D. Mackenzie.

1/6/16–5/10/16. Lieutenant the Hon. R. Coke, D.S.O.

6/10/16 until disbandment. Lieutenant H. H. Liddell-Grainger.

9,716 recruits passed through the battalion during its existence. Drafts totalling 388 officers, 10,813 other ranks, were dispatched to the Service Battalions.[1]

146 other ranks were transferred to the Guards M.G. Regiment on the formation of that regiment in March 1917. During January 1915 the recruits of the Brigade of Guards were accommodated at the White City under Major H. F. Maclean, but afterwards the system of recruits being received direct by the Depot was reverted to. At first the battalion was organized on a 4 Company basis (numbered 1 to 4), but in June 1915, owing to the large number of men on the strength, 4 extra Companies were formed. The Companies were then designated, R.F., " O," " P," " Q," " R," " S," " T," L.F., and on 1/3/19 the

---

[1] The difference between this number and that given on p. 328 is explained by the footnote on that page.

battalion was again reduced to 4 Companies (R.F., " O," " P," L.F.).

Until October 1915 all sick and wounded personnel from the battalions overseas rejoined the Reserve Battalion on discharge from hospital, but in that month Command Depots were formed to take all men on discharge from hospital who were not likely to be fit for service overseas within three months. The Command Depot of the London District was formed at Seaford, and moved later to Shoreham. Various forms of training were carried out daily by all companies of the Reserve Battalion, mainly in London and its vicinity. Physical training and bayonet fighting were carried out in barracks, in Kensington Gardens, and in Hyde Park. Musketry training in the miniature range in barracks, and at Rainham and Purfleet, and field firing on the Ash Range at Aldershot.

Route marches took place in London, and field days in Richmond Park and on Wimbledon Common.

Series of short regimental courses in anti-gas training, scouting, musketry, interior economy for officers, and senior N.C.O. classes were organized in barracks. Training in bombing was carried out in Burton Court, Earlsfield, and Chorley Wood, and by lectures in barracks. Until the formation of the Guards Machine-gun Regiment, in February 1917, machine-gun training was carried out regimentally by a detachment at Kensington Barracks, and later at Tadworth.

In addition to this, an extra company was formed from time to time of men who were fit to proceed on service overseas. These men were struck off all other duties for a period of intense field training, lasting usually about one month. The first Training Company was formed in January 1915, but remained quartered at Wellington Barracks, and was trained in London and its vicinity. On 5/6/15 a detachment was sent to Sandown Park, Esher, for summer training.

In February 1916 a Battalion Training Camp was formed at Corsham, and three detachments were sent there for periods of intensive training of about one month each. From June to December 1916 a Training Company was sent monthly from the battalion to Tadworth; in January and February 1917 to Corsham; and in May, June, and July 1917 to Tadworth.

In November 1917 forty men were detailed weekly by the Orderly Room to form a Training Platoon which was struck off all other duties, and exercised in the Green Park.

In June 1918 a Training Company was sent to Pirbright, and in November 1918 a Battalion Training Camp was formed at Sevenoaks, to which men fit to proceed on Service Overseas, and all Recruits from the Depot, were sent. The training of officers was carried out simultaneously with that of other ranks. Until February 1917 officers were given commissions in the Special Reserve of the Regiment, without previous training. Up to the end of September 1914 these officers were trained at the Guards Depot, but after that their training was carried out under regimental arrangements in the battalion.

In February 1917 the H.B. Cadet Battalion was formed, to train prospective officers for the Special Reserve of the Household Cavalry and Foot Guards. The Reserve Battalion was reduced to cadre on 7/3/19, and finally disbanded on 10/3/19, on which occasion the Lieut.-Colonel Commanding the Regiment said in a Special Order : " The strength of the battalion was generally equal to at least that of three battalions of peace-time strength. It is a great satisfaction to know that on no occasion was the battalion unable to find the drafts called for." The Colours of the battalion were taken to Buckingham Palace and handed over by the Lieut.-Colonel Commanding the Regiment to the Lord Chamberlain, who received them on behalf of H.M. the King, and deposited them in the Private Chapel.

During the 1915–16 football season the battalion won 30, drew 5, and lost 10 matches. In the succeeding season they won 19, drew 8, and lost 9.

The recruits for the Reserve Battalion all received their early training at the Guards Depot at Caterham. Lieut.-Colonel Sir W. H. Ingilby commanded there from the commencement to the end of the war.

CHAPTER XX

CASUALTIES, STRENGTH, AND DRAFTS—ORDERS, DECORA-
TIONS, AND MEDALS—BATTLE HONOURS

I

(a) OFFICERS, WARRANT OFFICERS, NON-COMMISSIONED
OFFICERS AND MEN OF THE REGIMENT KILLED AND DIED
OF WOUNDS DURING THE GREAT WAR:

> *Officers.*—One hundred and eleven.
> *Other Ranks.*—Two thousand seven hundred and
> thirty.

(b) OFFICERS, WARRANT OFFICERS, NON-COMMISSIONED
OFFICERS AND MEN OF THE REGIMENT WOUNDED DURING
THE GREAT WAR:

> *Officers.*—Two hundred and sixteen.
> *Other Ranks.*—Four thousand and two.

(c) STRENGTH OF THE BATTALIONS OF THE REGIMENT
ON EMBARKATION FOR SERVICE WITH THE BRITISH EX-
PEDITIONARY FORCE:

> 1ST BATTALION:
> > *Officers.*—Twenty-eight.
> > *Other Ranks.*—Nine hundred and sixty-five.
> 2ND BATTALION:
> > *Officers.*—Thirty-one.
> > *Other Ranks.*—Nine hundred and seventy-three.

(d) NUMBER OF OFFICERS, WARRANT OFFICERS, NON-
COMMISSIONED OFFICERS AND MEN OF THE REGIMENT,
WHO PROCEEDED TO JOIN THE BRITISH EXPEDITIONARY
FORCE AS REINFORCEMENTS DURING THE GREAT WAR:

> *Officers.*—Three hundred and eighty-eight.
> *Other Ranks.*—Ten thousand seven hundred and
> ten.[1]

---

[1] This number does not include a draft which proceeded to join the
B.E.F. on 25th November, 1918, after the Armistice had been signed.

II

ORDERS, DECORATIONS, AND MEDALS AWARDED TO MEMBERS OF THE REGIMENT DURING THE GREAT WAR FROM THE OUTBREAK OF HOSTILITIES TILL THE TERMINATION OF THE WAR, 31ST AUGUST, 1921

(a) BRITISH ORDERS, DECORATIONS, AND MEDALS :

THE VICTORIA CROSS :
Second-Lieutenant G. A. Boyd-Rochfort.
No. 10,053 Sergeant J. McAulay, D.C.M.
No. 13,301 Lance-Sergeant F. McNess.
No. 16,444 Lance-Sergeant H. B. Wood, M.M.
No. 8,185 Private J. Mackenzie.

THE ORDER OF THE BATH :
Knight Commander.—One officer.
Companions.—Eight officers.

THE ORDER OF ST. MICHAEL AND ST. GEORGE :
Knight Grand Cross.—One officer.
Knight Commander.—One officer.
Companions.—Eleven officers.

THE ORDER OF THE BRITISH EMPIRE :
Commanders.—Two officers.

THE DISTINGUISHED SERVICE ORDER :
Twenty-two officers whilst serving with the Regiment.
Four officers whilst attached to other units.

THE ROYAL VICTORIAN ORDER :
Members.—Two officers.

THE ORDER OF THE BRITISH EMPIRE :
Officers.—Nine officers.
Member.—One officer.

THE MILITARY CROSS :
Seventy-two officers and warrant officers whilst serving with the Regiment.
Thirteen officers and warrant officers whilst attached to other units.

THE GRAND PRIORY OF THE ORDER OF ST. JOHN OF
JERUSALEM IN ENGLAND :
Knight of Grace.—One officer.
THE ALBERT MEDAL :
(*In Gold*).—One officer.
THE DISTINGUISHED CONDUCT MEDAL :
Ninety-three other ranks whilst serving with the
Regiment.
Two other ranks whilst attached to other units.
THE MILITARY MEDAL :
Three hundred and thirty-eight other ranks.
THE MERITORIOUS SERVICE MEDAL :
Thirty-nine other ranks.

(*b*) ORDERS, DECORATIONS AND MEDALS AWARDED BY
ALLIED AND FOREIGN POWERS.

EGYPT :
THE ORDER OF THE NILE :
One officer.
FRANCE :
LÉGION D'HONNEUR :
Grand Croix.—One officer.
Croix de Commandeur.—One officer.
Croix d'Officier.—Three officers.
Croix de Chevalier.—Four officers.
CROIX DE GUERRE :
Thirteen officers.
Eighteen other ranks.
MÉDAILLE MILITAIRE :
Four other ranks.
ITALY :
THE ORDER OF ST. MAURICE AND ST. LAZARUS :
One officer.
THE ORDER OF THE CROWN OF ITALY :
Two officers.
THE MILITARY ORDER OF SAVOY :
One officer.
CROCE DI GUERRA :
One officer.
One other rank.

THE BRONZE MEDAL FOR MILITARY VALOUR :
One other rank.

BELGIUM :
OFFICIERS DE L'ORDRE DE LÉOPOLD :
Three officers.
L'ORDRE DE LA COURONNE :
Three officers.
CROIX DE GUERRE :
One officer.
Five other ranks.

RUSSIA :
THE ORDER OF ST. ANNE :
One officer.
THE ORDER OF ST. STANISLAUS :
One officer.
THE ORDER OF ST. GEORGE :
Two other ranks.
THE MEDAL OF ST. GEORGE :
Three other ranks.

JAPAN :
THE ORDER OF THE RISING SUN :
One officer.
THE ORDER OF THE SACRED TREASURE :
One other rank.

PORTUGAL :
THE MILITARY ORDER OF AVIS :
One officer.

GREECE :
THE ORDER OF THE REDEEMER :
One officer.

SERBIA :
THE ORDER OF THE WHITE EAGLE :
One officer.
THE ORDER OF ST. SAVA :
One officer.

RUMANIA :
THE ORDER OF THE STAR OF RUMANIA :
One officer.

MONTENEGRO:
>   THE ORDER OF DANILO:
>   One officer.
>   THE GOLD MEDAL FOR MERIT:
>   One officer.

CZECHO-SLOVAKIA:
>   THE MILITARY CROSS:
>   One officer.

PANAMA:
>   LA SOLIDARIDAD:
>   One officer.

III

HONORARY DISTINCTIONS GAINED DURING THE GREAT WAR AND BORNE ON THE KING'S AND REGIMENTAL COLOURS OF THE REGIMENT.

>   " RETREAT FROM MONS."
>   " MARNE, 1914."
>   " AISNE, 1914."
>   " YPRES, 1914, '17."
>   " FESTUBERT, 1915."
>   " LOOS."
>   " SOMME, 1916, '18."
>   " CAMBRAI, 1917, '18."
>   " HINDENBURG LINE."
>   " FRANCE AND FLANDERS, 1914–18."

HONORARY DISTINCTIONS GAINED DURING THE GREAT WAR, BUT NOT BORNE ON THE COLOURS OF THE REGIMENT.

>   " LANGEMARCK, 1914."
>   " GHELUVELT."
>   " NONNE BOSSCHEN."
>   " GIVENCHY, 1914."
>   " NEUVE CHAPELLE."
>   " AUBERS."
>   " FLERS-COURCELETTE."

" Morval."
" Pilckem."
" Poelcapelle."
" Passchendaele."
" St. Quentin."
" Albert, 1918."
" Bapaume, 1918."
" Arras, 1918."
" Drocourt-Quéant."
" Havrincourt."
" Canal du Nord."
" Selle."
" Sambre."

INDEX

23

MEMORIES OF THE XXᵀᴴ CENTURY

By the EARL OF MEATH, K.P., G.C.V.O., G.B.E. The cordial welcome accorded to Lord Meath's "Memories of the 19th Century" has encouraged him to offer the reading public this further volume covering the period down to 1922.　　　　　Frontispiece Portrait.　10s. 6d. net.

JOHN VISCOUNT MORLEY

An Appreciation and Some Reminiscences. By Brig.-Gen. J. H. MORGAN. This volume is in no sense a biography—but is a collection of personal reminiscences by one who knew him intimately. With a Photogravure Frontispiece.　　　　　　　　　　　10s. 6d. net.

SIXTY-THREE YEARS OF ENGINEERING

By Sir FRANCIS FOX, M.I.C.E., Hon. A.R.I.B.A. Sir Francis Fox has been intimately connected with most of the great engineering feats of the last half-century.　　　　　　Plans and Photographs.

THE ROYAL NAVY AS I SAW IT

By Captain G. H. R. WILLIS, C.B., R.N. Captain Willis writes of the days when masts and yards and smooth-bore ordnance were relied on. His book is full of good stories.　　　　　　　　　Illustrated.

REMINISCENCES, 1848-1890

By Major-Gen. Sir FRANCIS HOWARD, K.C.B., K.C.M.G. "Sir Francis has the knack of writing on all kinds of subjects and writing well. This is indeed a book that people with very different tastes can read with pleasure."—*Field*.　　　　　　　Portrait.　15s. net.

AUTOBIOGRAPHY GEN. GEORGE GREAVES,

G.C.B., K.C.M.G. Edited by Colonel F. SPRATT BOWRING, late R.E., C.B. With a Foreword by Field-Marshal EARL HAIG, K.T., G.C.M., O.M.　　　　　　　　　　　With Illustrations and Maps.

REMINISCENCES OF AN OLD PHYSICIAN

By ROBERT BELL, M.D., F.R.F.P.S. The author is a man of many interests—fisherman, scientist, gardener, sportsman, traveller—but is best known from his long study of Cancer.　　　Illustrated.　16s. net.

IN SOUTHERN SEAS

By W. RAMSAY SMITH, M.D., D.Sc., F.R.S. Edin. This book combines pleasant gossip, anecdotes and personal experiences with sound scientific knowledge and observation.　　　　　　Illustrations.

DAYS GONE BY

Some Account of Past Years, Chiefly in Central Africa. By Rt. Rev. J. E. HINE, M.A. Oxon., M.D. Lond., Hon. D.D. Oxon., Hon. D.C.L Durham, M.R.C.S., sometime Bishop (in the Universities Mission to Central Africa) of Likoma, of Zanzibar, and of N. Rhodesia; Rector of Stoke; Prebendary of Longford in Lincoln Cathedral; and Bishop Suffragan of Grantham. Bishop Hine holds a position possibly unique in having presided over three Dioceses in Central Africa extending over a period of 18 years. His reminiscences should especially appeal to the missionary, the traveller, and to the student.　　Illustrated.　16s. net.

THE TREFOIL.

WELLINGTON COLLEGE, LINCOLN AND TRURO. By A. C. BENSON, C.V.O., LL.D. Author of "The House of Quiet," etc. This is an experiment in personal biography, telling, as it was not possible to tell in the official "Life," the inner history of Archbishop Benson's Truro episcopate. Second impression. Illustrated. 12s. net.

MEMORIES AND FRIENDS.

By A. C. BENSON, C.V.O., LL.D. This volume includes personal recollections of well-known figures, such as Ruskin and Henry James, and of certain familiar Eton and Windsor personalities, Dr. Warre, Mr. Edward Austen Leigh, Dr. S. A. Donaldson, Mrs. Warre Cornish, Mr. J. D. Bourchier, Lady Ponsonby, and Mrs. Oliphant. With Portraits.

IONICUS.

By Viscount ESHER, G.C.B. "This handsomely printed volume enables us to see the great personality whose influence was exercised over the characters of such diverse men as Lord Balfour, Lord Rosebery, and Mr. Asquith."—*Daily Chronicle.* With Portrait. 15s. net.

WILLIAM BENTINCK AND WILLIAM III.

By (Mrs.) M. E. S. GREW. This life of William Bentinck, first Earl of Portland, includes the story of the complicated diplomatic missions in Europe undertaken by him in pursuance of William's design of forming the First European Coalition. With Portraits.

LETTERS OF ANNE THACKERAY RITCHIE.

With forty-one additional Letters from her father, William Makepeace Thackeray. Selected and Edited by HESTER RITCHIE. This record of the life of Lady Ritchie is founded on and chiefly composed of her own letters to her friends and of letters from her father, William Makepeace Thackeray. With Portraits and other Illustrations.

CONTEMPORARY CRITICISMS OF DR. SAMUEL JOHNSON: His Works and His

Biographers. Collected and Edited by JOHN KER SPITTAL. "It forms a biography that we shall place side by side with Boswell. For the Doctor really comes to life in these pages."—*Daily Chronicle.* With Portrait and Maps. 16s. net.

"EGO": RANDOM RECORDS OF SPORT, SERVICE AND TRAVEL IN MANY LANDS. By LORD CASTLETOWN OF UPPER

OSSORY, K.P. The author has had a full and, at times, exciting life in many parts of the world. Eton—The Life Guards—Parliament—sport and adventure in the Wild West and in India—these are some of the subjects told of. 10s. 6d. net.

OUT OF THE PAST.

By Mrs. W. W. VAUGHAN (MARGARET SYMONDS). This book is an account of John Addington Symonds written by his daughter (Margaret), Mrs. W. W. Vaughan, with a small memoir of her mother by Mrs. Walter Leaf. It includes many letters which illustrate the happiness and variety of his interests and of his friendships. With Illustrations.

THE ENGLISH, 1909-1922.

A gossip by FRANK FOX. "Here is English life seen from every angle, national and personal. Mr. Fox has known many men and women who have influenced our history in recent years. He tells stories of them and uses them as illustrations for his text."—*Morning Post.* 9s. net.

THE LETTERS OF QUEEN VICTORIA

Second Series. A selection from HER MAJESTY's Correspondence and Journals, 1862-1878. Published by authority of HIS MAJESTY THE KING. Edited by GEORGE EARLE BUCKLE, sometime Editor of *The Times* and author of the later volumes of "The Life of Disraeli." With Illustrations. In 2 Vols. £2 12s. 6d. net.

LIFE & LETTERS OF WM. BOYD CARPENTER

By the Rev. H. D. A. MAJOR, D.D., Author of "Reminiscences of Jesus by an Eye-Witness." 16s. net.

MEMORIES AND HOPES

By the Rev. the Hon. EDWARD LYTTELTON, D.D. With Illustrations. 16s. net.

BERNADOTTE : PRINCE AND KING, 1810-1844

By the Rt. Hon. Sir DUNBAR PLUNKET BARTON, Bt., P.C., K.C., Author of "Bernadotte: The First Phase," etc. Illustrated. 12s. net.

REMINISCENCES

By the Hon. EMILY KINNAIRD. Illustrated. 5s. net.

E. T. BUSK : A PIONEER IN FLIGHT

WITH A SHORT MEMOIR OF H. A. BUSK, FLIGHT-COMMANDER, R.N.A.S. By MARY BUSK. With Illustrations. 7s. 6d. net.

MEMORIES OF FORTY-EIGHT YEARS' SER-

VICE, 1876 TO 1924. Covering Campaigns from the Zulu to the Great War. By General Sir HORACE SMITH-DORRIEN, G.C.B., G.C.M.G., D.S.O., Grand Officer of the Legion of Honour. Maps; Illustrations. 2nd Edition. 25s. net.

MEMORIES

By the Rt. Hon. Sir ARTHUR GRIFFITH-BOSCAWEN. 10s. 6d. net.

OUT OF THE PAST

By MARGARET SYMONDS (Mrs. W. W. Vaughan). This volume is devoted to John Addington Symonds' home life. Illustrated. 16s. net.

EMPTY CHAIRS

By Sir SQUIRE BANCROFT. Photogravure Frontispiece. 2nd Edition. 10s. 6d. net.

A PRIME MINISTER AND HIS SON

Correspondence of the Third Earl of Bute and of General Sir Charles Stuart, based on the Stuart Correspondence at Highcliffe Castle. Edited by the Hon. Mrs. EDWARD STUART-WORTLEY. Illustrated. 16s. net.

MARY HAMILTON

At Court and at Home. Edited by ELIZABETH G. ANSON. Illustrations. 16s. net.

JOHN MURRAY, ALBEMARLE STREET, LONDON, W.1

THE REIGN OF KING EDWARD VII

By the Author of "The Victorian Age." This sketch of King Edward's reign is intended to convey to the reader a general view of that short period in a small compass. A briefer record and survey of the outstanding features and events of the time, may be of use to many who wish to gain fuller knowledge of the reign but have not sufficient leisure for more lengthy study.　5s. net.

THE PRIME MINISTERS OF BRITAIN, 1721-1921

With a Supplementary Chapter to 1924. By the Hon. CLIVE BIGHAM. "A history of British politics for the last two hundred years in a series of pen portraits. . . . How many well-educated persons could even name the thirty-nine Prime Ministers since 1721, much less give any account of their characters and careers."—*Morning Post.* Portraits of 39 Ministers.　10s. 6d. net

THE CHIEF MINISTERS OF ENGLAND, 920-1720

By the Hon. CLIVE BIGHAM. "Mr. Bigham has produced a book it would be difficult to overpraise; rich in the fruits of reading and research, written in a most lively and interesting style, sober and just in judgment."—*Sunday Times.* With Portraits of 28 Ministers.　Cheaper Edition, 10s. 6d. net.

WILLIAM BENTINCK AND WILLIAM III

(Prince of Orange). The Life of Bentinck, Earl of Portland, from the Welbeck Correspondence. By MARION E. GREW. "Mrs. Grew originally intended to write a life of Bentinck alone, but the many important diplomatic negotiations he undertook for the Prince of Orange gave it a setting of history impossible to ignore. The book has consequently a greatly enhanced value. . . . A human document of extraordinary interest."—*Graphic.* With Portraits. 21s. net

THE CONQUESTS OF CEAWLIN, THE SECOND BRETWALDA

By Major P. T. GODSAL. The author gives a coherent account of the Conquest from the coming of the West Saxons in the year 514, to the death of Ceawlin in 593, and thereby throws an entirely new light on this obscure chapter of our history. With Maps. 10s. 6d. net.

THE CHALLENGE OF ASIA

By STANLEY RICE, late Indian Civil Service. "It was a task well worth doing, and it could hardly have been better done than in this thoughtful and thought-provoking book."—*Punch.*　7s. 6d. net.

SHELTERED MARKETS

A Study of the Value of Empire Trade. By F. L. McDOUGALL. With a Preface by the Rt. Hon. Sir ROBERT HORNE, G.B.E., M.P. The solution of the Empire problems of "Men, Money and Markets" is here shown to be of greater economic importance to industrial Britain than even to the Dominions and Colonies themselves. 5s. net.

JOHN MURRAY, ALBEMARLE STREET, LONDON, W.1

Lightning Source UK Ltd.
Milton Keynes UK
27 August 2010
159094UK00001B/17/A